THE EARLY MEDIEVAL BALKANS

The Early Medieval Balkans

A Critical Survey from the Sixth to the Late Twelfth Century

JOHN V. A. FINE, JR.

Ann Arbor
The University of Michigan Press

First paperback edition 1991
Copyright © by The University of Michigan 1983
All rights reserved
Published in the United States of America by
The University of Michigan Press
Manufactured in the United States of America

1993   1992   6   5

Library of Congress Cataloging-in-Publication Data

Fine, John Van Antwerp.
  The early medieval Balkans.

  Bibliography: p.
  Includes index.
  1. Balkan Peninsula—History.   I. Title.
DR39.F56 1983   949.6   82-8452
ISBN 0-472-08149-7 (pbk.)   AACR2

A CIP catalogue record for this book is available from the British Library

To Gena, Sasha, and Paul

Preface

This book is a general survey of early medieval Balkan history. Geographically it covers the region that now is included in the states of Yugoslavia (Croatia, Bosnia, Serbia, Montenegro, and Macedonia), Bulgaria, Greece, and Albania. What are now Slovenia and Rumania are treated only peripherally. The book covers the period from the arrival of the Slavs in the second half of the sixth and early seventh centuries up to the 1180s. A second volume will continue the story from this point to the Turkish conquest, a process carried out over the late fourteenth and through much of the fifteenth centuries.

This book is, to the best of my knowledge, the first of its kind in any language. There are many works devoted to the history of the Byzantine Empire (which encompassed much of the Balkans). However, these works have stressed the history of Byzantium and its institutions; when the Slavic regions were not imperial provinces these works have treated the Slavic states only from the point of view of foreign relations. The various Balkan nations have produced a wide assortment of histories of their own individual states (or of regions within those states) in the Middle Ages, and foreign historians have also produced monographic surveys of specific regions (e.g., of Bulgaria, Serbia, or Croatia in the Middle Ages). However, no work has yet dealt with the various medieval Balkan peoples as a whole. Such a work seems necessary, particularly for this early period when much of the area was in a state of flux and the protostates' borders did not coincide with later state boundaries. Since the early medieval period was an era of both national and state formation, a study that treats the region as a whole may better trace and explain developments than a study focused on only one area. This is particularly to the point, since the regions that have usually been chosen for study by historians have been defined by what came later, namely by being included in a subsequent national state.

The early medieval period is a critical one for Balkan history. Enormous demographic changes occurred. If we exclude the Greeks, living in Thrace and Greece, the Albanians, and the Vlachs, scattered in various mountainous regions of the Balkans, the population of the classical Balkans disappeared in the sixth and seventh centuries to be replaced (partially by assimilation) by new ethnic groups which invaded and took over the Balkans: the Turkic Bulgars and the Slavic groups which produced the Serbo-Croatians and the Bulgaro-Macedonians.

In the period that followed, these new arrivals developed into identifiable nationalities, each acquiring an ethnic awareness which has survived to the present. Moreover, the first states created by each of these peoples (which of course greatly contributed to the development of each group's ethnic awareness) also appeared in the early medieval period.

Finally, during this period all these peoples were officially converted to Christianity. Though many of the peasants retained so many pagan beliefs that we might consider them semipagans and only nominal Christians, nevertheless the rulers and their people considered themselves Christians, and churches and a church hierarchy were established throughout their lands. Furthermore, during this period it was determined which regions were to end up under the religious jurisdiction of Constantinople (and later under that of independent national Orthodox churches) and which were to end up under Rome. Thus when the split in the church came to affect the Balkans, a gradual process occurring over a long period of time, which peoples were to be Eastern Orthodox and which Roman Catholic had already been settled. This differentiation, which has lasted to the present, has had a great impact on the history of the Balkans up to our own day.

Only Bosnia proved to be an exception. Though in the early medieval period it was nominally under Rome, it had so weak a church organization that Catholicism was not firmly established. Thus, despite its nominal Catholicism, it was more of a no-man's-land between faiths than Catholic; hence it is not surprising that it had a unique religious history in the later Middle Ages when it was to produce its own independent and somewhat heretical church. From that period to the present Bosnia has been an area of mixed faiths.

This work is to large extent a political history with a good dose of church history. Needless to say, this emphasis follows the emphasis of the surviving sources. I would have liked to treat at greater length social and economic matters. However, we have so few sources on these questions that broader or more detailed treatment is impossible. When documents like *The Farmer's Law* have survived, I have dealt with them at some length. However, for other matters or other periods—though sweeping generalizations about the activities of various social classes are often seen—I have limited myself to more narrow conclusions that can be supported by the sources. I have very little sympathy for "what must have been" or for conclusions about other lands based on what was occurring in the Byzantine Empire at the same time. I also see little value in works that fill in the blanks on the basis of the belief that societies pass through certain ordered stages.

The story told here of various people, movements, and events—including some major ones—differs from that found in previous scholarship, because the sources simply do not support many statements made in existing historical works. Thus it is important for historians to take each statement of fact found in these works and seek its source. By this means many items, which turn out to have no reliable source, can be removed. At this moment historians of the medieval Balkans should concern themselves primarily with determining what did happen, and it is as important to remove myths and fictions as it is to uncover new facts. Since this has been one of my main aims, this work has fewer broad generalizations than most survey histories. Until the facts can be established, these generalizations are not warranted, for trends based on hypotheses really are not trends. It is important to more or less forget all the myths and tales which generations of Balkan school children have been brought up on—many of which have a nationalistic origin, showing the heroic past of a people ever struggling to assert its nationality, and provide justification for preserving or changing modern borders—and turn back to the sources with a critical eye. On the sources depends all that we can know of the medieval Balkans. Yet, because many sources are tendentious or uninformed, the historian cannot simply take them at face value but must devote much of his attention to scrutinizing them closely.

It immediately becomes apparent that our sources on the whole are poor. The narrative sources were chiefly written by foreigners, often at a considerable distance from events, or by patriotic locals centuries later on the basis of oral traditions and documents of varying reliability, many of which no longer survive. Thus, frequently we do not know what a later author's source was. And even when we can identify what it must have been, the lack of the original document often makes it difficult to determine its reliability. Although there exists a considerable number of other documents, such as letters and charters, these rarely give us the details and explanations we would like; thus we are constantly faced with a scarcity of source material. However, such a lack is no justification to fill in the blanks with fiction and then, as has so often happened in the past, to serve up this mixture of fact and fiction as history. There is nothing shameful in admitting that we do not know things. Only when we admit our ignorance will it become clear which areas have the greatest need for further study. Then we can turn to these areas and problems with fresh minds and possibly uncover some new facts about them. If we cannot find further material, which will frequently be the case, then we must be satisfied that there are some things which we may never know.

Though this work is primarily aimed for the general reader and college student, I hope specialists will also find much in it to interest them. But, keeping in mind my general audience, I have kept notes to a minimum and have included only a brief bibliography of the most basic works. Unfortunately many of these are in foreign languages, since the literature in English is sparse.

Furthermore, because of the nature of the field—the scarcity of sources encouraging a great variety of scholarly hypotheses—it has been necessary to include a certain number of discussions about the interpretations of scholars and about the sources these interpretations rest on. Some readers may feel that for a general book I have included an excess of scholarly names and views in the text itself, especially when, as is sometimes the case, I subsequently take contrary positions. In almost all cases, however, when I present the views of a scholar—this is particularly true of the views of Zlatarski on Bulgaria—only to argue against them, these views have become "facts" in almost all the literature on the subject. Thus my readers may well have already come across them as facts; and if this book, as may be the case, is a reader's first taste of the medieval Balkans, still if he or she reads further about the Balkans, he or she will surely come across them. It is thus necessary to call attention to the existence of differences of opinion, point out that views other than my own exist, and justify the position which I have taken. Moreover, if attention were not called to these differences in views, readers finding one interpretation in my work and a differing interpretation presented as "fact" in a second work might well become confused. On the whole the names which I bring into the text are giants in the field (like Dujčev, Dvornik, N. Klaić, Ostrogorsky, Zlatarski), whose names should become known to my readers, for their work has had enormous impact on the historiography of the societies they have studied.

Moreover, such excursuses have their positive side. They present the reader with unsolved riddles, showing that medieval Balkan history is an exciting field, where much important work still remains to be done. They also show the nature of the sources upon which certain historical conclusions have been based and demonstrate how, at times, broad conclusions have been erected on little or no evidence. In this way they serve to correct past errors or point out that something frequently stated as a fact is really only a theory. Such discussions, by making readers reflect on the actual evidence standing behind assertions made by historians, may not only instill in readers a healthy scepticism about statements found in works on the medieval Balkans, but will serve in general to cultivate readers, who will be more critical of all the nonfiction which they read.

This book is to a large extent based upon the lectures for the first half of my course on the medieval Balkans which I have been giving over the past ten years at the University of Michigan. I owe a debt to my students' responses to these lectures; their comments and questions have compelled me constantly to rethink and clarify my thoughts. Thankfully, this book can be spared their major criticism: that I speak too fast.

Acknowledgments

The decision to write this work began when the American Council of Learned Societies (ACLS) Committee on Eastern Europe asked me to produce a major regional history of southeastern Europe in the Middle Ages, as part of a series for which they hoped to receive outside funding. When the funding efforts proved unsuccessful, I decided to go ahead with my part anyway, because there has long been a need for a book such as this one.

The first draft was read by one year's Medieval Balkan History class, whose students were well qualified to tell me what was clear and what was not. The glossaries at the end of this work owe their presence to student suggestion. The manuscript also was read by a variety of friends and colleagues; some were Balkan specialists and others were asked to read it to comment on manner of presentation, matters of clarity and interest for nonspecialists, and style. I am indebted to Professor Ivan Dujčev of the University of Sofija, Professor Michael B. Petrovich of the University of Wisconsin, Carol B. Stevens, and my parents, Professor John V. A. Fine and Elizabeth B. Fine, for their comments. I owe a particular debt to John H. Forsyth, Robert J. Donia, and Duncan M. Perry, former graduate students of mine who spent hours reading, pondering, and writing out detailed and valuable criticisms which have vastly improved the work. A teacher can have no better or closer friends than his past and present graduate students. I am also grateful to Professor Sima Ćirković of the University of Beograd for his thorough and careful responses to various questions that I put to him. Finally, I would like to express my appreciation to the ACLS Eastern European Committee, headed by Professor Michael Petrovich, for getting me started on the project. None of the individuals named, of course, bears any responsibility for errors of fact or interpretation that may appear in the work. I am also grateful to the Center for Russian and East European Studies at the University of Michigan which financed the typing of both the first draft and final version of this work.

I am most grateful to my wife Gena who, while suffering all the inconveniences a spouse must when such a project is being carried out, throughout gave me the strongest encouragement and support, as did our sons Alexander (Sasha) and Paul. Since she is Yugoslav, this work treats part of her and our boys' heritage. It is only fitting that this work be dedicated, with love and appreciation, to the three of them.

Note on Transliteration
and Place Names

Serbo-Croatian is a single language (with, of course, dialectical differences) written with two alphabets, Latin for Croatian and Cyrillic for Serbian. Thus the Croatian Latin scheme is a natural one to use for transliterating Serbian names. Furthermore, it seems to me a better system than any other now being used to transliterate Bulgarian and Russian as well. Thus, following Croatian, the following transliteration scheme is used:

> *c* = *ts* (except in words already accepted into English such as *tsar*)
> *ć* = *ch* (soft)
> *č* = *ch* (hard)
> *h* = guttural *kh* (though I have left the *kh*, since it is standard, for Turkic names such as Khazars, khagan, Isperikh)
> *j* = *y* (as in *yes*)
> *š* = *sh*
> *ž* = *zh*
> The Slavic softsign is indicated by a single apostrophe (').
> The Bulgarian hardsign has been rendered with a double apostrophe (").

Greek was undergoing evolution at this time with the *b* coming to be pronounced as a *v*. However, I have consistently stuck with the *b* in transliterating names, thus *Bardas* rather than *Vardas*. The same thing was happening to *v*, with its pronunciation shifting from *u* to *v*. I have almost always stuck to the *u;* thus *Staurakios* rather than *Stavrakios*. A major problem with Greek names is also the fact that their latinization has already become standard in English. Thus *k* tends to be rendered as *c* rather than *k*. I have reverted to the less ambiguous *k* in all cases (Kefalonia, Nikopolis, etc.) unless names have already become commonplace in English: e.g., Nicephorus, Lecapenus, etc. In the same way the Greek *os* tends to be latinized to *us*. In names already commonplace in the English literature I have stuck with the *us*, otherwise I have used the *os*.

Since control of particular territories in the Balkans has changed over time from Romans or Greeks to different Slavic people to Turks, it is not surprising that there are many different names for some cities. On the whole, I have chosen the name used in the Middle Ages by the power that controlled that place most. Upon first mention (and also in the index of place names) I give the variant names for each place (e.g., Philippopolis [modern Plovdiv], or Durazzo [Dyrrachium, Durres], etc.).

Contents

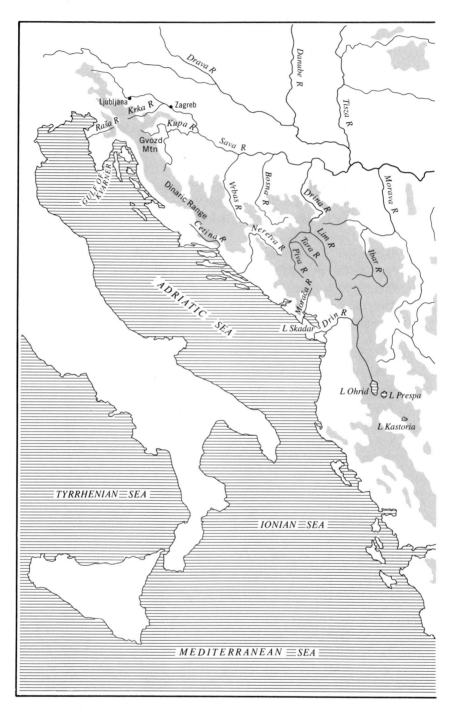

Map 1. Geographical features of the Balkan region

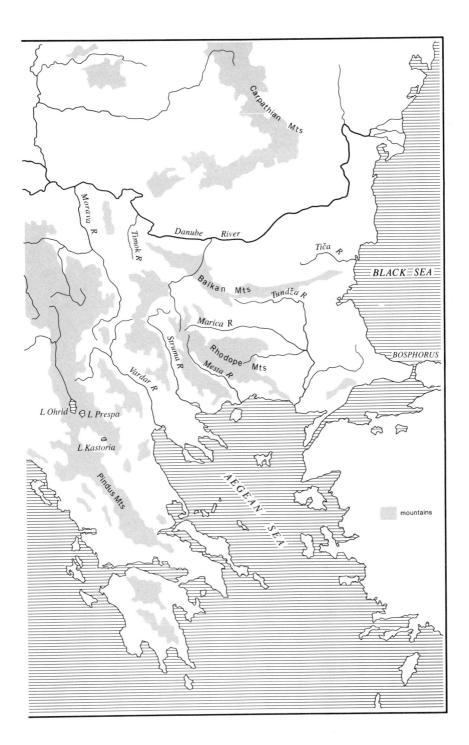

Carpathian Mts

Morava R

Timok R

Danube   River

Tiča R

BLACK=SEA

Balkan Mts

Tundža R

Marica R

Rhodope Mts

Mesta R

Struma R

Vardar R

BOSPHORUS

L Ohrid L Prespa

L Kastoria

Pindus Mts

AEGEAN SEA

mountains

Map 2. Early medieval Balkan regions

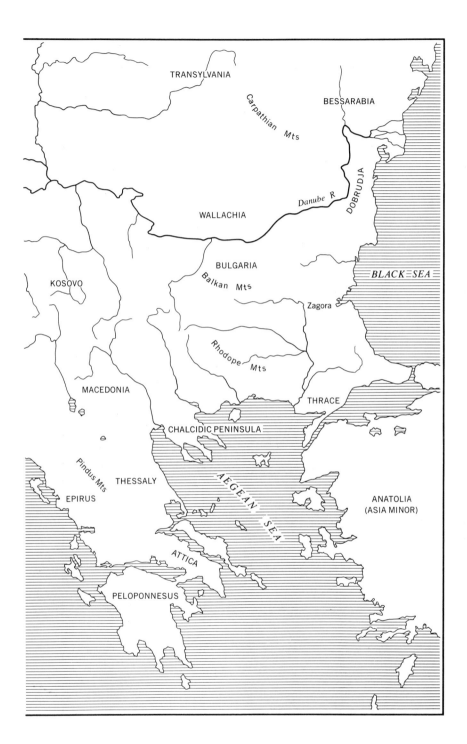

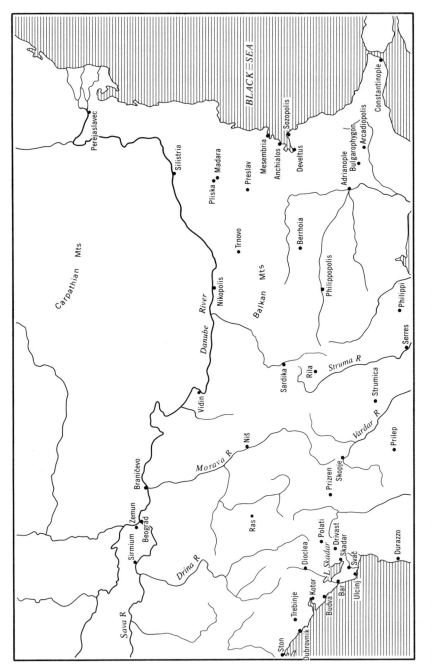

Map 3. Major early medieval towns in the eastern and northern Balkans

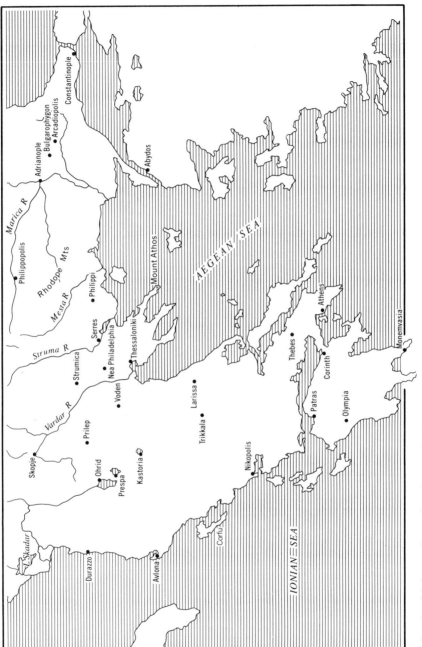

Map 4. Major early medieval towns in the southern Balkans

Map 5. Major early medieval towns in the western Balkans

Introduction: Balkan Geography and Society

Geography

Most general surveys of the Balkans begin with a survey of the geography, presenting the reader with a long list of rivers, mountains, and products. This, despite the great natural beauty of most of the geographical features, is usually fairly boring and virtually impossible to remember. It is my hope that the reader will familiarize himself with the maps of the Balkans provided in this text so that he can identify the major regions of the Balkans as well as the important towns, rivers, and mountain ranges. For the reader's benefit I have included maps. Thus here I shall simply try to generalize about some of the important features of Balkan geography and the impact these features had on Balkan developments.

First, the Balkans are an extremely mountainous region. It is said that if one ironed out Bosnia and Hercegovina this region alone would be as large as all of Europe. The regions now called Montenegro and Albania (particularly the northern part of the latter) are almost wholly mountainous. A major range runs parallel to the Dalmatian coast. This range—the Dinaric—to a considerable degree was responsible for the isolation of what became Bosnia, Hercegovina, and Montenegro and formed a border between the Italian culture of the coast and the Slavic culture of the interior. A large mountain range—the Pindus—divides the eastern and western parts of central Greece, and large numbers of mountains exist in the Peloponnesus. The Balkan range extending to join the Rhodope range separates Bulgaria from Thrace.

The mountains, by isolating peoples and encouraging localism, have hindered the development of states. They contributed to the fact that the South Slavs never created a single united nation state in the Balkans, and they have impeded the unification of individual peoples.

For example, lack of communication resulting from the presence of mountains encouraged the development of separate Greek dialects and has resulted in many Greeks feeling a stronger loyalty to a particular region than to a national ideal. But the mountains have also had positive effects. Their presence has meant that minority peoples have been able to take refuge in them to escape conquerors and large migrations and thereby to retain their identities rather than be entirely assimilated. Thus the Illyrians and Dacians were able to retreat into the mountains at the time of the Slavic invasions and retain their identities as Albanians and Vlachs.

The medieval Balkans had plentiful thick forests. These forests, along with the mountains, provided protection for brigands—a perpetual Balkan institution, be they out-and-out highwaymen, social bandits, or rebels against a dominant power. Guerrilla warfare was not new to the Balkans in the Second World War; it was a common feature in the early Middle Ages as well, and the same mountains that sheltered Partisan bands against the Fascists also had sheltered the Dukljans (proto-Montenegrins) resisting the Byzantines in the eleventh century.

The mountains gave rise to a particular form of society—the pastoral. The pastoralists were mobile, nomadic peoples, caring for flocks (chiefly sheep), who moved with their flocks from the valleys, where they wintered, up into the mountains for the summer, covering in some cases enormous distances each year. These groups—the Montenegrins, Vlachs, and northern Albanians—were organized according to tribes.

With the exception of the Balkan and Rhodope ranges, all of the major mountain chains run north-south. This meant that the Balkans were open to invasion from the north, and it was from the north that all the early major land invasions came, whether the invaders were Huns, Goths, Avars, Bulgars, Slavs, Pechenegs, Cumans, or Ghuzz. If we exclude the Normans, the Ottoman Turks, who appeared in the fourteenth century, were the first medieval invaders not from the north, and, of course, their invasion was possible because they had first conquered Anatolia.

The major mountain range that runs east-west is the Balkan range; it is not as high as some of the other ranges and thus was not a major barrier against the barbarian raiders. It had various passes through which armies could march; however, when military strength was adequate these could be defended. Thus for centuries this range formed the border between the Bulgarian state and the Byzantine Empire.

Most of the Balkan rivers are not navigable, though the Danube, the Sava, and the lower Neretva below modern Metković are. In fact, the lower Neretva opens up into a number of channels in the midst of thick marshes which were a retreat for the leading early medieval pirates—the Neretljani. Even to the present day many villages here have no land connections with the outside world and carry on all communication with it by boat. The major rivers, in particular the Danube, were important for transporting goods. Rivers, even medium-sized ones, often served as borders between states. The Danube was frequently a major border between civilization and "barbarism," and for long periods the Drina served as a border between Bosnia and Serbia while the Sava and Drava borders helped Slavonia maintain its identity. Furthermore, since rivers created valleys (often between high and difficult-to-pass mountains), land routes tended to follow rivers. For example, an important route running from the coast into Bosnia ran along the Neretva.

The main land routes through the Balkans went south from the Danube or from the coast inland. The most important inland highway is the one used in this century by the Orient Express. From central Europe it passes through Ljubljana and Zagreb across the plain to Beograd, where the Sava and Danube rivers meet and where an important route enters from across the Danube. Then from Beograd the route swings south along the Morava River to Niš where it splits in two with one branch running east through Sofija (medieval Sardika) and Plovdiv (medieval Philippopolis) to Constantinople, while the second runs south along the Vardar valley through the city of Skopje on to Thessaloniki (Salonica) and Athens. This road was both a major trade and a major invasion route. During invasions and raids the greatest devastation took place along its path. The earliest Slavic settlement, when the Slavs turned from raiding to settling, occurred along its Morava valley section. Subsequently the Crusaders, who came to the Balkans via Hungary, also used this route.

The second major road was the famous Via Egnatia which began at the important port of Durazzo (Dyrrachium, Durres) in modern Albania which was the major Byzantine naval base and military-administrative center on the Adriatic. From Durazzo the route passed through Ohrid and Thessaloniki (the second city of the empire in Europe and a major trade center) on to Constantinople. In addition roads ran inland from other major ports, like Kotor, Dubrovnik (Ragusa), and Split, through mountain passes and often along river valleys into the interior of Bosnia and on to northern Serbia or along southern routes through modern Hercegovina or modern Montenegro on to southern Serbia and Bulgaria.

For territories near the water, communications by sea were more important than by land. It was by sea that foreign products reached the Balkan ports. Much larger cargoes could be carried on ships than could be hauled overland by caravan. It was also much cheaper to transport goods by sea. During the late Roman period it was less expensive to ship goods from one end of the Mediterranean to the other than to cart them seventy-five miles overland. Thus a large portion of Balkan commerce went by sea routes along the Adriatic, Mediterranean, and Aegean. In keeping with this, most of the largest Balkan cities in the Middle Ages were seaports. At the time of the Slavic invasions many of the ports, behind their walls, were able to hold out, being provided with their necessities by sea. Sea connections with the Italian world also contributed to the success many of the Dalmatian cities had in retaining their Italian character. It should be noted that for much of our period many of the major ports, and thus a large portion of the sea commerce, remained Byzantine.

The Balkans were an underdeveloped area compared to Byzantium. They exported raw materials and imported manufactured goods. In the medieval period they chiefly exported pastoral products, such as cheese, and forest products, such as wood, wax, and honey. In the late Roman period, and again in the thirteenth and fourteenth centuries with the rise of independent Serbian and Bosnian states, products of the rich Balkan mines (silver, iron, lead) were exported. The people of the interior of the Balkans imported salt from the Dalmatian coast and manufactured goods, particularly luxury items—textiles and metal products—from the Byzantine Empire or from Italy. A nobleman often had to export a large portion of his estate's surplus to pay for his luxury imports; this did not aid the development of local markets or the local economy. Since none of the Balkan states had its own coinage until the thirteenth century, they used either barter or foreign currency (particularly Byzantine). Small-scale purchases at local markets presumably were chiefly by barter.

The Balkans have two climatic zones. Southern Greece and the Aegean and Adriatic coastal regions enjoy the hot and dry Mediterranean climate where olive trees, citrus fruit, and grapes thrive. The interior has a continental climate with a variation in seasons, often fairly rough winters, and sufficient rainfall for regular agriculture and the production of cereals.

Society

The overwhelming majority of Balkanites were rural—farmers or shepherds. There was a marked difference in character between town and countryside. This difference was not just the obvious occupational one of farmer versus urbanite, but was also ethnic and cultural. Along the Adriatic coast the old (pre-Slavic) Roman-Italian population predominated in many of the walled cities while the Slavs came to control the hinterland. A similar (though there quite temporary) phenomenon occurred in Greece. There, after the Slavic invasions and before imperial recovery, some walled cities and the islands remained Greek while much of the countryside came to be Slavic. In Dalmatia, throughout the Middle Ages, the old cities retained their Roman-Italian character and were more a part of the Italian than of the Slavic-Balkan world. There was a gradual influx of Slavs into these towns which in turn reacted to protect their own culture; thus, for example, in the fifteenth century Dubrovnik issued laws declaring Italian to be the official language of the town. All sorts of goods and cultural features, including Christianity, radiated from these towns into the hinterland, but the Slavs did not allow themselves to be latinized.

This dichotomy was true further inland as well. For example, for long stretches of time in what is now Serbia the Byzantines retained possession of towns like Niš. In Niš there was stationed a bishop, various administrative officials, and a garrison. But, though this town remained Byzantine in character, the surrounding countryside consisted of Slavs—sometimes paying tribute to the Roman Empire and sometimes loyal to a neighboring Slavic state. Later on in the thirteenth and following centuries within the Slavic states of Bosnia and Serbia the towns continued to retain a foreign flavor. Then, after the mines were reopened, the mining towns were dominated by people connected with that industry, particularly Saxons from Hungary and the Italian-speaking coastal merchants who established commercial colonies in these important centers. In addition the Serbian ruler Stefan Dušan established garrisons of foreign mercenaries (chiefly Germans) in various of his towns since they were more likely to be loyal to the central state than the fractious nobility. Each of these foreign communities had considerable autonomy, being run by its own leaders under its own laws. In this later period, for example, Dubrovnik established colonies in mining centers and market towns across the Balkans. In the early medieval period, since the mines, the chief incentive for major commerce, had not been reopened, we find much more limited activities by coastal merchants inland. In fact, after the Slavic invasions, commerce and the towns declined for a long period of time.

The medieval period was one of great demographic change, resulting not only from massive invasion or migration and the preservation of minority peoples through their seeking sanctuary in the mountains or other security zones, but also from large-scale forcible transplanting of populations which was a regular policy of the Byzantine Empire. Large numbers of captured Slavs were transferred to Anatolia and to regions further east. And large numbers of eastern peoples (Syrians, Armenians, etc.) were transferred as settlers along imperial borders with the Slavs, both to defend these frontiers against the Slavs and to break up their own dangerously large concentrations in eastern regions of the Byzantine Empire. Thus forcible resettlements introduced new ethnic elements into the Balkans and also imported heretics—the Paulicians—who were transferred in large numbers to Thrace (particularly around Philippopolis) in the ninth century. In addition this policy also brought large numbers of Greeks back to Greece at the beginning of the ninth century after Emperor Nicephorus I (802–11) had restored imperial rule over most of Greece; in this case the transfers contributed to halting the process of slavicization of Greece and to bringing about the area's rehellenization, thus guaranteeing that Greece remained Greek in culture.

The peoples of the Balkans—both the pre-Slavic population as well as those who arrived in the Balkans in the course of the early Middle Ages—will be discussed in the following chapters as they become relevant. However, a word should be said about families in these societies. Throughout the Balkans, families were organized patriarchally. This meant that generally the eldest male dominated. This organization was found among all classes of society—pastoralists, agriculturists, and the nobility. With the death of an elder the remaining males inherited equal shares; they might hold the inheritance collectively (with one heir acquiring seniority) or they might spilt into individual households. In the case of a collective, after a father's death generally the new elder was his eldest son, though on occasion a brother of the father would succeed before one of the sons. Charters have survived signed by "N. and sons" or "N. and brothers." On occasion even rulers left their realms to be divided among several sons. Cases of this will be discussed in the narrative that follows. Such divisions of a state seldom worked and generally led to civil war. In medieval Duklja (modern Montenegro) the principle of succession to sons conflicted with the principle of succession going to the deceased ruler's brother.

The father in a nuclear family or the eldest male in an extended one tended to be an autocrat, defining the duties of others and controlling the family's economy. Women had a minimal role in decision making. By the division of labor women had strictly defined duties which were carried out—in large households—under the direction of the elder's wife. Families tended to be larger in the mountain areas and there society was organized into clans and tribes. In these regions family honor became the basis for values. Since there were few or no "state" institutions to maintain order, the tribesmen kept order by self-help, relying on their family. As a result the blood feud became a major institution, which has survived into the twentieth century, particularly among the Montenegrins and northern Albanians.

In settled societies in later times large extended families were common. In the Slavic lands such a family is often called a *zadruga* by modern scholars, though this term was not used by the families themselves. Over the past two or three centuries when documentation exists about their size, a few of these zadrugas reached a hundred members, though it seems the average size was nearer to twenty. The elder ran the family, assigned all tasks, controlled the economy (all earnings went to him and he decided on all family expenditures) and arranged all family marriages. In the zadruga several generations lived under one roof; but though larger in size, the zadruga operated on the same principles as the normal patriarchal household.

A limit was generally kept to a zadruga's size by conflicts within the household which caused them to break up with the territory being divided into equal shares among the different sons; then the process could start again with each son assuming the role of household elder and coming to have more people under him as his sons married, brought in women, and began producing children. In the twentieth century for a series of economic and social reasons this institution has been dying out, and now the few that survive tend to be much smaller in size.

Scholars have long thought that the zadruga was an old institution going back to the primitive Slavs. However, there are no sources to show this. There is a theory that such an institution arises at a critical time when people feel the need to band together, for defense against raiders or for economic reasons. Thus an alternative view has it that, though the Slavs may have had large families from time to time in the past, it was not a primitive institution per se. This view holds that zadrugas arose and developed according to need at critical times, and that most of the zadrugas noted in sources of the early modern period were not of ancient origin but arose and developed into a common institution in the insecure years during and after the Ottoman conquest of the fourteenth and fifteenth centuries. This view finds confirmation in sources about southern France. There villages of nuclear families were replaced by extended households in the middle of the fourteenth century. Over the next century and a half (1350–1500), a period of great insecurity for the people of the south, extended households were common over much of southern France. A century or so later, with the return of more stable conditions, once again nuclear families predominated. This model could well also fit the medieval Balkans.

However, there are no sources to give us any information about household size among the medieval South Slavs. Thus, though extended households may have existed, it would be wrong to assume the existence of the zadruga then, and there is no basis to consider it a primitive Slavic institution. One might suspect that in periods of insecurity there would tend to be larger households and in periods of peace smaller ones. In addition, one should not expect that all families would have been organized in just one way or just the other; presumably at any given moment larger households coexisted with smaller ones. At times of insecurity the balance probably would have been in favor of the larger household. But at all times, irrespective of external conditions, internal conditions would have had an effect on the development of any given household, causing it to grow (as sons married) or causing it to split up (as brothers or other members inside the household quarreled).

And now, after these brief introductory remarks, let us turn to examine the Balkans on the eve of the Slavic invasions.

CHAPTER 1

Historical Background

This chapter will provide a brief summary of the historical background to set the stage for the major turning point with which this work begins—the Slavic invasions of the late sixth and early seventh centuries. In the pre-Slavic period and throughout the Middle Ages, the Balkans were underdeveloped—exporting raw materials and importing manufactured goods. In the late Roman or early Byzantine pre-Slavic period the Balkans became an important part of the Roman Empire. The regions now called Bosnia and Serbia possessed valuable mines. Thrace was a major granary and the Balkans as a whole were an important source of manpower for the armies. In particular, the Illyrians, who lived in Dalmatia, Istria, Epirus, northwestern Macedonia, and what is now Bosnia, Hercegovina, and western Serbia, constituted a significant portion of the Roman armies and had a well-deserved reputation as fine warriors.

The Indigenous Population

Before turning to the Roman Empire, its characteristics (particularly those which were to have an influence upon the Balkan peoples), and its problems on the eve of the Slavic invasions, let us first survey the indigenous population of the Balkans. First a line should be drawn running roughly through Albania, Macedonia, and Thrace on to Constantinople. South of this line were found chiefly Greeks. North of it, if the classical sources, which are far from ideal on this question, can be trusted, three peoples were to be found: the Illyrians, Thracians, and Dacians. (1) The Illyrians lived in the western portion (northwestern Greece, Albania, and a large portion of present-day Yugoslavia). However, some Yugoslav archaeologists of the prehistoric period, excavating in this region, have come to believe that the term *Illyrian* is an oversimplification that masks a variety of cultures. They have found significant cultural variations between findings from different so-called

Illyrian sites within what is now Bosnia and Hercegovina alone. This suggests to some of them that the "Illyrians" should be subdivided into different cultural groups. Whether this also means they should be divided into different ethnic groups is still not known. (2) The Thracians dwelled in Thrace, much of modern Bulgaria, and eastern Macedonia. (3) The Dacians inhabited Moesia (roughly what is now northern Bulgaria and northeastern Yugoslavia) and Dacia (what is now Rumania).

Linguistically these three peoples were all Indo-Europeans, and some scholars believe that the Thracians and Dacians until a millennium or so earlier had been one people. Various linguists disagree. Traditionally scholars have seen the Dacians as ancestors of the modern Rumanians and Vlachs and the Illyrians as the proto-Albanians. Perhaps (keeping in mind the frequent ethnic mixing as well as cultural and linguistic evolution) we should retain this view. However, from time to time these views have been challenged, very frequently for modern nationalistic reasons. For example, if the Illyrians were the ancestors of the Albanians, then the Albanians, as original inhabitants, have some historic right to that region and possibly rights to other regions which had been settled by Illyrians. And their Illyrian ancestry has been very important in Albanian nation-building myths. In the same vein, if the Dacians were proto-Rumanians then they were the original settlers and have historic rights to Rumania, particularly in the mixed region of Transylvania against claims of the late arriving (end of the ninth century) Hungarians. Not surprisingly, Hungarian scholars have been the leading critics of the claim that Dacians are Rumanians and argue that the Vlachs (or Rumanians) arrived in the eleventh and twelfth centuries when Vlachs first appear in the written sources.

Recently the Albanian-Illyrian identification has come under more serious challenge from linguists.[1] Before turning to the arguments, it must be pointed out that Dacian, Thracian, and Illyrian are not only dead languages but languages in which no texts have survived. Thus all that is known about these languages comes from personal and place names mentioned in classical texts or surviving place names (toponyms). V. Georgiev argues that Illyrian place names are found in a far smaller area than I have given above for Illyrian settlement. Secondly, he argues that, though the Albanians now live in what was Illyria, they themselves come from part of Moesia, from the Morava region of eastern Serbia. This was ethnically a Dacian region and thus he argues for a Dacian ancestry for the Albanians. These conclusions, he believes, are shown by the following: (1) Illyrian toponyms from antiquity do not follow Albanian phonetic laws. (2) Most ancient Latin loanwords in Albanian have the phonetic form of East Balkan Latin (i.e., proto-Rumanian) and not West Balkan (i.e., Old Dalmatian) Latin, suggesting the Albanians were descended from the Dacians. (3) The marine terminology in Albanian is borrowed from different languages, suggesting that the Albanians were not originally a coastal people. (4) Few ancient Greek loanwords exist in Albanian; if the Albanians had originated in the Albanian-Epirus region there should be more. (5) There is no reference in any source to Albanians in the Albanian region until the ninth century. (6) Roughly one hundred Rumanian words are similar only to Albanian words, and when this fact is combined with the similar treatment of Latin in Albanian and Rumanian, Georgiev concludes that the Albanians came from what is now Rumania (or the region of Yugoslavia close to modern Rumania) and that their language developed during the fourth to sixth centuries when proto-Rumanian was formed. Rumanian he sees as a completely romanized Dacian-Moesian language whereas Albanian is a semiromanized Dacian-Moesian language.

These are serious (nonchauvinistic) arguments and they cannot simply be dismissed. Furthermore, during the fourth to sixth centuries the Rumanian region was heavily affected by large-scale invasions of Goths and Slavs, and the Morava valley (in Serbia) was a main invasion route and the site of the earliest known Slavic sites. Thus this would have been a region from which an indigenous population would naturally have fled.

However, very little is known about the Dacian and Illyrian languages—and that little consists chiefly of certain place names and a few historical personal names. The Albanian language could well preserve large numbers of Illyrian features that simply are not known to linguists. The two languages, Dacian and Illyrian, may have been more similar than linguists think. And since the Morava region was near the border between Dacians and Illyrians, through direct contact possibly Illyrian was influenced by the Dacian language. The lack of early references to the Albanians is not significant. The centuries before the ninth are a period of few sources. And, if the Illyrians were proto-Albanians, the argument does not stand because sources mention Illyrians there earlier. We should also note that Vlachs are not mentioned anywhere in this period either.

But, though they are not conclusive, the arguments for the Dacian origin of the Albanians have strong points and cannot be summarily dismissed. More evidence is needed which, owing to the nature of our sources, may never be obtained; thus the question may well be one of many in early Balkan history which we may never be able to answer. Moreover, the Albanians did not have a single ancestor in one or the other of these pre-Slavic peoples; the present-day Albanians, like all Balkan peoples, are an ethnic mixture and in addition to this main ancestor they contain an admixture of Slavic, Greek, Vlach, and Romano-Italian ancestry.

In addition to these three Indo-European peoples, each living in its own zone of the pre-Slavic Balkans, other peoples had impact as well. Large numbers of Celts had passed through earlier, leaving their contribution to the gene pool as well as a wide variety of cultural (particularly artistic) influences. Large numbers of Roman veterans were settled in the Balkans (in particular, in what is now Yugoslavia). Different Germanic peoples (Ostrogoths, Visigoths, and Gepids) raided and settled (both on their own and as Roman federate troops) in the Balkans in large numbers over three centuries (third to sixth). And in the towns were merchants, officials, and soldiers, drawn from the whole empire, which included Italians, Germans, Greeks, Armenians, and other eastern peoples from Anatolia, Egypt, and Syria.

The Romans Acquire the Balkans

Roman influence during the period before Christ was chiefly along the coast and concentrated in coastal towns. Its impact was little felt in the interior before Augustus (27 B.C.–14 A.D.). In the period extending from the second century B.C. to early in the first century A.D. the Romans subdued the Illyrians. The first Roman successes were in Dalmatia. The Romans increased their influence by settling many veterans in and along Dalmatia. The Dalmatian towns were given various privileges, including autonomy, which they retained throughout the Middle Ages. At first there was considerable instability in Roman Dalmatia, owing to Illyrian pirates and raiders from the mountains who swept down upon the coast to plunder. But as the coast became romanized, its towns became very similar to those in Italy. Throughout the Middle Ages these old coastal towns were far more Italian than they were Balkan. Salona, which lay just outside of modern Split, was the chief Dalmatian city.

In the first century A.D. the Romans began pushing their frontiers inland across the Balkans (across modern Yugoslavia) toward the Danube. Following their conquest, they established forts and small towns (the ruins of some of which have been excavated), and built roads to connect the towns and fortresses with the coast. Other roads were built to link a variety of rich mines (particularly in Bosnia and Serbia) with the coast, and the Romans exported minerals and timber from the Balkans. The roads were kept in repair and were guarded (with key places garrisoned) to secure transport and communications. The rest of the region (i.e., most of the countryside) was still populated by the indigenous populations (Illyrians and any other peoples) and surely retained its "Illyrian" character, with limited Roman influence.

The boundary between eastern (Greek) and western (Roman) culture ran through what is now Albania and Macedonia. The Greeks, living to the south of this line, kept their Greek language and culture and maintained their own local administration and controlled their cities. In general the Greeks remained loyal to Rome. Many more towns existed in the Greek-Macedonian region than existed to its north. As in the interior of the northern Balkans, some Roman veterans were also settled in Greece. They established new Latin-speaking towns and villages within the Greek zone.

The Roman Empire and Its Balkan Provinces in the Third and Fourth Centuries

The third century A.D. was a period of chaos. The northern part of the Balkans, because its mountain ranges ran north-south, had no natural military defense and was easily accessible to invasion. In the third century intensive Goth raids were launched by land from across the Danube. At the same time Goth pirates began raiding Roman towns along the Black Sea coast. Frequently the Roman generals sent out to defend Roman territory against them revolted and claimed the throne. Throughout the third century there were civil wars; the throne changed hands on the average of every three or four years. There were also numerous revolts which did not succeed, and provinces broke away, loyal to this or that pretender. Thus, much of the Balkans was devastated by wars and raids and for much of the time was not really under the control of the ruler in Rome.

During all this internal chaos the Goth raids continued, lasting from the third to the fifth century. Yet, though these raids were frequent, they tended to be concentrated along major routes (e.g., the Orient Express route through the Morava valley) and roads leading off the main routes to other centers. Probably they rarely went further from these routes than was necessary to forage for food. Furthermore, along these main routes were concentrated the major cities (sources of the most booty) and the major concentrations of population (urbanites or nearby villagers supplying urban needs) for slaves. These areas were plundered time and again. But it probably is not accurate to picture the whole Balkan region (or even large parts of it) as being desolate; such a picture would be valid only for the region along the main routes. Much of the population probably reacted as people did later, at the time of the Turkish conquest, withdrawing into the hills and mountains further from the routes to avoid the invaders.

The result was probably the depopulation of villages and poorly fortified towns on and near main routes, with an accompanying reduction in commerce and the standard of living, while much of the interior presumably remained untouched (though probably less well supplied with the goods obtained by trade). Thus the Goth raids caused some devastation, depopulation of certain areas, flight of population to other areas, decline of commerce, and a dislocation of the tax base. All this must have weakened the area for subsequent invaders (the Slavs and Avars).

In the midst of these troubles Diocletian (284–305) assumed the throne. Feeling that the empire was too large for one ruler to administer, he divided it among two senior and two junior emperors, each one with specific territorial responsibilities. Despite the actual division the theoretical unity of the empire was retained. Diocletian, the leading senior emperor, then chose to move east. Peace was established during his reign, but after his abdication further power struggles and various territorial divisions followed, until Constantine emerged in 324 as the sole emperor.

Creation and Importance of Constantinople

Constantine chose to live in the east and he established a new center there, Constantinople. He began to build the city in 324 and it was dedicated in 330. Constantinople was given tremendous walls and defenses and was to hold out against all attacks from east and west (except for the Fourth Crusade in 1204) for over a thousand years. As long as the city remained unconquered, the empire survived. Constantinople soon became the chief city in the empire, though throughout the fourth century the imperial capital remained where the emperor and his suite were; and they were generally in transit moving from one city to another. At the end of the fourth century the emperors settled down permanently in Constantinople and it became the real capital. In a short time Constantinople became a great cultural center from which Christianity, literature, art, music, ideas, and goods spread. Its wealth attracted invaders and imitators. A great trade center, it became the richest and most advanced city of Europe. It was a key point in both east-west trade between Asia and Europe and in north-south trade between the Steppes and the Black Sea on the one hand and the Aegean and North Africa on the other.

Across the straits from Constantinople lay Anatolia. For centuries, except for occasional wars with Persia and later wars with the Arabs, Anatolia was untouched by invasion. Thus Anatolia was an intact source of manpower and grain to supply the capital and eastern heartland of the empire, allowing the empire to survive. So, while the west (including the Balkans) was ravaged by barbarians and collapsing, the city of Constantinople, located opposite Anatolia, was able to survive. Eventually after major losses in the Balkans, with the resources from the east, the empire was able to regroup its forces and recover most of the lost parts of the Balkans.

Constantinople's magnificent fortifications were not only a barrier preventing Balkan invaders from breaking through into Anatolia; they also prevented the great power invaders from the east—Persians and Arabs—from penetrating into the Balkans and Europe until finally the Ottoman Turks succeeded in circumventing these defenses and gaining a foothold in the Balkans during the second half of the fourteenth century. Within a century they had made themselves masters of the Balkans and the capital city itself.

Division of the Empire, 395

In 395 the emperor Theodosius I died, leaving the empire divided in two parts, west and east, to his two sons. Though in theory they were colleagues and it was still one empire, from here on the empire was never united in fact. The two different civilizations developed on their own: Latin and Greek (eventually each with its own Christian church). After the Slavic invasions of the late sixth and seventh centuries cut off east-west communications (overland via the Balkans while Slav [and later Arab] pirates cut off sea communications), these differences became even greater, making it impossible for the two to agree on certain major issues again. This was to be an important factor behind the later church quarrels and eventual (eleventh century) church split. The various differences that had always existed between Greek and Latin cultures increased as did separate political ambitions. The line dividing the two parts of the empire was basically the same as the old Greek-Latin cultural line and the later Orthodox–Roman Catholic line. This boundary ran through the Balkans from Sirmium on south to Skadar. Thus the Balkans became the border region between Old Rome and New Rome (Byzantium) and between Latin and Greek. The Balkans also served as a borderland between civilization (the empire) and the barbarian world beyond the Danube.

Characteristics of the Byzantine Empire

After its capital was established in the east, the empire became, in scholarly parlance, the Eastern Roman Empire. Furthermore, because Constantine and all of his successors (except Julian the Apostate, 361–63) were Christians, the empire from here on can also be called the Christian Roman Empire. As a consequence of these two changes the Roman Empire had become the Byzantine. However, though used by scholars, none of these three names was used at the time. Though the empire had its center in a Greek cultural and linguistic area, as a result of which there followed a gradual hellenization of its institutions and culture, the emperors recognized no change. The empire remained the Roman Empire and the citizens (even though Greeks came to dominate it) still called themselves Romans. The term *Hellene* (Greek) connoted a pagan. The term *Byzantine* was an invention of Renaissance scholars after the fall of the Byzantine Empire and was never used by its contemporaries. By the middle of the seventh century Greek had become the official language of all spheres of government and the army; nevertheless the empire remained "Roman" and despite divisions of its territory at times it was always seen as a single unit. Essentially the Byzantine Empire was a combination of three major cultural components: (1) Roman in political concepts, administration, law, and military organization, (2) Greek in language and culture, and (3) Christian in religion.

The Empire Becomes Christian

The empire became officially Christian under Constantine. Of course, the Christianization of many people (though a relatively small percentage) went back to the first century. Christianization was a long process and even after the imperial conversion it still was far from completed.

Under Constantine, the first Christian emperor, a major theological dispute broke out over the relationship of Jesus Christ to God the Father. It was known as the Arian dispute. We can ignore the theology here because with the exception of the Goths, who became Arians but who departed from the Balkans before the Slavs arrived, all the Balkan peoples became Nicenes, that is, followers of the form of Christianity that was defined at the Council of Nicea in 325 and which triumphed throughout the Byzantine east by the end of the fourth century. What is important for us is that the Christians were so glad at last to have an end to persecutions, a Christian emperor, and to have become a favored religion that they allowed the emperor to acquire a great role in church affairs. So when the Arian controversy became heated, Constantine called the council at Nicea, financed the passage of bishops to it, presided over it, and, though he was not a theologian at all, was allowed to press a compromise solution (in many ways theologically unacceptable) upon the assembled bishops which was adopted. Thus the emperor dominated the church council. Constantine then gave the decisions of Nicea the force of imperial law. This became the basis for state persecution of variant religions as heresy. Correct belief was to become a criterion for full citizenship. Heresy became a crime against the state.

Because religion (and loyalty to the state) became the criterion for citizenship, nationality (or ethnic group membership) had no importance for one's citizenship. The state remained, as it had been earlier, multinational. But now all Orthodox Christians in the empire regardless of nationality were defined as Romans; and such a criterion for citizenship was to be true also for the later medieval Slavic Orthodox Balkan states of Serbia and Bulgaria. In them too all Orthodox Christians were equally citizens and community was thus seen along these religious lines.[2] This was not only true in the Byzantine and Orthodox Balkan states but also later in the Hungarian Empire (though here it was Catholicism that defined the community) and in the Ottoman Empire which divided its people into different religious communities called *millets*.

At the same time at the Council of Nicea the emperor set the precedent that he had the final word in matters of faith and that the state had the duty to protect the church. This resulted in the church losing its independence and becoming a department of state. Thus from a spiritual point of view one can see how the conversion of the empire was to have many negative effects on the Christian religion. However, the church leaders of the early fourth century did not consider precedents. They were grateful to the Christian emperor, they tolerated his dominance, and quite possibly the leaders of the winning side were happy to have the state enforce their views.

Soon, as Constantinople became a true capital, the bishop of that city was elevated to patriarchal rank. But not surprisingly, with the church becoming a department of state, the emperor came to control the appointment and actions of the patriarch.

These models of emperor and patriarch and of the role of the ruler in church affairs were to be imitated later on, after their conversions, by the Bulgarians and Serbs. Byzantine culture (much of it religious culture) was also to be imitated; this culture, including literature, art, architecture, and music, was to accompany the Christianization of the Balkans, which was brought about by missionaries sent from Constantinople. In addition, various later Orthodox Balkan rulers, in imitation of Byzantium, sought to become emperors themselves and modeled their court ceremonial as well as the titles of their court officials on the Byzantine court.

The fourth and fifth centuries saw a gradual elimination not only of the Arian heresy but also of pagan cults. After Rome itself finally became Christian only Athens held out as a pagan center until Justinian finally closed the Academy in 529. Athens then declined to a second-rate provincial town. Yet though Christianity nominally triumphed, paganism (particularly as rites and specific beliefs rather than as a coherent religion) remained side by side with it. Old pagan customs received a Christian veneer. Christian holidays were set on pagan feast days and many of the old pagan rites connected with these days were retained under a Christian cover. Attributes of pagan gods became features of Christian saints, and often the saint whose day fell on the holiday of a former pagan deity acquired some of that god's attributes. Churches were erected on existing sacred spots and much of the ceremonial for a saint's day—such as the ritual meal—retained old pagan forms. Whereas some pagan rites were absorbed into Christian ones, others continued to exist in their old form, being practiced on specific days or for specific needs—e.g., for the welfare of family, animals, and crops. Thus many people, particularly villagers, even though they became nominally Christians, can be called more pagan than Christian.

Imperial Administration of the Balkans

When the Roman Empire was centered in Italy, the Balkans had been a distant borderland. The establishment of the capital in Constantinople brought the Balkans much nearer the center of things. More Roman influences penetrated the peninsula, which, owing to its proximity to the capital, became more important for the empire to defend and hold. Now there was more Roman activity here; more officials and troops were present than had been the case when the imperial center lay in Italy.

The Balkans were split among three imperial prefectures: (1) the Prefecture of the East, which in addition to Asia Minor and the other eastern provinces also included Constantinople and Thrace, (2) Illyricum with its capital in Thessaloniki, which included Greece and the central Balkans, and (3) Italy, which in addition to that peninsula included Pannonia, Istria, and Dalmatia. Dalmatia at that time included a great deal more of its hinterland than it does now. Thus, the

Italic Prefecture roughly contained the Balkan territory that later was to become Roman Catholic.

Diocletian and Constantine initiated a series of economic and administrative reforms which, on the whole, we can ignore in this survey. However, after their reforms the army was composed of two types of troops: (1) Frontier forces (*limitanei*) whose task was to defend the borders. Many of those so settled were barbarians: Goths and Slavs. (2) The elite troops which were the mobile armies, divided into five large units based in the interior, particularly around the capital; these were able to be sent on foreign operations or to any place of weakness where the frontier defenses were insufficient. Each of these five units was under a commander who reported directly to the emperor. In this period more and more barbarians (particularly Goths) were taken into the army. Some were integrated into the regular Roman units but large numbers became federates, settled on lands under their own leaders; their settlements tended to be drawn from just their one ethnic group and they fought in their own contingents under their own chiefs.

Since there was a shortage of cash, Diocletian instituted a new tax system. By it the state's major sources of revenue, the land and head taxes, were to be paid in kind (i.e., produce). They were assessed on the rural population which was, of course, the overwhelming majority of the empire's population. In addition, most civil officials' and military salaries were also paid in kind. Early in the fourth century the monetary system was reformed and the coinage was standardized. It remained at the same standard, undebased, until the eleventh century. It was far more stable than any modern coinage. The Byzantine *solidus* was used throughout the Balkans and remained in use through much of the Middle Ages even in the independent Slavic states. Finally in the twelfth century the Venetian ducat came more and more to replace the solidus, and it became the model for the independent Balkan coinages that began to be issued in the thirteenth and fourteenth centuries. In the Byzantine period and during the later independent period as well, much of the trade in the interior remained in kind. Local markets were certainly more based on barter than on cash.

Despite these reforms, disorder continued throughout much of the Balkans, particularly the large-scale raids, which were able to dislocate any system. However, it is evident that from the time of Diocletian there was more efficiency than previously in tax collection (with taxes raised in kind and chiefly used in the area where they were raised) and in the recruitment of soldiers. The military reforms also failed to solve the Goth problem. Goth raids continued through the fourth and fifth centuries and proved to be a major drain on the treasury, necessitating the hiring of soldiers to fight them or paying the Goths protection money (tribute) not to attack.

The Byzantines developed many diplomatic techniques which were to be utilized throughout the empire's history and whose fame added a new meaning to the term *Byzantine*. (The word *Byzantine*, in the sense of being wily and not completely honest, exists to the present day in many of the languages of Europe.) (1) The Byzantines created a chancellery to collect information on barbarians. (2) They paid tribute to buy peace or to buy allies. (3) They granted titles of honor to barbarian chiefs, bringing them into the imperial hierarchy of princes. (4) They granted them territories, generally territory which, though in theory imperial, had already been lost to the empire; either the receiving barbarians already held it and the empire, desiring peace, used the grant as a means for this, or some less friendly barbarian held it and the empire told a more friendly chief that if he won the lands, they could be his. (5) They educated the sons of barbarian chiefs in Constantinople, which also gave the empire possession of useful hostages. (6) They played one group of barbarians off against another. (7) They built up within barbarian nations pro-Byzantine factions which were supported against anti-Byzantine rulers or factions. The empire often financed its allies with gold. (8) The empire sent missionaries to convert to Christianity barbarians and then through the church hierarchy, under the patriarch of Constantinople, exerted Byzantine cultural and political influence.

Land, Magnates, and Peasants

One feature of the period from the fourth through the sixth centuries was the growth of large estates and the absorption of many state lands and the lands of many free peasants (including whole villages) by the great magnates. Some scholars seem to believe that this phenomenon was almost total; yet it is clear that although there were great increases in the holdings of the great magnates, many small holdings and free villages remained. The novels (new laws) of Justinian (mid-sixth century) included edicts against the absorption of free holdings in Thrace and Illyricum; since these were general laws it demonstrates clearly that a sufficient number of free holdings still existed to be worth protecting by general legislation. Saints' lives also show that in addition to the great estates free villages existed in all parts of the empire. The sources are far too meager to provide a general picture of landholding in the Balkans. But we must beware of the tendency of historians to carry real trends to the nth degree. Although there was an increase in the size of many great estates, in the percentage of lands under their control, and even in the number of such estates, still many small holders and free villages continued to exist. In addition it is certain that the ratio of great to small and the percentage of land under the great magnates varied from province to province.

At the same time various peasants, probably in large numbers, were fleeing to the mountains or to other distant regions out of the reach of tax collectors. Others sought the protection of patrons by becoming serfs on estates; and the number of serfs increased in this period. Since many magnates had tax exemptions—or enough pull to evade taxes—the peasant often found himself better off financially as a serf than as a free peasant. The effect of abandoned lands and of free men becoming serfs was to reduce the income of the state at this critical time when it needed cash to raise armies to fight the barbarian invaders.

To try to keep the peasants on land and taxpaying artisans in their places, the state passed laws intended to bind men to their trades (and sons to the trades of their fathers) and the peasants to the land. Many studies describe the empire in these terms. However, we may wonder how rigid life really was. How was the empire able effectively to enforce such laws? The fact that these laws were reissued frequently suggests that the problem continued and the policy was not effective. Thus it is doubtful that life in the Balkans (a particularly chaotic region) was really as rigid as the laws demanded. However, binding men to professions clearly was the aim of the government. And since the main tax was on land, and since land to be taxable needed a cultivator, the state did try to bind the peasants to the land. In good times, people on the whole probably followed these laws willingly. The artisans, as a result of state limitations on the number of artisans in any trade, had a guaranteed income, and the peasant, who was guaranteed the right to his plot, probably also was usually content to remain on his land. However, raids and increasing tax demands, which often were impossible to meet, caused flights and the dislocation of the system. In these insecure centuries when people were killed, carried off by raiders, or fled to the hills (often to become brigands) to escape taxes, population decreased. And this of course meant reduced income for the state, which was faced with ever increasing budgetary needs.

Withdrawal of the Goths

In 476 the Goth Odovacar overthrew in Italy the last weak western emperor. The emperor Zeno in the east could do nothing to prevent this so he accepted Odovacar's pledges of loyalty and his recognition of Zeno's suzerainty. Zeno made Odovacar part of the court hierarchy with the rank of patrician. In theory there was still one empire and Italy was still part of it.

However, the eastern emperors were unhappy with the situation and soon nicely killed two birds with one stone by persuading the Ostrogoth Theodoric, who had been a troublemaker in the Balkans, to march against Odovacar in Italy. Theodoric eliminated Odovacar and set up an Ostrogothic kingdom in Italy in 493 against which some forty years later Justinian campaigned in his attempt to restore the old Roman Empire. This kingdom included some of the western Balkans, Istria, Dalmatia, and part of Pannonia. With the establishment of this kingdom most of the Goths in the Balkans migrated thither leaving the Balkans (except the regions noted above) more or less clear of them, and the Goths ceased to be a Balkan problem. The Goths left little long-term influence on the area. However, their exodus surely made the Balkans more inviting for the Slavs and Bulgars, now living across the Danube, to raid; for the Goths, whether they were fighting for the empire or for their own interests, were sturdy soldiers who could resist plundering by these other peoples. Moreover, after the centuries of destruction and unrest caused by the Goths, the Balkan peoples surely were weaker and less able to resist the newcomers.

The Effects of Justinian's Wars of Reconquest

At the start of his reign, the emperor Justinian (527–65) was concerned with the barbarians beyond the Danube. He built fortresses along the Danube (or ordered them built, for probably in general the localities had the actual responsibility to build them) to tighten defenses against the barbarians. Older fortresses were repaired. He also repaired the walls and fortifications of various cities in the interior of the Balkans. Such walls, even if not manned, could give shelter for urban populations and neighboring peasants when raids came. However, Justinian was primarily concerned with the loss of Rome and Italy to the Ostrogothic kingdom which Theodoric established in 493. Caught up by the imperial idea and his desire to restore the old Roman Empire, he fought an almost continual war for forty years to recover Italy, Spain, and North Africa. The parts of the Balkans held by the Goths were restored early, Dalmatia by 537, Istria by 539. By the end of his reign Justinian seemed successful; he had recovered Italy, the coast of North Africa and much of Spain. However, he achieved this at enormous loss of manpower and an exhausted treasury. The recovered territories were full of barbarians hostile to Roman rule and awaiting their chance to revolt. Thus these lands required further manpower and state expense to hold. And just three years after his death, the Avars drove the Lombards out of Pannonia into northern Italy, which undid half of his work of Italian reconquest. Thus much of his work went for naught.

In order to carry out these western campaigns Justinian ignored two major problems: the Persians in the east and the barbarians to the north of the Balkans. Not only did he not concentrate serious efforts on these two frontiers, but, lacking sufficient manpower to carry out his western conquests, he had to take troops away from them to send west, leaving these frontiers relatively unprotected. This led not only to the weakening of imperial defenses but also to all sorts of financial problems. For with insufficient troops (a problem which had increased with the departure of the Goths) he had to hire mercenaries and to bribe barbarians with tribute not to attack, both of which were costly. And raids continued anyway, since the empire was faced with many individual tribes, each under its own leader; tribute paid to one had no effect on others. The result of these raids was, of course, reduction of manpower and tax income.

Since Justinian needed cash for his ventures, he was then forced to increase the rate of taxes on the remaining peasants. Many could not pay and fled. Some of these became brigands, which increased the law and order problem. These flights also increased the depopulation and led to more lands being out of cultivation which caused further decline, both in productivity and in the state's income. The shortage of troops caused many of the Danube frontier forts to be left unmanned or undermanned and consequently worthless, a fact which encouraged the barbarians to raid, which in turn intensified the economic problems of the area.

Moreover, Justinian's whole policy was pointless, for it was already too late to unite the two parts of the empire, which were already divided in fact and whose unity was an anachronism. Justinian did it by force but the empire lacked the resources to retain these conquests; and by exhausting his manpower and economic resources, he left an empire with an empty treasury, unable to face serious threats from the Persians and Slavs. (The treasury had been further emptied by the fact that Justinian had carried out a guns *and* butter policy; he had also directed a massive and expensive building program of churches, palaces, etc.) Had he concentrated on the enemies on his two frontiers, he might well have been able to achieve success. However, he left both problems to his successors. Shortly after his death in 565, the empire found itself involved in a costly Persian war. To make matters worse, the Slavs had from the late 550s become a serious threat to the empire; they were to become even more dangerous after Justinian's death, when their raids across the weakly defended Danube frontier became almost annual. Justinian thus left an enormous empire with huge commitments which spread its limited resources far too thin.

NOTES

1. V. Georgiev, "The Genesis of the Balkan Peoples," *Slavonic and East European Review* 44, no. 103 (July, 1966): 285–97.

2. By the fourteenth century the pastoral Vlachs in Serbia had acquired certain specific variant legal requirements; these might be seen as somewhat altering the equality of citizenship between them and the settled agriculturists. These distinctions, however, probably arose for logical occupational-economic reasons rather than ethnic prejudice.

CHAPTER 2

The Slavic Invasions

The Slavs Settle in the Balkans, ca. 550–ca. 630

In the fifth century Slavs first show up north of the Danube in the written sources. Many scholars feel that they had arrived in that region even earlier than that. Where they had come from has long been a most controversial point. Yet it is a point that really is not too important for the history of the Balkans, because we know so little about the possible homelands and the cultures of the various peoples in them during these centuries. The evidence used for locating the homeland of the Slavs—that is, the region where they became a distinct people from their Indo-European cousins—is all linguistic and archaeological. Much new evidence is being uncovered now which may eventually settle the point, but at present the best case can be made for the Ukraine, possibly between the Bug and the Dnepr. The Ukrainian theory has been advanced by a variety of scholars.[1] Adherents of this view believe that the Slavs followed the path toward the Danube used by a large number of Turkic peoples—including Huns, Avars, Bulgars, Pechenegs, and Cumans.

The sources speak of many disunited tribes divided into two groups north of the Danube in the fifth and sixth centuries—the Slaveni and the Antes. Some linguists have argued that the word *Antes* is not Slavic but Iranian. However, Procopius, a sixth-century historian who is a major source for this period, says the two groups (Slaveni and Antes) speak the same language and in looks do not differ from one another. The *Strategikon* (a military manual from the late sixth or early seventh century attributed to the emperor Maurice) confirms Procopius by stating that the two groups lived in the same way and had the same customs. To a Byzantine speaking about Slavic languages, the word *same* could really mean *similar*. But, in any case, if the Antes really were not originally Slavs, it seems most likely that they had been a conquering group which had asserted authority over

25

various Slavic tribes and had thereby donated their name, but had in time become linguistically and culturally assimilated by the larger number of Slavs. Thus there seem to have existed two groups linguistically Slavic and ethnically probably more Slavic than anything else but certainly not pure Slavs. Some scholars, such as the prominent Bulgarian historian V. Zlatarski, think, and it is perfectly plausible, that the Slaveni to the west were the ancestors of the linguistic group that became Serbo-Croatians while the Antes were the ancestors of those who were to become Bulgaro-Macedonians.

The name *Antes* suggests this people was intermixed with Iranians, and linguists point to a large number of Iranian loanwords in Slavic that were acquired very early. This would not be surprising if the Slavs came from the Ukraine because there they would have had contact with both Iranian Scythians and Sarmatians. Indeed, the Sarmatians were still to be found in Bačka and the Banat near the Danube at the time the Slavs arrived there. Archaeologists working in that area speak of cultural borrowings by the Slavs from Sarmatians living in the Banat.

There are also in Slavic a large number of early Germanic loanwords. In the southern Ukraine as well as along their whole route to the Danube, the Slavs would have run into many Germanic peoples; Germans were still to be found in the Danubian region when the Slavs arrived and were to remain there for a considerable time thereafter. In what is now Rumania these Slavs met Dacians. Rumanian archaeologists have discovered a variety of cultural borrowings by the Slavs from the indigenous population of Rumania. They have even unearthed what they claim to be joint sites, showing Slavs and Dacians living in the same communities.

Byzantine Descriptions of Slavs' Way of Life

What were these early Slavs like and how did they live? Brief descriptions are given by several Byzantine writers. The Slavs were wild and free (i.e., not subjected by anyone else) and without leaders. Procopius stresses that they were not ruled by one man but from ancient times had lived in "democracy." (Needless to say, too much has been made of this last word by various Slavic scholars.) They had public gatherings to decide on policies. The *Strategikon*, attributed to the emperor Maurice, states that the Slavs lived without authority and in mutual hatred (i.e., in hatred between groups); they did not recognize military ranks; they had many chiefs but no supreme chief. The different tribes disagreed with each other and it was not difficult to play one tribe off against another. (However, it proved impossible for the Byzantines to solve the Slavic problem or defeat them for the same reason; for if the Byzantines defeated or made a pact with one tribe, that arrangement was valid for just one small group and had no effect on any other tribe, and a vast number of small tribes existed.)

Procopius says that the Slavs lived in poor huts spread far apart and that they frequently moved (i.e., either they were pastoral or else primitive farmers who quickly exhausted the soil and had to move on). They tended to war on foot with spears and bows and arrows; other than shields they had no armor. They did not keep captives long in slavery. They tried to ransom them quickly and send them home; those who were not ransomed were soon allowed to live freely within their society like everyone else. The Slavs had much endurance, poor food, were very hospitable, and avenged injuries to their guests. They lived in or near woods, swamps, or along rivers; they generally had secret exits for escape routes and hid their valuables. When fleeing, they often hid under water, breathing through straws. In battle they stressed guerrilla tactics and specialized in hit-and-run ambushes. The Byzantine strategists felt it was best to attack them in the winter when their tracks could be seen in the snow, when it was easy to cross frozen rivers, and when their stock was at home.

Slavic Religion

Procopius reports that the Slavs had a chief god of lightning, their only lord of the world, to whom they sacrificed animals. It is generally felt that this one god was Perun, a leading deity and the master of thunder and lightning. He was worshiped by many Slavic peoples; and though his name is not given in any written source about the South Slavs, many toponyms derived from his name exist in the Balkans. Procopius also says they worshiped springs (possibly this should mean they worshiped *at* springs) and nymphs to whom they also sacrificed. This last item is probably accurate, since nymphs (*vilas*) have played an important part in South Slavic folklore to the present.

Much has been written about ancient Slavic religion; but a great deal of it is worthless, for we really know almost nothing about it because we have so little information. There has been a strong tendency among scholars to take any ancient Slavic deity or belief found anywhere—be it in Russia, among the Baltic Slavs, or in Procopius—and make it common to all Slavs, and then to combine all this material into some sort of conglomerate system of early Slavic belief. There is no evidence that such a common system ever existed, and thus it is most dubious that such a composite picture could be accurate.

For instance, scholars have written a great deal about early Slavic dualism, i.e., that the primitive Slavs had good and bad gods, two opposing supernatural camps at war with one another. However, there is little evidence for this. First, the presence of a supreme deity (Perun) argues against a dualist cosmology. Secondly, the later legends about saints and their attributes and behavior, much of which is inherited from pre-Christian spirits and gods, depict the saints as saints of function. This suggests that the pre-Christian spirits and gods had been so too. Thus there would have been, e.g., a god of rain who could help people by bringing rain for crops or hurt them by floods and droughts. This amoral functional depiction of gods does not coincide with a dualist world view. The only evidence for the existence of dualism comes from the Christian period (chiefly from among the Baltic Slavs), when sources mention a black god whose negative characteristics may simply reflect the common tendency of pre-Christian deities to become demons after the victory of the new religion.

Thus it seems most probable that the early Slavs were not dualists; they seem to have had a pantheon of gods of functions (e.g., of thunder, sea, crops, and animals) who could help people or hurt them depending on whether or not they carried out appropriate rites. These rites included sacrifices and seem to have been held at particular sacred spots. In addition to the gods, there seem to have been other supernatural creatures which also had to be appeased, including nymphs.

Slavic Activities in the Balkans in the Mid-Sixth Century

Though some Slavic incursions had occurred earlier, the number of raids increased in the second half of Justinian's reign. If we can believe Procopius, they were an annual affair, and the number of specific raids mentioned in sources confirms this generalization. Procopius also speaks of Slavs living in the vicinity of certain Thracian cities, suggesting that by the middle of the sixth century a certain amount of Slavic settlement (as opposed to raiders coming, raiding, and then returning beyond the Danube) had begun in the Balkans. Procopius confirms his own statements by giving in the course of his works a fairly large number of Slavic place-names in what is now north and east central Yugoslavia (particularly along the Morava and Timok river valleys) and northern Bulgaria. These places were clearly well established by the early 550s when Procopius wrote.

Some Slavs were settled as federates in the Balkans (their settlements could be responsible for some of the place-names) and others were already fighting for Justinian in Italy. Thus at least in the north-eastern Balkans, south of the Danube, by the middle of the sixth century there already was a fair number of Slavic settlements. Probably, though, this settlement was relatively small-scale (compared to what was to follow), for there is no evidence that regions had lost their Roman character and become slavicized yet.

The basic pattern of Slavic activity up to the late 560s was raiding. The bands crossed the Danube, in general following the main routes into Thrace or Macedonia, occasionally penetrating into Greece (on one occasion as far south as Corinth). The bands were lightly armed and mobile. Since walls could stop them, they could not conquer cities or whole regions. In this period, though some towns were taken, no major cities fell.

When the Slavic raiders arrived in an area, the urban and local village populations fled to walled enclosures. Generally local militias defended the walls in smaller places. However, the countryside was open to pillage. Thus the peasants suffered the greatest misery, for their crops were often ruined and they might be taken prisoner. The raiders got what booty they could; particularly often it was captives, hence they could profit by attacking villages. Then they returned home across the Danube. The Balkan peninsula was thus open for annual plunder but was not occupied by the Slavs in a major way. Though there was some limited Slavic settlement, much of it could have been colonies of federates with military responsibilities settled by the Byzantines inside the Balkans.

The Avars and Their Impact on the Slavs

Large-scale Slavic settlement began in the Balkans in the late 570s and early 580s. These larger population movements, still on the level of individual tribes, are associated with the arrival of the Turkic Avars, a nomadic group who, having lost a major war to other nomads in the east, had then migrated west, subjecting various Caucasian tribes and other groups north of the Sea of Azov and the Black Sea. They annihilated the Antes as a political force and subjected various Turkic Bulgar groups. They appeared north of the Danube at the end of the 550s and in the mid-560s established themselves in what later became known as the Hungarian plain, with their main settlements between the Danube (after it bends north) and the Tisza rivers.

In the Balkans archaeologists have found vestiges of Avar settlements along the Sava and Danube rivers as far east as the mouth of the

Morava. Further east along the Rumanian and Bulgarian sides of the Danube, Slavic sites are found but not Avar. Thus the Avars settled to the west of the main Slavic concentrations. The Avars were excellent soldiers and horsemen; they were tightly organized with their ruler, called a khagan, supreme over the various Avar groups. They made treaties with their neighbors and fixed frontiers. Below them was a vast array of subject peoples, various Slavic and Bulgar tribes plus the remnants of the Huns. In addition to subject tribes, they also had large numbers of vassal tribes while others were allies.

The Avars asserted their authority over many Slavs and other peoples north of the Danube. Since the Slavs were divided into numerous petty tribes, they were easily subjugated. The presence of the Avars also surely sent other Slavs scurrying south across the Danube to escape subjection or tribute. Rumanian archaeologists think still other Slavs were driven up into Transylvania, and they date the arrival of the Slavs in that region to the coming of the Avars. The presence of the Avars also curtailed the pattern of gradual settlement of Slavs in the Balkans. This had been the pattern up to then, and had it been allowed to continue at the same slow rate, the empire in time probably could have gradually hellenized them. For, despite some Slavic settlement, there was up to that time no sign that the Roman Balkans had lost their Roman character. However, the presence of the Avars, who either mobilized Slavs as troops or caused them to flee in large numbers, was an impetus for large-scale Slavic settlement to the south of the Danube.

The settlement of the Slavs was also facilitated by Byzantine involvement during much of this period in a war with the Persians; thus they could not bring troops to the Balkans. Furthermore, the Slavs were aided in their conquest by their large numbers; they simply infiltrated and eventually submerged whole regions. Their lack of organization was also a help; they had no overall political leader to defeat in battle and thereby force their retreat. It was necessary to defeat each individual little chief and tribe and that was impossible.

The Avars were masters of sieges, and now cities began falling to them and their Slav clients. The loss of cities often led to the loss of imperial control over whole regions. In 582 the Avars conquered the Byzantine border fortress of Sirmium (modern Sremska Mitrovica), which eliminated a major Byzantine border defense post, and soon the Slavs were pouring into the Balkans. The fall of Sirmium has always been depicted as a major event. Possibly its importance is somewhat exaggerated, for before its fall it was possible to bypass Sirmium and cross the Danube elsewhere. In addition, various sources mention large-scale Slavic campaigns in the year before Sirmium's fall. In any case, it fell in the period (581–84) during which most scholars date the first massive Slavic invasion-settlement.

John of Ephesus—a contemporary but not local writer—states,

> Three years after the death of Justin II under Tiberius [i.e., 581] the cursed nation of Slavs campaigned, overran all Hellas, the provinces of Thessaly and all of Thrace, taking many towns and castles, laid waste, burned, pillaged, and seized the country. And dwelt there in full liberty and without fear, as if it belonged to them. This went on for four years, and until the present, because the emperor was involved with the Persian war and the armies were in the east.

He goes on to explain that the Slavs had a free hand to do what they wanted, expanding where they would in the Balkans, and treating the land like a conquered province up to the outer walls of Constantinople, and "today they still are established and installed in Roman provinces, killing, burning, and pillaging, having learned to make war better than the Romans."

Most scholars feel this long stay in the Balkans (581–84) is the beginning of large-scale Slavic settlement, and it is close to the time the sources give for the beginning of the Slavic occupation of Greece. Menander—a late-sixth-century historian whose work only partially survives in extracts incorporated in the works of later authors—speaks of a hundred thousand Slavs in Thrace and of Greece being pillaged by Slavs in 582. Evagrius—a church historian who died near the end of the sixth century—states that in these years the Slavs twice reached the Long Wall, captured Beograd and all of Hellas. And the Chronicle of Monemvasia—a late-tenth- or early-eleventh-century source based on earlier material—dates the beginning of Slavic settlement in Greece in 587. Thus the first half of the 580s were peak years for raids, warfare, and destruction; the Slavs were relatively unopposed since the main Byzantine forces were tied up in the east fighting the Persians.

For the period that follows, we have a major source about Thessaloniki and its environs in *The Miracles of Saint Demetrius*. These hagiographic tales recount how the great saint reappeared from the beyond to rescue his city from various crises, many of which were Slavic and Avaro-Slavic sieges and attacks. The tales make it clear that by the second decade of the seventh century massive Slavic settlements existed in the environs of Thessaloniki. In fact, that city had become virtually a Roman island in a Slavic sea.

The Byzantine Counteroffensive against the Avars

The Persian war ended in 591 and now at last the emperor Maurice (582–602), a skilled general, was free to turn to the Balkans. He dispatched various military forces into the Balkans during the next decade. The outline of the campaigns that follows is accurate but the actual dates are not always certain. Thus the reader may find discrepancies of a year or so between dates given here and those given elsewhere. In the absence of clearer sources, however, all that is certain is the correct sequence of events; the actual dates must remain questionable.

Maurice rightly realized that the Avars were the key problem and aimed his campaigns against them. He sent troops into the Balkans which retook Beograd and pushed the Slavs and Avars back across the old Danube-Sava frontier. This victory amounted to no more than driving out the military peoples who had been in occupation of cities; it certainly had little effect on the numerous nonmilitary Slavic settlers scattered around the Balkans. Maurice's war lasted ten years; on the whole it was successful despite various checks and small defeats. These reverses usually occurred when Maurice became jealous of his successful and able general Priscus. When this happened he recalled him, replacing him with his own brother Peter who was a mediocre commander. Peter was usually soundly trounced, necessitating Priscus being sent back to pick up the pieces.

The Avars did not give up without a fight and after their expulsion they returned to lay siege to Beograd in 593 and 596. In 597 they sent a massive raid through Dalmatia (then a broad province including also most of modern Bosnia), which destroyed some forty fortresses. In roughly 599 the Avars with a massive army broke through Byzantine defenses all the way to the walls of Constantinople, where a plague struck them, killing off large numbers, including several sons of the khagan. The khagan at this point retreated, carting off many prisoners; we are told he took seventeen thousand and demanded a ransom of half a gold piece for each. When Maurice refused to pay the sum, the Avars slaughtered them all. His failure to buy back the captives did much to destroy Maurice's popularity, which was to influence the events that followed. Byzantine armies were back in the field in 600, when they regained Sirmium which reestablished the Danube as the frontier. Peace was then agreed to by both sides for the sum of one hundred twenty thousand gold pieces a year tribute to the Avars as protection money.

But now for a change it was the Byzantines who broke the treaty, and they did so almost immediately, still in 600; after campaigning for about a month, they crossed the Danube, probably with the aim of destroying the centers of Avar power. However, it was hard to make permanent gains since the tribes beneath the Avars were loosely bound to them; if one was defeated, it had no effect on others, and if one alliance was smashed, others were formed. It was decided to attack the real center of Avar power. So in 601 new forces were sent across the Danube, marching up toward the Tisza River where they won a major victory over the Avars. Hoping to follow this up and eliminate the Avars once and for all, Maurice ordered the troops to winter there across the Danube and then to continue the campaign the next year; possibly he also was following the advice in the military manual attributed to him to campaign against the Slavs in the winter. However, the troops were not used to wintering away from imperial territory and morale was bad (it seems partly owing to Maurice's failure to ransom the seventeen thousand captives), so a revolt broke out under an officer named Phocas. He brought the forces back over the Danube and marched on Constantinople; civil war broke out at home and Phocas was admitted into the capital. Maurice and his family, captured trying to escape, were all butchered.

Byzantium Loses the Balkans

Almost immediately the Persian king of kings declared war on Phocas to avenge Maurice, who had previously restored him to his throne. This initiated a twenty-year war with Persia. Factions of what were more or less street gangs ran wild in the capital. Phocas, who was extremely suspicious, began purging large numbers of the highest and most experienced military officers. Flunkies rose to high positions and there seems to have been considerable financial corruption. The Balkan frontier along the Danube and Sava, which Maurice had restored, seems to have collapsed almost immediately and the Balkans were opened once again to Slavic raids. Once again, as in the 580s, these included large-scale settlement. Owing to the new Persian war, few imperial troops were available to defend the Balkans. By 604 the Avars, who had not been destroyed, regrouped, and, as a result of their demands, received a considerably increased tribute.

In the years that followed, under Phocas (602–10) and during the early years of Heraclius (610–41), the Byzantine Empire, lacking in money and manpower, was in no position to oppose the Slavs. The Persian war continued, and in 615 Persian troops reached the Bosphorus. The Balkans were now freely overrun by Slavs who settled in even larger numbers than previously. Slavic settlement at this time seems to have been chiefly in what is now Bulgaria, Serbia, Macedonia, and parts of Greece. Presumably this new settlement dates from the reign of Phocas when the empire began to be beset by major difficulties. However, Barišić dates it from Heraclius' reign. He notes that no source mentions Slavic activity in the Balkans during the reign of Phocas; the many disasters that the sources mention all occurred after Heraclius had taken the throne in 610.[2]

Whereas the eastern lands were overrun by Slavs, the more western territories of what is now Yugoslavia (western Bosnia, Croatia, and Dalmatia) seem to have chiefly suffered Avar raids. It has long been believed that in these regions the Avars did not settle and that the settlement which did occur was by Slavs who were under the Avars. However, recently a strong case has been made that in these western regions large-scale settlement by actual Avars occurred;[3] the mid-tenth-century work known as *De Administrando Imperio* by the emperor Constantine VII Porphyrogenitus repeatedly states that Avars settled this region. In addition, there is a variety of toponyms in this region derived from early Turkish words (probably Avar), which confirms Constantine's information on Avar settlement. Furthermore, archaeologists have turned up Turkic (probably Avar) sites and objects in these western regions as far south as what is now Montenegro. Finally, up to the present, archaeologists have found no Slavic settlements in this area from the sixth or early seventh centuries.

The raids increased in frequency in the second decade of the seventh century. Slavs, having increased their numbers in what were to become Bulgaria and Serbia, pressed south into Macedonia and reached the Aegean. This settlement provided the basis for the Slavic states that were to appear in these regions later. They penetrated into Thessaly and on occasion ravaged Thrace where they also established some settlements. They also raided some of the Greek islands.

Other marauders reached the Dalmatian coast which, after the departure of the Goths, had, until then, suffered few incursions. It seems likely that the Avars themselves played a major role in the onslaught upon Dalmatia. Salona (near modern Split), the capital city of the province of Dalmatia, which stretched from Kotor north to Istria, was sacked and destroyed in 614. The population fled to Diocletian's walled palace at Split which was able to hold out. Thereafter Split rose quickly in importance as one of Dalmatia's major cities. Constantine Porphyrogenitus in the *De Administrando Imperio* gives two accounts of the sack of Salona: one (chap. 29) is confused, at times calling the attackers Avars, at other times calling them Slavs, and at still other times making the two terms synonymous. His other account (chap. 30) mentions only Avars. One can suggest that the account emphasized the Avars not only because they were prominent participants but also because they directed the attacks. Since the numbers of actual Avars seem to have been limited, it seems likely that Slavs would have accompanied them. However, in this region the Avars retained direct control until they were driven out a decade or two later by the Croats.

Constantine Porphyrogenitus then goes on to describe the conquest at this time of Zahumlje, Dioclea (Duklja, modern Montenegro), and the mouth of the Neretva. In these chapters he mentions only Avars and makes no mention of Slavs, again crediting the Avars with the major role. The evidence from toponyms and archaeology, as has been noted, shows that there was some direct Avar settlement in these regions as well. This, of course, does not rule out early settlement by some Slav clients of the ruling Avars in these western regions. For it is natural for a source to stress the role of the dominant people who directed an attack and at times to ignore other peoples in their armies, even if numerous. As a result of these Avar offensives in the second decade of the seventh century the western part of what is now Yugoslavia seems to have fallen under direct Avar rule, while the eastern territories were under Slavs, some of whom may have been connected with the Avars; but in the east Avar control, being nothing more than indirect rule, was much looser than in the west.

In Dalmatia, besides Salona, the city of Epidaurus fell and the inhabitants of that town fled to a more defensible spot where they founded Dubrovnik (Ragusa). When the Avar campaigns were completed in Dalmatia, only Zadar, Trogir, Split, Dubrovnik, Budva, Kotor, and most of the islands had withstood their attacks. The islands, which had not had much importance until now, became a place of asylum for refugees from the coast and, in particular, Rab, Krk, and Cres became major food suppliers for the surviving cities of the mainland which had lost control of the territory beyond their walls. Thus the islands expanded both their fishing activities and agricultural production. The major Dalmatian islands acquired a role they had not had previously and were to have no longer after a Croatian state was established in Dalmatia in the ninth century.

The surviving Dalmatian towns bore many similarities to the Greek coastal towns which held out. The Greek towns remained centers of Greek and Christian culture and were to play a major role in rehellenizing Greece after Slavic occupation there. These Dalmatian coastal towns, though failing to romanize the barbarians settling all around them, would survive as Roman-Italian cities and would in time serve as conduits for Christianity and urban literate culture to the peoples of the interior.

Meanwhile within the interior of the Balkans most major cities fell to the invaders, including Niš and Sardika (Sofija). Beograd somehow managed to remain in Byzantine hands; Constantine Porphyrogenitus mentions its governor dealing with the Serbs in about 630. Thessaloniki also held out. But besides these two cities and various coastal towns, the Balkan towns were overrun and imperial authority disappeared.

In the lost areas urban life disappeared or declined; many of the towns became little more than villages. Commerce as well as communication across the Balkans virtually ceased owing to both urban decline and the insecurity of the roads. Christianity as a religion of the Balkan population almost disappeared in the interior. Literate culture more or less died out.

Greece, except for certain coastal cities and certain mountainous regions, was overrun by large numbers of Slavs and was lost to imperial control. Slavs poured down to the tip of the Peloponnesus in Greece. This Slavic settlement was on such a large scale that the Balkans were lost for several centuries to the empire. When the dust settled, the empire held only most of Thrace, a few walled cities along the Dalmatian and Greek coasts, and many islands.

That so much territory was lost to imperial control suggests that the invasions were massive. This conclusion is confirmed by source references (possibly sometimes somewhat exaggerated) to large numbers of raiders (in one case to one hundred thousand participating in a particular raid in Thrace). Since imperial control was lost from such a large area, we can assume that, though the Balkans were not evenly settled throughout, the Slavs must have had large numbers of settlements in every region of the Balkans lost to the empire. At the same time other Slavs settled in territory that remained imperial. Byzantine sources tell of Slavs in Thrace who were not always as loyal as the authorities might have liked.

Most of the Balkans was settled by Slavs of one of two types (excluding the smaller groups of Slavic Slovenes and Turkic Avars in the western Balkans). Each of these two main Slavic groups was to be named for a second conquering group who appeared later in the seventh century.

The first of these two groups was the Bulgaro-Macedonians, whose Slavic component the Bulgarian historian Zlatarski derives from the Antes. They were conquered in the late seventh century by the Turkic Bulgars. The Slavs eventually assimilated them, but the Bulgars' name survived. It denoted this Slavic group from the ninth century throughout the rest of the medieval period into modern times. Until the late nineteenth century both outside observers and those Bulgaro-Macedonians who had an ethnic consciousness believed that their group, which is now two separate nationalities, comprised a single people, the Bulgarians. Thus the reader should ignore references to ethnic Macedonians in the Middle Ages which appear in some modern works. In the Middle Ages and into the nineteenth century, the term *Macedonian* was used entirely in reference to a geographical region. Anyone who lived within its confines, regardless of nationality, could be called a Macedonian. Nevertheless, the absence of a national consciousness in the past is no grounds to reject the Macedonians as a nationality today.

The second of the two Slavic groups settling in the Balkans was the Serbo-Croatian Slavs, whom Zlatarski derives from the Slaveni. These Slavs came to be dominated by two different but similar tribal peoples called Serbs and Croats in the second quarter of the seventh century. But though subjected by a smaller military elite of true Serbs and Croats, who gave to the larger number of Slavs these new names, the masses who made up these peoples go back to a single group of Slavs (probably Slaveni) who settled in the Balkans during the sixth and early seventh centuries. Though in the twentieth century increasing numbers of their descendants have come to feel otherwise, they were a single people (though one broken up into many small tribal groups).

Fate of the Indigenous Balkan Population

What was the fate of the indigenous population? Many were killed, while others were carried off beyond the Danube as captives (some of whom were ransomed and returned), or fled to walled cities or to the islands. Still others withdrew to the mountains or remote regions, and their descendants reappeared later as Vlachs or Albanians who begin to turn up in written sources in the eleventh and twelfth centuries. The Thracians disappeared from history. But many indigenous peoples surely simply remained; perhaps in their original homes or perhaps moving a short distance to establish new homes in the same general area. Thus there came to be Slavs in every region of the Balkans (including imperial territory like Thrace) but they were not everywhere; considerable numbers of the indigenous population remained, sometimes in isolated pockets and sometimes in close proximity or even in the same communities with the Slavs. Presumably Slavic concentrations were heaviest along the main routes. For example, along the Orient Express route (Beograd, Niš, to either Sofija or Thessaloniki) are found references to early settlement, and many Slavic place-names show up there early. Along this route, owing to constant raids, the greatest depopulation would have occurred, leaving lands vacant to be taken by the newcomers. Presumably also in the nearby fertile regions of central Serbia there was large-scale early settlement.

Probably fewer Slavs penetrated early into more remote or less fertile regions, e.g., Lika, much of Bosnia and Hercegovina, and Montenegro. Here were refuge areas where the original population could have remained in larger numbers, possibly joined by refugees from other areas. Such a process would have been more likely if in fact these regions had been areas of direct Avar rule. Because the Avars were primarily pastoralists and not numerous, one would not expect them to have completely depopulated an area when they took it over but rather to have ruled over the existing population, collecting tribute or taxes. In these western refuge areas, then, it is likely that the ratio of indigenous people to Slavs would have been higher. If so, this probably would have led to more indigenous influence on these Slavs, and the greater the number of remaining pre-Slavic peoples, the greater would have been the intermixture of the two groups and the greater the likelihood of their forming joint communities of the type for which Rumanian archaeologists think they have found evidence in Rumania.

Archaeology in western Yugoslavia shows considerable cultural continuity from the pre-Slavic to the Slavic population. Frequently the same towns continued to function as did many fortresses; the Croatian župa (territorial) organization seems to have been heavily influenced by the earlier Illyrian territorial organization. A continuity of cult and graveyard sites exists; the Slavs took over the techniques of the indigenous population in tomb construction. The Slavs acquired indigenous metallurgical techniques, leading them to produce many of the same type of metal farm implements and household objects as their predecessors. Slavic house construction also reflects many indigenous influences. The acquisition of such things as metalworking techniques and architectural and grave-construction features suggests that close and friendly contacts existed in places between the two populations.

The Archaeological Evidence

In general, archaeologists have dated Slavic settlement in the Balkans to the seventh century. They claim the scarcity of (and some even feel the total lack of) Slavic sites in the Balkans from the sixth century is evidence for initial Slavic settlement in the seventh rather than the sixth century.

However, Irma Čremošnik presents good evidence for at least two sixth-century Slavic sites in eastern Bosnia (Dvorovi near Bijeljina and Mušići near Višegrad).[4] Despite the date of these two sites, some scholars argue that the basic conclusion of archaeologists still is tenable. Yet, if two such settlements existed in relatively remote places like Višegrad and Bijeljina, it seems probable that were funds available for massive exploration and excavation many other sixth-century sites might be discovered. Furthermore, the most intensively studied areas lie in western Yugoslavia, which seems to have been chiefly a region of Avar settlement. The two sixth-century Bosnian sites are in easternmost Bosnia along the Drina River, which forms the border with Serbia. Presumably, if one is seeking sixth-century Slavic sites, intensive work must be done in more eastern regions.

Professor Barišić also points out that because most Slavs were agriculturists, their settlements would have been in rural areas outside the cities. Because most archaeologists (particularly in Serbia where one would expect the earliest Slavic settlement along the Morava and Timok rivers) have concentrated their work on cities, it is hardly surprising that few sixth-century Slavic sites have been found.[5] Furthermore, peasant villages would have left fewer and less monumental remains; thus peasant sites would be harder to discover.

In Serbia archaeologists have based their conclusions for no sixth-century Slavic settlement on their excavations of cities. They point to the discovery of Byzantine coins in cities throughout the Balkans from the reigns of most all of the sixth-century emperors up to and including the reigns of Phocas (602–10) and Heraclius (610–41). They believe this shows that the Byzantines kept the cities into the seventh century. Some scholars feel this means the Byzantines held the surrounding countryside as well. However, again we must pause. The situation of Thessaloniki has been noted; this city remained Roman while its surrounding countryside was largely Slavic. Such could easily have been the pattern for other cities as well. Moreover, the presence of Byzantine coins from dates well into the seventh century need not mean Byzantine possession. Slavs could have come by these coins through looting and trade.

Misdating of sites may be another reason for there seeming to be fewer sixth-century localities than there actually are. In many cases dating is done on very tenuous grounds, and some so-called seventh-century sites could well be sixth-century and, conversely, localities declared to be extremely early could really be from a century or so later. But at present, assuming that the dating of known sites is correct, it is a fact that there is very little archaeological evidence of Slavic settlement from the sixth century. However, regardless of archaeological finds, written sources provide material for a different conclusion. The Slavic place-names mentioned by Procopius, and noted earlier, are clear evidence of some sixth-century Slavic settlement.

A second problem with the conclusions of archaeologists has been their attributing sites to particular peoples. It seems to me that there is frequently a great leap of faith in labeling many of the early sites. How can one be sure whether a site is pre-Slavic or Slavic? To date it is not sufficient since pre-Slavic peoples survived into and after the seventh century. Frequently few objects are found in graves to give us a basis to assign a site to one group or another. Often the few objects found are not conclusive to label the site even though certain archaeologists may claim certainty. For example, wavy-line pottery motifs are often credited to the Slavs; they did have such motifs but this motif was found all over Europe. The so-called Slavic button types seem not to be unique; the so-called Slavic fibula is found among Germans into the seventh century, and Visigoths ruled Bosnia from 490 to 535. Thus many of the "proof" items are not certain. To this situation must be added the subjective factors of the excavators, some of whom want the sites they uncover to belong to their own special period or peoples or to their own ancestors; such archaeologists may exercise special pleading and pass off hypotheses as facts. In addition, since cultural borrowings occurred and objects were acquired in commerce, so-called Slavic items can turn up in non-Slavic graves and vice versa. Frequently it is impossible to ascertain to whom a site belongs.

One further problem remains. If the indigenous population remained in some areas in large numbers, then why did Christianity die out throughout the interior? For archaeologists have concluded that this is indeed what happened. Though the dating of early Balkan churches is a most controversial subject, with archaeologists disagreeing as to whether certain churches are pre-Slavic (fourth to sixth century) or early Slavic Christian (ninth to eleventh), they do agree that there was a gap without churches that included the seventh and eighth centuries.

Their conclusions leave three possibilities: (1) the generally accepted view believes that as a result of the Slavic invasions the indigenous Christians were more or less eliminated from the area and Christianity in the interior almost completely died out; (2) the dating of some of the churches is incorrect and actually there are churches from every century, in which case Christianity did not entirely disappear; and (3) since few pre-Slavic churches have been found in the interior, possibly the indigenous population was not really that deeply Christianized. When the invasions came the priests and missionaries fled, and the indigenous peoples, though remaining in numbers in the Balkans, in time lost what Christian beliefs they had had and reverted to paganism. In any case, the fate of Christianity shows that either the balance between indigenous population and Slav was heavily in favor of the latter or else the indigenous populations had been shaky Christians who easily shed this religion for other rites.

In conclusion, in many regions of the Balkans after the invasions there were two populations—old-timers and newcomers. In time, owing to the superior numbers of Slavs (again suggesting the invasions were massive), the descendants of the indigenous population on the whole were assimilated and became Slavic-speaking, whereas in Greece (in time, aided by more Greeks being settled there in the ninth century, plus the role of church and administration) the smaller number of Slavs scattered throughout Greece came to be hellenized.

The Avars: From Peak Strength to Decline, 614–ca. 635

Slavic and Avar Threats to Thessaloniki, 614–17

Between 614 and 616, at the same time that the Avars were leading their major offensive against Dalmatia, *The Miracles of Saint Demetrius* describes the attacks by five named Slavic tribes by sea in small boats along the coasts of Thessaly, western Anatolia, and various Greek islands. They then decided to capture Thessaloniki in a combined land and sea attack. Under the walls of the city they camped with whole families. They were led by a chief (the Greek title used is exarch) named Chatzon. During the sea attack, a vision of Saint Demetrius was seen by the whole town population, including the Jews, showing that the famous Jewish colony in Thessaloniki was already established. Right after this vision a sudden shift of the wind occurred and many boats capsized. The sailors who had been spilled out tried to climb into other canoes which now became overloaded and capsized in their turn. To save themselves, those still in boats beat off the others with oars and many drowned. Following this disaster, the Slavs retreated and many of their prisoners escaped.

Shortly thereafter Chatzon received a safe conduct and was allowed to visit the city; however, within the city a mob rioted, and the leaders of the city were unable to protect Chatzon, who was killed. His furious tribesmen then sent an embassy to the Avars. The embassy brought gifts and offered gold and prisoners to the Avars if they would help the local Slavs take Thessaloniki. The Slavs told the khagan that to take the city would be an easy task because Thessaloniki was entirely encircled by Slavs who had depopulated all the other towns; it stood alone, attracting refugees from the Danube, Pannonia, and Dacia. The *Miracles* specifically refers to refugees from Niš and Sardika, showing that these cities had already fallen. The khagan accepted the offer and assembled an army of Avars, Slavs, Bulgars, and other peoples. After two years of preparations, the khagan arrived and demanded that the city surrender. His demands were refused and the city suffered a thirty-three-day siege during which the environs were plundered. Then finally a treaty was drawn up, the Avars were paid off and the prisoners held by the Avars were ransomed. This story shows that the Slavic settlement was well advanced and provides evidence of the fall of two major cities from the interior.

Avar Threats to Constantinople

At roughly the same time—the date is disputed but most scholars accept 617—the Avars sent envoys to treat with the emperor Heraclius. The emperor went out to meet them, but as he approached the place set for the meeting, he was warned of a large number of armed Avars preparing an ambush. He fled and just managed to find the safety of Constantinople's walls in time. Angry at the failure to capture the emperor, the khagan ravaged the environs of Constantinople. Two years later, in 619 (unless it is actually the aftermath of the event just described from 617), there seems to have been a second Avar attack which ravaged Thrace and then returned to the Danube carrying off, we are told, two hundred seventy thousand people.

In 621 peace was concluded between the empire and the Avars, giving Heraclius briefly a free hand to turn against the Persians who in 619 had conquered Egypt, which, among other things, was the main source of grain for Constantinople. In 622 the Avars demanded and received increased tribute, and some relatives of the emperor had to be sent off to the Avars as hostages; but the peace allowed Heraclius to continue his campaigns in the east. Four years later in 626, however, the emperor's worst fears were realized when the Avars and Persians seem to have teamed up to attack the capital. A horde of Avars, Slavs, Bulgars, Gepids (a Germanic tribe), and other barbarians under the command of the khagan appeared before the walls of Constantinople. A small Persian army appeared on the Asiatic side. Whether their appearance was by prearrangement or whether the Persians, hearing of the Avar attack, sent a squadron thither to get in on the act and obtain some of the fruits of victory is a matter of scholarly debate. At the time Heraclius was in Armenia recruiting soldiers to lead an attack on Persia itself, and the defense of the capital was in the hands of the patriarch. Persian envoys sailed across to Europe to meet with the Avars, but on their way back they were captured by the Byzantines.

The khagan demanded the surrender and evacuation of Constantinople; the citizens were told they would be allowed to leave with only their clothes on their backs, but with no baggage. The Slavs were mentioned as being on foot with no armor, a description which agrees with those from the previous century. The Slavs also had their fleet of small boats there, presumably having sailed down from the Black Sea; but this fleet was annihilated by the Byzantine fleet, and, according to the Byzantine sources, after this defeat the enraged khagan butchered all the surviving Slavic sailors who fell into his hands. The khagan was not prepared for a long siege, and, having failed by sea, he retreated. Many Slavs then deserted.

Most scholars see this as the beginning of the end for the Avars; this was their last attack on Constantinople. After its failure the Byzantines ceased to pay the Avars tribute. In 629 a battle occurred between Slavs and Avars. Shortly thereafter the Avars suffered two major defeats. The first was at the hands of the Croats, who then set up an independent state in Illyricum. Secondly, the Bulgars near the Sea of Azov under Kovrat's leadership liberated themselves around 635. In addition, prior to the attack on Constantinople (a western chronicle dates it 623) some Czechs under Samo, allied to the Franks, successfully broke away from the Avars and established their own state. But though various Avar defeats and Avar decline followed the 626 events, it would be difficult to show how the failure of an offensive campaign and a quarrel with certain Slavic subjects were responsible for that decline.

The Bulgar Revolt of Kovrat, ca. 635

From the late fifth century the Bulgars, a Turkic people, had been living in scattered tribes north of the Black Sea and the Sea of Azov and along the lower Don. They were in two major groups: Kutrigurs who had moved west of the Black Sea in the 490s and the Utigurs to their east. In the first half of the sixth century both groups raided the empire from time to time, and Justinian was fairly effective at either buying them off with tribute or playing off one group against the other. In the second half of the sixth century both of these groups were subjected by other nomads, the more westerly Kutrigurs by the Avars and the more easterly Utigurs by a group known as the West Turks.

By the 630s the sources mention a group of Onogur Bulgars living in the region between the Caucasus and the Sea of Azov under a ruler named Kovrat. He had already established good relations with the empire. Two ninth-century historians, Theophanes and Nicephorus (probably from a common source, however), report that in 619 an Onogur Bulgar prince Organa (Orhan) and his nephew Kovrat had come to Constantinople, made a treaty with the empire, and accepted Christianity. After a lengthy visit in the capital, the two Onogurs returned to their people in the east.

Soon Kovrat became the ruler of the Onogurs and in 635 he threw off Avar rule, drove the Avars from his lands, and once again concluded an alliance with the empire. He also succeeded in uniting all the eastern Bulgar groups who were living north of the Black Sea, Sea of Azov, and the Caucasus. Kovrat died in roughly 642, leaving five sons. No sign of Christianity is seen among any of them. Each of the five sons, probably around 660, migrated to a different place with a following. Two of the five are important to us. First, an unnamed son with his supporters moved west and settled in Pannonia, accepting Avar suzerainty. (The Avars, despite a series of seventh-century defeats leading to the loss of much of their empire, continued to retain their centers in the Hungarian plain until Charlemagne defeated them in the 790s.) Second, another son, Isperikh (or Asparukh) moved into what is now Bessarabia, and then in the 670s crossed the Danube into Bulgaria. He conquered the Slavic tribes there and eventually established a Bulgarian state. It was centered in the northeast of present-day Bulgaria, stretching along both sides of the lower Danube, and extending south to the Balkan mountains. In passing, we may note that a third son established the Volga Bulgars who eventually accepted Islam and acquired an important role in that region.

The Controversy over Kuver

The Miracles of Saint Demetrius (*Miracle* II, 5) describes a certain chief called Kuver—generally thought to be a Bulgar—who had been made governor by the Avars over a mixed population of Christian Bulgars, Greeks, and other people in the region of Sirmium. This mixed population had been made captive "about sixty years before" at the time of the unsuccessful attack against Thessaloniki by the Slavs under Chatzon (described in *Miracle* II, 1) and the Avar intervention that followed. These events occurred between 614 and 618 and, if we add sixty years to this, we obtain a date in the late 670s. It is even possible that these people were the descendants of the two hundred seventy thousand captives taken in Thrace and carried off beyond the Danube in about 619. Though they had long been cut off from their roots, these subjects under Kuver had retained their Christianity and their desire to return to their ancestral homeland (which most scholars place in Thrace and/or Macedonia). Kuver, learning of their sentiments, revolted; his subjects supported him.

They began a migration south; the Avars attacked them five or six times and each time Kuver was victorious; finally, the Avar khagan had to withdraw with those still faithful to him further to the west, i.e., to the northwest of his state. Kuver then crossed the Danube with his people and came to "our region" (i.e., near Thessaloniki) and occupied a plain whose name is given but which means nothing to us now. Zlatarski claims the plain was near Bitola; however, Bitola seems a bit far from Thessaloniki to be considered in "our region."

Kuver sent an envoy to the Byzantine emperor (who unfortunately is unnamed) for permission to settle there with his people and requested that the Slavs of Dragovica supply him with food. These Slavs were one of the five tribes mentioned in 614. They were to give their name to a region in Thrace for which a later dualist church was to be named. Kuver's request was granted and he and his followers settled inside imperial territory; possibly the empire saw him and his people in the role of federates. This event must have occurred after 658, the date of a campaign by the emperor Constans II into this region, because prior to the 658 campaign no imperial control existed in this region and there would have been no reason to seek imperial permission.[6] In addition, prior to 658 no emperor would have had any authority over the Dragovica Slavs. Once settled there, Kuver's people in Thrace and Macedonia wanted to disperse and return to their original or ancestral homes. Kuver's advisors opposed this for they wanted to keep them together as a group with Kuver as khagan; for if they were allowed to disperse he would lose his whole power base. Kuver now requested the emperor to oppose this dispersal and to sanction Kuver's authority over them.

Possibly rebuffed, Kuver soon thereafter turned against the empire. Realizing that he needed a base and fortified center, he decided to capture Thessaloniki. He tried to take the city by ruse: he set off a civil war in the city in the midst of which the gates were to be opened to him. However, his agents were unmasked by Saint Demetrius and the city did not fall, and there the story ends, for the purpose of the story was to show how the saint saved the city, and the preceding was given just to provide the context for the miracle. The *Miracles* say no more about Kuver and his following, and other sources do not mention him by name though one event, mentioned in a Byzantine chronicle which shall be discussed at the end of this chapter, may involve his Bulgars.

The Bulgarian scholar Zlatarski suggests that Kuver, whose revolt he dates ca. 670–75, was the unnamed son of Kovrat who had left the Steppes in the 660s. This son, as mentioned, had moved west to Pannonia with his following and had accepted Avar suzerainty. Once there, presumably since he was an important prince, the khagan assigned him to rule the territory on which these descendants of earlier Byzantine captives lived. Thus Zlatarski concludes that, after the arrival of Isperikh (Asparukh) and his Bulgars in the northeast of modern Bulgaria in the 670s, there were two Bulgar states in the Balkans, the rulers of which were brothers: (1) Isperikh's in northeastern Bulgaria on the Danube, extending south toward, but not beyond, the Balkan mountains, and (2) Kuver's state in Macedonia.

The chronological pattern of the *Miracle* anecdotes themselves confirms the above dating of Kuver's revolt to the 670s (i.e., sixty years after Chatzon's attack). Book II of the *Miracles,* consisting of six episodes, was compiled in the 680s and describes events occurring between the 610s and 670s–80s. Episodes 1–2 on Chatzon and on the Avar attack that was its aftermath clearly took place in the middle to second half of the second decade of the seventh century; episode 3 consists of minor events that seem to have occurred around 630; episode 4 is almost certainly in the late 670s. Episodes 5 and 6 convey the Kuver story and, other than the reference to the sixty years, contain no specific dates or names of figures we can date from other sources. But the fact that the preceding episodes are in chronological order with number 4 in the 670s suggests that Kuver's revolt occurred after number 4 in the late 670s or early 680s. This gives the same result as adding sixty years to 618.

This all seems quite clear-cut, and Barišić, Zlatarski, Dujčev, and, most recently, Charanis have all made strong cases for this dating. However, many scholars have not accepted the dating of ca. 680 for Kuver; instead they have posited the revolt around 635–40. Simply ignoring the clear link to Chatzon's revolt, they have dated the Kuver story sixty years from the major Slav attacks mentioned by John of Ephesus around 581–84. It was possible, these scholars have argued, that the author of the *Miracles,* who is often not precise on earlier events, might have been confused over time duration, or that he might not have known which raid had been responsible for carrying off the captives.

Though the source refers to Kuver "in our times" (with Book II being composed in the 680s) some have argued that the author in the 680s was simply copying an earlier source from ca. 640 (for clearly the author had used earlier sources when he compiled the anecdotes in *Miracles*, II, 1–3) and failed to alter that phrase in his copying. It has also been argued that the 618 date for the captives was accurate, but the figure sixty was not only a round number but a highly inaccurate one. Sixty years, it has been argued, is a very long time to hold customs and wish to return "home"; and though the source says the parents had taught their children their old traditions, still their behavior on returning to the empire—when they did not wish to remain near Thessaloniki under Kuver but desired to return to their own villages— seems more like that of first-generation people. And if it was a first generation which was involved, then the date for these events would be nearer 635–40.

But why this dickering in the face of all the internal evidence given above? (1) The 630s and 640s were a time of general revolt against the Avars; (2) Fredegar's chronicle—a late-seventh-century Frankish source—refers to a civil war for succession within the Avar empire in which the Bulgars had their own candidate (whose name is not given) for the throne. This, if nothing else, shows the strength of the Bulgars within the Avar empire (in having their own candidate for the throne). Fredegar's Bulgar rebels were forced to flee and nine thousand of them, together with women and children, were chased out of Pannonia and sought refuge with Dagobert of Bavaria from whom they asked asylum in the Frankish land. Once there Dagobert split them up and tried to massacre them all. In the end only seven hundred were able to escape. Fredegar dates this event 631–32.

Some scholars have assumed that this story refers to Kuver's revolt and have made slight of the differences in the story, noting that Fredegar as a distant western source probably received his information third or fourth hand. Fredegar's rebels lost in battle against the Avars whereas Kuver won; but in both cases the rebels revolted in Pannonia and then emigrated.

However, what is important is that they departed to entirely different places and met entirely different fates; for we have detailed accounts of where Kuver and his people went and what happened to them in Macedonia when they got there, and we have a detailed account of where the unnamed Bulgar rebel and his following went and what happened to them in Bavaria. Thus I think it is safe to conclude that Fredegar was speaking of an entirely different event, one which occurred in 631–32 as he dates it but which has no bearing on the separate Kuver revolt which has to be dated on the basis of the other evidence we have and which evidence, as seen above, suggests it was in the late 670s or early 680s.

Also influencing many scholars to choose the earlier date is the Byzantine chronicles' mention of a Bulgar leader named Kovrat or Kuvrat revolting against the Avars in ca. 635. Many scholars, influenced by the similarity of the names, have concluded that Kuver was the same man as Kovrat. They point out that, in addition to similar names, they both revolted against the Avars. If one dates Kuver early, then they are contemporaries. Both sent envoys to the emperor (in Kuver's case to the unnamed emperor). Lemerle and Gregoire have concluded that the two men are the same. However, there are serious difficulties with this identification. In addition to the evidence that Kuver may well be a generation later is the fact that the two revolts are clearly described as taking place in entirely different regions. Kovrat's revolt was in the vicinity of the Sea of Azov, while Kuver's was far from there in Pannonia. And, according to the Byzantine historians, Kovrat and his family, after their revolt, remained in the Steppe region. It is only much later in the 660s that two sons moved west. Thus the two revolts took place in different places and the aftermath of the two is different. In Kuver's case there was a migration to the region of Thessaloniki while Kovrat, having liberated his own territory near Azov, did not move at all.

In my opinion, these arguments make this identification impossible; and though the names Kuver and Kovrat are similar, both are foreign names (one certainly and the other probably Bulgar) rendered into Greek. The Greeks were notorious for distorting foreign names when rendering them into the Greek phonetic system, and as cultural snobs, they never had any interest in getting barbarian names correctly. Possibly Kovrat and Kuver in the original Turkic were not really that similar. A later Bulgar kings' list mentions a seventh-century ruler named Kurt whom most scholars have, I think correctly, identified with Kovrat. Thus if Kovrat's real name was Kurt (and this form, coming from a Bulgar source, is probably closer to the original), then there is considerable distortion in the Greek giving the name as Kovrat. Moreover, even if Kuver and Kovrat are different versions of the same name, it is possible that this was a very common Bulgar name. If Zlatarski is correct in making Kuver Kovrat's son, it very likely was the same name, with the son being named for his father.

Thus the Kovrat-Kuver identity does not hold up, and Kovrat cannot be used as evidence to date Kuver in the 630s. However, though Kovrat is not Kuver, this is not absolute proof that Kuver must be assigned to ca. 680. But it does seem that the weight of evidence strongly adds up to Kuver being active in the late 670s.

The Establishment of the Croatians and Serbs

There were several revolts against the Avars in the period from the 620s to about 640: Samo's revolt in what is now Czechoslovakia in 623, the reference to fighting between Slavs and Avars in 629, and Kovrat's Bulgar revolt in 635. There was one other major offensive against the Avars, that of the Croatians who liberated much of the western Balkans from the Avars during the reign of Heraclius. At the same time the Serbs arrived, and though they did not actually battle the Avars, they did assert their authority over some Slavs who had been under Avar suzerainty.

The major source on the arrival in the Balkans of the Croatians and Serbs is Constantine Porphyrogenitus's *De Administrando Imperio*[7] written by the emperor in the late 940s or early 950s as a foreign policy guide for his son and heir. This is not an ideal source for these migrations because Constantine is describing events that occurred in the second quarter of the seventh century. However, the Byzantines had a chancellery which kept information on barbarian tribes and much of the information for this book evidently came from there; furthermore the empire kept records over the centuries, for at times in treaties references are made to former treaties from several centuries before. Thus much of this information, if it was derived from chancellery records, was probably accurate. However, this does not mean that all of Constantine's information came from the chancellery nor is there any guarantee that everything preserved in the chancellery was reliable.

Constantine's discussion of what is now Yugoslavia is contained in chapters 29 to 36. He swings back and forth in time, covering events before the appearance of the Slavs and Avars, their arrival, the subsequent arrival of the Croatians and Serbs a bit later in the seventh century, and various items from the ninth century. Chapters 29, 31–36 are a consecutive text. Chapter 30 is a later addition but still presumably dates from the time of the emperor Constantine; it was probably written by a second author. However, chapter 30 was composed independently of the others and contains a mixture of material contained in the other chapters and new material not found in them. The author seems unaware of what was said in 29 and 31. Thus the book evidently never received its final editing, which presumably would have incorporated 30 into the other relevant chapters and would have come to some decisions on contradictory material. This conclusion is reasonable because it is evident that the book was not completed; some of the most important neighbors of the empire, far more important to Constantine's son than the more distant Serbs and Croatians, are never discussed. For example, the Bulgarians, Khazars, and Russians never receive specific treatment but are mentioned only in passing references in discussions of other peoples. Presumably Constantine intended to discuss them but never got to it.

In chapter 30, Constantine first gives a clearly legendary account of how the Avars crossed the Danube, defeated the Romans and occupied, partly by guile, much of the Roman province of Dalmatia. This province, as noted before, was far broader than the narrow strip we now think of as Dalmatia, and included much of western Bosnia. In this account, Constantine makes the Avars the leading actors and does not mention Slavs at all. However, in chapter 29 Constantine at times speaks of Slavs and at times of Avars, and at times uses the two words as synonyms. It has been concluded previously that this territory was under the direct rule of the Avars and in it there were actual Avar settlements. However, there probably also was some settlement in this territory by Slavs who were clients of the Avars. Constantine goes on to say in chapter 30:

> [And the Avars] thereafter made themselves masters of all the country of Dalmatia and settled down in it. Only the townships on the coast held out against them, and continued to be in the hands of the Romans, because they obtained their livelihood from the sea. The Avars, then seeing this land to be most fair, settled down in it. But the Croats at this time were dwelling beyond Bavaria, where the Belocroats [White Croats] are now. From them split off a family of five brothers, Kloukas and Lobelos and Kosentzis and Mouchlo and Chrobatos, and two sisters, Touga and Bouga, who came with their folk to Dalmatia and found the Avars in possession of that land. After they had fought one another for some years, the Croats prevailed and killed some of the Avars and the remainder they compelled to be subject to them. And so from that time this land was possessed by the Croats, and there are still in Croatia some who are of Avar descent and are recognized as Avars. The rest of the Croats stayed over against Francia, and are now called Belocroats, that is, white Croats, and have their own prince; they are subject to Otto, the great king of Francia, or Saxony, and are unbaptized, and intermarry and are friendly with the Turks [i.e., the Hungarians, whom Constantine consistently

calls Turks]. From the Croats who came to Dalmatia a part split off and possessed themselves of Illyricum and Pannonia; they too had an independent prince, who used to maintain friendly contact, though through envoys only, with the prince of Croatia [i.e., in Dalmatia]. For a number of years the Croats of Dalmatia also were subject to the Franks, as they had formerly been in their own country [i.e., in White Croatia]; but the Franks treated them with such brutality that . . . the Croats, unable to endure such treatment from the Franks, revolted from them, and slew those of them whom they had for princes. On this, a large army from Francia marched against them, and after they had fought one another for seven years, at last the Croats managed to prevail and destroyed all the Franks with their leader, who was called Kotzilis. From that time they remained independent and autonomous, and they requested the holy baptism from the the bishop of Rome, and bishops were sent who baptized them in the time of Porinos their prince. Their country was divided into 11 'zupanijas' [which he then goes on to name].

Most of this material concerns later events and will be dealt with in a later chapter. We shall see that there were to be two different Croatian states, one in Dalmatia and one in Pannonia. This account telescopes matters; the Franks did not gain control of these Croatian regions until the 790s and the first decade of the ninth century. The revolts against the Franks occurred in the third quarter of the ninth century. The missionary activities from Rome also are ninth-century events. The material about the war against the Avars shall be considered after we have examined the account given in chapter 31. Here it is just worth noting that Constantine stresses the actual presence of Avars (as opposed to Slavs) and notes that in Croatia in his time there were still people recognizable as Avars. And archaeologists have found in western Bosnia Avar artifacts which they have dated as late as the ninth century.

In chapter 31 Constantine says:

The Croats who now live in the region of Dalmatia are descended from the unbaptized Croats, also called 'white,' who live beyond Turkey [i.e., Hungary] and next to Francia, and have for Slav neighbours the unbaptized Serbs. 'Croats' in the Slav tongue means 'those who occupy much territory.' [?] These same Croats arrived to claim the protection of the emperor of the Romans Heraclius before the Serbs claimed the protection of the same emperor Heraclius, at that time when the Avars had fought and expelled from those parts the Romani. . . . These same Romani having been expelled by the Avars in the days of this same emperor of the Romans Heraclius, their countries were made desolate. And so, by command of the emperor Heraclius these same Croats defeated and expelled the Avars from those parts, and by mandate of Heraclius the emperor they settled down in that same country of the Avars, where they now dwell. These same Croats had at that time for prince the father of Porgas. The emperor Heraclius sent and brought priests from Rome, and made of them an archbishop and a bishop and elders and deacons, and baptized the Croats; and at that time these Croats had Porgas for their prince. . . . The prince of Croatia has from the beginning, that is, ever since the reign of Heraclius the emperor, been in servitude and submission to the emperor of the Romans, and was never made subject to. the prince of Bulgaria. Nor has the Bulgarian ever gone to war with the Croats, except when Michael Boris, prince of Bulgaria, went and fought them and, unable to make any headway, concluded peace with them.

Constantine then goes on to stress the traditional friendship and gifts exchanged between the Bulgarians and Croatians and ends his account by noting that Great Croatia called White was still unbaptized in his day as were the Serbs who are neighboring on it.

It is interesting to note that Constantine, in this chapter, denies the established fact that the Croatians had once been subject to the Franks. Moreover, he strangely mentions a minor Bulgarian-Croatian skirmish almost a century earlier and ignores the massive conflict between the Bulgarians and Croatians in his own lifetime (in 926) when Symeon, Byzantium's major enemy, invaded Croatia and was trounced soundly by Tomislav, a Byzantine ally.

In chapter 32 Constantine discusses the Serbs. He also makes them originate from some unbaptized peoples called "White." This Serbia lay beyond Hungary, neighboring on Francia and White Croatia. Two brothers, whose names are not given, took half the Serbian folk and claimed the protection of the emperor Heraclius. The emperor received them and gave them land in the province of Thessaloniki (a province settled by many Slavs prior to that reign) at a place called Serblia. He then gives us a folk etymology, deriving the word *Serb* from the Latin *servus* (slave), and claims the Serbs were slaves of the Roman emperor. After some time they decided to depart home and the emperor sent them off but having crossed the Danube they sought permission to return from the Byzantine military governor representing Heraclius at Beograd. Thus all this movement happened during that emperor's reign. They were then given land to settle on in what is now Serbia (i.e., the region of the Lim and Piva rivers), Pagania (the lower Neretva), Zahumlje, Trebinje, and Konavli, regions which had been made desolate by the Avars.

Constantine makes no mention of Serbs fighting the Avars and there is no evidence that the Serbs did fight them, even though the Avars had previously directly controlled at least part of this territory. In these territories listed as Serbian Constantine informs us that the emperor settled the Serbs here and they were subject to the emperor and thus imperial power was restored here. This last remark can be taken as a convenient fiction. Once again he reports that elders came from Rome to convert these Serbs. However, it is doubtful that they had any success. The Serbs settled far to the south of what we now think of as the center of Serbia. Later, when the first state of Serbia (Raška) was established, it also was to be located in what we think of as southern Serbia centered near modern Novi Pazar.

Thus Constantine describes the Serbs settling in southern Serbia, Zahumlje, Trebinje, Pagania, and Konavli. This situates some of them in the southern part of the Dalmatian coast. The Croats were settled in Croatia, Dalmatia, and western Bosnia. The rest of Bosnia seems to have been a territory between Serb and Croatian rule. In time, though, Bosnia came to form a unit under a ruler calling himself Bosnian. Constantine gives no data as to Serb settlement in Duklja (Dioclea); however, since Serbs settled in regions along its borders, presumably this would have been a Serb region. However, as we shall soon see, this may be an artificial issue.

The mass of Slavs (Slaveni) who had settled over most of what is now Yugoslavia during the preceding decades were one people. The Serbs and Croats whom Constantine mentions were a second migration of a different people who do not seem to have been particularly numerous. In his discussion, Constantine describes which element emerged as the ruling one over which particular territories. Thus by the end of the seventh century Slaveni were settled over most all of what is now Yugoslavia, except for Slovenia and Macedonia, and some of these Slaveni were ruled by a Croatian military aristocracy and some by a Serbian one. If few Slaveni had come into the western territories under the Avars, probably many more did so now, in the wake of the new conquerors.

The most controversial chapters are the two on the Croatians, chapters 30 and 31. In them there is considerable overlap, with certain items repeated in both. There is also a certain amount of contradiction (e.g., there was a period of Frankish overlordship as opposed to Croatia being constantly under Byzantine suzerainty). Constantine never tried to combine or reconcile the two accounts. Chapter 30 noticeably never mentions Heraclius and contains little on Byzantium at all. It simply describes a Croatian invasion which expels the Avars by defeating them in battle; then it has the Croatians take over as rulers, though remaining subjected to the Franks (a subjection which actually occurred considerably later, in the 790s). This subjection lasted until they eventually liberated themselves from the Franks in the mid-ninth century. Chapter 30 gives the names of the tribal leaders (five brothers and two sisters) from the time of the migration. Chapter 31 states the Croatians arrived at the invitation of Heraclius; there is no mention of the five brothers or tribal origins. This chapter ascribes the establishment of the Croatians and the missionary effort to the command and the blessing of the emperor Heraclius. The constant reference to Heraclius and the claim that Croatia was always under Byzantine overlordship clearly was aimed at furthering Byzantium's claims of suzerainty.

Scholars have correctly noted that chapter 30 must be the Croatian account and chapter 31 the Byzantine account. Presumably, then, 31 was at least partially based on the records of the Byzantine foreign office; but it is impossible to say how much Constantine may have added to the Byzantine records to strengthen imperial claims. It is also possible that some earlier official had added this material on Heraclius to records that Constantine used. The Croatian account naturally ignores any such claims over the Croatians. The only former suzerain it notes is the Franks (though it misdates when that suzerainty was established) and it contains an account of the Croats' later successful struggle to become independent of the Franks. Much of this material is correct, but accuracy on recent events does not guarantee the accuracy of information about events two centuries earlier, particularly since the chapter contains errors in respect to the alleged establishment of Frankish overlordship then. Much in the Croatian account, particularly the five brothers and two sisters, sounds legendary and was quite likely part of an oral tradition. Thus each story presents a view of the Croatian past; both views have considerable in common, but in its variants each presents this past as was convenient for its own (Byzantine or Croatian) ends. How can we choose between them?

The early seventh century was a period of chaos for the empire; the Balkans were swamped by Slavic settlement (much of it under Avar direction). At the same time the empire was involved in an all-out war with the Persians. Thus, if the Croatians had wanted to move into the Balkans, there was little or nothing the empire could have done to stop them. In addition, after they had arrived—if they had arrived on their own—the best the empire could have done was to try to make peace with the newcomers so as not to have them as enemies on a second front. Byzantium could possibly then, and certainly later, have tried to represent the Croatian conquest as having taken place with Byzantium's blessing and therefore under some sort of Byzantine overlordship. If the early Croatian leaders received court titles such a fiction could have had further support.

On the other hand, in the period from about 617 to the crisis of the Avar-Persian attack of 626, the empire was in desperate straits. The empire must have known of the existence of the Croatian state north of the Carpathians and known that this state had hostile relations with the Avars who lived to its southwest. It would have been logical for Heraclius to have sought an alliance with these tribesmen against the Avars. In this way the empire's western enemies could be taken care of while Heraclius concentrated on the Persians in the east. Thus it is not at all impossible that Heraclius did send envoys thither to invite the Croatians to come. Of course, once they came they clearly could have done as they wanted, for regardless of the Byzantine invitation and any claims of Byzantine suzerainty (which might have been included in some sort of treaty), Byzantine overlordship could have been only nominal. Between these two choices there is no reason to favor one over the other.

One argument used against the Byzantine account is the story of the baptism of the Croats. Constantine here could not deny the role of Rome, but he still tried to give the empire credit for it by having Heraclius invite the pope to send the priests. Various scholars have felt this was impossible and Heraclius would never have turned to Rome. And though the definitive split between the churches had not yet occurred, relations between the two religious centers were then bad because Heraclius, in trying to solve a schism in his church, had come up with a compromise doctrine on the nature of Jesus Christ which most popes considered heretical. Thus it has been argued that the two ecclesiastical camps would not have been working on such a joint project under Heraclius. However, since one pope, Honorius (625–38), did have cordial relations with Heraclius, such an arrangement could have taken place during his reign. It is also possible that the priests simply were sent from Rome, and Byzantium, to increase its claims for suzerainty, later invented this role for Heraclius to take some of the credit. In any case, none of these early missions to Croatians or Serbs had any lasting effect.

Both traditions stress that in the seventh century (after the initial Slavic invasions) there was a second migration of Croatians and Serbs. The Byzantine tradition dates it to the reign of Heraclius (610–41). The Croatian tradition assigns it no date but simply has it follow the Avar occupation; it gives no data that would disagree with a Heraclian dating. Thus, first there was a Slavic migration into what is now Yugoslavia under the Avars (with a strong suggestion of Avar settlement as well) and later under Heraclius a second migration composed of Croatians and Serbs. When the Avars were driven out, these new people then settled in particular regions and became the rulers of the population living in those regions; this population presumably consisted of indigenous peoples and the Slavs who subsequently had settled there.

Scholars, accepting Constantine's account, have then turned to the existing data on the Croatians. First, linguists have taken the names of the five brothers and two sisters which are given and claim that these names are not Slavic. They find the word *Croat* (related to the brother Chrobatos) also is not Slavic; most linguists believe it is similar to an Iranian place-name, Choroathos, on the lower Don. Scholars also have found references in various scattered sources to a White Croatia which lay then north of the Carpathians. This state continued to exist in the tenth century in Constantine's time even after some of its members migrated south. It lay in the general area that Constantine says the Croats came from. White Croatia is referred to in a variety of sources independent of one another, such as Russian chronicles and tenth-century Arab geographers. One Arab geographer, Al-Mas'ūdī, says the White Croat chief drank fermented mare's milk, a characteristic of Turko-Tatar nomads rather than of the Slavs. Linguists have arrived at similar conclusions for the Serbs; confirmation in other sources is found for the state of White Serbia. The name *Serb* is also not thought to be Slavic; around the time of Christ there was an Iranian tribe on the Don known to Greek geographers as Serbi-Serboi, and in the tenth century an Arab geographer noted a Sarban tribe in the Caucasus. These two tribes are clearly not Slavic.

Thus there is considerable evidence to suggest that the Serbs and Croats who came into the Balkans in the early seventh century were not Slavs but members of another ethnic group (probably Iranian). But though their names probably are Iranian, it does not rule out the possibility that some or even all the Croats and Serbs were then Slavic-speaking. For such groups are named after their leadership. Thus many Slavs could have participated in their armies and have migrated to the Balkans with them. Furthermore, assimilation of the actual

Iranians could already have been taking place beyond the Carpathians. After all, names may survive long after linguistic change. As we have seen, the Antes, though slavicized, still bore an Iranian name. The Croats and Serbs seem to have been relatively few in number, but as warrior horsemen fighting against disunited small tribal groups of Slavs on foot, they were greatly superior militarily. They arrived, expelled the Avars, and then, as tough, tightly knit groups of warriors, were able to dominate the disorganized Slavic tribes. They were able to provide a ruling class and be a source of unity for the different Slavic groups. Soon the newcomers came to provide a general name for all the people (the majority of whom were Slavs) under them. But they did not establish a single Serbian or a single Croatian state but several different smaller states (e.g., Zahumlje, Trebinje, Konavli, etc.); within the Croatian area we have noted the formation of eleven fairly autonomous župas (counties) which eventually coalesced into two different states, in each of which the nobles retained great local independence. However, since the Slavs were the vast majority, as the Serbs and Croats intermarried with them, in time the conquerors came to speak Slavic too, and ironically, the Slavic language they came to speak and which had been spoken by the earlier arriving Slavs (the Slaveni) came to be named after the Iranian newcomers. This is an almost identical process to that exhibited by the Turkic Bulgars who conquered the Slavs in what is now Bulgaria. They came to be slavicized in time, but provided the name for the Slavic people, language, and state established in Bulgaria.

The fact that the Serbs and Croats were not Slavic but Iranian is not important in the long run since the Iranians were a small minority in a population of Slavs. They quickly became assimilated by the Slavs and the resulting society was clearly Slavic (despite the non-Slavic name and the non-Slavic origin of its ruling class).

What must be understood is that in dealing with Constantine Porphyrogenitus one must accept his accounts for both Serbs and Croats or reject both. It is beyond belief that one of these stories could be correct and the other false, particularly when verification exists for both a White Serbia and a White Croatia beyond the Carpathians. Yet in this century, as nationalistic squabbles and hatreds developed between Serbs and Croats in prewar Yugoslavia, various chauvinists (in this case particularly Croatians) have wanted to prove the Croatians have nothing in common with the Serbs and have taken as accurate only the Croatian material from Constantine. In general these Croatians (under the influence of the Habsburgs under whose empire they lived until the First World War and whose universities they attended) have felt that Slavs were inferior to Iranians and have tried to assert that Constantine was correct in providing evidence for the Iranian origin of the Croats, but incorrect in regard to the Serbs who were Slavs. However, one cannot pick and choose what is desirable in Constantine and reject less satisfying statements with no further evidence to back one up. Thus, if one takes him as basically accurate, then it is evident that both the Serbs and Croats were Iranian peoples who were close cousins and who conquered a Slavic population that was basically a single people.

There is a second school of thought which formerly was the dominant one but whose popularity has been declining over the last thirty years or so. Espoused by the eminent philologist Vatroslav Jagić around the turn of the century, it can be called the "Slavic" school. In general its adherents were willing to view the Serbs and Croats as one people but were unwilling to see the leadership in establishing the Croatian and Serbian societies in the hands of non-Slavic peoples. This school visualized one migration of Slav Serbs and Slav Croats in the late sixth and early seventh century and believed that these same migrants later, when the Avars grew weaker, overthrew them and eventually established Croatian and Serbian states in what is now Yugoslavia. This school rejected the testimony of Constantine Porphyrogenitus, stressing the fact that the emperor was writing in the tenth century and that much in his account was clearly legendary (e.g., the two sisters and five brothers). They argued that the early (seventh-century) material in his account was either legend or bits of fact so mixed up with legend that it was now impossible to extract a true story. They, of course, stressed all Constantine's contradictions and errors in fact. They also pointed out that the seventh century was a period from which few Byzantine sources survive and wondered how much material from that century was extant when Constantine was writing.

At the beginning of this century most scholars agreed with Jagić, one of the greatest minds in the field; and, of course, there is a great deal of truth in all of his objections. There certainly is much to be sceptical about in Constantine's account, for it is not an ideal source for the seventh century. But in the last thirty years more and more scholars have come to put more faith in the tenth-century emperor. Much of this change in attitude is due to the discovery of other independent sources (Russian and Arabic) which verify the existence of White Croatia and White Serbia north of the Carpathians. This evidence was not available to those late in the last century who rejected Constantine's account.

Thus the general view now is to accept in general terms Constantine Porphyrogenitus's two-migration account—first a large migration of Slavs driven into the Balkans by the Avars and then later, probably in the 620s, a second migration of Iranian Croats and Serbs who moved into the Balkans, drove out the Avars, subjected the Slavs, and in time were assimilated by them.

The Slavs in Greece

Also extremely controversial is the question of the Slavic settlement in Greece. This controversy dates back to the 1830s when a German scholar, J. P. Fallmerayer, wrote his history of the Morea (Peloponnesus). Fallmerayer was reacting to the romantic exaggeration of the Philhellenes at the time of the Greek war against the Turks. Fallmerayer wrote:

> The Hellenic race in Europe is completely exterminated. The physical beauty, the sublimity of spirit, the simplicity of customs, the artistic creativeness, the races, cities and villages, the splendor of columns and temples, even the name of the people itself, have disappeared from the Greek continent. A double layer of ruins and the mire of two new and different races cover the graves of the ancient Greeks. The immortal works of the spirit of Hellas and some ancient ruins on native Greek soil are now the only evidence of the fact that long ago there was such a people as the Hellenes. And were it not for these ruins, grave-hills and mausoleums, were it not for the site and the wretched fate of its inhabitants, upon whom the Europeans of our day in an outburst of human emotions have poured all their tenderness, their admiration, their tears, and their eloquence, we would have to say that it was only an empty vision, a lifeless image, a being outside the nature of things that has aroused the innermost depths of their souls. For not a single drop of real pure Hellenic blood flows in the veins of the Christian population of modern Greece. A terrific hurricane has dispersed throughout the space between the Ister and most distant corner of the Peloponnesus a new tribe akin to the great Slavonic race. The Scythian Slavs, the Illyrian Arnauts, children of Northern lands, the blood relation of the Serbs, and Bulgars, the Dalmatians and Moscovites—those are the people whom we call Greeks at present and whose genealogy, to their own surprise we have traced back to Pericles and Philopoemen. . . . A population with Slavonic facial features and with bow-shaped eyelashes and sharp features of Albanian

mountain shepherds, of course, did not come from the blood of
Narcissus, Alcibiades, and Antinous; and only a romantic eager
imagination can still dream of a revival in our days of the ancient
Hellenes with their Sophocleses and Platos.[8]

Needless to say, this denial that there were any "pure" Greeks left
and the claim that all the modern Greeks were descendants of Slavs
and Albanians provoked a violent reaction, first from the Philhellenes
and then from the Greeks themselves. The opposition started by denying that the Slavs really penetrated into Greece at all. But the sources
clearly refuted such an extreme position and we have already seen
documentation that Slavs settled in Macedonia and Thessaly. So many
Slavs were settled around Thessaloniki that the town was described as
a Roman island in a Slavic sea by a local source. So the Greek historians have had to retreat on this point and admit large-scale Slavic
settlement in northern and central Greece, though some have deem-
phasized its significance. The controversy then came to be centered on
the Peloponnesus. Did the Slavs settle here too? Some Greeks still
refuse to admit that there was Slavic settlement here. Let us look at
the evidence on this question.

The major source on this question is the Chronicle of Monemvasia, which states that the Slavs came into the Peloponnesus in 587,
presumably in conjunction with the major raids of the early 580s. This
chronicle then states that the eastern Peloponnesus was almost immediately recovered; Corinth was clearly recovered by ca. 600, when an
imperial governor was sent thither. But it is possible that just the
walled city remained in Byzantine possession with little—or even without any—of its hinterland. The French scholar Bon feels that this was
the case, and that after further invasions from the beginning of the
seventh century, the Peloponnesus was overwhelmed and the Byzantines lost control of the whole peninsula. The chronicle reports that
many Greeks emigrated to the islands, the few surviving coastal cities,
and to Sicily and southern Italy. Thus Bon concludes that all of the
Peloponnesus, except for a tiny number of walled cities like Monemvasia and Corinth, was in the hands of Slavs until the beginning of the
ninth century.

The American Byzantinist Charanis on the whole agrees, but he
believes that Corinth and its hinterland were recovered quickly, and
though there probably were some Slavs living there, Corinth and the
eastern part of the Peloponnesus were Byzantine through the seventh
and eighth centuries. Charanis points out that fewer Slavic place-
names are found in the eastern Peloponnesus than elsewhere on the

peninsula and he notes the evidence for the recovery of this region in the Chronicle of Monemvasia. Corinth was Byzantine from 600 to as late as 662, for Constans II on his way west stopped at Athens and Corinth. This shows the two cities were imperial. Athens was clearly still imperial in the 770s when Irene was brought from there to become the bride of Leo IV. Byzantine coins are also found in considerable numbers in Corinth through Constans II (641–68). Two hundred twenty-five coins have been uncovered there for the period 582–668. Only seventeen have been found from 668 until the reign of Nicephorus I (802–11). Thus it has been suggested that Corinth fell at some point after 662. Since Corinth is clearly Byzantine at the beginning of the ninth century, if it did fall, it presumably was recovered in the campaign of Staurakios in 782–83, which we shall discuss later.

Charanis, however, has argued strongly and persuasively against the idea that after 600 Corinth might ever have ceased to be Byzantine. First, the Chronicle of Monemvasia states it was Byzantine throughout the seventh and eighth centuries. Secondly, Athens—which remained Byzantine—on the whole exhibits a similar pattern of coins found to that of Corinth. Thus Charanis believes the paucity of coins from these two cities is indicative merely of a state of economic decline in both these cities which he believes was caused more by Arab pirates than by the Slavs.[9] This is also strong evidence for the decline of urban life and commerce in this period. Even in Byzantine-held cities, it seems, coins became rare.

In any case, to return to our initial question, both Bon and Charanis admit that the Byzantines lost control of the western, central, and southern parts of the Peloponnesus, that this region was heavily settled with Slavs, and that this situation lasted from the late sixth century until the recovery in the beginning of the ninth century. The only difference between the views of the two scholars is the question of the eastern Peloponnesus which Charanis would make Byzantine and Bon would not.

The Greek Byzantinist Zakythinos, however, would greatly modify the above position. He argues that the Chronicle of Monemvasia is not a reliable source and that it is based on oral tradition. He believes that the Slavs came into the Peloponnesus only after 746 and since Byzantine recovery was carried out between the 780s and early in the ninth century, they had very little influence. Thus one cannot speak of a slavicization of the Greek population. His view, as we shall see, conflicts with a great deal of contrary evidence.

Charanis has convincingly shown that the Chronicle of Monemvasia is a reliable source and though it is late—late-tenth or early-eleventh century—it is based on earlier written sources; and Charanis finds passages in it similar to other (albeit late) written sources. Thus he argues that it was based on earlier (no longer surviving) written sources and should not be discredited as being based on oral tradition. In addition, there is considerable other evidence of massive Slavic presence in the Peloponnesus. Unfortunately, none of it is drawn from ideal sources, but the weight of their numbers and the fact that they are independent sources, all of which support the same conclusions, make it plain that the Slavs did settle in large numbers in the Peloponnesus.

First, there are toponyms; Slavic place-names are found throughout Greece. The German linguist Vasmer has listed some 429 from the Peloponnesus alone. Certain of his specific examples might be challenged, but the fact remains that many clearly Slavic names do exist there. Byzantine coins are common in the Peloponnesus into the seventh century, become rare after the middle of the century and then reappear early in the ninth century, becoming common from the 820s. For example, the last coins from Olympia in the western Peloponnesus are from the reign of Phocas (602–10). Archaeologists have found no pre–seventh century building intact in the Peloponnesus. This numismatic and archaeological evidence suggests a major upheaval in the area.

The written sources confirm this conclusion. None of the written sources is ideal but their combined weight is significant: (1) Isidore of Seville states that in the fifth year of Heraclius (i.e., 615) the Slavs took Greece from the Romans. (2) Willibald, a pilgrim to Jerusalem, states that Monemvasia (in the southern tip of the Peloponnesus) was a Slavic territory. (3) The abbreviator of Strabo states that the Slavs occupy all Epirus, most all of Hellas, the Peloponnesus, and Macedonia. (4) The Chronicle of Monemvasia dates the Slavic settlement of the Peloponnesus from 587. (5) The patriarch Nicholas III of Constantinople, writing in the late eleventh century, states that for 218 years from 589 (i.e., to 807) there were no Byzantine officials in the Peloponnesus. (807 was roughly the date of recovery; his statement should be qualified for there seem to have been Byzantine officials in a few Peloponnesian ports.) (6) Constantine VII Porphyrogenitus in *De Thematibus* (his book of themes—i.e., of Byzantine military provinces) states,

> And the whole country [the Peloponnesus] was Slavonized and became barbarous when the deadly plague ravaged the universe and when Constantine [V] the one named after dung held the sceptre of the Romans.

Since the plague during Constantine V's reign occurred around 744–47, this statement can be dated. This is confirmation of the Slavic presence, though not of dating it back as far as other sources state; it is on the basis of Constantine VII that Zakythinos dates large-scale settlement to around 746. However, the other sources make it clear that the Slavs were there earlier; thus, if the 740s were of any major significance, presumably the already present Slavs took advantage of the plague to assert their authority over certain regions that had previously not fallen and in the course of this to assert their authority over most all the Peloponnesus.

From the above it seems clear that Slavs settled in large numbers in the Peloponnesus; thus they settled in every region of mainland Greece. In the Peloponnesus, as in the region of Thessaloniki, Slavs lived in the countryside and hinterland, while Greeks held certain fortified coastal towns (like Corinth), which remained cultural centers. Yet it is apparent that such Greek positions could not have been in a state of siege all the time. The Slavs, practicing agriculture in the region of these towns, in all likelihood went to the towns to trade. Presumably only off and on did hostility break out between the two groups or did a particular Slavic tribe attack a town for plunder. After the initial settlement relations were probably fairly peaceful and both sides lived and let live.

Furthermore the Slavs surely did not occupy the whole interior or eliminate the whole Greek population of Greece. Some Greek villages must have remained in the countryside too; presumably there would have been pure Greek, pure Slavic, and even mixed villages, and in time, with intermarriage, assimilation. Probably it worked in both directions, depending on which population was dominant in what area. Quite possibly some of the assimilation or hellenization of Slavs by the Greeks of the Peloponnesus took place in the period before Byzantine recovery.

No real state replaced Byzantine rule; when the sources state the Peloponnesus went to the Slavs, they just mean that Byzantine rule disappeared and different regions remained in the hands of various Slavic groups while others presumably were left in the hands of local Greeks; very likely, in some places the local Greeks continued to administer themselves, simply paying tribute to the newcomers.

At the time of Byzantine recovery in the early ninth century (to be discussed subsequently) many Greeks from Sicily and Asia Minor were resettled in the interior of Greece, which increased the number of Greek-speakers. With the restoration of Byzantine administration, which strongly supported an active church missionary program during the ninth century, there followed the Christianization and hellenization of many Slavs. With the tide moving in this direction in the period after recovery, assimilation worked in favor of the Greeks with Slavs becoming grecized. Thus by the tenth century, except for pockets here and there, all the Peloponnesus was "Greek" again (i.e., Greek in culture and language).

The fact that the rehellenization of Greece was successful, through recolonization and the cultural activities of the church, suggests that the Slavs found themselves in the midst of many Greeks. It is doubtful that such large numbers could have been transplanted into Greece in the ninth century; thus there surely had been many Greeks remaining in Greece and continuing to speak Greek throughout the period of Slavic occupation. This success in rehellenization also suggests that the number of Slavs in Greece was far smaller than the numbers found in what is now Yugoslavia and Bulgaria. For Bulgaria could not be hellenized when Byzantine administration was established over the Bulgarians in 1018 to last for well over a century, until 1186.

It is evident that in this period a great deal of ethnic mixture between Slavs and Greeks occurred; probably few pure-blooded Greeks—if such existed prior to the Slavic invasions—were left. A few centuries later many Albanians migrated into these regions and further increased the ethnic mixtures. Thus there is no reason to believe that the Greeks now are any purer-blooded than any of the other Balkan peoples. But, of course, it is culture rather than blood lines that matters. As Charanis points out, what is important is not the fact that Slavs were present throughout Greece but rather what their impact was on the subsequent Greek people. And despite much genetic mixture, there was no question of any permanent slavicization of Greek territory. Though the resultant population was ethnically mixed, Greek language and culture triumphed and, by the tenth century, most all the population of Greece (including that of the Peloponnesus) believed itself to be Greek and therefore can be so considered.

Byzantium and the Balkans in the Seventh Century to 658

By the middle of the seventh century the Slavs had settled throughout the Balkans, except for a few walled cities (generally along the sea coasts) and many Greek and Dalmatian islands and parts of Thrace near the capital. Over most of this area, through this settlement, different Slavic languages came to dominate and thus were formed the bases for the medieval and modern Slavic states in what is now Yugoslavia and Bulgaria. Though many Slavs settled in Greece, their numbers seem to have been fewer; after the Byzantine recovery in the ninth century, the tide turned and that region was rehellenized.

Though the Byzantines had lost control of most of the Balkans in the seventh century, the Slavs had formed no states as yet. They continued to live in small tribal units independent of one another, on occasion cooperating together but not forming by themselves any lasting larger units. At first, many of these groups were under the Avars, but by 640 the Avar influence in the Balkans was greatly reduced.

Larger units of Slavs were first to be created by the Turkic Bulgars who established, in the late seventh century, the first real state in the Balkans. However, early in the seventh century, since no other state existed, the Byzantines, even though they had lost control of the Balkans, were able to retain the fiction that imperial rule continued; in keeping with this theory, they referred to the Balkans as *Sclavinias:* lands where the Slavs lived.

Roads through the Sclavinias, such as the Via Egnatia, were unsafe. As late as the ninth century the saint's life of Gregory the Decapolite says land traffic was paralyzed across the Balkans. Thus commerce with or across the Balkans greatly declined.

These conditions cut off land ties between Constantinople and the few surviving Roman cities in Dalmatia. The sea routes between them were also insecure because of pirates. At first the pirates were primarily Slavs, but by the end of the seventh century Arab pirates had become especially menacing. Thus Dalmatia came to have far closer ties with Italy than with the centers of the empire of which its cities theoretically formed a part.

Another major result of the Slavic invasions was that Constantinople and Rome, which had already significantly drifted apart, were cut off from communication with one another. They now became even more separated culturally and politically. The people of each region ceased studying the other's language. What remained of the Roman Empire became more or less ignorant of Latin. Byzantine historians make few references to western events for the whole period of the seventh to the ninth centuries. They stop recording the names of popes from 570 to the eighth century, and when they start mentioning them again they make errors (e.g., popes Gregory II and III are listed as one pope).

For a long time Byzantium was helpless to act; the Persian war was not finally ended until 629. Then almost immediately the Arabs began launching attacks against the empire. Once again its very existence was threatened, and eventually it lost all its eastern lands except Anatolia. Thus in the seventh century it could make only a few small-scale attempts at recovering its Balkan losses. After Maurice's final campaign in 602, the Byzantines made no serious efforts to reverse the situation in the Balkans until 658. Then Heraclius's grandson Constans II launched a large-scale campaign against the Slavs.

The chronicles state that Constans attacked "Sclavinias," many prisoners were taken, and many Slavs were brought under his control. Thus, it seems, some Macedonian Slavs were forced to accept Byzantine suzerainty. Many of the captured Slavs were transplanted to Anatolia. It was normal Byzantine policy to resettle people, both to improve defenses in the new homeland (in this case against the Arabs) and to break up concentrations of untrustworthy people where they had been living. Many Slavs from here on served in the imperial armies in the east; in 665 a Slav division of five thousand men deserted to the Arabs, who then settled them in Syria. Constans's campaign was to be the last major military effort in the Balkans until the 680s.

Migration and Establishment of the Bulgars in Bulgaria, 670s

The territory of modern Bulgaria, extending up into modern Wallachia and down into Macedonia, had meanwhile been settled by the Bulgaro-Macedonian Slavs. They belonged to a different linguistic group from those who became the Serbs and Croatians. They spoke an old form of modern Bulgarian which surely then differed less from the language of their western neighbors than it does now. Zlatarski has speculated that these Bulgaro-Macedonians were descended from the Antes who were living north of the Danube in the fifth century. These Slavs had not formed a state but were living as tribes. Since in the 670s the sources mention "The Seven Tribes" being subjected by the Bulgars, it seems that different tribal groups were beginning to coalesce and form federations which might well have been a first step toward state formation.

Meanwhile in the Steppes and the region around the Sea of Azov dwelled the Onogur Bulgars. They were a seminomadic, ethnically mixed people under a Bulgar chief. According to their traditions their ruling family, known as the House of Dulo, was descended from Attila the Hun. Though scholars have advanced many theories, the origin and meaning of the name *Dulo* remain obscure. In 635 the Onogur chief Kovrat led a revolt against the Avars which succeeded in driving them from his lands and putting an end to Avar suzerainty over the Onogurs. He soon united under his own rule the various Bulgar groups living north of the Black Sea, the Sea of Azov, and the Caucasus.

Kovrat died in about 642, leaving five sons. Some scholars have claimed that this number and even some of the names given are legendary, but an Armenian geographer from the second half of the seventh century confirms that there were four groups of Bulgars in the east. This then seems confirmation of the Byzantine story of the five brothers. Possibly the Armenian missed one group, or possibly he was writing after one brother—possibly Kuver—had already departed for Pannonia. These Bulgar groups were attacked by another Turkic people from further east, the Khazars, who were soon to establish a great Steppe empire, centered on the lower Volga.

As a result of this Khazar attack, the Onogur Bulgars were scattered and, according to Byzantine historians, the tribe split into five groups, each under one son. The most important son for us, Isperikh or Asparukh, moved through what is now Bessarabia and then settled briefly at the mouth of the Danube. He subdued the territory north of the Danube in modern Wallachia. Then in the 670s Isperikh's Bulgars began crossing the Danube and set about subjecting or pushing out the Slavic tribes living in modern Bulgaria north of the Balkan mountains.

The Byzantines had enjoyed good relations with these Bulgar tribes as long as they stayed on the other side of the Danube; they had had good relations with Isperikh's father Kovrat. However, the emperor Constantine IV was upset when these warriors began entering the Balkans. He led an army to oppose their entry. The Bulgars, however, defeated the imperial army and the empire was forced to sign a treaty in 681, recognizing the Bulgar state.

This is the first state that the Byzantines recognized in the Balkans; until then, though much territory had been occupied by Slavs, leading to the disappearance of imperial control, no state had replaced imperial rule and the empire had been able to keep up the fiction that all the Balkans were still in theory imperial. In 681, for the first time, the empire legally surrendered claim to some of its Balkan territory.

The Bulgar state extended south to the Balkan mountains and east to the Black Sea. At this time its northern border was probably not much beyond the Danube. Most of the land from the Danube up to the Carpathians probably still remained under Avar suzerainty. Eventually, in the beginning of the ninth century, after the fall of the Avar khaganate, the Bulgars acquired overlordship over this territory between the Danube and the Carpathians. The western border of Isperikh's state is vague. Since the Bulgars themselves were concentrated in the northeast of their state, whatever control they had in the west was surely indirect, with these western regions in the hands of various Slavic chiefs who rendered tribute to them. Since which tribes actually paid them tribute probably varied from year to year, the western border must have regularly been in a state of flux.

The Bulgars themselves do not seem to have been particularly numerous. A twelfth-century source gives their numbers as ten thousand. The Bulgars were concentrated in northeastern Bulgaria, along the Danube, particularly its right bank (though early Bulgar sites are found on both banks) east to the Black Sea including the Dobrudja.

The Bulgars established their capital at Pliska which was a huge walled camp, lying on a plain, encompassing some twenty-three square kilometers. Inside were the khan's palace, the yurts of his fellow tribesmen, warehouses, shops, and space for flocks and horses. Nearby Madara was their religious center; it exhibits a fine carved horseman on the face of a steep cliff rising above a temple at its base. Archaeology shows that for a while many Bulgars kept their settlements distinct from those of the Slavs. They had a mixed pastoral and agricultural economy. Trade was important; the ruins of Pliska show caravanserai, warehouses, and many shops, and an early treaty with Byzantium, in 716, had commercial clauses. Most of the trade seems to have been barter; the Bulgars had no coins and Byzantine coins are not found in Bulgaria from the early seventh century until the mid-tenth century.

The Bulgar sites show variations in burial practices, suggesting that the Bulgars were drawn from more than one ethnic group. The cultural syntheses between Slavic and Bulgar practices (and Byzantine influences) varied from region to region.[10] The pre-Slavic population (of Thracians and Dacians), whose culture had acquired many Byzantine features, seems to have had relatively little influence on the Slavs and Bulgars. Some scholars attribute this to the fact that the indigenous population's numbers had already been greatly reduced—owing to Goth and Hun raids and settlement—before the appearance of the Slavs.

The Slavic and Bulgar migrations created a sharp cultural break. The old populations disappear from the sources. (The Thracians are not to be mentioned again; some Dacians found refuge in the mountains and survived to reappear in sources of the eleventh century as Vlachs.) The existing towns more or less died out. Archaeologists have shown that the Bulgar towns were new ones rather than continuations of earlier cities. In some cases, however, these new towns were built near classical ones, whose ruins supplied the newcomers with building materials. In most cases, there is a gap from the sixth to the ninth century at the sites of classical towns. Christianity also almost entirely disappeared and there is a hiatus in church building over the same centuries.

The Bulgars found a variety of Slavic tribes in the regions they occupied. Theophanes says the Bulgars became masters of the Slavs (i.e., conquered them), the Seven Tribes were subjected, and the Severi (a Slavic tribe) were made to move east to the shore of the Black Sea. The Severi seem to have retained at least semi-independence, for in 767 a Severite prince raided Byzantine territory; presumably they maintained relations with the Bulgars, probably paying them tribute.

Zlatarski tries to soft-pedal the conquest aspect and idealizes the relationship between Slavs and Bulgars. He claims the Slavs did not resist the Bulgars but made an agreement with the Bulgars which allowed the Slavs to keep their own rights, and the two peoples thus formed a mutual federation against the common enemy, Byzantium. This is far too romantic and there are no sources to support it at all. Dujčev clearly shows that the Greek expression used by Theophanes refers to a conquest and not an alliance.

The Slavs were settled agriculturists, chiefly living in villages. They, with a loose tribal structure, were too weak to resist the Bulgars who were superior militarily and organizationally. Presumably, having been subdued, the Slavs were allowed to retain their own chiefs. Thus Zlatarski is probably right that they were allowed to keep their own customs; for it is unlikely that the Bulgars sent officials out to govern them. The Slavs paid tribute in kind and provided foot soldiers to the Bulgars. In time (and it seems in some cases quite early) mixed settlements of Slavs and Bulgars appeared in some places, as archaeology has shown. The dating of these sites is not clearly established.

Into the ninth century the Byzantine authors distinguish between two groups in Bulgaria—Slavs and Bulgars—and the sources show that the less numerous Turkic Bulgars retained their specific names and titles that long. By the late ninth and early tenth centuries the more numerous Slavs had succeeded in slavicizing the Bulgars, who came to speak Slavic. Linguists claim that fewer than a dozen words in modern Bulgarian go back to the language of the Turkic Bulgars. The overwhelming majority of Turkish words in Bulgarian date from the Ottoman period. The Bulgar elite, however, though a minority, was able to remain a close-knit military leadership caste into the ninth century.

The Theme System and the Beginning of Byzantine Recovery in the Balkans

Under Heraclius and his successors a new military system was formed within the empire known as the *theme* system. The word *theme* meant an army corps and soon came to refer also to the province on which

that corps was settled. The actual chronology of the system's development as well as whether it was a piecemeal reform or a system worked
out and then imposed on the whole empire at once is a matter of
controversy which need not concern us. In any case, by the late seventh century this system was in effect over the territory which the
empire actually controlled; this territory was divided up into military
provinces, called themes, under the command of a general, usually
entitled a *strategos,* who was military commander for the province and
also had a considerable civil role. In each province military units were
settled under the strategos' control. In time many of these soldiers
were to be locally recruited, and assigned lands to support their service. At what point the link between land and service was established
is also controversial. But after it was established the land base for the
troops eased the burden on the treasury; it also created a hereditary
local militia able to come quickly to the defense of the province if it
was attacked. These militias could also be mobilized and sent elsewhere for offensive military operations. The Slavs provided some of
the manpower for the thematic armies, both in the Balkans and in
Anatolia (where many Slavs were to be resettled).

According to the Yugoslav Byzantinist Ostrogorsky, once the system was established, it was imposed upon all parts of the empire which
were under the actual control of Constantinople; thus by the end of the
seventh century if sources refer to a theme, then imperial administration existed there. If there were no themes listed in a region, Byzantine administration did not exist there. Following this formula, an ex-
amination of theme lists shows that the Byzantines had no control over
most of the Balkans for most of the seventh century.

The First Two Balkan Themes

The gradual appearance of new themes in the Balkans over the late
seventh, late eighth, and early ninth centuries illustrates the process
and chronology of the Byzantine recovery. The first theme established
in the Balkans was the Thracian theme which was created by 687. It is
first found mentioned, as the only Balkan theme, in a list of themes
given in a letter of Justinian II in 687. The actual date of its foundation
is unknown. Constantine Porphyrogenitus's *Book of Themes* credits
Constantine IV (668–85) with its establishment. Most scholars believe
he created it during the 680s. This theme was located in Thrace, the
region nearest Constantinople; its actual borders are unknown. From
the name it could include all or some part of that region. This then was

the first territory recovered, and part of Thrace had remained in imperial hands throughout.

At the end of the century a second theme, of the Helladikoi—of the Greeks—was established. This theme is not mentioned in the list of themes given in Justinian II's 687 letter. In 695 the strategos of the Helladikoi participated in overthrowing Justinian. Thus this theme was established at some point between 687 and 695. Again its boundaries are in doubt. The term is derived from the word *Greek*. Some scholars want it to include all of Greece; however, it is evident that most of Greece was still not recovered. The term *Greek* could signify one or both of two things, either a territory with a Greek population or a territory on which a Greek army unit was stationed. For example, the Armeniakoi theme in Anatolia was a theme in which Armenian troops were stationed and had nothing to do with Armenia, which lay well to the theme's eastern borders. All scholars, however, feel that this theme included some Greek territory. Ostrogorsky locates it in east central Greece, and most scholars agree it included part of Macedonia and part of northern Greece (probably much of northern Thessaly). Some scholars, including Ostrogorsky, have brought its boundaries as far south as Attica to include Athens.

No more themes were to be established in the Balkans for another hundred years until the end of the eighth century; thus after this small initial recovery late in the seventh century little or no territory was recovered from the Slavs for another hundred years. Thus throughout the eighth century the bulk of the Balkans remained Slavic, or as the Byzantines would say, Sclavinias.

Justinian II's Balkan Campaign of 688/89

In the late seventh century Byzantium carried out a new Balkan campaign which presumably led to the establishment of the Helladikoi theme. Events connected with this campaign also shed some light on the state of Balkan politics at the time as well. In 688/89 the emperor Justinian II marched through Thrace where at least enough Byzantine rule had been restored for a theme administration to be established; as stated above, it is not known how much of Thrace was actually under the control of the Thracian strategos. The purpose of this campaign was to punish the Bulgars and Slavs. Justinian successfully subdued many Slavs (taking many captives) and reached Thessaloniki. On his return toward Constantinople in 689 he was ambushed by the Bulgars who wiped out most of his army. The emperor just managed to escape with his life but he lost his booty, prisoners, and most of his soldiers. Possibly the intervention by the Bulgars shows they had good relations with these Slavs; they may even have exerted suzerainty over them. It is also possible they simply wanted to capture the booty won by the Byzantines.

These Bulgars are generally believed to have been those following Isperikh. However, Isperikh, who had signed the treaty in 681, was probably at peace with the Byzantines then. Furthermore, though treaties could be and often were broken, Isperikh's state, lying beyond the Balkan Mountains, was at considerable distance from Thrace. Thus a reasonable alternative view has been advanced by Zlatarski (and various other Bulgarian scholars including Cankova-Petkova have adopted it) that the Bulgars who attacked Justinian were not Isperikh's at all, but those of the second Bulgar "state" which Kuver established shortly before (in approximately 680) in Macedonia. Whether Kuver was still alive in 689 or whether a successor ruled his Bulgars is not known. Although the source account is too brief to allow certainty about which Bulgars attacked Justinian, it seems to me that attributing the attack to Kuver is more plausible than ascribing it to Isperikh.

While nothing specific has been heard about Kuver or his people after his attempt on Thessaloniki in ca. 680–85, the attack on Justinian happened so soon after those events that his Bulgars could well have still been in the area. Furthermore, hostile relations existed between Kuver and Byzantium over the Thessaloniki events, which gave Kuver reason to attack Justinian and Justinian reason to seek to punish these Bulgars, the motivation given by the Byzantine source for the campaign, whereas there is no known reason for Justinian to have wanted to punish Isperikh. Isperikh's state had a treaty with Byzantium, and in the beginning of the eighth century warm relations existed between Justinian II and Isperikh's successor, Tervel. Tervel, in fact, was to be instrumental in restoring Justinian to his throne in 705. He might not have been willing to do this had Justinian been making war upon his predecessor.

Thus I would agree with Zlatarski that Justinian was attacked by Kuver's Bulgars who in the decades that followed were assimilated by the more numerous Slavs and disappeared as any sort of coherent unit or semistate.

NOTES

1. A brief persuasive summary article presenting this view is: H. Birnbaum, "The Original Homeland of the Slavs and the Problem of Early Slavic Linguistic Contacts," *Indo-European Studies* 1, no. 4 (Winter 1973):407–21.

2. F. Barišić, "Car Foka (602–610) i podunavski Avaro-Sloveni," *Zbornik radova Vizantološkog Instituta* (*ZRVI*) (Serbian Academy of Sciences) 4 (1956):73–86.

3. J. Kovačević, in *Istorija Crne Gore,* vol. 1 (Titograd, 1967), pp. 282–90.

4. I. Čremošnik, "Die Chronologien der aeltesten slavischen Funde in Bosnien und der Herzegovina," *Archaeologia Iugoslavica* (Beograd) 11 (1970):99–103.

5. F. Barišić, "Proces slovenske kolonizacije istočnog Balkana," in *Simpozijum predslavenski etnički elementi na Balkanu u etnogenezi južnih Slovena,* ed. A. Benac (Sarajevo, 1969), pp. 11–27; and his remarks in the general discussion, ibid., pp. 122–23.

6. P. Charanis, "Kouver, the Chronology of His Activities and Their Ethnic Effect on the Regions around Thessalonica," *Balkan Studies* 11, no. 2 (1970):229–47.

7. Constantine Porphyrogenitus, *De Administrando Imperio,* ed. Gy. Moravcsik and R. Jenkins, with English translation, Dumbarton Oaks Texts, vol. 1 (Washington, D.C., 1967). See also vol. 2 commentary, edited by R. Jenkins (London, 1962).

8. Translation taken from A. Vasiliev, *History of the Byzantine Empire, 324–1453* (Madison, 1958), p. 177.

9. P. Charanis, "The Significance of Coins as Evidence for the History of Athens and Corinth in the Seventh and Eighth Centuries," *Historia* 4 (1955):163–72.

10. Regional cultural variations, which influences existed in which region and to what extent, where Bulgars and where Slavs were settled, and where their settlements remained separate and where they coexisted are all discussed in detail by S. Vaklinov, *Formirane na starob"lgarskata kultura* (Sofija, 1977).

CHAPTER 3

The Balkans in the Eighth Century

Bulgaria and Byzantium in the Eighth Century

Tervel and Byzantium

In 695 Justinian II was deposed. After spending nearly a decade with the Khazars (a Turkic tribe which controlled a Steppe empire) from whom he had acquired his wife, he arrived in Bulgaria to seek the aid of Khan Tervel (701–18). Receiving help, Justinian appeared in 705 before the walls of Constantinople with a Bulgar-Slavic army. The army was not equipped for a successful siege but after a few days, Justinian II entered the city through a drainpipe, contacted supporters in the city and engineered a successful uprising to restore himself to the throne. Once in power again, Justinian granted Tervel the title caesar (the second highest title in the empire) and agreed to pay a large tribute to the Bulgars.

Despite claims by many historians, there is no evidence that Justinian II gave Tervel any more territory. Some scholars, like Zlatarski, state that Justinian rewarded Tervel with the territory of Zagora, a small region just south of the Balkan Mountains near the Black Sea shore. However, another Bulgarian scholar, Cankova-Petkova, has shown that all references to such a grant are in sources written after 865; no contemporary or pre-ninth century source mentions any territorial grant to Bulgaria.[1] Thus she reasonably concludes that the Bulgarian-Byzantine border remained the Balkan Mountains throughout the seventh and eighth centuries.

Friction soon followed between the two states; in 708 Justinian grew tired of paying tribute and began preparations to invade Bulgaria, but a Bulgarian surprise attack on Byzantine territory forestalled this. When in 711 Justinian was again overthrown, Tervel found avenging him an excuse to ravage Thrace. Skirmishes continued until peace was concluded in 716 on the eve of a major Arab offensive against Byzantium which threatened both the empire and Bulgaria. The treaty set the frontiers, and the amount of Byzantine tribute, provided for an exchange of prisoners, and defined commercial relations. Thereafter all merchandise had to be accompanied by a diploma and seal put on by both parties. This indicates that the Bulgars had a sufficiently well developed state organization to control and regulate the behavior of merchants. The Bulgarians soon had an active market operating in Constantinople.

When the Arabs appeared and laid siege to Constantinople in 717, Tervel sent troops to the aid of the Byzantines. They played a role in breaking the siege that led to the Arabs' withdrawal. This was one of three major Arab offensives against Europe (the other two being one up through the Caucasus toward the Steppes, which the Khazars turned back in 737, and the Battle of Tours where Charles Martel stopped the Saracens in France in 731 or 732); most scholars feel the Byzantine victory was the most significant of the three.

Civil Wars and Anarchy in Bulgaria

In 739 the Bulgar royal house of Dulo died out. A period of civil war followed between boyar factions. Unfortunately for scholars studying this period, all the early sources on Bulgaria (except for one Bulgar kings' list, which is little more than a list, and a handful of inscriptions conveying overall a very limited amount of information) are Byzantine. Thus the modern reader sees Bulgaria through Byzantine eyes and learns about things that were of interest to the Byzantines. The Byzantine sources describe two opposing factions, struggling for power in Bulgaria: a pro-Byzantine party which sought peace with the empire and was dominant in Bulgaria until 755 and an anti-Byzantine party, the boyar aristocracy, which sought war with the empire. The Byzantine writers made Bulgaria's relationship to Byzantium the key issue in the Bulgarian struggle. These sources ignore other issues that may well have been far more important for the Bulgarians themselves. These descriptions could be compared to some American descriptions of Latin American revolutions in the twentieth century which note only the attitudes of the rival factions toward the United States and ignore all other issues even though these frequently were the true causes of the revolutions.

Zlatarski, probably correctly, believes that the most important issue within Bulgaria in the eighth century (and the one that was to have the greatest historical significance) was the relations between

Slavs and Bulgars. Zlatarski makes this issue the focal point in his description of the civil wars; he depicts the struggle as one between the old Bulgars (whom he calls the Hunno-Bulgars and who, he believes, particularly wanted war with Byzantium) and those Bulgars allied to the Slavs whom he sees as the party of peace. However, there is no source base for any of this.

Zlatarski is correct in wanting to highlight the relationship between Slavs and Bulgars. After all, the state was composed of these two peoples, one (the Bulgar minority) was politically dominant and the other (the more numerous Slavs) was gradually assimilating the Bulgars linguistically. Surely the complex and changing relations between these two peoples would have had effect on many Bulgarian events. However, when there are no sources about these relations, scholars should do no more than suggest that the mutual relations between these peoples probably played some role; they are not justified in going on to create hypothetical situations. We do not know for a fact that this issue played a major role in the dynastic struggle; we do not know that one Bulgar side was more favorable to the Slavs than the other. And though Slavs may well have been active on one or even both sides in the struggle, it is also possible that the Slavs were merely passive onlookers. Thus, Zlatarski's description of the civil war is highly speculative and, as such, must be rejected.

Constantine V's Wars against Bulgaria

In 756 the emperor Constantine V built a series of fortresses along the Byzantine-Bulgarian border. Since these fortresses were in violation of an earlier treaty's terms, the Bulgars demanded compensation. Constantine refused and the Bulgars, interpreting his actions—probably quite correctly—as hostile, invaded Byzantine territory only to be routed by imperial troops. This was the first of nine wars between Constantine V and the Bulgars. This defeat led to the overthrow of the Bulgar khan. Civil war followed again, at the end of which, in 761 or 762, a certain Telec came to the throne.

With Telec's accession, according to a contemporary Byzantine source, "two hundred eight thousand Slavs" emigrated to Byzantium and were allowed to settle in western Asia Minor. Zlatarski, not surprisingly, puts great emphasis on this and depicts Telec as the leader of the Hunno-Bulgar party whose triumph meant that large numbers of Slavs who had opposed him had to flee. Such a construction is not impossible, but it cannot be proved. The two hundred eight thousand could have been a mixed group casually labeled "Slav" by the Byzantine writer; it is also possible that the emigration was motivated by some other factor, such as a famine. However, even if the emigrants were political opponents of Telec (who possibly had been in some defeated army), this single case is not sufficient to demonstrate the character of the two parties throughout some three-quarters of a century of friction.

Telec immediately built up his army, fortified his frontier with Byzantium, and then advanced into Thrace. Constantine V went out to meet him and after a furious battle the Bulgars were again routed. This defeat seems to have been the cause of the new disturbances in Bulgaria which led to Telec's overthrow in about 764. The new khan, Sabin, tried to make peace with Byzantium, was accused of handing the country over to the Byzantines, and had to flee with his relatives to Constantinople. Peace was soon made, however, by a khan named Pagan, but the struggle for the throne continued with different figures in and out of power. On a couple of occasions (one of which was in 766), Byzantium intervened with armies on behalf of its candidates. When it intervened, the empire was able to impose its will upon the Bulgarians, whose land was in anarchy. In 767 the Byzantines kidnapped the prince of the Slavic Severi tribe who had been making trouble in Thrace. His activities against the empire do not coincide with Zlatarski's depictions of the Slavs as advocates of peace with Byzantium.

In 770 Telerig became khan; he is credited by Zlatarski with reestablishing order. However, warfare resumed in 773 when Constantine V successfully attacked the Bulgars. In the same year the Bulgars raided as far south as Thessaly where they were stopped by the Byzantines. The chronology of these two events as well as the causes are unknown. Zlatarski makes Telerig into an able figure who was trying to restore the authority of the khan, increase centralization, and give the Slavs a greater role. Sources are lacking to support or refute this characterization.

It seems that the next year, in 774, Constantine V was planning a new attack. Telerig wrote to the emperor saying that he might have to flee to Constantinople; whom in Bulgaria could he trust? Constantine stupidly sent him a list of Byzantine agents in Bulgaria. Telerig seized and executed them all. From this story we learn that Byzantine intelligence agents were active and intervening in the internal affairs of Bulgaria. Constantine V then set about planning his next expedition against the Bulgarians; however, his death at the beginning of the campaign put an end to the war.

In all this warfare the Byzantines proved that they were superior militarily. Each time they were able to defeat the Bulgarians, and frequently they were able to place their candidates on the Bulgarian throne as well. However, despite their victories, the Byzantines were unable to deal the final blow and either conquer Bulgaria or impose imperial suzerainty and a lasting peace. These wars, most of which were fought on Bulgarian soil, must have left Bulgaria partially devastated with considerable manpower losses; in addition they greatly increased the disorder and anarchy within Bulgaria. The wars could also have had the effect of rallying the Slavs behind the Bulgars and of uniting the two groups against the common Byzantine enemy. After nine wars, the Bulgarians probably had greatly increased their dislike of the Byzantines. Thus, the Byzantine successes were gained at the expense of making their Balkan neighbor into a hostile one. More hostilities were to occur in the 790s between the two peoples; though there were no major victories, the Bulgarians were by then more successful because they no longer were fighting the able general Constantine V but his incapable grandson Constantine VI.

Collapse of the Avars

Meanwhile in the 790s the Frankish king, Charlemagne, campaigned against the Avars. He won a major victory in 796 (in which the Pannonian Croatian duke Vojnomir aided Charles) and the Franks made themselves overlords over the Croatians of northern Dalmatia, Slavonia, and Pannonia; Frankish missionaries soon entered the area. A second major blow to Avar power, but this time from the east, soon followed under a new Bulgar khan Krum. As a result of these two victories, the Franks and Bulgars soon came to have a common border along the River Tisza. A second result of the Avar collapse seems to have been to allow the Bulgars to extend their overlordship over the territory north of the Danube up to the Carpathians.

The Avars did not disappear at once. West of the Danube a khaganate, which was vassal to the Franks and under a Christian khagan, was established. Frankish sources mention envoys from it visiting the Frankish court between 805 and 822. After that nothing more is heard of any Avar khaganate. However, Frankish troops defeated an attack by some Avars in 863. And in 889 mention is made of the Hungarians seizing the pastures of some free Avars in lower Pannonia. After that sources cease mentioning the Avars; presumably the descendants of those who survived the Hungarian conquest of the Hungarian plain in the 890s were absorbed by the Hungarians.

The Byzantine Recovery of Greece

According to the sources examined earlier, there were Slavs living throughout Greece during the seventh and eighth centuries. All of Greece except the islands and certain coastal cities such as Corinth, which may have retained some of its hinterland, were out of imperial control until Byzantine offensives began to regain some territory during the 780s.

Staurakios's Greek Campaign, 782–84

In 782–83, since things were peaceful in the east and the Bulgars were then quiet, it became possible for the empire to launch an offensive against the Slavs. The imperial armies, led by the eunuch general Staurakios, first attacked the Slavs around Thessaloniki and then marched south through Thessaly into central Greece, where they attacked the Slavs there and then marched into the Peloponnesus. They won victories in Hellas (probably meaning Thessaly) and the Peloponnesus; they took many prisoners and returned to the capital in 784 where Staurakios was given a great triumph. Staurakios clearly did not recover all the Peloponnesus. In fact, the campaign may not have aimed at extending Byzantine control in the Peloponnesus but may have simply been a raiding party. It is not known whether any new territory was restored to imperial authority in the Peloponnesus on this occasion, though it is possible some was. And though he clearly won victories and may well have made some defeated Slavs pay homage, the loose organization of the Slavs would have made it impossible for him to have subdued all of them in so short a time; whatever submissions he received might well have been lost after his departure.

Creation of the Macedonian Theme

No more campaigns into Greece are known until the reign of the emperor Nicephorus I (802–11). The preceding chapter discussed the restoration of Byzantine administration in the regions closest to the capital, with the creation of the themes of Thrace and the Helladikoi (probably including parts of eastern Macedonia and Thessaly) at the end of the seventh century. No more themes were created for a century thereafter. Between 789 and 802 the theme of Macedonia was established. This name is misleading since the theme contained little of geographical Macedonia. It consisted of western Thrace and its strategos resided in Adrianople. Its creation probably did not reflect new conquests. Most of its territory seems to have been taken away from the two seventh-century themes and made into a separate theme.

Nicephorus I's Recovery of Greece

A serious and successful effort to recover the Peloponnesus was launched by Nicephorus I (802–11). Most scholars date the establishment of the Peloponnesian theme to the early ninth century, at some time around 805, when Nicephorus's Greek campaign was in full swing. Ostrogorsky has argued that the Peloponnesian theme dates back to the 780s, a result of Staurakios's campaign. Let us now turn to the source accounts of the campaigns in the Peloponnesus in the early ninth century.

The Chronicle of Monemvasia dates the Slavic occupation of the Peloponnesus 587–805. Charanis points out that this does not necessarily mean the Slavs held the Peloponnesus to 805 but that they were independent of any imperial authority until then. He argues, supported by the Chronicle of Monemvasia, that some areas in the Peloponnesus, like the northeast corner around Corinth, were Greek more or less throughout this period. The Chronicle of Monemvasia states that the Slavs were in occupation of the rest of the peninsula until 805 when they were defeated and subdued by the governor of Corinth who went to war with the Slavs, conquered and obliterated them, and allowed the ancient inhabitants to recover their own. Nicephorus was pleased and wanted to rebuild cities and churches; he rebuilt the city of Patras, reestablished a bishop there, and settled the town with a mixed people (including Thracians, Armenians, and others brought from various places). Thus this chronicle sees 805 as the beginning of the real recovery and implies that Patras was recovered at that time; however, Charanis feels that Patras may have been held by the Greeks before 805.

A second account of the Slavs in the Peloponnesus and Patras comes from Constantine Porphyrogenitus's *De Administrando Imperio*. He gives no specific date but simply states that the Slavs who were in the Peloponnesus decided to revolt during the reign of Nicephorus (802–11), attacked their Greek neighbors' dwellings, and then attacked the Greek city of Patras. The Greek citizens of Patras sought the aid of the "strategos of the theme" who resided in the fortress of Corinth. He was slow in coming but the city was saved by the miraculous intervention of St. Andrew, who aided the citizens in a sortie to defeat the Slavs. The captured Slavs were made slaves of a new church dedicated to St. Andrew in Patras; this story provides a fine example of the use made of the church to hellenize the Slavs.

Since Constantine gives no specific date, there is a controversy over his story. (1) Some scholars see the events he describes as a revolt after the initial recovery and rebuilding of Patras in 805 or 806. Thus they believe it should be seen as a second military event around Patras taking place sometime between ca. 807 and 811 (the last year of Nicephorus's reign). The reference to a theme and strategos signifies that the Peloponnesian theme had already been established; this had most probably occurred in association with the events which the Monemvasia chronicle dates 805. (2) Others feel that possibly Constantine is giving a distorted version of the initial recovery. If so, his story should probably be dated 805. In this case the reference to a strategos of a theme, if it is not an anachronism introduced by the mid-tenth-century author, means that the Peloponnesian theme's establishment precedes the events of 805. Some want to establish the theme immediately before these events; possibly the first step in the campaign was a decision to raise the military governor of the Byzantine city of Corinth to the rank of strategos. Others have tried to date the theme back to the 780s and Staurakios's campaign.

Since I do not find at all odd two military engagements around Patras at a critical time of Byzantine recovery, a recovery which would surely stir up the opposition of some Slavs, and since Constantine clearly has the Slavs attacking a Greek-held city, I strongly favor the first alternative given above. This makes 805 the year that part of the Peloponnesus including Patras was recovered and the Peloponnesian theme established. Then, three to five years later rebel Slavs attacked Patras and failed to capture it.

There is a third reference to these events. Theophanes, who was very hostile to the emperor Nicephorus for his church policy, lists a series of "wickednesses" of that emperor. One wickedness is relevant to us. Theophanes says that Nicephorus transferred Christians from every province of the empire to the Sclavinias, and the people wept over the graves of their fathers and felt that the dead were more blessed than the living. Some hanged themselves to escape their dreadful fate. Poor and rich alike were helpless. This forcible population transfer was begun in September 810 and completed by Easter 811. Such transfers were common Byzantine policy.

The term *Sclavinias* is vague, for it refers to any one of the numerous regions throughout the Balkans where the Slavs were. The two most likely places to transfer Greeks to in the first decade of the ninth century would be (1) Greece, at the time being recovered in order to have in the area larger numbers of Greeks and Christians to Christianize and rehellenize the area as well as loyal Byzantines to oppose militarily any Slavic revolts, and (2) the newly established Macedonian theme and Thrace, which was an area threatened at the time by the warlike Bulgar khan Krum. Such a transfer would increase the number of defenders ranged against Krum and would dilute the Slavs who might be loyal to the Bulgars. Possibly Greeks were sent to both places. That some were sent to Greece is evident because the Chronicle of Monemvasia states that under Nicephorus in 805–6 Greeks were sent to repopulate the region of Patras. It is possible that Theophanes was referring to this very transfer mentioned in the Chronicle of Monemvasia; if this was the case, then this wickedness noted by Theophanes should be dated 806 and not 810. But quite likely population transfers were a regular policy from 805 on to the end of Nicephorus's reign.

In any case, with the restoration of Byzantine power, a theme of the Peloponnesus was established. It appears for the first time on a theme list of 812. Presumably its creation was the result of one of the two imperial campaigns to recover the peninsula. Thus it would date from the mid-780s or from around 805. I lean toward the later date. Corinth, the chief fortress of the theme, had long been held by the Byzantines. So presumably with increased territory after 805, the military governor there received the increased title of strategos, and his old territory would have been combined with the newly recovered lands to form a new theme. However, the existence of a theme of the Peloponnesus does not prove that all of the peninsula was recovered.

The resettlement of Greek-speakers was accompanied by the reestablishment of the church organization. Besides the new metropolitanate of Patras, a metropolitanate of Athens was created between 805 and 810. The resettlement of Greeks and the establishment of a metropolitan in Patras contributed to the rehellenization of the Peloponnesus; and great credit for this must be given to the policy of the emperor Nicephorus. By his campaigns and resettlement policy (made possible by his successful campaigns), Greek-speakers who were brought into the area came to absorb and dominate the Slavs (aided by the restored administration and the church whose conversion of Slavs was a major factor in their rehellenization). Even after a Slavonic liturgy was created in the middle of the ninth century (which was supported by the Byzantines for foreign Slavic states), the Byzantines did not permit the Slavonic liturgy inside what were felt to be Greek territories. The Slavs of Greece all attended Greek-language churches.

New Byzantine Themes of the Ninth Century

In the ninth century other regional themes were created. (1) The theme of Kefalonia (including the Ionian Islands) is first referred to in

809 when its strategos is mentioned. (2) The theme of Nikopolis in Epirus dates from the second half of the ninth century; there is no reference to it in a military manual (known as the *Taktikon* of Uspenskij after its scholarly editor) which is dated from between 842 and 856, but its strategos is referred to in a protocol list (the *Kletorologion* of Philotheus) from 899. (3) A small theme of Thessaloniki and its environs is first referred to in 836. It may well have been created by Nicephorus I (802–11). (4) The port of Durazzo with its environs is referred to as a theme in the *Taktikon* of Uspenskij (842–56). Ferluga persuasively argues that it dates back to the time of Nicephorus I.[2] This is a particularly important theme for our study because Durazzo was the main Byzantine port on the Adriatic. And later it was to be the major center for dealing with the independent Slavic state of Duklja, formed in the eleventh century in what is now Montenegro. (5) The theme of Strymon included the territory between the themes of Macedonia and Thessaloniki and was centered in Serres. Its territory lay between the Struma and Mesta rivers. Its strategos is not referred to in the *Taktikon* of Uspenskij but is mentioned in the 899 protocol list.

From all these administrative centers, Byzantine laws and culture flowed into the interior; thus administration complemented the work of the actual Greek citizens and the church in hellenizing and Christianizing the people of the interior. The coastal cities (some of which had been imperial throughout, like Corinth, or resettled as Greek centers upon their recovery, like Patras) were particularly important for this. Slavs surely remained in large numbers in the Greek interior, but they were soon to be subdued and assimilated by the superior culture of the Greeks. By the end of the ninth century most of Greece was culturally and administratively Greek again except for a few small Slavic tribes living in the mountains. For example, the Melingi and Ezeritae were able to retain their independent identity up to the Ottoman conquest.

Yet these two tribes were the exception. The process of rehellenization begun under Nicephorus was continued throughout the ninth century. Surely other Greek-speakers came to Greece on their own; some may have emigrated from northern Greece and Thrace to escape Bulgar attacks, while others may well have fled from Sicily, which was taken over by the Arabs. A Byzantine bishop, Arethas (writing in the early tenth century), refers to Greeks from Calabria coming to the Peloponnesus in the ninth century. The process, though it seems very rapid to us, occurring in something less than a century, went on gradually throughout that century. Thus the emperor Leo VI was able to credit his father, Basil I (867–86), with grecizing the Slavs and converting them.

The Farmer's Law

The Farmer's Law is a Byzantine code concerned with adjudicating problems likely to arise within a village. It is a most controversial document because it does not tell us when, by whom, and for what communities it was written. The text is in Greek; there are several Greek manuscripts extant—most of them clearly late copies. There are also even later Slavic translations. In general scholars assign the text to the late seventh century (during the reign of Justinian II) or to the first half of the eighth century. The data they have assembled makes this dating reasonable.

Region of Its Validity

Next comes the question, was the code valid for the whole empire or just for a particular region? Since the document focuses on the internal affairs of a single village, it is difficult to believe that the code had empire-wide application. Local customs varied significantly throughout the Byzantine Empire; therefore if the text was relevant, say, to Thrace, it probably violated the customs of an eastern Anatolian village and would have caused unrest if it had been forced on villagers there. Furthermore, there is no evidence that the empire cared about standardizing such local matters; its concern went little beyond making certain that taxes were paid and soldiers were recruited. Disputes about borders inside a village would not have interested the capital. Moreover, if the empire had been issuing a code to make things uniform, the state could be expected to have been looking out for its own interests (tax rates, collection of taxes, military recruitment, and the like) and to have stressed such matters in the articles of the code. However, the text does not treat such issues at all. Thus, most scholars feel it had local validity and was drawn up for a particular region. If this was the case, then, since the South Slavs later became familiar with it and translated it, this region was probably the Balkans.

Since the text is written in Greek (and there are various Greek texts), it is evident that the law was valid for some imperial territory; therefore, if the dating of it to the late seventh or early eighth century is accurate and if its validity is for a particular Balkan region, then it must have been valid for imperial Thrace (held by the empire throughout) and/or for the territory regained late in the seventh century and included in the Thracian and Helladikoi themes, for no more territory was recovered until the end of the eighth century. Thus it is safe to say the text was valid for Thrace, parts of Macedonia, and parts of Thessaly or some smaller region within this large territory.

This view is similar to that reached by scholars through study of the code itself. For example, in its eighty-five articles there are references to vineyards and figyards but no reference to olive trees. Because olives were a major crop in much of Greece and Dalmatia, their absence eliminates these two regions as the territory for which the code was drawn up. However, Macedonia and the interior of Thrace have figs and no olives (a rarity since most areas with figs also have olives) which suggests again the code was valid for some part of this region. One objection could be raised to this last argument; the code does have reference to trees in general and though scholars have interpreted "trees" as meaning fruit trees, it is not absolutely certain that olive trees could not have been included under that term.

Its Purpose and Authority

Virtually the entire code is devoted to relations within a village. The code makes only a couple of references to relations between villages, when it discusses common borders and disputes about them. There is much about thefts, accidents, and peasant problems, and very little about matters which would interest the government. It contains little on taxes except insofar as it discusses who was liable for the payment of taxes of a peasant who abandoned his property. Because the whole village owed a set sum in taxes, the government was not concerned with how much a particular peasant paid. The code's concern to divide fairly the burden left by deserters reflects the interests of the peasants. That the concerns of the law are peasant concerns (and not those of the state), is further evidence that it was a local code. Yet evidently it was not written by the local villagers to whom it pertained; presumably they would have been illiterate and normally they would have settled their disputes by customary (oral) law through their own village assemblies or judgments by village elders.

It seems most probable that the code was designed for a petty provincial judge who on occasion would have heard disputes between peasants in villages under his jurisdiction. Probably, he would have chiefly been faced with appeals when village losers would try to go over the heads of village justice. So we may suppose that the code was drawn up by a Byzantine provincial official as a guide for judges under him; at the same time it was probably not theoretical but based to a considerable extent on local customs, though it is impossible to say to what extent. And with a Byzantine author the code would be likely to include customs of local Greek villages—a question we shall return to later.

Since only one such code has been found, presumably it was not based on an imperial order or any sort of general requirement or reform demand, but rather was the independent act of a high local official (possibly the strategos of a theme) for use in the territory under his jurisdiction. Its aim would have been to guide subordinates who might be judging village cases by providing them with local customs of which they could well be ignorant. After all, the strategos and the other high-ranking military officers (e.g., tourmarchs who also had a civil judiciary role in the themes), as military types, were probably ignorant of peasant customs; furthermore, it was usual to assign these military leaders to provinces other than their own; thus frequently Anatolians, who would have had little background on Balkan customs, would have been administering Balkan courts.

Eighth-Century Village Society as Seen in The Farmer's Law

The Farmer's Law indicates the existence of independent villages—i.e., the farmers were not subject to a landlord; their taxes went directly to the state. They had private farm plots and if they met their tax obligations from their new residences, were free to leave their lands. Thus they were not bound to the soil. Besides the private plots, the village as a unit held common land for pastures and woods. The villagers also hired herdsmen to watch the animals of several families at a time. The village was taxed a certain sum and the villagers were jointly responsible for the full sum; if someone forfeited, the others were responsible for his share; thus, the code discusses the taxes owed by men who left. If such an absentee failed to meet his village tax obligations, the other villagers, responsible for his taxes, might make use of (but not take in ownership) his land to aid them in paying his taxes.

Reference is also made to slaves; thus some farmers were prosperous enough to own slaves. Since there is little mention of them, slaves were probably not common in villages. The code also mentions hired workers working on land. Most scholars think of them as landless peasants. This is not necessarily so; at least in modern villages the average man who is hired to help with particular chores lives in the village and owns some land (often a small parcel). However, he needs more income than his lands provide and thus he hires himself out part time to supplement the income from his own farm. There is no sign of large landlords in the code. This, of course, does not mean that they did not exist elsewhere; they were just not relevant to the contents of *The Farmer's Law.*

The code, then, speaks of three types of people: farmers (peasants), hired workers, and slaves. The village was broken up into individual plots and each farmer had shares or strips of each sort of land—strips of first quality land, second quality land, a piece of vineyard, and so on. When the owner died, each of his heirs inherited a strip of each type of land. This, in time, if families were large, led to dwarf holdings. It also meant that usually the possessions of a farmer were scattered around the village instead of being a consolidated farm plot.

The type of village described, though presumably in a theme, does not seem to be connected with the theme structure; in other words, because the code makes no reference to military service or shares in the support of a soldier, it did not pertain to a village supporting thematic troops.

The code is of interest for what it shows, not only about the internal affairs of a village, but also about the place of villages in society. Since it concerns free villages (i.e., those not part of an estate but which paid taxes directly to the state), it shows that free villages existed, and presumably existed in sufficient numbers to make a general document of this sort worthwhile. However, it proves only this. The absence of reference to great estates does not mean, as some claim, that there were few or no great estates. It is simply a code legislating for (or guiding in the handling of cases about) affairs in a free village. It makes no claim to do anything more. Great estates could well have existed throughout the province but they would have handled legal affairs in a different manner. After all, landlords had authority to judge the peasants on their own estates, and it would have been rare to find a peasant appealing to the state over the head of his own landlord. Thus the state would rarely or never have been faced with a dispute between two villagers living in a village that formed part of a great estate.

Free Villages and Great Estates

Some scholars have exaggerated two trends, that toward large estates in the sixth century prior to the Slavic invasions and that toward free villages in the end of the seventh and eighth century; in so doing they have come up with the following distorted picture, which finds its way into some of the literature on Byzantine-Balkan history: At the time of Justinian I, the empire was composed chiefly of great estates under landlords who had enserfed all (almost all) the peasants. The Slavic invasions followed, killing or driving out the landlords (at least those in the Balkans). The Slavs settled throughout the Balkans, setting up their own villages. Then, after Byzantine recovery the Byzantine Balkans was found to be full of Slavic settlers amidst whom were no great estates. This situation of free villages remained for years thereafter, reinforced by the settling of soldiers (thematic troops) on small holdings.

There are problems with this oversimplified picture. Although there were many enormous estates in the sixth century and although the trend was for their growth and for the percentage of overall land becoming part of such great estates to increase, the whole empire (and certainly the Balkans) did not consist just of great estates. Free villages survived throughout this period, despite declining numbers and constantly dwindling holdings. References to them throughout the empire appear in saints' lives, and Justinian's edict against foreclosures on free holdings in Thrace and Illyricum shows free holdings were widespread enough to warrant a general law.

The Slavic invasions followed and disrupted land tenure in the Balkans. In the Sclavinias surely the great landlords did not remain. The former peasants on their estates in some cases disappeared, either fleeing or being killed; others certainly remained, eking out their subsistence on their former plots or on new lands as free villagers. So, in the territory lost to imperial control which was to be regained, at the moment of recovery no great estates existed.

Imperial Thrace around the capital and Adrianople did not fall; because this region suffered most frequent raids, some of the local landlords may have sold their estates and moved to Asia Minor, but many certainly kept their lands with serfs and simply spent more time residing inside walled cities. In fact, even in peaceful times the landed aristocracy generally spent most of its time living in town houses in the capitals. Thus great estates probably remained in effect in much of imperial Thrace, though presumably their prosperity had declined as a result of the unsettled conditions in the countryside. In this period the number of free peasants must have risen, even in imperial Thrace; some Slavs migrated into this area and presumably the villages they established were free. The sources mention various captives and eastern peoples being settled here—often as soldiers—to bolster the area's defenses. Such people would have been settled on free—often thematic—villages.

After the reconquest of Macedonia, Thessaly, and the rest of Thrace by the empire, more people were resettled in these regions.

Most of those so settled were peasants and presumably most of them would have been established in free villages. Furthermore, whatever people were brought in to be thematic units would have been established in free villages. Thus there would have been an increased number of free elements being added to the numbers of Slavs already living in free villages in this reconquered territory. However, though at the time of recovery no great estates were found in these regions, this situation would not have continued.

Recovery meant added security to the church, and this was a period of great donations to the church and the rise of monastic estates. Since estates would have been of little value without labor, peasants were certainly settled on most of these newly donated monastic lands. And we noted Constantine Porphyrogenitus's mention of Slav peasants being given as slaves to the Church of Saint Andrew in Patras. Surely this was not a unique case. Thus we see that the church from the moment of reconquest was acquiring lands and serfs.

Officials and wealthy citizens were also presumably buying lands and starting to build up estates. Since commerce was looked down upon, there was little other than land to invest one's money in. Thus in secure, recovered areas the rich could be expected to start buying lands immediately, and though there would have been a preponderance of small holdings for a while, from the time of reconquest the process of estate formation would have begun.

Saints' lives of the eighth and ninth centuries refer to these great estates throughout the empire, including the Balkans. The sources mention enormous estates in Thessaly and the Peloponnesus in the ninth century, and by the tenth century great estates were becoming a problem for the economy of the empire, just as they had been back in the time of Justinian. The widow Danielis, who was patroness for Basil the Macedonian before he became emperor, for example, had vast estates near Patras. She not only had a great amount of land, but also hundreds of slaves who manned a whole series of shops and other enterprises. Particularly impressive were her textile works. She continued to favor Basil with gifts after he became emperor and a source claims she annually gave him more than sovereigns were able to offer one another.

Things were never static and it was never a question of there being all one or all the other type of landholding. Free villages always coexisted with great estates, and it was just a question of what moment one is thinking of as to which form predominated. The end of the seventh century and the eighth century was a period in which there were large numbers of free villages.

Influence of the Slavs on Rural Customs

The Slavs had a great effect on landholding; they totally disrupted the old land tenure relationships in the areas they occupied, and probably by their raids, which produced conditions of insecurity, they to some extent disrupted land tenure in imperial Thrace. Before and after recovery they certainly provided much of the manpower for the free villages in the Balkans—like those described in *The Farmer's Law*—and also a portion of the thematic troops. In addition, because of the increased population in the area—from the Slavs—there was less reason to bind people to the soil, be it to the soil of an estate or of a tax-paying independent village. Hence the Slavic invasions contributed greatly to eliminating great estates, to providing the population which made possible free villages with people not bound to the soil, and to reviving the rural economy. *The Farmer's Law* depicts the society that resulted from the Slavic invasions. This is probably the extent of the Slavs' influence on *The Farmer's Law*.

Nevertheless, some Slavic scholars have wanted to go much further. They argue that the bulk of the rural population after the invasions (and even after recovery in the recovered territories) was Slavic. Since the code was based on local customs, they maintain, it must depict primitive Slavic institutions and customs which later received imperial recognition as the basic rural institutions for the empire. Some of these scholars then compare the society described in *The Farmer's Law* with the Russian *obščina* (commune) in the seventeenth century and claim that the obščina was based on primitive Slavic customs; since the contents of *The Farmer's Law* are similar to obščina customs, they maintain that this confirms the theory that *The Farmer's Law* was based on early Slavic customs.

However, this is not valid. The obščina customs in Russia are shown to be of more recent origin, imposed in the sixteenth century by the Muscovite state to facilitate its tax collection. There is no evidence that the obščina preserves primitive Slavic customs, and we are not justified in falling back on Marxist or other theoretical models that posit stages through which societies must pass (and stress an early communal one) and assume such a theoretical construct is a fact. Theories must be based on sources.

Some Slavic scholars, to show *The Farmer's Law*'s Slavic character, claim that the code establishes the periodic redistribution of land, which they claim is an old Russian (therefore Slavic) custom. But here they are on very shaky ground. Periodic redistribution of land would be a logical way to deal with dwarf holdings and cannot be taken as unique for any particular society. Furthermore, it is not clear that the code really does establish the periodic redistribution of land. Finally, this practice also is not an old Russian institution but one that was later imposed by the state in the sixteenth and seventeenth centuries for tax purposes.

Now let us see what the code establishes. It mentions family property and common lands. If periodic redistribution of land can exist on a village scale, there must be some general village ownership of land that is higher than that of individual families. For without such a concept there would be no authority to redistribute lands. In trying to solve this question, we must turn to the so-called right of departure. Did a man lose his property rights if he left his land? The code states that as long as he paid his taxes from wherever he went, he did not. If he failed to meet his taxes, then the villagers might utilize his lands to help meet the tax burden (for the villagers did have joint responsibility to pay taxes) but they could not take his lands. Only if he did not return and did not pay taxes for a period of thirty years did he lose the land. But then he lost it for tax default and the land was taken not by the village but by the state for reassignment to someone who would pay the taxes. Though presumably the state would have frequently reassigned the land to someone within the village, the fact that the state and not the village took this land for reassignment implies that the village had no such authority on its own.

Now, does *The Farmer's Law* actually speak of a periodic redistribution of land? There are three references that have been taken by scholars to refer to it, Articles 8, 32, and 82. Article 8 states, "If a division wronged people in their lots or lands let them have license to undo the division." This does not show periodic redistribution; this could refer to an initial division in the establishment of a village or more likely a division among heirs of a deceased father's estate. It gives to the heirs a right to challenge what is seen as an unfair division of an estate. Nothing in the article even suggests that the whole village is faced with some sort of redivision. Scholars have argued whether the Greek word used, *merismos* (division), has a specific or technical connotation, but it seems to many (and I feel correctly) that the Greek word is as unspecific as to what is being divided as our word *division*.

Article 32 states, "If a tree is cultivated by someone in an undivided place and afterwards an allotment took place and it fell to another in his lot, let no one have possession of the tree but him who cultivated it." Here it seems that the allotment referred to is an initial one. Possibly the village had expanded into the common woodland where someone had cultivated a fruit tree. Possibly it again refers to a division of a father's estate previously undivided, now being divided among his heirs. There is nothing here that suggests periodic redistribution of land, and Article 32 could only create a chaotic situation if it were valid for a society which practiced such redistribution.

Article 82 states, "If after the land of the district has been divided a man finds in his own lot a place suitable for the erection of a mill and sets about it, the farmers of the other lots are not entitled to say anything about the mill." This again seems to be an original allotment, possibly at the establishment of a new village. There is no suggestion here of any second or later divisions.

One also suspects that in conditions of low population density, if a family found its holdings too small, it would simply expand its holdings into some neighboring woodland by chopping down trees. This practice was still being followed in nineteenth-century Serbia. Thus in many—but not all—regions redistribution would not even have been a necessary institution. Agricultural techniques were then primitive, so presumably on occasion the soil became exhausted and a whole village would have moved. But this would have entailed clearing new land and creating an initial division rather than redistributing old lands. Possibly this sometimes occurred and some of the divisions referred to in the articles cited previously refer to the right to challenge a division made in the case of initial divisions when a village moved to a new location.

We can see, therefore, that there is no evidence that periodic redistribution of land is an old Slavic custom. It also is not clear that *The Farmer's Law* even refers to it; in fact, it probably does not.

Common sense also argues against Slavic influence on the text. The Byzantine state was primarily concerned with tax collection and military recruitment. It had laws to cover these needs. What went on within a village beyond these issues was of little interest to the state. Thus Slavic villages would have been allowed to handle their quarrels by themselves and the state would not interfere. Furthermore, there were many Greeks throughout the parts of the Balkans which the empire then held; many had remained during the period of Slavic occupation and many others were resettled in recovered regions to rehellenize the area and dilute the Slavs. Thus regions were not as heavily populated by Slavs as some scholars might have it (though surely in much of the territory Slavs were a majority). The extent of the region to which *The Farmer's Law* was applied is not known, so it is not known whether Slavs formed a majority of the population of that region.

The empire, fostering its rehellenization policy, would presumably have been concerned primarily with new Greek villages, that things went smoothly for them, that land was broken in and farmed for the needs of the state. Thus more government concern could be expected for these new settlers than for the Slavs. Furthermore, Byzantine arrogance probably prevented the administration from giving legal sanction to purely Slavic customs or allowing such customs general validity to supersede customs of Greek villages in the area.

Probably each village judged its own internal matters by its own customs and the state judges became involved inside a village only when villagers failed to meet their tax or military obligations or when a villager appealed to the state over the heads of local village justice. Only in this last situation would *The Farmer's Law* have come into play as a guide for the judge. Since *The Farmer's Law* is written in Greek, drawn up, presumably, by Greeks, insofar as local customs had a part, more weight surely was given to local Greek customs.

There is nothing in the code which is specifically Slavic. In fact, it is impossible to show that particular points are Slavic because no documentation about Slavic village customs exists until centuries later. Since by that time *The Farmer's Law* had already been translated into Slavonic, Slavic customs found in later sources, instead of being primitive Slavic traditions, could well have been patterns acquired from *The Farmer's Law*. Most of the code, however, exemplifies commonsense peasant reasoning and could have been drawn from the customs of any nationality. It is likely that village legal customs between Slavic and Greek villages were quite similar. Thus most scholars have rejected the theory of Slavic influence on *The Farmer's Law* and the idea that it depicts Slavic villages and their customs.

NOTES

1. G. Cankova-Petkova, "O territorii bolgarskogo gosudarstva, v VII–IX vv," *Vizantijskij vremennik* 17 (1960):124–43.
2. J. Ferluga, "Sur la date de la création du Thème de Dyrrachium," in J. Ferluga, *Byzantium on the Balkans* (Amsterdam, 1976), pp. 215–24.

CHAPTER 4

Bulgaria in the Ninth Century

Krum

Krum, one of Bulgaria's greatest warrior rulers, came to the Bulgarian throne in about 803. He was originally a Bulgarian chieftain from Pannonia. Nothing is known about his activities there nor about his acquisition of the Bulgarian throne.

It is tempting to associate him with the old royal house, and make him a descendant of Kovrat's son who migrated to Pannonia in the 660s. If that son were Kuver, possibly he left sons behind him when he migrated south to Macedonia; then Krum might have been a descendant of Kuver. This is idle speculation. But it is likely that the warfare in Pannonia between the Avars and Franks caused various defeated Avars and their clients (who could well have included some Bulgars) to become dislocated and move east as a compact unit. We have discussed the instability existing in the Bulgarian state, where a struggle for the throne had been going on for decades. Possibly these immigrants appeared at a moment of crisis and took over.

Wars with the Avars

Shortly thereafter, in 805, Krum was at war with the Avars who had already lost their western territories to the Franks and their Croatian allies. Krum was successful. After a brief encounter he defeated the Avars and united the Bulgarians of the west (Pannonia) to those of the east and thereby created a far more powerful state. The Bulgarian state then may have extended to the Tisza River, which was the eastern border of the expanding Frank state. However, Cankova-Petkova believes Krum's western borders did not even reach the Timok River. In the territory to the west of the original Bulgar state around the Timok and beyond were small tribal groups. She argues that these peoples were only subjected by Krum's son, Omurtag, in 827.[1] At whatever moment—be it under Krum or Omurtag—the Bulgars acquired this territory, the Bulgars and Franks came to have a common border for the first time. In addition, with the fall of the Avar khaganate the Bulgars replaced the Avars as overlords over the Slavs and proto-Rumanians living in the territory north of the Danube up to the Carpathians and as far east as the Dnepr.

Wars with Byzantium

Very little is known about Krum's state until warfare broke out with Byzantium. It seems the event that set things off was a Byzantine raid launched against Bulgaria in 807. It is not known whether this was an aggressive act or retaliation for some earlier Bulgar action. In any case the raid had hardly begun when a plot against the emperor Nicephorus was uncovered, leading to the immediate recall of the imperial army. Krum, however, did not take this lightly. In 808 Bulgarian troops raided into imperial territory along the Struma River and in 809 Krum's armies took Sardika (Sofija). According to Byzantine sources, having massacred the garrison (supposedly six thousand men), he razed the walls and returned to Bulgaria.[2] In retaliation, it seems, later in 809, the emperor Nicephorus marched against the Bulgarian capital of Pliska and ravaged its environs. However, time was short, forcing him to withdraw.

At this juncture (810–11) Theophanes notes the "wickednesses" of Nicephorus and mentions the relocation of Greeks from elsewhere in the empire (presumably chiefly from Anatolia) to the Sclavinias. Most studies associate these shifts of population with the wars against Krum and conclude that these people were settled in Thrace along the Bulgarian border. This is perfectly plausible, but the Chronicle of Monemvasia mentions population transfers to the Patras region in 806. Further relocations of people to recovered Greece cannot be ruled out. Thus the new settlers could have been settled in Thrace near the Bulgarian border and/or the regions of Greece which were being recovered in the first decade of the ninth century. If they were sent to Thrace, they would have strengthened defenses against the Bulgarian raiders and have diluted the Slavs in Thrace, some of whom may well have had ties with Krum or with other Slavs living within his state.

Nicephorus was angry over the sack of Sardika and also believed that various Byzantine commanders and officials had not done all that they might have to defend the town. Word reached these people of the emperor's displeasure and they learned that they would not be pardoned. These people, including some engineers, fled to Krum. The

Byzantine authors report that these refugees, especially the engineers, proved useful to Krum; in particular they helped improve his siege machinery. While this may have been true, it might also be taken as a typically arrogant Byzantine interpretation to believe that no barbarians could develop technical improvements on their own and to thus assign credit to the imperial brains which deserted. Such a view may not be warranted. After all, Krum's predecessors, and presumably former masters in Pannonia, the Avars, were masters at siege warfare and Krum himself took Sardika seemingly with little difficulty prior to these desertions.

In any case Nicephorus, unhappy with developments in Bulgaria, in 811 led a massive campaign to destroy the upstart Krum. A brief account of the campaign is given by Theophanes but a much fuller account is preserved in a manuscript recently found by I. Dujčev in a Vatican collection of saints' lives. According to this source, Krum was not prepared for a major invasion and he held out offers of peace to Nicephorus, who refused them. Seeing no chance to defend Pliska against this massive army, Krum abandoned his capital and fled to the mountains, leaving a small garrison behind at Pliska. The newly found manuscript states that this garrison was composed of twelve thousand men, but possibly this figure is exaggerated. Nicephorus took Pliska without difficulty, penetrated the khan's residence, and massacred the garrison. He then succeeded in wiping out a late-arriving small Bulgarian force sent to aid the defenders.

Having occupied Pliska, Nicephorus plundered the city. The anonymous manuscript reports that he divided the wealth, gold, and wine with his soldiers. According to the strongly biased monk Theophanes, who detested Nicephorus for the emperor's church policy at home, Nicephorus put his personal seal on all the goods and refused to allow his soldiers to receive any booty; those soldiers who touched things had their ears and other members cut off. The anonymous manuscript gives a brief description of the khan's palace at Pliska. It was enormous, and had a series of terraces with alleys running through it. Nicephorus decided he wanted to erect a new Byzantine town here to be named for himself. To prepare the way for this he burned down the entire town, much of which—including a major portion of Krum's palace—was built of wood.

Then, leaving Pliska in ruins, he ordered a march in the direction of Sardika, hoping for an engagement with Krum in order to destroy him. Krum again sent envoys requesting peace, and once again Nicephorus refused the offer. The anonymous author presents us with an account of the disastrous end of the campaign. Previously, only the results were known but not how they had come about. Probably the story should be accepted as accurate, though it must be noted that the tale of Nicephorus was told to illustrate his hubris and how the sin of pride (illustrated by his ambitions to build a city named for himself on the ruins of the Bulgarian capital) preceded a fall. According to the story, his sin was punished almost immediately.

After a few days' march southwest from Pliska, Nicephorus began to neglect affairs. His spirit was no longer the same; he was like a man outside of himself; he lost his mind and suffered mental confusion and a paralyzed will. He retired to his tent. The army camped around him with its tents spread at some distance from one another as a precaution against a surprise attack. Nicephorus remained in his tent constantly, refused to see anyone, and issued no orders. His generals and officials did not dare to force their way into his presence. Finally they persuaded his son Staurakios to go and reason with him in an effort to convince him to leave this place located dangerously beneath a mountain range. Nicephorus lost his temper with his son and wanted to hit him; the army remained camped where it was. Some soldiers, seeing what was happening, broke discipline and began pillaging the area, burning fields, stealing animals, feasting and carousing, while other soldiers simply deserted and went home.

The Bulgarians, camped in the mountains above the Byzantines, watched the disintegration of the Byzantine army. Krum had already sent embassies to neighboring Avars and Slavs for aid. This shows that Krum had good relations with some Slavic tribes who lived outside of his state. Most probably they were Slavs from Thrace or Macedonia. Krum then armed his women as well as his men and ordered a dawn surprise strike upon the Byzantine camp. As noted, the Byzantine tents were spread widely apart; when the attackers struck word of the attack was slow to circulate. The Bulgars immediately directed their attack toward the imperial tent; Nicephorus was killed and his son and heir Staurakios was mortally wounded. A massacre followed and the Bulgars enjoyed a complete victory. Krum then in triumph had the emperor's head carried back on a pole to Pliska where it was cleaned out, lined with silver and made into a goblet which he allowed his Slavic princes (archons) to drink from with him.

With the emperor dead, and his only son and heir lingering on his deathbed for several months, the empire was in considerable chaos. No army stood between Krum and Constantinople. However, he did not immediately take advantage of the situation; almost a year passed before he attacked. Then in 812 he launched his invasion against the important fortress of Develtus near the Black Sea. After taking the city, he destroyed it, leveling all the fortifications so that they could not be used against him. Its inhabitants were forcibly transferred to Bulgaria. He then sent an ultimatum for a truce to the empire.

By this time the empire had found a new ruler, Michael I Rangabe, the husband of Nicephorus's daughter. Michael was incompetent in all respects as a statesman, but since he favored the party of the Extremist monks and listened to their advice, he receives praise from the chronicler Theophanes. The Byzantines were slow to respond to Krum's ultimatum, so Krum captured the important Black Sea port of Mesembria from which he took great booty.

Meanwhile, in Constantinople the Byzantines were debating over the treaty; in particular they were arguing over whether to accept a clause calling for the handing over of all Bulgarian deserters who had sought refuge in imperial territory. The Byzantine officials wanted to agree to this clause and completely accept the proposed treaty but Theodore of Studios and the Extremist monks convinced the emperor Michael that he must reject this point for it would be a sin to return the deserters. They persuaded the emperor to reject the clause by citing John 6:37, "All that the Father giveth me shall come to me; and him that cometh to me I will in no wise cast out." So the clause was rejected and Krum resumed his attack.

Zlatarski speculates that there may have been more to the clause's rejection than Christian ethics; those who deserted to Byzantium frequently included high officials and members of various political factions which had been struggling for the throne. Byzantium liked to have such people around to use whenever an opportunity presented itself to meddle in Bulgarian affairs. As noted, Byzantium installed its puppets on the Bulgarian throne on occasions during the eighth century. Thus Zlatarski may be right in thinking that there were also political reasons to reject this clause.

In 813 Krum raided imperial territory again and an imperial army was sent out against him. Poor Byzantine leadership and dissensions within the army resulted in a major victory for Krum. As a result of this defeat the emperor Michael was deposed and a general, Leo, took the throne as Leo V. A later source accuses Leo of deliberately losing the battle against Krum to discredit Michael and obtain the throne for himself. After his victory, with no further imperial troops around to oppose him, and with a change of rulers being effected in the capital, Krum advanced on the major city of Adrianople which he besieged. Leaving his brother to capture it, he then marched on Constantinople; arriving with his armies, he was given an invitation and a promise of safe conduct to meet with the new emperor. Accepting this at face value, Krum set out unarmed for the capital with only a small escort. Suddenly he found himself in an ambush; he wheeled around and managed to escape. Needless to say, this treachery infuriated him and he ravaged the countryside beyond the walls of the capital and destroyed the suburbs. One source reports that he even carted off large pillars to redecorate Pliska, which he was rebuilding after its destruction by Nicephorus.

Unable to take Constantinople, he returned to Adrianople, which had fallen to his brother. There he captured a large number of inhabitants, including the archbishop of Adrianople, Manuel. These people were carried off beyond the Danube. As noted above, the Bulgarian state by then occupied both sides of the Danube and extended north up to the Carpathians. In these years many captives were taken to Bulgaria from the empire. Probably they included Slavs as well as Greeks; but clearly many of them were Christians (and the archbishop has been noted). As a result, many Christians came to be found inside of Bulgaria who soon began to sow the seeds of their religion there.

In 814 Krum assembled a huge army, which, the sources say, included Slavs and Avars, and launched a new campaign that was aimed at Constantinople. However, on the way he suffered a stroke and died. Thus the empire was spared further pillaging at the hands of this able warrior prince. Though Krum is usually depicted as a major enemy of Byzantium, it should be noted that Byzantium seems to have initiated the wars. In the early stages Krum sought peace but was rebuffed by the Byzantines. He turned to a major assault against the empire only after his great victory over Nicephorus in a war Nicephorus forced upon him. Even after this triumph, he waited to strike the empire and only pressed war upon it when his peace offers were rejected.

Krum's Achievements

Krum is credited by scholars with many achievements: he united the western Bulgars to his state and extended Bulgaria's borders to the west where they may have reached as far as the Tisza River. He also expanded Bulgaria's territory to the north and east. He did a great deal to strengthen Bulgaria's armies; he won victories over the Byzantines, though his greatest successes began when the emperor Nicephorus had what could be called a nervous breakdown and then continued through a disastrous two-year reign of an incompetent emperor followed by a palace revolution. Thus the empire was not able to offer Krum the opposition it could have at other times. But he showed himself able in besieging and capturing cities (and he was able to take a series of well-fortified towns). He did not try to hold all of them; at times he just razed the walls so that they could not be used against him. He did not permanently expand Bulgarian boundaries to the south against Byzantium; he occupied some territory there briefly but after his death the boundary again was to be the Balkan mountains.

Krum also issued a law code; unfortunately its text has not been preserved and only a couple of items from it were preserved by a tenth-century compiler who wrote under the name of Suidas. The code prescribed the death penalty for false oaths and false accusations and ordered the uprooting of vines; the last is usually interpreted as a measure against drunkenness. As far as is known this was the first law code issued for the Bulgarian state. Zlatarski believes it was valid for everyone. If so, the code would have put an end to specific laws and privileges for different elements in the society and would have placed everyone under a single set of laws. Though Zlatarski's is a reasonable hypothesis, it is not certain that the code was intended to put an end to all local self-rule privileges, and even if this was Krum's intent, he may not have been successful.

Sources exist to support the preceding statements about Krum's achievements. However, Krum is also credited, with little basis, with having achieved a variety of other things. First, historians claim that he centralized the state and built up more of a state apparatus to put down the individual boyars who had been governing independently in the provinces. Such could have been the case but no sources exist to prove it. All that can be said is that his military success suggests he was able to obtain obedience from the boyars. However, he may have achieved this by being a successful military leader who brought much booty to those following his standard. Through such rewards he could have built up a large following, by means of which he could have forced others to obey or be subject to punitive raids. It is also possible that he won the support of the boyars by allowing them great independence in their provinces, and that he avoided revolts against his rule by recognizing boyar privilege. If this second hypothesis is correct, there would have been no reason for the boyars to oppose him, and he could have been successful in battle without increasing the central government's authority at all. In fact, he would have had foreign successes as a result of not trying to centralize.

The law code might suggest an attempt at centralization; however, since its text has not survived, its thrust and aims remain unknown. Furthermore, even if the code gave great authority to the khan and his servants it would not demonstrate centralization unless it could be shown that the khan was able to enforce its articles. The fact that no revolts against him are known might suggest that he crushed the oligarchy. However, if he was popular with its members, there would have been no reason for them to revolt. Reigns of eleven years without revolt occurred earlier without scholars suggesting centralization.

Krum's Relations with the Slavs

Krum is also credited with showing no favoritism to the Bulgar boyars over the Slavs, and it has been said that he built his state into an autocracy as opposed to an oligarchy by relying on the Slavic element. This may be true but it cannot be proven. First, no evidence exists to show that he did replace an oligarchy by an autocracy; and, secondly, the sources report so little about his relations with the Slavs that it is impossible to say what role they played in government. If the initial agreements with the defeated Slavs back in the seventh century, despite making them pay tribute, allowed them much local autonomy, possibly they would not have been interested in strengthening the central government at all. In addition, the limited sources provide no information to show that Krum played the Slavs off against the old Bulgar boyars or that he included many Slavs in his government. Except for the references to Slavs in his armies or Slavs coming to aid him on his summonses—which were occasions which had nothing to do with internal affairs but instead involved fighting a foreign enemy— there are only two sources that suggest any particular friendship toward Slavic elements.

The first of these is a Byzantine chronicle which reports that having made Nicephorus's skull into a goblet, Krum gave it to Slav princes (archons) to drink from. Since the passage does not refer to Bulgars or boyars, some scholars have suggested this shows some favored position to the Slavs. Others have even interpreted it to mean that Slavs had been brought into dominant positions at court and in the retinue, forcing out the old Bulgar aristocracy (possibly even sending them off to their own estates in the provinces) and thereby paving the way for the khan to deprive the boyars of their hereditary role and raise himself up as an autocrat. This all could be true, but it is reading a great deal into this one simple story.

An alternative explanation could be the following: the anonymous manuscript reports that when Nicephorus was experiencing his victories, taking Pliska and then heading south in pursuit of Krum, Krum had sent for aid to the neighboring Slavs and Avars. If the neighboring Slavs (who evidently lived as independent tribes and were not members of the Bulgar state, since the source calls them neighboring) had sent aid, then very likely Krum would have invited their leaders to a victory banquet after his triumph. If so, then the archons referred to could well have been these foreign Slav leaders. In fact, Byzantine sources usually used the term *archon* to designate a prince; it would seem to be a very high title for this source to use if the Slavs were simply high officials at his court.

Finally, common sense suggests that if Krum needed a force to use against the old Bulgars (the boyars living in the northeast, in the central part of the old state) and if he was really from Pannonia, then he would have relied upon his own tribesmen and cohorts from the west who had presumably come east with him as his retinue when he obtained the throne and who very likely provided the muscle which allowed him to obtain the throne in the first place. That this was perhaps his policy is seen in the fact that his second in command—who took Adrianople and who probably governed it after its conquest—was his own brother. If Krum relied heavily on these Pannonians, this policy could have somewhat limited the privileges and positions of the old court boyars from the eastern part of the state.

The second source suggesting Krum's friendship toward the Slavs simply reports that Krum sent a man named Dragomir as an ambassador to Constantinople in 812. This is clearly a Slavic name. However, names may not have been given strictly according to nationality at this time; after over a century of probable intermarrying much mixing could be expected to have taken place in the society. Thus names could have crossed ethnic lines. In fact, Krum's own grandson was to have the Slavic name of Malamir. However, if Dragomir was really a Slav, which is perfectly likely, it merely shows that one Slav attained a trusted position. Though it is probable that others were in high positions as well, this one remark is by no means proof that Krum used Slavs exclusively or even that he used more than one.

In fact, the one source that lists high officials—an inscription we shall turn to shortly—gives the names of the three highest men in the state; and not surprisingly all three are Bulgars. Thus it is wrong to state—as some scholars have—that the old boyars were exiled from court to provincial posts to be replaced by Slavs. No source exists to suggest such an expulsion occurred and there is continued evidence of Bulgar boyars at the top of the administration.

However, as a ruler in a multiethnic state in the nonnationalist Middle Ages, who would have wanted to have his whole country behind him to fight a dangerous foreign enemy, Krum surely would have tolerated all ethnic elements in his state. There is no known reason for him to have persecuted Slavs—and ethnic persecution was a very rare phenomenon in the medieval Balkans. Thus it would be plausible to assume that he maintained good relations with both ethnic groups and utilized members of each in civil and military posts. And if he did this, it, along with the regular contacts between the two peoples living in one society in close proximity to one another, would have contributed to mixing the two elements. This in itself would have played a role in limiting the old Bulgar privileges. Presumably through intermarriages, the Bulgar minority was gradually being linguistically (and possibly culturally) assimilated by the larger number of Slavs. This assimilation was probably occurring under Krum, but there is no reason to think it was happening more rapidly under him than under his predecessors.

In short, there is nothing in the sources to show that Krum relied exclusively on the Slavs or gave them any particular or new privileges or that he persecuted in any way or exiled from court the old boyar aristocracy. In fact, common sense suggests he would not have persecuted the boyars as a group. Such a policy would probably have led to civil war and Krum would not have wanted to provoke internal friction when he was involved in a major foreign war for seven of the eleven years he reigned.

Krum's Relations with the Greeks

It is also worth noting that Krum was not always harsh to Greeks. Theophanes mentions various Byzantine notables and malcontents deserting to Krum and offering him their services. There were those who feared Nicephorus's wrath after the fall of Sardika. In 811 a high official—a domesticus—close to Nicephorus deserted to Krum, as did a certain Constantine Pabikos who was later to marry Krum's sister. The sources also mention an Arab who instructed the Bulgars in the construction of siege machinery. The presence of these Greeks and the Arab serving Krum supports our contention that he was working to strengthen his state and would not have played on animosities between groups.

This policy of good relations with Greeks is also reflected in an inscription from Hambarli in Thrace. As noted above, Krum took various Byzantine cities in Thrace and along the Black Sea coast which, though they soon reverted to Byzantium, seem to have remained Bulgarian throughout the remainder of Krum's lifetime. The inscription, which cannot be read in its entirety, states after an initial lacuna that the strategos Leo is subordinate to Krum's brother, that from Berrhoia . . . the Interior Boyar Tuk is chief of the right side of the kingdom and beneath him are the Strategoi Bardas and Jannis. For the left side of my [Krum's] empire, Anchialos, Develtus, Sozopolis, Ranuli, are under the boyar Kavkhan Iratais, and the Strategoi Kordylas and Gregoras are his subordinates.

This extremely important inscription describes the division of the newly added Greek regions. No old Bulgar places are mentioned, thus this is simply a public notice of the administration of the regions Krum had conquered. Since the inscription was placed in Thrace and written in Greek, it can be taken as a notice about the occupation government to the local Greek-speaking inhabitants. What region was to be administered by Krum's brother is lost in a lacuna, but presumably it would be the region around Adrianople because the brother conquered that.[3] The extent of Tuk's territory is lost since all that survives of the text is the city of Berrhoia on one end.

The three major figures mentioned were all Bulgars: Krum's brother, Tuk, and Iratais. The title kavkhan is usually taken for the second position in Bulgaria, regent in the absence of the khan, like the count palatine in later Hungary. This office was held by a Bulgar, so there was clearly no replacement of Bulgars by Slavs in the very top positions. By establishing this new administration, it is apparent that Krum intended to retain this territory for Bulgaria; of course, this was not to be realized since shortly after his death it reverted to Byzantium.

Subordinate to these three leading Bulgars were Byzantines (shown by their Christian—Greek or Armenian—names) in official positions, called strategoi. *Strategos* is a Greek term for general; by this time it usually was used for the commander of a theme. Whether some or all of them had been strategoi earlier under Byzantium is not known. Possibly Krum, since they were Greeks being given important administrative roles in a Greek-speaking area, simply gave them this Greek title. It is quite possible that the so-called strategoi were earlier deserters to Krum, whom he trusted and decided to put over these captured areas. In any case, Krum used Greek strategoi in each of the three occupied regions as his seconds in command. They were under the close control of Bulgarian superiors, but it seems that he was making a serious effort to make Bulgarian rule more acceptable to the Greek population by using Greek administrators.

Two of the five strategoi (Leo and Jannis) were eventually to be executed as Christian martyrs under Krum's son and successor Omurtag. Two others are also mentioned later. Evidently, under Krum these five strategoi, left in the newly occupied territory, were believed to be trustworthy or sufficiently under Bulgar control to assure their loyalty. However, it is evident that his successors felt it unsafe to have Greeks in high positions on the border with Byzantium, for in 836 sources mention some Greek peasants called Macedonians (i.e., their place of origin earlier, a geographic rather than an ethnic term) who sent a secret embassy to Constantinople to ask for boats to take them to Byzantine territory. They were living on Bulgaria's northeast frontier beyond the Danube where the Bulgars used them to defend it. This military role was the same as that which they had earlier had in Byzantium. They had served under the strategos Kordylas and his son Bardas (who surely is the same man as the inscription's Bardas). The Byzantines sent aid and as a result ten thousand peasants were able to flee to Byzantine territory.

This shows that the Bulgars utilized not only Greek leaders but whole Greek thematic units. Presumably Krum's successor immediately on Krum's death, before the Byzantines recovered the Thracian-Macedonian territory, uprooted whole villages of thematic troops (soldier-peasants) to utilize in their regular defensive role for Bulgaria's benefit. Since Krum's inscription shows their leaders were still in the south, presumably Krum felt it safe to use them—and possibly these Greek troops under them as well—there. But then his successor, not wanting to return the troops to Byzantium when the territory was given back and not wanting to leave them inside Bulgaria on a border with the empire, removed them and sent them to the northern border with the Steppes where they would oppose non-Greeks.

This was in keeping with Omurtag's policy which showed great distrust of the Byzantines (in fact, he would execute two of the original five strategoi). In the north these Greeks could not have aided the empire but could have been useful as defenders of the dangerous northeastern border, from which it would have been hard for them to escape and return to Byzantium because of the distance. Furthermore, Krum and his successors left the troops under Greek commanders, probably expecting them to fight more loyally under their own leaders. Thus Krum also used Byzantines in running his state. He seems to have favored no nationality but to have aimed at administering a multinational state. This was an accepted concept of his time; the multinational Byzantine Empire also did not favor one ethnic element over another.

Bulgaria, 814 to 852

Omurtag's Relations with Byzantium

After brief disorders—and possibly one or two extremely brief reigns or perhaps regencies lasting only a few weeks—Krum's son Omurtag (814–31) came to the throne. Local order was reestablished. Peace soon followed with Byzantium in 816. It was a thirty-year peace which lasted from 816 to 846. The old frontiers seem to have been more or less restored. The Balkan Mountains became the border again and Byzantium regained its lost Black Sea cities, several of which had had their fortifications and walls demolished. The treaty included the clause Krum had sought about returning deserters; they were to be returned to both sides. To seal the treaty each side swore also by the other's religion; it was horrifying to some Byzantines to see the new emperor Leo V swearing by a sword and sacrificed dogs and to have the heathen Bulgars touching and profaning the Gospels.

The Bulgars were to cross the frontier only twice before 846. The first instance was in 822–23 when Constantinople was besieged by the rebel Thomas the Slav and Omurtag came to the aid of Michael II. In fact the Bulgarians played a major role in breaking the rebel's siege of the city. Secondly, in 836/37 small skirmishes, noted previously, followed Byzantium's aid in allowing the ten thousand former Macedonians to return to the empire from Bulgaria's northern border.

Though peace was maintained with Byzantium, the hostility of the Bulgars toward the Greeks remained, as can be seen by an inscription from Preslav—a town founded by Omurtag which later, in 893, replaced Pliska as the Bulgarian capital.

> The Sublime Khan Omurtag is divine ruler in the land where he was born. Abiding in the plain of Pliska he made a palace on the Tiča [River] displaying his power to the Greeks and Slavs. And he constructed with skill a bridge over the Tiča and he set up in his fortress four columns and between the columns he placed two bronze lions. May God grant that the divine ruler may press down the emperor with his foot so long as the Tiča flows, that he may procure many captives for the Bulgarians and that subduing his foes he may in joy and happiness live for a hundred years. The date of the foundation [of Preslav was the Bulgar year] Shegor alem or the 15th indiction of the Greeks [821/22].

The inscription was in Greek. Since there was as yet no written Bulgarian language, Greek was the official written language for the state.

Many inscriptions from the pre-Christian Bulgars survive; except for a small number of runic ones, all are in Greek.

The inscription not only proclaims Omurtag's superiority over the Byzantines, but also in its opening line asserts his authority over the boyars by claiming divine origin for his rule. The inscription's references to the newly erected bridge and palace at Preslav also reflect a major aspect of Omurtag's reign, his building activity. He rebuilt Pliska, destroyed by Nicephorus I, using massive blocks of stone and making the city and its palace more grandiose than they had been before. He also erected another splendid palace on the Danube. He built a variety of shrines including a great temple at the religious center of Madara.

Omurtag's Activities to the West

Peace with Byzantium enabled Omurtag to turn to affairs on his western border. There the Slavs on the Timok River, who had been allied to the Bulgars, broke that alliance and in 818 contacted the Franks. However, soon they switched that allegiance and allied themselves with Ljudevit, the Croatian župan of Pannonian Croatia, who was then trying to assert his independence from the Franks. Thus some of the territory (or better to say peoples) which had been added to Bulgaria by Krum now broke away, and Omurtag lost control over or tribute from this region. However, Omurtag was patient and moved slowly. In 823 the Franks subdued Ljudevit, ending his secession, and now the Timok Slavs who had been allied to Ljudevit found themselves under the Franks whose eastern border (if borders go with the territory of tributary peoples) had been extended considerably further and was now encompassing territory the Bulgars thought was theirs.

The Bulgarians sent embassies to the Franks in 824 and again in 826 to request a definition of the Bulgar-Frank border. The Franks hedged, so finally in 827 Omurtag launched an attack to the west and penetrated into this disputed territory; it seems he pressed well into Pannonia. He expelled the local Slavic chiefs and installed Bulgar governors over these tribes to tighten control over them. Thus once again after 827 Bulgaria was in control of this western territory as far as part of Pannonia, including the cities of Beograd, Braničevo, and Sirmium as well as most of eastern Slavonia.

Omurtag and Christianity

Omurtag was hostile to Christianity, which seems to have been spreading inside Bulgaria, even though the state and most of the ruling class were to remain pagan until Boris's conversion in 864. The spread of the new religion was facilitated by the influence of Greek refugees and captives who were settled in large numbers in Bulgaria. The Bulgar boyars were hostile to Christianity because it threatened the old order upon which their privileges were based. Each boyar clan—having its own totem—was believed to have been divinely established. This derivation entitled each family to high positions in state and society. The boyars thus could be expected to have put pressure on Omurtag to act against the Christian religion. Furthermore, Omurtag also seems to have felt that Christianity (with its hierarchy based in Byzantium) was a threat to Bulgarian independence. He presumably saw Christians as Byzantine agents and seems to have believed that if his nation should become Christian it would be little better than a Byzantine colony. Thus he persecuted Christians, possibly as much because he saw them as imperial spies as for the interests of his own religion. There were some executions: Leo and Jannis, two of the five strategoi from the Hambarli inscription, and various high clerics who had been captured and taken to Bulgaria, including the bishop of Develtus and the metropolitan of Adrianople, all died for their faith. Despite the persecution, the religion continued to spread.

Malamir, Persian, and the 836 War with Byzantium

Omurtag died in 831. He left three sons; the eldest, Enravota, did not succeed. He was converted to Christianity by one of his slaves and soon was to be executed when he refused to give up that faith. It is likely that his religious beliefs excluded him from the throne. Succession went to the youngest son, Malamir, the first khan to have a Slavic name. How long he reigned is controversial; some scholars believe he ruled until 852, others believe he was replaced by a certain Persian (or Presiam), who was to rule from 836 to 852. For our purposes it is not a major question because almost nothing is known about the period or the two men in question—if indeed they really were different men.

There are three sources relating to this question: Constantine Porphyrogenitus refers to Persian attacking the Serbs at the time of the Serb ruler Vlastimir. He gives Persian the title of archon; this title need not be the head of state but when used by Constantine it usually has this meaning. For example, Constantine uses the title of archon for Khan Boris, whom he calls Persian's son. Thus the use of the title archon suggests—but does not prove—Persian was the ruler. If Boris was really his son, this might be further confirmation of that supposition. A much later writer, Theophylact of Ohrid (ca. 1090–1109), who drew his information from earlier sources—though unfortunately we do not know anything about what they were or their reliability—however, claims Boris was the son of Omurtag's third son Svenica.

There are also two inscriptions. The first states that the Greeks violated the peace. Malamir with Kavkhan Isbul marched against them, took several fortresses in Thrace, and then marched against Philippi from which the Byzantines fled. The second states that Khan Persian sent Kavkhan Isbul against the Smoljane (a Slavic tribe in Byzantine territory near the Struma River) and gained a victory which punished the Christians for their transgressions. Neither is dated, but since from 816 to 846 a thirty-year peace existed between Bulgaria and Byzantium broken only by the brief skirmishes in 836 after the Byzantine rescue of the Macedonians from Bulgaria's northern frontier, which the Bulgarians saw as a violation of the treaty, most scholars have concluded these inscriptions refer to the events of 836/7. This would explain the first inscription's statement that the Greeks violated the peace and the second's reference to Christian transgressions.

The close connection of the information conveyed in the two inscriptions can also be seen in the major role which Kavkhan Isbul had in both campaigns. Thus the Belgian Byzantinist Gregoire has reasonably proposed that, since only one war is known of in this general period of peace, these must refer to the same campaign. And since it would be odd to have the same campaign directed by two different rulers, then presumably Malamir and Persian are two names for the same man, possibly a Slav name and a Bulgar name. Such double names are perfectly common among the medieval Balkan peoples. This is a logical proposal, which would mean that one man, Malamir-Persian, ruled from 831 to 852. However, others argue that the two inscriptions refer to two different campaigns in the same war, and that Malamir was replaced by Persian in 836/7 in the course of the war at some time between the two campaigns. Since scholars are divided on this issue, secondary works list the rulers between 831 and 852 differently.

The inscriptions are also important for the information conveyed about Bulgarian troop movements and successes in 836/7 and for the references to the kavkhan Isbul, which shows that the key post of kavkhan was still held by a man with a Bulgar name, despite whatever slavicization had occurred. Isbul was immensely rich. Another inscription announces that he paid for an aqueduct which he donated to the khan.

Serb-Bulgar Relations

Byzantine-Bulgar relations were relatively quiet in this period. The Serbs, however, were increasingly becoming major rivals to the Bulgars. Where the Bulgarian-Serbian border then ran is not known. But as the Bulgars pressed into the region along the Morava River—where they subdued the rebellious Timok Slavs—they became a threat to the Serbs living there; presumably this danger proved to be a catalyst in the uniting of various Serbian tribes to oppose it. The Byzantines also, seeking a check to the Bulgarians, were interested in building up a stronger Serbia in Bulgaria's rear. The Serbs, being more distant, were then of little worry to Byzantium; as a result, Byzantine diplomats and gold were active in encouraging Serbian unity. These actions mark the beginnings of a Serbian state; this newfound Serbian unity caused the Bulgars to see the Serbs as increasingly dangerous to Bulgaria. Thus Serbian unity would have been a factor both in provoking the Bulgars to attack and also in increasing the effectiveness of the Serbs to resist such an attack. The immediate causes of the war are unknown as is its actual date, but at some time between 839 and 850 the Bulgarians invaded Serbia. The Serbs, after several years of fighting, successfully drove them out.

The Serb ruler, Vlastimir, who defeated the Bulgars, also expanded his state to the west. He married his daughter to the župan of Trebinje and raised his son-in-law's title to prince. Vlastimir was overlord of Trebinje and this relationship continued throughout the next century, for Constantine Porphyrogenitus reports, "The princes of Terbounia [Trebinje] have always been at the command of the prince of Serbia." Most probably Vlastimir and his heirs were also overlords of Konavli, for Constantine Porphyrogenitus says that Konavli was subordinate to Trebinje. Vlastimir had three sons, among whom civil war broke out in the 860s.

Bulgarian-Byzantine Wars: 846, 852, and Bulgarian
Expansion into Macedonia

In 846 the Bulgar peace treaty with Byzantium expired. The Bulgarians invaded Macedonia along the Struma River. Possibly, as some scholars suggest, they chose a moment when the empire was involved in suppressing some Slavic revolts. However, there are chronological problems about these Slavic uprisings and no major one can be shown occurring in 846. The best-known one broke out among the Slavs of the Peloponnesus during the reign of Theophilus (829–42). They liberated themselves and ravaged the area before they were subdued by a Byzantine commander sent thither with a large army in the early years of Michael III's reign. It has been argued that this subjection occurred immediately on Michael's accession, still in 842. If so, this revolt would have been over well before the Bulgarian treaty expired in 846. The *Life of St. Gregory the Decapolite* describes a Slavic revolt in the vicinity of Thessaloniki. Though this uprising has been placed about 846 by some scholars, Dvornik, the editor of that saint's life, believes it took place some time between 831 and 838.[4] In any case, whether in conjunction with Slavic rebellions or not, the Bulgarians invaded imperial territory in 846. A new truce followed shortly thereafter.

Many historians believe that this 846 campaign also marks the beginning of Bulgarian expansion into Macedonia west of the Vardar. Unfortunately, the chronology of this expansion (and which khan to credit it to) is unknown. Boris clearly had possession of Macedonia as far west as Ohrid by the 880s and, since there were no Bulgarian wars against Byzantium after 860, it is evident that de facto Bulgarian possession predated the 860s. Thus the Bulgarians either annexed this territory in the 846 campaign—an annexation unrecognized by Byzantium—or else annexation occurred in a later campaign—unknown to us—by Malamir-Persian prior to 852 or by Boris subsequent to his accession in 852.

Only one campaign by Boris against Byzantium is noted in the sources. In an undated reference—assigned reasonably to 852 by Cankova-Petkova[5]—Theophanes Continuatus states, "Boris learning a woman reigned in the empire became more brave and he sent messengers to say that he denounced the treaties of peace and he began a campaign against the territory of the empire." The chronicler does not state which lands he attacked or whether he acquired territory. However, it is possible that some or all of Macedonia was acquired by Boris at this time. A treaty, probably signed in 853, seems to have ended this conflict and Boris remained at peace with the empire until ca. 860, when he entered into a Frankish alliance probably chiefly aimed against the expanding Moravian state. There is no evidence that Bulgaria went on the offensive against Byzantium after 860. Thus we may conclude that Bulgarian expansion into Macedonia occurred in the course of one or both of these two campaigns—846 and 852—though Byzantine recognition of this territory's loss came only in a 904 treaty with Boris's son Symeon.

The above argument assumes Byzantium had restored its authority over western Macedonia at some time in the ninth century. Such a recovery, though often assumed, is not documented. Thus, possibly western Macedonia remained Sclavinias up to Bulgaria's acquisition. In this case, Bulgaria would simply have asserted control over various independent tribes—an act which being unrelated to a war with Byzantium, could have occurred at any time in the ninth century.

If much of this Bulgar expansion into Macedonia had occurred around 846 it might be plausible to date the Serbian war to shortly after 846 and to connect it with that expansion; for such southwesterly expansion, which was to the south of Serbia, when taken in conjunction with Omurtag's previous gains to include the lands to Serbia's north along the Timok and Morava rivers, would have had the effect of putting the newly developing Serbian state into a pincer. Thus either the Serbs, feeling threatened, could have initiated hostilities or the Bulgars may have decided to annex the territory in the center of their newly gained western possessions.

Boris's Accession and Early Military Activities

In 852 Persian or Malamir died and Boris (852–89) succeeded. According to Constantine Porphyrogenitus, he was the son of Persian; according to Theophylact of Ohrid, he was the son of Svenica, Malamir's other brother. The question of Boris's relationship to his predecessors cannot be resolved without further sources.

During his first decade as ruler Boris was involved in a variety of military campaigns. In 853 Boris formed an alliance against the Franks with Rastislav of Moravia, whose state had expanded south into Pannonia as far as the Danube. The Bulgarians seem to have been badly defeated in battle against the Franks. At least Theophylact of Ohrid, writing in the eleventh century on the basis of earlier but now lost sources, states that a German cloud covered Bulgaria. This defeat forced Boris to mend relations with the Franks and break off the Moravian alliance. By the end of the 850s, because of this new orientation, Boris found himself threatened by Moravia. As a result Boris went to war with the Moravians in the early 860s.

At the outset of his reign, Boris sent a Bulgarian army into Serbia, where it was ambushed. His son and twelve leading boyars were captured and had to be ransomed. After this defeat, peace was made with the Serbs and good relations with them followed. Early on Boris also had an unsuccessful minor skirmish against the Croatians with whom he shared a border. In addition, as noted, he attacked the Byzantines in a brief campaign, probably in 852. This campaign, whose objectives and theatres are unknown, could well have been directed into Macedonia—possibly it was the initial Bulgarian expansion there or possibly it added to what had been gained in 846.

Except for perhaps the 852 war with Byzantium, all Boris's early military ventures were unsuccessful. However, through skillful diplomacy Boris suffered no territorial losses from them. His outstanding qualities as a diplomat were to serve him well throughout his reign.

Christianization of Bulgaria

The single most important event of Boris's reign was Bulgaria's conversion to Christianity. This religion had been gradually spreading in Bulgaria, presumably greatly influenced by Greeks who had come thither as captives or deserters. Both Greek and Bulgarian Christians had been persecuted under Omurtag and Malamir. Now under Boris the state officially became Christian; for, after his conversion, he ordered his people to follow suit. The conversion of Bulgaria involved a three-way struggle for control of the new Bulgarian church between Boris, Rome (supported by some Frankish activity), and Byzantium. Moreover, the quarrel between Byzantium and Rome over Bulgaria took place simultaneously with a major conflict within the Byzantine church in which the papacy sought to intervene.

The Constantine-Methodius Slavonic Mission to Moravia

The story begins with a fourth actor, Rastislav, the prince of Moravia (846–70), a successful warrior who had expanded his state to the Danube, which gave Moravia a common border with Bulgaria. By about 860 Rastislav found himself under strong political pressure from the Franks, who were his neighbors to the west. He was interested in accepting Christianity but was afraid that if he supported Frankish missionaries, it would merely contribute to Frankish domination of his country. So, in 862 he sent envoys to Constantinople to request missionaries.

Two brothers, sons of an imperial official in Thessaloniki, named Constantine and Methodius, were chosen. They were well educated and fluent in the dialect of Slavic spoken in the environs of Thessaloniki. They devised an alphabet to convey Slavic phonetics. Then they worked out a Slavic language based on this dialect; but since this Slavic vernacular did not contain a sufficiently subtle or comprehensive lexicon to convey complicated theological ideas, they imposed upon this dialect a large number of Greek words as well as certain Greek grammatical forms. This composite language is what is now called Old Church Slavonic (OCS). Next they translated the Gospels and various other church writings into this language and set off for Moravia in 863.

Since Constantine and Methodius were able to have both language and translations ready so promptly, they must have been at work upon this project for some time prior to Rastislav's request. If so, presumably their efforts had been originally aimed at a future mission for Bulgaria. This also would explain why Old Church Slavonic had a Bulgaro-Macedonian base; this dialect was well suited as a missionary language for Bulgaria. One would expect that if the project were an answer to Rastislav's request the Slavic component of the language would have been a form of contemporary Czech. In any case, Constantine and Methodius appeared in Moravia in 863 and immediately set to work educating and preaching.

The Franks complained to the pope, who summoned the two brothers to Rome. This meeting went smoothly since the Byzantines accepted papal jurisdiction over Moravia and recognized that any bishoprics founded there would be under the pope. Seeing no threat from the Byzantine Slavonic mission, the pope gave the brothers his blessing to continue their work in Moravia. He even approved of their use of Slavonic. However, Constantine was taken ill in Rome; he became a monk, taking the name of Cyril (from which the present alphabet of the Russians, Serbs, Bulgarians, and Macedonians takes its name of Cyrillic), and died in February 869. His brother Methodius, however, returned to Moravia to continue his work.

The following year, during the winter of 869–70, Rastislav was overthrown by a member of a pro-Frank party in Moravia and soon Frankish priests, using Latin, were invited in; the Slavonic mission was expelled. Subsequent popes supported the Frankish clerics in their hostility to Slavic as a church language. Various late-ninth-century popes condemned the Slavonic liturgy and declared that since there were only three holy languages—Greek, Latin, and Hebrew—it was wrong to translate the word of God into any other tongue. As a result the Slavonic liturgy died out in Moravia. It was to become extremely important, however, in the Slavic lands under Byzantine jurisdiction—Russia, Bulgaria, Serbia—for the Byzantine church did not oppose the liturgy in the vernacular in foreign territory. This Byzantine tolerance of local languages for the liturgy eventually became a major difference between the eastern and western branches of the church.

Extremist-Moderate Feud in the Byzantine Church

For years an extremist faction within the Byzantine church had been feuding with a moderate one. The quarrel began in the late eighth century when the first period of banning icons (Iconoclasm) was declared ended. The Iconodules (proicon people) then split over what the church should do with the repentant ex-Iconoclasts. The Extremists felt they should undergo stiff penalties and that bishops who had accepted iconoclasm should be removed. The Moderates wanted to forgive and forget and allow repentant ex-Iconoclasts to remain in church offices and communion. The state officials, seeking peace, wanted everyone back in communion and an end to quarrels; thus the state tended to support the Moderate view. However, many monks, who had throughout been faithful to images and had suffered persecutions, disagreed with this Moderate policy. Wanting revenge on their former persecutors, they demanded long penances from them.

As time went on, other differences emerged. The Extremists took church canons literally and would not authorize exceptions; the Moderates tended to be willing to stretch church law at times, particularly for imperial needs. Thus the Moderates allowed the emperor Constantine VI in 795 to divorce his wife and marry another woman. The Extremists called those who allowed this "adulterers," and that term was to be used for the next seventy years by Extremists for the Moderates.

This particular phase of the conflict died down in 815 when icons were again banned. This put both factions of Iconodules back into the same camp to battle on behalf of icons. However, in 843, when the empress Theodora—regent for her young son Michael III—again restored the icons, the old issue returned—what should be done about the 843 vintage repentant ex-Iconoclasts? Thus the Byzantine church in the mid-ninth century was split into two warring camps. In 847 the empress Theodora had installed as patriarch a man named Ignatius, who was the castrated son of the deposed emperor Michael I Rangabe (811–13). To avoid the quarrels and bitter friction that would have taken place at a synod, Theodora had dispensed with the canonically required synod and had simply appointed Ignatius. Once in power, he became closely associated with the Extremists, though he seems to have been more their tool than their leader.

In 855 a palace coup ousted Theodora as regent for her minor son Michael III; she was replaced by her brother Bardas who had little love for the Extremists. Various plots which the Extremists and Ignatius were accused of supporting were formed to restore Theodora. Because of his alleged political role, Bardas wanted to depose Ignatius. It was possible to do this with relative ease since Ignatius's appointment (by just the empress) was not canonical. Ignatius was incensed by the thought of removal from office but Bardas succeeded in 858 in procuring a resignation from him. Bardas then selected as patriarch Photius, a layman who had suffered for icons, who was one of the most learned men of his time, and who had had up to this time little or no involvement with either party. Photius was put through all the church ranks in a week and became patriarch. The pope was simply informed of the change. The details were not supplied to the pope because the Byzantines felt it a matter of internal discipline.

Pope Nicholas I Enters the Byzantine Quarrel

Pope Nicholas I (858–67) wrote back that the whole matter sounded most irregular. He demanded a new hearing with the final decision belonging to Rome. He sent legates east who were expected to carry out this arrogant order. The emperor Michael and Photius informed the legates that the case was closed. For the sake of good relations, however, they would let the legates examine the matter. But the legates must reach a verdict themselves. Because of the slow communications between Rome and Constantinople, the Byzantines could not afford to wait six months to a year without a head to their church until news of a papal decision could reach them. The legates were distressed because these terms violated their instructions, which stipulated that the pope should judge in person. They decided, however, that their being allowed to judge the case would be a precedent for Roman primacy—Rome's right to settle matters within the eastern diocese—and agreed to these conditions. At the hearing the legates recognized Ignatius's deposition. Since his original election was irregular, they concluded that he had never rightfully been patriarch.

When word reached the pope, he was at first satisfied. In allowing the legates to hold the hearing, the Byzantines, in the pope's mind, had recognized papal primacy. Moreover, he still felt he had a weapon to use against Constantinople to satisfy another ambition. For though the legates had recognized that Ignatius was deposed, they had not accepted Photius as patriarch. So Pope Nicholas decided to make his recognition of Photius conditional on Byzantium's restoring to papal jurisdiction the province of Illyricum (which included more or less the whole Balkans except Greece, Dalmatia, and Thrace).

In 731 the iconoclastic emperor Leo III, angry at Rome for condemning him and iconoclasm as heretical, had removed Illyricum, Sicily, and Calabria from the jurisdiction of the pope and transferred them to that of the Constantinopolitan patriarch. In the eighth century Illyricum, settled with pagans, was not of much importance. In the mid-ninth century it was becoming more significant because the Bulgars were about to accept Christianity. Rome wanted to have Bulgaria under its jurisdiction. The Byzantines could not accept this. The Bulgarians, poised right on their borders, were frequently dangerous enemies. Thus the empire hoped to have the future Bulgarian church under the Greek patriarch as a conduit for influence on Bulgarian politics. Furthermore the Byzantines could not allow Bulgaria to become a military tool of the pope which could be used to attack Byzantium to enforce papal wishes.

When the Byzantines refused the papal demand, Nicholas declared that the legates had not had the authority to judge Ignatius. He demanded that the case be reopened. The two legates were defrocked and excommunicated. The Ignatian party meanwhile sent envoys to Rome who were received warmly by the pope; they began to fill his ears with all sorts of wild stories about Photius. Nicholas made it clear to these Ignatian envoys that he would acquit Ignatius on condition that Ignatius, upon his restoration as patriarch, accept Rome's rights over Bulgaria.

The emperor Michael, hearing of Ignatian agitation in Rome, wrote an angry letter in 863 to the pope, demanding that the pope send the agitators home. Michael stated that he had made a great concession to the pope, for the sake of good will, by letting the legates reopen a closed case. The issue was one of discipline and none of Rome's business. In the course of the letter he referred to Latin as a barbaric and Scythian language—a clear indication of the great distance that had grown between East and West.

The pope replied that no patriarch could be deposed without a trial by a higher court (i.e., the pope). He then remarked that if Latin was a barbaric tongue, why did the emperor call himself the Emperor of the Romans; and noted that most of the Byzantine emperors since the seventh century had been heretics anyway (i.e., iconoclasts). He concluded by ordering both Photius and Ignatius to appear before him in person for him to decide the case. Since the Byzantine emperor could not yield on such an important issue, the correspondence for a time ceased.

Boris of Bulgaria's Conversion

At virtually the same time—863—Boris had decided to accept Christianity. Since no sources speak of his aims, the reasons behind this decision are unknown. He probably had both religious and political motivations for his conversion. His sister was already a Christian and another relative whom he was to use as an envoy to Rome was clearly already one as well, since he was named Peter. Boris may well have been convinced of the truth of Christianity; his later abdication to enter a monastery in 889 signifies that by then he had become a deeply religious man. It is not possible to ascertain when he acquired such religious fervor, but it is not impossible that he was beginning to do so back in the 860s.

There were also many political goals that could be realized through the new religion. How many of them could have been foreseen by Boris and to what extent any of them were factors in his decision to adopt Christianity are unknown. However, as shall be seen, Christianity was a means to crush the religious and ideological basis of boyar privileges, and advance Boris's position as an autocrat. The new religion allowed him to stand high above the boyars and, in imitation of the Christian emperor, be prince "by Grace of God" and God's representative on earth. Moreover Christianity was a way to equalize both his nationalities (Slavs and Bulgars), and the possession of a common religion was a force to unite them into a single people.

Having made his decision to convert to Christianity, Boris in 863 sought a mission from the Franks. He had been allied with them since about 860 as both states were alarmed at the growing power of Moravia. Furthermore, from their distant homeland, the Franks were not in a position to interfere extensively in the development of the Bulgarian church; for what Boris seems especially to have been seeking was a church under his own control, modeled probably on the Byzantine system with a patriarch of a domestic church seated beside and appointed by the ruler.

The Byzantines seemed a far less satisfactory source for a Christian mission. As a neighbor, Byzantium clearly would interfere more in Bulgarian church matters than would the Franks. He also realized that Byzantium might well utilize the church for its own political ends—a fear that seems to have existed in Bulgaria throughout the century and to have been one of the causes for the persecution of Christians previously. So, just as Rastislav turned to a distant power (Byzantium) rather than to his strong neighbor (the Franks) for Christian missionaries, Boris requested the more distant Franks to send a mission.

However, the Byzantines, flushed with triumph from a major victory over the Arabs in 863, were not about to let this happen. They quickly sent a fleet into the Black Sea and launched an army toward Bulgaria. Boris was not prepared for this; at the time his armies were in the northwest campaigning against Moravia. So, when the Byzantine forces appeared on his borders in late 863, he yielded immediately. He promised to break the Frankish alliance, to accept Christianity from Byzantium, and to allow the entry into Bulgaria of Greek clergy. As a concession he was allowed to annex a strip of territory just southeast of the Balkan mountains between Sider and Develtus known as Zagora. Presumably he held this territory already, for it is unlikely that the Byzantines, operating from a position of strength, would voluntarily have surrendered it. Whether this territory had been acquired in the 846 or 852 campaigns or even earlier is not known. Boris was then baptized, with the emperor Michael III as his sponsor, sometime in

864. As a result, he took the name of Michael after his sponsor, and some modern works and sources so refer to Boris after this date.

Various other leading Bulgarians accepted Christianity at the same time. Many pagan temples were ordered destroyed while others were converted into Christian churches. Greek priests entered and began establishing a church organization and converting the populace. These first Greek priests preached and held services in Greek. Further adding to the confusion of the newly converted Bulgarians was the presence of other missionaries. Some were Christians—Franks and Armenians—who had various practices which differed from those of the Greeks. But the sources report that there were also some Islamic missionaries preaching in Bulgaria as well. These Moslems left no lasting mark on Bulgaria.

The Boyars and Boris

In 866 a group of boyars revolted against the new religion and the new legal order. The latter may have been equally galling to them, because Boris wanted to create a new legal basis for his state modeled more on Byzantium than on the old Bulgar customs, based on their paganism, which supported privileges to the old Bulgar families. Boris had obtained Byzantine legal texts, and their influence is already seen in 866 in some of the questions on legal practice which he directed at Pope Nicholas I. Thus, the boyars' position, long guaranteed through belief in divinely established clans, was threatened. Furthermore Boris no longer claimed to be first among equal clan leaders but prince by grace of God. Finally, many of the boyars had long resented Byzantium; they surely considered the entering Byzantine mission a threat to Bulgarian independence.

The boyars marched on Pliska and Boris suppressed the revolt. Our only source about this event, a western one, Hincmar, attributes his victory to miracles. Boris executed fifty-two leading boyars and their families, while he pardoned the lesser rebels. This weakened the old aristocracy and probably enabled him to advance some of his own people into positions of power, thus possibly laying a basis for a service nobility and to some degree strengthening his central administration. But though Boris's suppression of the boyar rebellion surely weakened the boyars, it did not, as some scholars have claimed, have the effect of smashing the boyar class. This class continued to exist, with some boyars continuing to oppose Christianity; for in the early 890s boyars supported (or even dominated) Boris's eldest son Vladimir when he tried to restore paganism.

On the basis of our limited sources, it is very difficult to determine the position of the boyars in Boris's state. Bulgaria was then divided into ten regions, each under a great nobleman. In the First Bulgarian State (681–1018)—except for the governors sent out to the Timok region by Omurtag—it is not known whether regional governors were local magnates or appointees of the prince. Under Boris many of the important old boyar families were liquidated and some scholars have assumed that they were replaced by a service nobility dependent not on birth but on the prince. Though plausible, this view cannot be proven owing to the meager details supplied by the sources. Some boyars evidently remained influential under Boris, for popes wrote to individual boyars, urging them to exert influence on Boris. In Boris's period we hear of "greater" and "lesser" boyars. In the tenth century, Constantine Porphyrogenitus refers to "inner" and "outer" boyars. Most probably the outer boyars were those living out in the provinces with their own local power bases and the inner ones were those based at court and presumably dependent on the prince. It would be interesting to know to what extent the prince succeeded in appointing inner boyars to positions of provincial authority. But references to outer boyars in the tenth century suggests that Boris, despite eliminating certain powerful families, did not break the power of provincial boyars as a class.

Boris Turns to Rome

Like the boyars, Boris worried about the large number of Greek priests active in Bulgaria and the increasing Byzantine influence in his state being exercised through the church organization. An independent Bulgarian church would lessen this danger to Bulgarian independence. So he asked Photius to allow Bulgaria to have its own patriarch. Besides seeking permission to more or less run his own church, he posed various questions to Photius about matters of correct practice. Photius ignored his request for a patriarch and instead of responding to the specific questions Boris asked him, wrote a long and pompous treatise on the duties of a Christian prince, as well as a detailed history of the church (focusing on doctrine, esoteric theological disputes, and church councils from centuries past). On receiving this, Boris, not surprisingly, felt rebuffed.

As a result of this rebuff by Byzantium, Boris decided to turn to Rome. This was probably a popular move at court and was more in keeping with Boris's initial intent of obtaining a mission from the Franks. Furthermore, since many of the boyars seemed to oppose Christianity, partly from fear of Byzantine penetration of Bulgaria, this act could well have diffused opposition in that quarter. It is likely that boyar opposition still was smouldering after Boris's suppression of the 866 revolt. On 29 August 866, an embassy headed by Boris's relative, the kavkhan Peter, arrived unexpectedly at the papal court, bearing a letter from Boris. In the missive the khan requested a patriarch for his realm, secular and canon law texts, and answers to a series of questions on church practices. The pope, thrilled at the opportunity to obtain from the Bulgarians what he had been seeking, immediately dispatched to Bulgaria legates, led by Formosus, an Italian bishop. This papal mission arrived in Bulgaria in November, 866, and Formosus immediately took over the direction of the Bulgarian church. He condemned various Greek customs which had been taught in Bulgaria, such as the marriage of priests and hands crossed on the chest for prayer.

Furthermore, when Boris had sent his envoys to Rome, he had directed a second embassy to the Franks. As a result a Frankish embassy arrived in Bulgaria in 867. It too included a contingent of missionaries. They and the legates sent by Nicholas seem to have gained the support of the anti-Byzantine party at court.

Formosus also brought Pope Nicholas's answers to all of Boris's 115 questions. The text of Nicholas's answer which survives is a major source on Bulgarian popular customs at the time. It depicts the confusion found among these people at the moment they were accepting Christianity. The pope's answers were moderate and sensible. He permitted the Bulgarians to continue to follow various old customs and, when he wanted to abolish one, he explained why its abolition was necessary. Not surprisingly, all of Boris's questions related to matters of practice (fasts, dress, rites) rather than doctrine. Nicholas informed Boris that, though Bulgaria, having been so recently converted, was not ready to have its own patriarch, he would give Boris bishops and maybe soon an archbishop, which was almost the same as a patriarch.

Boris was now in a position to deal with western Christians. The war in the northwest by then was over; his armies were ready if Byzantium should decide to invade again.

Not surprisingly, Photius was upset by this change. In retaliation he made a new papal embassy to Byzantium wait forty days on the Byzantine border. Meanwhile the Greek missionaries whom Boris had expelled from Bulgaria returned to Constantinople where they reported on various strange customs of the Franks: e.g., that it was permissible to eat milk and cheese in Lent, that priests were forbidden to marry. These Franks were even advancing a heresy, for they had added to the Nicene Creed. Instead of saying that the Holy Spirit descended from the Father, they said from the Father *and the Son* (*Filioque*). Photius wrote to the papal legates condemning these practices. He then convened early in 867 a small church council, composed only of the clergy of the city of Constantinople and its immediate environs, which also condemned these items. He then sent Boris a letter stating that the Roman priests were teaching him a false Christianity by which the Bulgarians could not be saved. This was exactly the sort of thing which would have alarmed a new convert and increased his feelings of insecurity. Photius then planned a large synod on the same issue which was to include all the eastern bishops.

The pope meanwhile received from Boris the results of the local Constantinopolitan synod. Its purpose had not been to cause an East-West break but to condemn certain practices and to frighten Boris into returning to Byzantine jurisdiction. Its decisions did not condemn the pope or the western church or even the Frankish church, but only certain practices of Frankish missionaries taught in Bulgaria. It was therefore aimed solely at Bulgaria. Nowhere did it state that the heresy and these practices were to be found in the Frankish empire itself, though of course they were.

The pope, for his part, was alarmed by Photius's activities. In addition to the issue of Bulgaria, he was afraid of a Byzantine-Frankish alliance against him in Italy (for despite the Byzantine attack on the Frankish Bulgarian mission, relations between the two empires were fairly good; they had a common policy and some degree of cooperation against the Arabs in Italy). In order to drum up more support and prevent the Franks from siding with Byzantium, the pope generalized the specific accusations and claimed that the Byzantine synod had made a general attack on the western church (Rome and the Frankish empire).

Photius next held a major synod in the summer of 867; it again condemned these practices and *Filioque*. This time, the synod attended by the other eastern bishops excommunicated and declared deposed Pope Nicholas I. At the same time it recognized Emperor Louis of the Franks. This recognition clearly signified that Byzantium had nothing against Louis and aimed to maintain good relations with his state; the Byzantine quarrel was just with the pope. Possibly Photius even hoped that Louis would carry out the sentence and unseat Nicholas, but in November, 867, Nicholas died before news of his sentence reached him; he was succeeded by Hadrian II.

Meanwhile, in September, 867, in Constantinople, Basil the Macedonian (formerly a groom in the imperial stables) murdered Michael III; since Michael had drawn his support from the Moderates, the new emperor Basil turned for allies to the Extremists. They were willing to support Basil only if he accepted their program, which at first he did. He reversed Michael's major church policies: he removed Photius, restored Ignatius, and attempted to pacify Rome by declaring Photius's synod of 867 invalid. Pope Hadrian II, who was infuriated with the impudence of a patriarch of Constantinople trying to excommunicate a pope, was in no mood to compromise with the East. When he received word of Photius's deposition and Ignatius's restoration, he believed this demonstrated that Nicholas had been right all along. Thus a strict policy toward the East was thought to be the only correct one.

Meanwhile, in Bulgaria, the papal legate, Formosus, had won Boris's confidence; so in the fall of 867 Boris requested Nicholas to grant him the promised archbishop and to allow Formosus to fill that post. Pope Nicholas, sensible up to this point in his dealings with Boris, recoiled; it seems he did not like the idea of a prince (particularly a newly converted one) telling him whom to appoint as a bishop. Clearly this was an appropriate moment for diplomacy, because Bulgaria's permanent status was still undecided. Furthermore the man Boris had requested was one trusted by Rome, the pope's own legate. Yet Nicholas refused; moreover he recalled Formosus on the pretext that he was needed at his own see in Italy. Hadrian continued this policy; for he, believing the new Byzantine emperor Basil to be pro-Roman, felt the papacy was free to do what it wanted in Bulgaria. Thus Hadrian denied Boris's request in February, 868, that Deacon Marin, another papal legate, be made the Bulgarian archbishop. These papal rebuffs alienated Boris, who, regardless of the state of direct Byzantine-papal relations, was an independent actor making his own decisions.

In the meantime Hadrian decided to take advantage of the changed situation in Constantinople to assert Roman control over the Byzantine church. He convoked a council in Rome in 869 which condemned Photius and declared that all bishops appointed by Photius were deposed. This affected a large number of prelates because Photius had been patriarch for nine years. Then Hadrian sent two legates to Constantinople to convoke a synod there to implement the decisions of the Roman council. This, of course, was a much more stringent policy than Basil had wanted; for though he had accepted Ignatius, he wanted peace in his church.

The two legates arrived with orders not to discuss matters nor to negotiate but to execute the decisions of the 869 Council of Rome. Aware of the excommunication of the two legates, sent by Nicholas, who had not carried out Nicholas's exact instructions, they were not about to repeat the mistake of their predecessors. Thus, they insisted that every bishop in the Byzantine Empire, to retain his see, must come to the council and sign a libellus which condemned Photius and recognized papal primacy. Bishops ordained by Photius could only receive lay communion henceforth, and Ignatians who had accepted him were to suffer long penances. No discussion was to be allowed.

When the synod was convened in October, 869, Ignatius and Basil, though shocked, signed the libellus; but a mere twelve bishops signed it during the first session. By the ninth session only 103—a small minority of eastern bishops—had signed. Rome clearly had misunderstood the situation in the East; otherwise the pope could not have been so uncompromising. The majority of the eastern bishops were Moderates. Moreover, the way papal policy was carried out insulted everyone, including Ignatius and the Extremists. Photius refused to sign his own excommunication and went into exile.

However, despite tensions, relations between the two churches were never broken at any point in this quarrel. (Photius's excommunication of Nicholas was annulled by Basil before word of it reached Rome.) It was in the midst of this quarrel that the Byzantine brothers, Constantine and Methodius, were summoned to Rome where they were well received, and given papal blessing for their work. In fact, Hadrian appointed Methodius bishop of Sirmium, a newly revamped see combining considerable territory in Pannonia and subject to Rome.

Bulgaria Returns to Byzantine Church Jurisdiction

Boris, unhappy with the two popes' refusals to appoint the bishops he wanted, sent delegates again led by his relative Kavkhan Peter early in 870 to the council in Constantinople which the two papal legates had convened in 869. These envoys were instructed to ask the council whether Bulgaria belonged to Rome or to Constantinople. The council, whose membership was overwhelmingly from the East, declared for Constantinople. Ignatius then appointed an archbishop for Bulgaria who was promised considerable autonomy. He stood over at least five dioceses. Byzantium then resumed sending Greek priests to Bulgaria.

Thus Ignatius and Basil, despite their attempts to have good relations with Rome, could not sacrifice imperial interests to the extent of giving up Bulgaria. Furthermore both Moderates and Extremists shared the same ambitions regarding Bulgaria. Ignatius and many of the Extremists (some of whom never did sign the libellus) must also have been so exasperated by Roman behavior and arrogance by

870 that they would have wanted to thwart Rome in any way they could. In any event, from this time there began a gradual reconciliation between Photius and Ignatius as well as between members of the two Byzantine factions.

Boris was satisfied with the council's decision which gave him a semiautonomous archbishop. The extent of this prelate's independence is not known. However, it has been plausibly argued that the role of Byzantium in the Bulgarian church was limited to appointing the archbishop; once in Bulgaria he had complete autonomy.[6] If Boris had in fact obtained so independent a prelate, his reasons for satisfaction with his renewed ties with the Byzantine church are obvious. He again admitted Greek priests and began expelling Latin ones. Thereafter (excluding a brief period, to be discussed later, when Bulgaria may have nominally belonged to Rome but during which Rome had no actual influence on Bulgarian church policy), Bulgaria was to remain under the ecclesiastical jurisdiction of Constantinople and part of the Orthodox world. Such a connection suited the interests of Bulgaria's rulers. It removed a major cause of tensions between Bulgaria and its neighbor, Byzantium. Furthermore, excluding the period from the 1030s to 1186, when Bulgaria, annexed by Byzantium, had lost its independence, the head of the Bulgarian church maintained this autonomous position. The degree of autonomy allowed by Constantinople was far greater than Bulgaria could have obtained from the pope.

The pope vehemently protested the council's decision on Bulgaria; Hadrian claimed that Ignatius's reinstatement was based on his recognition of Rome's rights in Bulgaria. A papal letter written in 874 by John VIII makes this clear.

> If Ignatius ever undertook anything against the apostolic rights in connection with Bulgaria, which not even Photius dared to attempt, he would, despite his acquittal, remain under sentence of his previous condemnation. . . . therefore he [Ignatius] stands acquitted if he respects the rights of the apostolic see on the Bulgarian question. If he does not, he falls back under the previous ban.[7]

Byzantium could not succumb to these demands; its foreign policy interests were too important. At the same time secular and church leaders of both parties were losing patience with papal behavior. This meant there was less and less to be gained by making concessions to Rome. So Basil wrote Hadrian asking him to reduce the sentences on Photius's supporters. When the pope refused in 872, Basil saw no further reason to follow the pro-Roman policy which had produced a situation offensive to all Byzantines. Instead Basil made peace with the Moderates. Photius returned from exile and was appointed tutor to Basil's children.

It was also important for Byzantine policy to restore the Moderates to favor because they included educated people (like Photius, Constantine, Methodius) who would be valuable to the state. Basil then succeeded in mediating the differences between the two sides; he made peace between Ignatius and Photius, leaving Ignatius in office with it understood that when he died Photius would succeed him. The pope continued to write to Ignatius to withdraw his priests from Bulgaria and to Boris to expel them, but these letters were ignored.

Ignatius died in 877 and Photius was again named patriarch. At that time Basil convened a council, the purpose of which was to reconcile the last remnants of the feuding factions. Some legates from Pope John VIII arrived in Constantinople at this moment. Unaware of Ignatius's death, they had no instructions on how to handle the new situation; Basil suggested they write the pope and delayed the council until his reply arrived. John wrote back that Photius must apologize for his past behavior and Byzantium must give up Bulgaria in order to gain his recognition of Photius. When Photius refused to apologize, the legates saw that schism would follow over this petty issue. So they agreed to drop that point if Byzantium agreed to surrender Bulgaria to Rome.

Photius now expressed his willingness to subject Bulgaria to Rome. He knew that, after the Byzantines' establishment of a Bulgarian archbishopric with considerable autonomy and almost a decade of Byzantine missionary effort, Boris was content. He saw that, regardless of what the council should decide, Boris, as an independent ruler, would do precisely what he wanted. But in consenting, Photius said that the actual decision would have to be left up to the emperor. The legates, having learned that the emperor Basil would agree to give Bulgaria to Rome, agreed to this condition. Thus a precedent was set that the emperor should decide matters of church jurisdiction. Over the next few years Bulgaria was not included in lists of sees subject to the patriarch of Constantinople. However, Greek priests remained there and it is evident that the Byzantine rulers did not care who sent the pallium, the symbol of office, to the Bulgarian archbishop so long as Byzantine priests ran the Bulgarian church. Moreover, as Photius had anticipated, the council's decision had no practical effect, because Boris refused to pay any attention to it. He did not reply to papal letters about his church and it is almost certain that no Bulgarian archbishop received the pallium from Rome. Thus the onus fell on Boris.

The Slavonic Mission in Bulgaria

Until this time, the Greek priests in Bulgaria had been Greeks preaching in Greek and using Greek texts. How many of them knew Slavic is not known. Methodius's mission had been in Moravia. The papacy had briefly supported his use of Slavonic there, and had made him bishop of Sirmium. But after Rastislav was overthrown in 870, Methodius was arrested. The Moravian state entered a period of close relations with the Franks, which led to a ban upon the Slavonic liturgy. Pope John VIII (872–82) procured Methodius's release from prison, but he supported the ban upon the Slavonic liturgy in Moravia. The papacy was to maintain this position from then on. Methodius tried to ignore the order; but soon, in April, 885, he died and his disciples were then expelled from Moravia. This signalled the end of the Slavonic liturgy in central Europe.

In 886 some of the Slavonic liturgists expelled from Moravia arrived in Bulgaria, where they were welcomed by Boris. They began to preach in Bulgaria; further they brought with them religious texts in Slavonic and began to translate other texts. Thus the work of the Slavonic mission was saved and Bulgaria acquired church services and a literature in the vernacular (for Old Church Slavonic, the language of the mission, was based on Bulgaro-Macedonian Slavic).

Over the following years more Slavonic liturgists came to Bulgaria from Byzantium where many of them had been trained as missionaries at the Patriarchal School. Thus two groups of clerics, one Slavic-speaking, the other Greek-speaking, both from Byzantium, were active in Bulgaria.

At first many of the Slavonic priests were sent into regions which were heavily Slavic, in particular to Macedonia. Zlatarski has observed that by the conquest of Macedonia Persian and/or Boris had united in one state almost all the Bulgaro-Macedonian Slavs. But though these tribes were all inside Bulgaria's borders, they were not yet sufficiently united to guarantee the permanence of the state. Still lacking were both a strong state organization and a common culture to bind them together with each other and with the Bulgarian state. Surely their loyalties and sense of identity were chiefly to tribe or region rather than to any state. Thus there was a Bulgarian state but as yet there were many people in it who did not have a sense of being Bulgarian. The Slavonic mission was to be a major means of making these Slavs in Macedonia—and other Slavs within the Bulgarian state as well—into Bulgarians.

A religious educational center was established on Lake Ohrid in

Macedonia by Saint Clement. At this center some translations were carried out and various religious literary works written. Most importantly, a school was established there where, according to the *Life of Saint Clement,* some thirty-five hundred were educated between 886 and 907. Possibly the figure is somewhat exaggerated. Saint Clement's closest associate, Saint Naum, briefly worked in the vicinity of Pliska, then he too was sent off to Ohrid.

The use of Slavonic-liturgy priests was useful in winning Slavic converts. Furthermore, the creation of a Slavic clergy was a first step toward liberating the Bulgarians from the Greek clergy (who were heavily under Byzantine influence). By the next generation, a large percentage of the Slavonic-liturgy clergy was to be of Slavic (rather than of Byzantine) origin, men trained by Clement and Naum. In this way the Slavonic liturgy enabled the Bulgarian church to utilize as its clerics native Bulgarians.

Boris furthered this process by making Clement—established at Ohrid—independent of the Greek who was archbishop of Bulgaria and based in Pliska. This action too increased the prestige of the Slavonic mission and of the Slavic language. These actions suggest that Boris was making a major effort to acquire Slavic support. Clement's *vita* states that Clement was the khan's representative among these Slavic subjects. This implies that Clement was also given a political administrative role over the Macedonians.

At the same time the Slavonic mission's activities contributed to an intensification of the slavicization of the Bulgars. By this time, after some two hundred years of living together, the more numerous Slavs seem to have been well on their way to assimilating the Bulgars. The process had been gradual, but the final stages seem to have occurred under Boris. It may be partially attributed to his liquidating many leading Bulgar families after their revolt. Christianity also dealt a crushing blow to their customs and privileged position in the state. Furthermore, many Bulgarians of Bulgar origin presumably were by then speaking Slavic. The Bulgars had always been a relatively small group and the number of people still speaking Bulgar would not have justified either a mission preaching in Bulgar or translations into that language. As far as we know, nothing was ever carried out along these lines. Thus after the official conversion the prestige of Slavic rose as it became a sacred-text language while that of Bulgar declined, being irrelevant to the new religion. But though Slavic was triumphing as the state language, the Bulgars could still be drawn into and identify with the national culture because this culture was not Slavic. For Boris made it national policy to use a new doctrine (Christianity), neither

Slavic nor Bulgar in origin, as cement to bind the two peoples into a single culture. Until now there had been a Bulgarian state, in which lived Slavs and Bulgars, but there were no Bulgarian people. This Boris's policies created. By the end of the ninth century, with Christianity making a strong contribution, the Bulgarians had become a basically Slavic nation with an ethnic awareness that was to survive through triumph and tragedy (including nearly two hundred years of Byzantine rule from 1018 to 1186) to the present.

After Boris's reign, the sources no longer distinguish between Bulgars and Slavs. Instead they refer to Bulgarians. This name, despite its origins, came to signify the ethnically mixed population of Bulgaria among whom the Slavic language triumphed. The Bulgar tongue died out and modern Bulgarian retains less than a dozen words from it.

Presumably the use of the Slavic language, the employment of a Slavic clergy, and Boris's policies which raised the Slavs to full membership in society did much to win the Slavs' loyalty to the khan and to his state and thus to make it a state with popular backing. Over two centuries an enormous change is visible; in the 680s the Bulgar khan had been a warrior chief leading bands of horsemen and nomads primarily seeking grazing grounds and booty. By the 880s he had become a Christian, Slavic prince presiding over a settled state with defined territorial boundaries (on the whole) and having a nascent system of law and administration.

Throughout his reign Boris concerned himself with legal matters. His letter to Pope Nicholas in 866 sought legal texts, secular as well as religious. Subsequently under him, the text of *Zakon sudnyi ljud'm (Court Law for the People)* based heavily on the Byzantine law code (*The Ecloga*), but adapted for Bulgarian conditions, appeared in Bulgaria. Whether it was compiled in Bulgaria or brought there from Moravia is heatedly debated among scholars but need not concern us.

The *Court Law for the People* deals with such matters as penalties for paganism, testimony of witnesses, distribution of war booty, sexual morality, marital relations, arson, theft, illegal enslavement, responsibility of a master for the behavior of his slave, and offenses involving horses and livestock. It imposed penalties for violations of its norms. The code has been characterized as combining "elements of canon law, military law, civil law, and criminal law, private and public law, substantive norms and procedural guidelines."[8]

Boris erected many churches including seven cathedrals in different dioceses of Bulgaria. The most spectacular was the great basilica built at his capital of Pliska, the seat of the archbishop. At ninety-nine meters in length, roughly the length of a football field, it was the longest church in Europe of its day. During this time many pagan temples were converted into churches. Boris also encouraged the development of monasticism. Various monasteries were built, some, as noted, becoming intellectual centers. They began to acquire tracts of land through donations.

Thus Boris Christianized his state, laid the basis for a Slavic literary culture (which, based on translations from Byzantine texts, meant bringing to Bulgaria elements of the rich Byzantine culture), presided over the final phase in the slavicization of the Bulgars, and reduced to some extent the position of the old boyars. Furthermore, after the series of unsuccessful military conflicts in the first decade of his reign, he kept Bulgaria at peace during the final twenty-five years he ruled. Considering Bulgaria's neighbors and the tensions existing between them and Bulgaria at the time, this too was a remarkable achievement.

Vladimir (889–93) Reverses Boris's Policies

Having seen his country through this great revolution, Boris fell seriously ill. Apparently genuinely religious, he abdicated in 889 and retired to a monastery. His eldest son Vladimir succeeded. Vladimir fell under the influence of the old boyars, many of whom had remained anti-Christian and anti-Byzantine. He attempted to restore the former Frankish alliance and also to reestablish paganism. The Bulgarian archbishop was martyred and many churches, including Boris's great basilica at Pliska, were seriously defaced or destroyed.

The Overthrow of Vladimir and the Preslav Council, 893

Afraid that his life's work might be undone, Boris left his monastery in 893 to lead a coup that overthrew his son Vladimir, who was deposed and blinded. After this triumph, Boris convoked that same year a large council, *not* at Pliska (the capital and long the Bulgar center) but at Preslav, which, though in the same general area, seems to have been chiefly a Slavic town and a Christian center. Near it was located the royal monastery of Tiča where Boris's second son Symeon and probably Boris were resident. The council recognized Vladimir's deposition. It then released Symeon from his monastic vows and proclaimed him the new ruler. Next it declared Christianity the religion of state. And, if a later Russian chronicle is accurate, Slavonic was proclaimed the official language of church and state. Finally it decreed that henceforth Preslav should be the capital of Bulgaria. Then Boris, having restored matters to what he felt were a more satisfactory state, returned to the nearby Tiča monastery from which he presumably kept an eye on things.

Thus Pliska, the Bulgar center where boyar influence still seems to have been strong, was abandoned as an administrative center and the capital was established in a Slavic and Christian town. Probably behind this decision also was Preslav's proximity to the monastery in which Boris was resident. If Preslav was the capital, Boris could be much more closely in touch with events and have more impact upon them. This shift of capitals was to further diminish the influence of the old boyars and encourage further slavicization of the already well-slavicized state. Furthermore in Preslav the influence of Christianity was stronger than that of paganism.

Certain scholars have claimed that state councils, like the Preslav gathering, were regular institutions. However, there is danger in trying to overformalize the institutional structure of a relatively primitive state. Such gatherings may have been common on a clan or tribal level, but no evidence exists that they were regular on a state level. This council is the first one known and it clearly was called to meet an extraordinary situation.

NOTES

1. G. Cankova-Petkova, "O territorii bolgarskogo gosudarstva v VII–IX vv.," *Vizantijskij vremennik* 17 (1960):124–43.

2. The Byzantine description of Krum's actions suggests that he did not plan to retain Sardika. However, recently Bulgarian archaeologists have raised doubts about the accuracy of the Byzantine account. Their excavations suggest that the walls had not been destroyed. In any event, Sardika and environs seem to have remained in Bulgarian hands. The city itself probably was more or less abandoned after the events of 809. Gradually a Slavic town grew up near the fortress.

3. I. Venedikov, "La population byzantine en Bulgarie au début du IX[c] siècle," *Byzantinobulgarica* 1 (1962):265–66.

4. F. Dvornik, "Deux inscriptions Greco-Bulgares de Philippes," *Bulletin de Correspondance Hellenique* 52 (1928):140–43.

5. G. Cankova-Petkova, "Contribution au sujet de la conversion des Bulgares au Christianisme," *Byzantinobulgarica* 4 (1973):21–39.

6. V. Swoboda, "L'origine de l'organisation de l'église en Bulgarie et ses rapports avec le patriarcat de Constantinople (870–919)," *Byzantinobulgarica* 2 (1966):67–81.

7. F. Dvornik, *The Photian Schism in History and Legend* (Cambridge, 1948), p. 156. This section on Photius's activities and Byzantine-papal relations is heavily indebted to this outstanding study.

8. H. W. Dewey and A. M. Kleimola, *Zakon sudnyi ljudem (Court Law for the People)*, Michigan Slavic Materials, no. 14 (Ann Arbor, Mich., 1977), p. vi. This volume contains both a short and expanded version of the code; both are given in the original Slavonic and in English translation.

CHAPTER 5

Bulgaria under Symeon, 893–927

Symeon's Background and Character

Symeon (893–927) was the most colorful ruler in Bulgarian, if not medieval Balkan, history. After Boris had designated Symeon's elder brother Vladimir heir to the throne, Symeon had been trained for a religious career; Boris may have intended him to become the Bulgarian archbishop (whose rank he hoped would be raised to patriarch). Symeon had been born about the time of Boris's conversion, and thus had been a Christian all his life. He was sent to Constantinople when he was about thirteen or fourteen. There he became a novice in a monastery, taking the name Symeon by which he was to be known for the rest of his life. He spent almost a decade there studying (ca. 878–888).

Much has been written about those whom Symeon might have studied with (e.g., Photius), but since no source tells us anything about his teachers, such speculations are fruitless. However, presumably as a foreign prince for whose education the emperor Basil was responsible, he would have had excellent tutors. During his decade there, he clearly learned Greek well; he is even called "the half-Greek" in Byzantine sources. One hostile oration delivered after Symeon met with the emperor Romanus in 923 says he spoke much [Greek] in a barbarous accent and made many errors in grammar; but as this source was out to mock Symeon, its criticisms may not be accurate.

In approximately 888 he returned to Bulgaria where he established himself at the new royal monastery of Tiča at Preslav. He was accompanied by various students from the Slavonic school in Constantinople. Symeon quickly became the leader of a massive translation project (Greek to Slavonic) at this monastery. After he left the monastery to become ruler, he seems to have remained interested in literature and sponsored many translations. These included both legal texts and religious works (in particular liturgical texts and the writings of

Greek church fathers). In addition, Byzantine historical chronicles were now translated. Symeon was associated with a major collection (sbornik), probably the translation of a popular Byzantine encyclopedia; this compilation is usually named after a Kievan prince Svjatoslav (1073–76) because the text survived in his copy. Under Symeon the first original Bulgarian works appeared: the treatise of Hrabr, the first saints' lives, and the writings of John the Exarch, which in addition to their religious content shed light on social and religious conditions in Bulgaria. John's major work is the *Šestodnev* (The Six Days), an account of the creation, which is quite heavily derived from the *Hexaemeron* of Saint Basil. Its preface is a panegyric addressed to Symeon which also praises the town of Preslav.

Symeon encouraged monasticism; at least eight monasteries existed in and around his new capital of Preslav. That city grew under Symeon's supervision. Its palace was renovated, new churches were built, and its commercial quarter had active shops in which artisans specialized in ceramics, stone, glass, wood, and metals (in particular gold and silver). Exquisite examples of these craftsmen's skills are now displayed in the National Historical Museum in Sofija. Bulgarian tile work (in the "Preslav style") was particularly famous. Beautiful examples of these tiles have survived. Because Bulgarian tiles achieved a higher quality than Byzantine, they were imported by Byzantium and Russia.

Though little is known about Symeon as a man, a few details do slip through in the letters written to him by the Byzantine patriarch Nicholas Mysticus in the second decade of the tenth century. In these letters, Nicholas, who was seeking peace in the midst of the Bulgaro-Byzantine wars of that time, was clearly trying to flatter Symeon; however, his statements could not have been effective if the flattery was entirely fictitious. In one Nicholas says the following:

> For who could ever have anticipated that Symeon, who for his great wisdom, for the favor shown him by heaven, has led the Bulgarian nation to a height of glory, who more than any man detests knavery, who honors justice, who abominates injustice, who is above sensual pleasures, who stints his belly like a hermit on the mountains, who tastes no wine. . . . [1]

In another letter Nicholas refers to Symeon's interest in ancient history. Presumably his historical interests and dietary asceticism can be accepted as facts.

The Slavonic Rite and Hrabr's Defense of Slavonic

As noted earlier, Boris had made Clement, who headed the Slavonic mission at Ohrid, independent of the Greek who was archbishop of Bulgaria. In 894 Symeon raised Clement to the rank of bishop and placed him over a newly established see (generally thought to include all of Macedonia as far east as Skopje) in a purely Slavic region. He was the first Slavonic-rite bishop in Bulgaria, a position he held until his death in July 916. Soon the rest of Bulgaria (the older core area in the northeast) received a Slavic bishop too. This bishop, named Constantine, resided at the important Tiča monastery. Thus, following the council of 893, the Slavonic rite triumphed completely.

These acts marked the end of the Greek liturgy in Bulgaria, and Greek-speaking priests began to leave. They were replaced by the new generation of actual Bulgarians, who had been taught by the Slavonic missionaries. Bulgaria thus was well on its way to having its own entirely independent church staffed by Bulgarians rather than Greeks.

Generally it has been stated that there was no Byzantine protest over either Symeon's appointments or his ousting of the Greek-language clerics. This would have been in keeping with Byzantine policy because the language of the liturgy for peoples beyond the imperial borders was not an important issue for the Greeks. But though there is no sign of any official Byzantine protest or of any Byzantine political acts against Bulgaria, it seems that some objections were made—quite likely by the individual clerics who were being expelled. From Symeon's time the following defense of the Slavic language and letters written by a monk, Hrabr (the Brave One), has survived. Presumably it was written in response to some Greek protests.

> The Slavs at first had no books, but, being pagans, they read and divined by means of lines and notches. When they became Christians they had to write the Slavic tongue with unadapted Roman and Greek letters. But how can one write well with Greek letters БОГЪ or ЖИВОТЪ or СѢЛО or ЦРЬКВЫ . . . . And so it was for many years.
>
> Then, God who loves man and who takes care of everything and does not leave mankind senseless but leads all to reason and salvation, took mercy upon the Slavic race and sent it St. Constantine the Philosopher, called Cyril. . . . He devised for them 38 letters, some modeled on the Greek letters, others to fit the Slavic speech. He started from the Greek alphabet: they say "alpha" and he says "az." Both alphabets thus begin with "a." Just as the

Greeks made their letters imitating the Jewish, he modeled his on the Greek. . . .

Some say: "Why did he devise 38 letters when fewer would be enough, just as the Greeks write with 24 letters?" However, they do not know how many letters the Greeks use. They have indeed 24 letters, but there are also 11 diphthongs and 3 for the numbers 6, 90, and 900. They add up to 38. Similarly and in the same manner St. Cyril devised 38 letters.

Then others say: "Why should there be Slavic books? They have not been created by God or by the angels, and they are not original like the Jewish, Latin, and Greek books which go back to the beginning and are accepted by God?" Still others think that God himself created the letters. They do not know, wretched souls, what they are talking about, and they think that God has ordered books to be written in three languages because it is written in the Gospel: "And there was a board with writing in Hebrew, Latin, and Greek." Since the Slavic language was not there, the Slavic books are not God-given. What can we say to that and what can we reply to such fools? Let us answer as we have been taught from the holy texts, that all comes in its turn from God and from no one else. God did not first create the Hebrew or the Greek language, but the Syrian which Adam spoke and was spoken from Adam to the Deluge, and from the Deluge to God's creation of the languages in the Tower of Babel, or the "Confusion of Tongues," as it is written.

Before then the Greeks had no alphabet of their own but wrote their speech with Phoenician letters. And so it was for many years. Then came Palamedes who started with alpha and beta and devised only 16 letters for the Greeks. Cadmos of Miletus added 3 letters. . . . Thus many men over many years barely managed to assemble 38 letters. Then, after many years, by God's will 70 men were found to translate [the Old Testament] from Hebrew into Greek. The Slavic books, however, were translated, and the letters were invented, by Cyril alone in a few years, whereas many men—seven—invented over many years the Greek letters and seventy made the translation. For this reason the Slavic letters are holier and more respectable because they were devised by a saint whereas the Greek letters were devised by pagan Greeks.

If you ask the Greek bookmen, "Who invented your letters and translated the books and when," few of them know. If you ask, however, the Slavic bookmen, "Who invented your letters and translated the books," they all know and will reply, "St. Constantine the Philosopher; he and his brother, Methodius, invented our letters and translated the books," because there are still men alive who saw them. And if you ask them at what time, they know and will say that it was in the time of the Byzantine Emperor Michael and the Bulgarian Prince Boris. . . . There are other answers which we will give elsewhere, for there is no time now. Thus, brothers, God has enlightened the Slavs.[2]

It seems clear that Hrabr's text is a defense of Slavonic written in response to Greek criticisms. This view has many defenders among scholars. Others, however, noting the similarity between Greek letters and Cyrillic, have seen Hrabr's text as a defense of the Glagolitic Slavic alphabet against Cyrillic.

Originally Old Church Slavonic had been written in Glagolitic, which bore little resemblance to any other alphabet. The missionaries who came to Bulgaria from Moravia brought texts in this alphabet and began teaching it to Bulgarians. Soon, however, Slavonic came also to be written in a second alphabet known as Cyrillic, named for Methodius's brother Saint Cyril. This alphabet was modeled on Greek letters, though written somewhat differently. Furthermore, original letters were created for sounds not existing in Greek. Probably Cyrillic first came into use during Symeon's reign. Dujčev gives Clement much credit for its introduction. In the decades that followed, Cyrillic gradually replaced Glagolitic as the Slavic alphabet used in Bulgaria. Eventually it came to be the alphabet used in all Orthodox Slavic lands. Today Bulgarian, Macedonian, Russian, and Serbian are written in versions of Cyrillic. On the whole these languages utilize the same letters, but each is distinguished from the others by the presence of certain specific letters that convey specific local sounds. Each of these alphabets has undergone various orthographic reforms in the modern era which have eliminated certain medieval letters.

Hrabr's own text makes it clear that he is defending Slavic letters against Greek rather than one Slavic alphabet against another. On the subject of the alphabet he is defending Hrabr states, "Some letters are modelled on Greek letters." Since Cyrillic alone resembles the Greek alphabet, clearly Hrabr was speaking about Cyrillic. Moreover, he states that the Slavic alphabet has thirty-eight letters; this statement would not make a contrast between the two Slavic alphabets which both had the same number of letters but makes a contrast with the twenty-four Greek letters. He also is evidently speaking of a Slavic alphabet when he defends the idea of the Gospels in Slavonic against the idea that there are only three holy languages. This argument would be irrelevant if one were differentiating between two Slavic alphabets.

Linguists have often assumed that, before Cyrillic triumphed over the earlier Glagolitic alphabet, some sort of conflict occurred between proponents of the two Slavic alphabets. However, in our sources there is no sign of any conflict between proponents of one against the other. As Cyrillic triumphed, there is no evidence of a resistance movement by defenders of Glagolitic.

The 894–97 War with Byzantium

Shortly after Symeon's accession a quarrel developed between Byzantium and Bulgaria. Most of the treaties concluded previously between Byzantium and Bulgaria had commercial clauses regulating on a most-favored-nation basis trade between the two nations. Bulgarian merchants were allowed to reside in Constantinople where they lived in their own colony and paid favorable tariffs. In 894, however, the position of these merchants was threatened. Under the emperor Leo VI (886–912), Stylianus Zautzes, the father of the emperor's mistress and later wife, gained tremendous influence, and granted all sorts of favors to his cronies. Stylianus persuaded Leo to move the Bulgarian market from Constantinople to Thessaloniki. This had the effect of expelling the Bulgarian merchants from the capital and meant that they could not buy eastern goods directly but had to buy them through Byzantine middlemen (i.e., the two cronies of Zautzes). Furthermore these goods, because of additional shipping costs, became more expensive. Possibly more important, the relocation of the market from the capital diminished imperial control over the duties being collected, allowing Zautzes's two friends to enrich themselves by increasing tariffs.

Symeon protested this change. Although Byzantium was then involved in a war on the eastern front and thus in no position to fight Bulgaria, Leo ignored Symeon's protests. Symeon then mobilized his troops and invaded imperial territory, ravaging the countryside.

Various scholars claim that Symeon already had great ambitions and had been waiting for an excuse for war; thus this commercial issue was the pretext he was looking for. However, there is danger in projecting his later behavior back some twenty years. Who knows what Symeon's ambitions were in the 890s? Because Symeon was at war with Byzantium from 913 to 927 is no reason to conclude he sought an excuse for a war in 894. When this first war was ended in 897, a period of sixteen years of peace until 913 followed; this long peace also belies that interpretation.

A small Byzantine force was sent out against the Bulgarians (still in 894) but was defeated. Captured members of the imperial guard had their noses cut off and were then sent home. After this failure, the Byzantines decided they needed outside aid and called on the Magyars (or Hungarians), then living between the Dnepr and the Danube, to attack Bulgaria in the rear from the north. After crossing the Danube on Byzantine ships, the Magyars ravaged Bulgarian territory and Symeon had to seek refuge in the fortress of Silistria while the Magyars ran riot; they even sacked Preslav. This was the first Hungarian intervention in European affairs.

Simultaneously, Byzantine armies attacked Bulgaria from the south, and the imperial fleet blockaded the mouth of the Danube. Symeon had no choice but to send envoys to Byzantium to seek peace. However, at the same time he sent off a second embassy to a Turkic tribe known as the Pechenegs (or Patzinaks) who lived in the Steppes to the east of the Magyars and who could strike at them in the rear. The Pechenegs agreed to help.

The Byzantines responded to Symeon's request for a truce by sending to him an envoy named Leo Choerosphaktes. Annoyed by the whole situation, Symeon pitched the envoy in jail and carried on all his negotiations with him there. Needless to say, the Byzantines were not pleased with the treatment of their envoy. A truce was arranged but the two sides continued bickering as to the terms of the treaty that was to follow; a point of contention was the exchange of prisoners.

Symeon clearly was in no hurry, for he burned for revenge on the Byzantines for calling in a non-Christian people (the Hungarians) against Christian Bulgaria. Thus he did not want a real treaty but rather wanted to mark time until the Pechenegs sent aid which would free his own armies to punish the Byzantines. Therefore Symeon continued to stall over the negotiations and showed constant suspicion over the wording of Byzantine notes; however, the worries he expressed may not have only been intended to stall, for Byzantine behavior was rarely above suspicion and probably Symeon really expected the empire to try to trick him. He constantly sought further clarifications and exact meanings of words. When the Byzantines grew impatient, Symeon replied to the envoy:

> The eclipse of the sun, and its date, not only to the month, week, or day, but to the hour and second, your emperor prophesied to us the year before last in the most marvellous fashion. And he also explained how long the eclipse of the moon will last. And they say he knows many other things about the movements of

heavenly bodies. If this is true, he must also know about the prisoners; and if he knows, he will have told you whether I am going to release them or keep them. So prophesy one thing or the other, and if you know my intentions, you shall get the prisoners as reward for your prophecy and your embassy, by God! Greetings![3]

While these negotiations dragged on, the Pechenegs attacked and occupied the Magyars' homeland. This forced the Magyars to withdraw from Bulgaria. However, the stronger Pechenegs prevented them from returning to their former lands. The Magyars were thus forced to migrate to new pastures, which they found in the plains of present-day Hungary. In this way a new people was established in Europe. Soon they created a major state which has existed to the present.

The Hungarians' arrival led to the collapse of the state of Moravia by 906. The Hungarians also seem to have occupied some Bulgarian territory north of the Danube. The extent of Bulgarian territorial losses in what is now Rumania is not known. Moreover, the arrival of the Hungarians drove a non-Slavic wedge between the West Slavs and South Slavs and eliminated the possibility that Slavonic language or literature would have long-term influence on the West Slavs; this was a factor (though not the major one) contributing to the triumph of Latin over Slavic among the West Slavs (Czechs, Slovaks, Poles). Finally, the arrival of the Pechenegs in Bessarabia split the Magyars from the Khazars with whom they had close ties. This had the effect of greatly weakening the Khazars as a Steppe power; eventually in 965 they were destroyed by Svjatoslav of Kiev.

With the Magyars out of Bulgaria, Symeon rebuilt his shattered army and demanded that Leo immediately return all Bulgarian captives. Leo, faced with the Arab danger in the east, agreed. Symeon seems to have seen this as a sign of weakness. A few months later, claiming that all the Bulgarian prisoners had not been restored, he invaded Thrace and marched on Constantinople. Byzantine troops were sent out to meet him. The two armies met at Bulgarophygon and the Bulgarians won an overwhelming triumph. Leo was in such a panic that he even considered arming his Arab prisoners and sending them out against the Bulgarians, though in the end he thought better of this wild idea. Further negotiations followed.

Finally the Byzantines agreed to Bulgarian terms and a treaty was signed in 897. In this treaty the Byzantines agreed to pay the Bulgarians tribute; Bulgaria regained its most-favored-nation commercial status, all commercial restrictions were abolished, and its market was restored to

Constantinople; there was a rectification of the frontier with some gains for Symeon along the frontier (unfortunately, it is not known where the boundaries established by this treaty lay); and in exchange Symeon restored some occupied Byzantine cities in Thrace. This peace remained in force from 897 to 913 with one brief break in 904.

Despite official delimitations in treaties the boundaries between the two nations were not and could not be absolutely clear; these regions were settled to a large extent by semi-independent Slavic tribes. In much of this territory there were neither Byzantine nor Bulgar officials and whatever the two states might decide, the Slavs might choose to ignore. Tribal boundaries (often not permanent) could well overlap state boundaries. Very likely some Slavs in what was theoretically Byzantine territory were loyal to—and possibly even paying tribute to— the Bulgars. Thus the loyalty of tribes may not have coincided with the state boundaries within which they lived. In short, certain borders might have been more theoretical than real.

The 904 Bulgarian-Byzantine Treaty

In the beginning of the tenth century, as noted above, the Arabs had completed the conquest of Sicily and Arab pirates terrorized the Aegean. In 902 they laid waste to the coast of Thessaly and the Peloponnesus. Then in 904 they captured Thessaloniki. After carrying out a bloodbath, the Arabs withdrew with many prisoners and a tremendous amount of booty. This was the first time in centuries that that great, and often threatened, city had been taken. After the Arabs had departed, Symeon's armies appeared in the vicinity; Thessaloniki lay open to them. Symeon capitalized on the situation to open negotiations with Byzantium. In exchange for not taking Thessaloniki Symeon received great territorial compensation—some new territory and recognition of other territories long held but never recognized as Bulgarian by the empire. He extended his borders up to Nea Philadelphia (Nareš) some twenty-two kilometers north of Thessaloniki. He also acquired some Thracian territory. In addition the Byzantines finally recognized Bulgarian possession of most of Macedonia. Most or all of this Macedonian territory had been held by the Bulgarian state since the middle of the ninth century. During that time the Bulgarians had consolidated their actual hold over it. Now, with their possession recognized, the Bulgarians completed their annexation of the Bulgaro-Macedonian Slavic tribes to the west of the original Bulgarian state. Whether Symeon would have been wiser to have grabbed, refortified, and tried to hold Thessaloniki is a matter of debate.

Serbia in the Second Half of the Ninth Century

Serbia meanwhile had been—and soon was to be even more so—a pawn in the Byzantine-Bulgarian struggle. In the middle of the ninth century Serbia had achieved some sort of statehood as various Serbian tribes, faced with the Bulgarian threat, united under a prince named Vlastimir. He became the knez (prince) and through the marriage of his daughter extended his overlordship over Trebinje and Konavli. He died leaving his state divided among three sons—Mutimir, Strojimir, and Gojnik. Among the Slavs it was not unusual to divide one's territory among one's heirs rather than to leave everything to the eldest son. In roughly 853 or 854 Boris of Bulgaria, as noted previously, sent an army led by his son Vladimir against the Serbs. The Serbs defeated this force and captured Vladimir and twelve leading boyars. This capture brought about a peace treaty, and an alliance was arranged between the two Slavic states.

Shortly thereafter Mutimir seized the Serbian throne and exiled his two brothers to the Bulgarian court. Gojnik's son, Peter, fled to Croatia. Mutimir ruled in Serbia until about 890 or 891 when he died leaving the throne to his sons, led by the eldest, Prvoslav. Prvoslav's reign lasted less than a year before Gojnik's son, Peter (whose name shows that he had converted to Christianity), reappeared from Croatia and after a battle ousted Prvoslav and took over in Serbia. This occurred in approximately 892. Prvoslav fled to Croatia and shortly thereafter his son Zaharije appeared in Constantinople, where he remained for many years before reappearing in Serbia. After the failure of a couple of more attempts by other relatives to capture the throne, including one supported by Bulgaria, Symeon agreed to recognize Peter's rule and Peter placed himself under Symeon's protection. This resulted in a twenty-year peace inside of Serbia and a Serbian-Bulgarian alliance, 897–917. Peter probably was not altogether happy with his subordinate position and may have dreamed of reasserting his independence. His situation as well as the feud between the three branches of Vlastimir's children's descendants—the Mutimirovići, Strojimirovići, and Gojnikovići—should be kept in mind because Peter's allegiances and this feud were to play a part in the major Bulgarian-Byzantine war to come.

Christianity presumably was spreading gradually at this time in Serbia. Unfortunately almost no sources touch on this process. Whatever missions and subsequent conversions may have followed Heraclius's alleged acceptance of the Serbian presence in the Balkans probably had little long-term effect. The Serbs in the ninth century seem to have been chiefly pagans. However, Peter's name shows him to have been a Christian; possibly during his long reign he encouraged the spread of that religion. Also since Serbia bordered on Bulgaria presumably Christian influences and perhaps missionaries came from there. Such contacts may well have increased during the twenty-year peace and alliance which existed between the two nations from 897 to 917.

War Breaks Out between Bulgaria and Byzantium, 913

The emperor Leo VI died on the eleventh of May, 912. His brother, Alexander, is depicted as hardly being able to wait to seize the throne. He came to the deathbed and Leo's last recorded utterance supposedly was "here comes the man of thirteen months." This, according to Jenkins, meant that the brother was an evil omen like the intercalary year which added an extra month to square the solar and the lunar cycles; but when Alexander died after thirteen months this was seen as prophetic and added to Leo's reputation as a wizard.

Almost all the sources are hostile to Alexander and thus he has for a long time been depicted by scholars as one of the worst of all the Byzantine emperors. Recently, however, Karlin-Hayter has turned out a fine study, demonstrating the bias of all the sources as well as their inconsistencies, and suggesting that perhaps Alexander was really not the incompetent debauched drunkard that the sources make him seem.[4] Unfortunately, sources are lacking to prove the point, but at least we should pause before accepting all the statements made against him.

In any case Alexander set about reversing various of Leo's policies, removing Leo's advisors and officers and bringing in other people, some of whom clearly were his own cronies. Among the people he put into power was Nicholas Mysticus. Nicholas had been patriarch under Leo but had been deposed when he refused to allow Leo's uncanonical fourth marriage. Leo had then ousted Nicholas and replaced him with a monk named Euthymius. Alexander clearly had little to gain by recognizing the fourth marriage since by it was legitimized the heir to the throne, Leo's sickly and minor son Constantine Porphyrogenitus, the future emperor and author, whose writings provide one of our most valuable collections of sources. Thus it probably made sense to restore to power the former patriarch who did not recognize the boy's legitimacy. Nicholas was to remain in office and be a major figure in subsequent relations with Bulgaria. The partisans of Euthymius, whom Alexander deposed, needless to say had little love for either Alexander or Nicholas. Since one of our major sources is a life of Euthymius, it perhaps is not surprising that Alexander has been treated so harshly by scholars.

Other than his appointments, Alexander carried out only one known significant political act. When Bulgarian envoys came to collect their tribute (according to the terms of the 897 treaty), Alexander not only refused to pay it but insulted the envoys. Alexander's behavior has been blamed for setting off the war that followed. It is evident that he did refuse the tribute though it is not certain that he did it as insultingly as the sources, hostile to him, say. However, an oration known as "On the Bulgarian Peace" states that Symeon had long been seeking a pretext for war and making claims on the imperial title. The oration claims that only Leo's diplomacy had held him in check. That Symeon wanted war is confirmed by the speed with which he launched his troops; they were already active in Thrace in the spring of 913. Clearly Symeon wanted war by then; possibly there was nothing Alexander or anyone else could have done to keep it from breaking out, particularly if we take into consideration the unstable situation in Constantinople, where an unpopular, inexperienced, ill, and possibly alcoholic emperor sat on the throne and where the heir was a sickly small boy considered by many to be illegitimate.

While the Bulgarians prepared for war, the situation in Constantinople was becoming more unstable.

Meanwhile the miserable Alexander sank from bad to worse. His excesses enfeebled his body. He indulged in a whole series of cruelties and follies. Once he became convinced that a bronze boar in the Hippodrome was his fetch and supplied it with a new set of teeth and generative organs by way of mending his own deficiencies in those departments. He led pagan processions in which sacred vestments were misused. The only good thing about him was that he could not possibly last long. On 4 June 913 he got drunk and went to play a ball game. A cerebral haemorrhage followed. He was picked up dying, and ended his life two days afterwards, leaving the Patriarch Nicholas, with a council chiefly composed of Slavs [*sic,* only two of seven], to govern as regents for his seven-year-old nephew Constantine Porphyrogenitus. Such was the end of the thirteen-months man. He was forty-two years old.[5]

This was an ideal time for Symeon to attack Byzantium. The child emperor was in the hands of a regent who considered him illegitimate and the boy's mother, Zoe, had been exiled against her will to a monastery, from where she was presumably plotting her return. In the midst of this chaos in August 913 Symeon appeared before the walls of

Constantinople with an army; he was not seeking plunder, Symeon wanted nothing less than the crown. He had been educated in Constantinople and had swallowed hook, line, and sinker imperial ideology; he did not seek a Bulgarian "empire" existing side by side with Byzantium, as Boris had. Boris had visualized himself as emperor of Bulgaria, having his own patriarch to preside over an independent Bulgarian church. Symeon, in the Byzantine tradition, understood there could be only one empire on earth, that of the Romans. He wanted to gain Constantinople so that he could become *the* emperor and rule over a joint Greek-Bulgarian state called the Roman Empire. Thus the threat from Symeon was different from that posed by Krum and other barbarian raiders. Symeon did not primarily seek plunder and new territories to add to a second state, he sought to take over the existing state and rule over it as the Roman emperor. But like previous invaders, Symeon found the walls impenetrable. He began negotiating via envoys with the regent, the patriarch Nicholas Mysticus.[6]

Nicholas had been in Constantinople when Symeon had been a student. Both seem to have studied at the Patriarchal School, though not necessarily at the same time. It is sometimes claimed by scholars that the two knew each other well. However, the sources mention only two meetings between them (one in 913 and a second meeting in 923). I doubt the two had known one another from Symeon's student days in the capital, since Nicholas wrote Symeon soon after the 913 meeting: "I know the greatness of your wisdom, not by rumor but by personal experience: for *that time* when we came together in mutual conversation, *short though it was,* yet gave me sufficient knowledge of your most perfect wisdom" [italics added].[7]

Symeon's Coronation

Negotiations led to a meeting between the patriarch-regent Nicholas and Symeon. What happened at that meeting—though often presented in straightforward fashion in our secondary works—is in fact a tantalizing riddle. Symeon had demanded a meeting with the emperor and patriarch. The Logothete's chronicle reports that Symeon's two sons were received inside Constantinople but the patriarch Nicholas "went out" to meet Symeon. Thus Symeon met the patriarch outside the walls, presumably the meeting taking place in the midst of Symeon's entourage. Symeon prostrated himself before the patriarch who, after reciting some prayers, placed upon his head instead of a crown (*stemma*) his own patriarchal headpiece (*epirrhiptarion*). Honored with many gifts, Symeon returned home.

In addition, it seems, from two other and later sources, Nicholas agreed that Symeon's daughter should be betrothed to the boy emperor, Constantine. This would have made Symeon, when the marriage took place, the father-in-law of the emperor, which, as will be seen, could be a quick route to becoming coemperor.

Now let us turn to the sticky questions surrounding Symeon's "coronation." Did Nicholas crown him emperor (probably of the Bulgarians) or caesar (then the second title in the empire)? This question immediately leads to a second one: was the coronation—be it as emperor or as caesar—a serious one or a sham? The chronicle account of the Logothete—which was then repeated in a series of other chronicles—clearly depicted it as a sham, stating that Nicholas crowned Symeon with a crown made from a church headdress (not a real crown); therefore, it is to be understood, the ceremony had no meaning. A court orator, to be discussed subsequently, also depicts the ceremony as a sham. But these two authors were writing later to defend Nicholas against the charge of knuckling under to the barbarian; consequently their words should not necessarily be taken as fact.

Though there has been considerable controversy among scholars as to whether Nicholas crowned Symeon caesar or emperor, recent scholarship has demonstrated that Symeon was almost certainly crowned emperor (basileus) of the Bulgarians.

First, Ostrogorsky noticed that the Byzantine chronicle account by the Logothete in referring to the coronation calls the crown that should have been placed upon Symeon's head a *stemma*. Ostrogorsky then traces this term through Byzantine sources and shows that, excluding one eleventh-century exception, it is always used to refer to the emperor's crown. The crown (or, more correctly, wreath) placed upon the head of a caesar was consistently called *stefanos*.[8] Since the Byzantines were clearly intent on denying Symeon's claims, it is inconceivable that a Byzantine source could make an error here and inflate the value of Symeon's crown. Had the source said *stefanos*, one might have argued that the author had substituted that term for *stemma* to suggest the coronation was for a lower title. But the error could not be the other way around. The Byzantines were sticklers for ceremony and protocol. The Logothete who wrote the chronicle was a high court official who clearly was aware of such distinctions. Thus if he said *stemma* he meant *stemma*, and therefore Symeon was crowned emperor. But though crowned emperor, one still may argue that the coronation was a sham. This possibility will be discussed below.

A second source supporting an "emperor's" coronation is a court oration from about 927, thus a contemporary source but one written some fourteen years after the 913 "coronation." I shall quote the text, inserting in brackets various words of explanation; the identification of individuals referred to in the text was made by the source's editor, Romilly Jenkins, whose translation I use:[9]

> For at once the torrent of vainglory, the whirlwind of ambition, the rainstorm and snowstorm swept into the heart of the archon [the normal title used by Byzantines for designating Bulgarian rulers up to this time, hence a reference to Symeon]. . . . Then followed insurrection or rather apostasy for the proclamation [of some title for Symeon] came and the other titles with which he profaned his seals and the evil was born and he [Symeon] appropriated the fruits of his father. [The father means the Byzantine emperor according to the Byzantine concept of the family of princes, thus here Constantine VII.]
>
> But he [Patriarch Nicholas] after enquiring of what he already knew excluded for that time [the 913 "coronation" meeting] the lords of the senate out of reverence for the Imperial office and him who gave it.

Thus Symeon insisted on a coronation, presumably with an imperial crown, and Nicholas, though feeling compelled to comply, wanted to make it as unofficial as possible, while still making it acceptable to Symeon. Thus he arranged the meeting outside the city, as the Logothete informs us, and avoided a major part of the coronation ceremony, the obeisance from the senate, by not having the senators present. To continue with our text:

> But he [Symeon] hidden beneath his helmet of darkness [Jenkins says this phrase refers to the patriarchal headpiece, the *epirrhiptarion*] called for his fellow celebrants and proposed the confirmation of the covenant [i.e., the necessary obeisance which Nicholas had foreseen]. But he [Nicholas] opposed this and said straight out that it was abominable for Romans to do obeisance to an emperor unless he was a Roman [and in any case the senate had been excluded]. "Rather" (says he) "wear your makeshift diadem for a little and let your fellow celebrants do you obeisance" [i.e., receive obeisance from your fellow Bulgarians who presumably were in attendance since the meeting "outside the city" probably took place near or at the Bulgarian camp].

Quite clearly Nicholas did not say the words attributed to him since Symeon would have been furious at the very least and nothing would have been achieved by the meeting and ceremony. The ravaging of the environs of the capital would have begun again. Thus this must be taken as the orator's explanation of what happened and what Nicholas's ceremony meant, but presented by the orator in an amusing way for the benefit of the court audience listening to him in 927.

> Who could number the devices, the expedients, the impositions of that man [Nicholas]? . . . But it is impossible to tell the devices whereby without force he [Nicholas] cunningly maintained and restrained Symeon throughout his life. So [in 913] he [Symeon] accepted the honorary peace and as yet honored by it, quietly took rule over a quiet folk and the *Imperial brother* [italics added] went off by the same way that he had come, leaving the sceptre to the child [Constantine VII].

The italicized phrase *Imperial brother* is the vital point here; it seems to signify that Symeon had received the title of emperor (presumably of the Bulgarians); for if he had received the title of caesar (or any other lesser title) he would have been the *Imperial son*. In Jenkins's opinion, that phrase absolutely settles matters; Symeon was crowned emperor, for certainly no court oration, hostile to Symeon, would have suggested that he was given a title higher than he actually received.

This oration, then, clearly implies that Symeon was given the title of basileus. But it also represents the whole ceremony as a sham. Ostrogorsky, however, argues that Symeon was too bright and also too experienced, having been in Constantinople ten years, to have fallen for a sham. He could not have fallen for a fake headgear, and thus Ostrogorsky believes all of the oration's contents were invented later to cover up a perfectly valid (according to the proper ceremony) coronation. Jenkins believes that even though Symeon had been ten years in Constantinople he had very likely never seen a real coronation. In the whole period during which Symeon had probably been in Constantinople, there had been only one, Leo VI's in 886, and Symeon may not have attended it. Thus, Jenkins feels, possibly Symeon could have been fooled by a sham ceremony.

There is no doubt that the orator depicts the whole ceremony as a sham. Thus either it was really more or less this way (for the orator was speaking before an in-group who knew the truth) or else the sham story had previously been created and propagated as a cover-up and the official Byzantine version, and the in-group audience, knowing the whole story, would have been amused at the presentation and not have been looking for accuracy. In any case, regardless of how serious the ceremony was, Jenkins believes that Symeon left it believing that he had been crowned basileus of the Bulgarians.

It seems safe to conclude that Symeon did not think he had been made a fool of. He evidently did leave the meeting thinking he had been crowned in a real ceremony with the title that he expected. Thus he felt that he had achieved his aims and was able to return to Bulgaria, vowing peace with Byzantium. Clearly he was satisfied; otherwise, and particularly if he felt the Byzantines were making fun of him, he would have resumed the war.

War with Byzantium, 913–27

However, once again the situation was quickly altered by a major change in Constantinople. Constantine VII's mother, Zoe, entered the scene. She had been chafing at the bit because of her incarceration in a convent and her desire for political power. Moreover she was furious at Nicholas's total capitulation to Symeon and at the idea that her son should marry a Bulgarian princess. The capitulation also seems to have been unpopular with the populace of the capital. So Zoe led a palace coup and ousted Nicholas as regent. She had long hated him for his attacks on her, the fourth wife whose marriage to Leo he would not accept. However, Nicholas was allowed to remain as patriarch and a hostile source states that he was now free to return to the church, for, as regent, even though he had been patriarch, he had not entered a church in eight months. Zoe, as regent, repudiated the title granted to Symeon and nullified the marriage plans made for her son by Nicholas.

This provoked Symeon into war again; he ravaged Thrace and conquered (though he did not try to retain) Adrianople. Over the next decade he carried out a continuing war to conquer the Byzantine Empire.

Byzantium, hard pressed, had no choice but to look for allies; the empire sent envoys to the Magyars, Pechenegs, and Serbs. The results of the discussions with the Magyars are not known (the Magyars remained idle in any case). The Pechenegs promised to help. The Serbs were then ruled by Peter Gojniković, since 897 theoretically a Bulgarian vassal, though not necessarily a willing one. Peter was now offered money and a chance for greater independence by the strategos of Durazzo. With these inducements it seems Peter agreed to join the coalition against Bulgaria. However, during the previous years he had been expanding his state to the west, defeating Tišemir of Bosnia, annexing the valley of the River Bosna and then expanding along the Neretva, where he seems to have come into some sort of territorial conflict with Michael of Zahumlje (who also ruled Trebinje and most of Duklja [modern Montenegro]). Michael, who was a loyal ally of Symeon, warned him of the alliance that Peter was making with Byzantium.

Some scholars feel that Symeon immediately (early in 917) attacked Serbia and eliminated Peter and then turned to face the major Byzantine attack. If the chronology of events went this way, then it explains why there is no sign of Serbian activity at the Byzantine-Bulgarian battle in August 917. However, most scholars accept Constantine Porphyrogenitus's version, which places the battle against Byzantium prior to the Bulgaro-Serbian war—a war which no source dates any more precisely than the year 917. Here I shall follow the majority view—supported by the contemporary author Constantine—and describe first the Byzantine war and then the Serbian war.

Byzantium, regardless of the results of its negotiations with the Serbs, did obtain the Pechenegs as allies and planned a massive attack on Bulgaria in 917. The Byzantine army was to be led by Leo Phocas and the fleet was to be commanded by an Armenian peasant who had risen to the rank of admiral, Romanus Lecapenus. The two military leaders were jealous of each other; furthermore each was ambitious to become regent. As a result each was out to discredit the other as well as Zoe's regency. The Pechenegs, realizing that the situation did not bode well for their survival in the coming battle and having already been richly paid, simply withdrew on the eve of the battle.

A Byzantine ex post facto justification and explanation for the empire's attack on Bulgaria states that the Bulgarians had been negotiating with the Pechenegs. Perhaps the Pecheneg withdrawal was the result of such negotiations. However, the truth of the Byzantine charge is not known: was it an excuse invented for attacking Bulgaria, was it based on false rumors circulating, or had the Bulgarians really been trying to create an alliance with the Pechenegs?

In any case the invasion was set for Anchialos on the Black Sea coast, where the army was to be landed. The Bulgarians with a huge army waited in the mountains overlooking the landing spot. On 20 August 917 Symeon surprised this uncoordinated venture with little difficulty and massacred the bulk of the Byzantine army. A Byzantine chronicle written a hundred years later refers to the site of the battle as still piled high with bones. Following the battle there were no imperial troops left between Symeon and the walls of Constantinople.

As the head of the church, Nicholas Mysticus was called on by the government to do something to restrain Symeon; the patriarch wrote the Bulgarian ruler to plead for peace and mercy. His letter presents the Byzantine side. It explains why the empire attacked Bulgaria or at least gives the reasons the empire issued for public consumption. Nicholas admits that the empire had been wrong to attack Symeon and claims that he had opposed the attack all along but had been unable to influence the planners, who were upset by Bulgarian raids on Byzantine Thrace and Symeon's negotiations with the Pechenegs. The purpose of the attack, he claims, had been to force Symeon to evacuate the regions around Thessaloniki and Durazzo; but though this was the reason, Nicholas admits this was still no excuse for the invasion. Nicholas exhorts Symeon to be a good Christian and forgive his fellow Christian Byzantines. Symeon's victory resulted from the will of God as punishment for the sins of the Byzantines; let not Symeon become overconfident or haughty lest God strike his armies down, particularly if he should wickedly invade the empire now.[10]

After Anchialos, and still in 917, Symeon invaded Serbia and deposed Peter whom he took back to Bulgaria and imprisoned. Peter died in jail within the year. Then Symeon placed Mutimir's grandson Pavel (the son of Bran Mutimirović who had led an unsuccessful rebellion against Peter in 894) on the Serbian throne. Pavel had long been living in Bulgaria. If in fact this Serbian war occurred after Anchialos, then the making of Serbia into a puppet state, a situation which would last until the conflict in 921, was a second result of that great victory over the Byzantines. In any case by the end of 917 Pavel, the Bulgarian candidate, was on the Serbian throne.

It seems that in 918 or 919 Symeon launched a major raid on Greece with his troops reaching the Gulf of Corinth. Why did he do this now rather than direct an attack against Constantinople? Did he hope to divert Byzantine troops thither away from the defense of the capital? Did he need booty to support his army? His motives are not known.

In any case, the empire was in desperate straits. The population seems to have believed that Zoe was incompetent to do anything and that it was necessary to have a man, and presumably a military leader, as emperor. This gave Romanus Lecapenus, the admiral, the opportunity to seize power in 919. Symeon's involvement in Greece certainly made it easier for Romanus to act freely in the capital without fear of outside interference. In May 919 Romanus married Constantine VII to his own daughter Helena, thus thwarting Symeon's ambition and making himself father-in-law to the emperor. What Constantine at the time thought of these events is unknown but as Jenkins nicely put it: "Constantine may be accounted lucky to have lived in the tenth rather than in the ninth century. He was neither murdered nor mutilated, only married."[11] Romanus soon took the title of caesar in September 920. Then in December 920 he had himself crowned coemperor, thus realizing Symeon's ambitions. Though Constantine's name stood first on protocol lists, Romanus was the real ruler. Nevertheless, he had to tolerate the boy, for the populace of the capital loved him.

Symeon's Relations with Romanus

The patriarch Nicholas tried desperately to mediate between the enraged Symeon and Romanus (who to Symeon was nothing but a usurper of his own promised position). Only the patriarch's side of the correspondence survives but it conveys the flavor of Symeon's letters to which Nicholas is replying: "But you my son—have written in derision of my old age that you are not demanding the impossible since you are not demanding the resurrection of the Bulgarian dead; you are only asking for those things which can be brought to pass," namely, that Romanus abdicate. This of course was impossible and Nicholas offered Symeon money, clothing, and "perhaps even a portion of territory." But these offers had no effect and the angry Symeon refused any discussions until Romanus was deposed; he even refused to respond to Romanus's letters. Nicholas, writing Symeon, reports,

> For when you received a letter from those appointed by God to be emperors of the Roman people [i.e., the Lecapeni and Constantine VII] you wrote back, not to them, but to the council; which is strange conduct to hear of, and unseemly and exposing you to censure. For who on earth, if he receives a letter from a prince, ever ignores the prince and writes back to the prince's underlings?

Symeon remained firm in his resolve. When Romanus offered one of his children to marry one of Symeon's, Symeon did not deign to reply. Instead he ravaged Thrace. But though Symeon could destroy the countryside and the Byzantine Balkan towns, he could not penetrate the walls of Constantinople. The capital was able to survive with the products of Anatolia, untouched by this warfare. Behind his walls, in spite of Symeon's activities in the Balkans, Romanus remained the emperor.

Serbia between Byzantium and Bulgaria

Meanwhile the Byzantines were unhappy with the turn of events in Serbia where the man whom they supported, Peter, had been ousted for Symeon's candidate, Pavel. The Byzantines now turned to Zaharije (the son of Prvoslav, who was discussed earlier) who had long been in Constantinople. He was sent off for Serbia in about 920 (Zlatarski says 921). He never made it, but was captured by Symeon on the way and spirited off to Bulgaria. After this failure the Byzantines began sending envoys to woo Pavel over to their side while the Bulgarians started indoctrinating Zaharije. The Byzantines seem to have lavished much gold on Pavel in an effort to win him over. Presumably they also played on the dangers that a strong Bulgaria must pose for Serbia.

Since at this time (921), Bulgarian troops were again besieging Adrianople and thus were concentrated in Thrace, Pavel allowed himself to be won over by the Byzantines. He began to prepare for a surprise attack on Bulgaria while its armies were thus involved; however, once again Symeon was warned. He spared a few troops and sent them west taking Zaharije along, having offered him the Serbian throne if he defeated his cousin Pavel. This intervention was successful and Zaharije's Bulgarian forces gained control of Serbia. Zlatarski places this campaign in 922; other scholars give varying dates that fall between 921 and 923. Once again the Bulgarian candidate was in power in Serbia.

But this situation was not to last, for Zaharije had long lived in Constantinople where he had been heavily influenced by the Byzantines; he also probably resented being captured by the Bulgarians and very likely was not truly won over. After all, it was natural for a Serb to be pro-Byzantine and anti-Bulgarian, because the former, a distant state, was offering Serbia greater independence from the latter, a powerful interfering neighbor. In any case, Zaharije stirred up various Slavic tribes along their common border to rebel against Bulgaria. Symeon sent an insufficient number of troops to quell these disturbances. Some Bulgarian generals were killed and their heads and weapons were sent on to Constantinople. This conflict probably occurred in 923.

Meanwhile (roughly 922 or 923) Symeon came to the realization that he could never capture Constantinople without a fleet. Not possessing one himself, he sought an alliance that would procure him one. He sent an embassy via Zahumlje (the state of his ally Michael) to the Fātimids in North Africa. While awaiting the return of this mission he refused to treat with the Byzantines or to answer Nicholas's letters. In addition he took Adrianople again and carried off a great number of captives. The Fātimids accepted his proposal but on the way home the envoys were captured by the Byzantines who imprisoned them and then quickly sent their own embassy to North Africa to outbid Symeon. The Arabs then agreed, for a price, not to aid Symeon. Symeon meanwhile spent a long period in ignorance of these developments, killing time by pillaging Thrace. When word finally reached him of what had happened, he responded by jailing a Byzantine embassy which he kept imprisoned in Preslav.

After his failure to obtain a fleet and the defeat of his small army at the hands of Zaharije in Serbia, Symeon finally decided to meet with the emperor Romanus. Possibly he saw this meeting as a means of establishing a truce to secure his eastern border so that he could attack the Serbs. At least, that is what was to happen; however, the result may not have been his initial intent. In any case, in September 923 he appeared before the walls of Constantinople with his army, which pillaged the suburbs of the capital and burned a church of the Virgin of great age. Symeon demanded an interview with the emperor and a meeting was arranged.

Symeon appeared on a magnificent horse surrounded by armed soldiers shouting in Greek "Glory to Symeon, the Emperor (Basileus)." This was presumably intended to be insulting. It is not evidence, as some have claimed, that the Bulgarian soldiers knew Greek. They could easily have learned one phrase in a foreign tongue. The insult was lessened by the fact that Constantine, the people of the capital's real emperor, was not there.

After the two rulers had kissed, the emperor Romanus asked Symeon to stop shedding Christian blood; he offered Symeon all the wealth he could dream of if he would make peace and directed a small sermon at Symeon about his mortality. How could Symeon face God with all that blood on his hands? According to the Byzantine sources, Symeon had no reply for these stirring words. But if he had no replies for the emperor—which is quite doubtful—he certainly had plenty to say to the patriarch, for in a subsequent letter, Nicholas complains to him:

But I now proceed to speak to you of the accusations and insults which you implied against me in the presence of our God-crowned Emperor, in derision, as it were, of my Wretchedness. You said, with a sarcasm against me, that you were riding the horse which in battle received the cut meant for you; and you added, with a sneer at me, that this had been the result of my prayer! And when I protested that I knew of no such thing, had never countenanced the war, and had made no such prayer, you answered that, as I sat on the patriarchal throne, it was in my power to forbid the war, or, at all events, temporarily to expel from the Church those who refused to obey my exhortations.[12]

After the interview Symeon rode away. At the same moment, the chronicler reports, two eagles were seen flying high in the air over the assemblage. Then they parted with one flying over the city, while the other winged its way northwards into Thrace. This was seen as an omen representing the fates of the two rulers. However, though a peace was discussed, Symeon quickly left before signing and swearing to any terms. Presumably he had no intention of making peace with Byzantium, but expressed such a desire to keep the Greeks at peace so he could settle Serbian affairs to his liking.

In 924 Symeon sent a large army against Zaharije in Serbia. The army was accompanied by Časlav (the son of Klonimir Strojimirović whom Symeon had unsuccessfully supported against Peter back in 896). Časlav had long been a hostage in Bulgaria. The Bulgarian armies ravaged a good part of Serbia and forced Zaharije to flee to Croatia. Symeon then summoned the Serbian župans (county lords) to pay homage to Časlav. When they came, he took them all prisoner and arrested Časlav as well and sent them all back to Bulgaria as captives. Symeon thus annexed Serbia directly, a necessary move since the Serbs had proved to be unreliable allies. This annexation considerably expanded Symeon's state, which came to border directly on that of his ally, Michael of Zahumlje, and on Croatia (where Zaharije had sought refuge). Croatia was then under the greatest of its medieval rulers, King Tomislav, who also had good relations with Byzantium. This was a dangerous neighbor.

In the fall of 924, after his successful Serbian venture, Symeon's armies reoccupied various imperial towns in Thrace. After the death of Nicholas Mysticus in May 925, Symeon wrote to Romanus; unfortunately once again only Romanus's reply survives (preserved in a twelfth-century manuscript). In this reply Romanus objects to Symeon's styling himself "emperor of the Bulgarians and Romans," stating that he personally does not care what Symeon calls himself; he could call himself the caliph of Baghdad for all he cares. Important only is the power sanctioned by God. Neither force nor the shedding of blood gives one the right to rule. Symeon's conquest of provinces had been the fruit of rapine and does not give him legitimate sovereignty over the conquered provinces. How can he call himself emperor of the Bulgarians when twenty thousand of his own people had sought refuge in the Byzantine Empire? (This figure is possibly exaggerated, and Zlatarski reasonably wonders, since this was written in 925, the year after the annexation of

Serbia, whether these "Bulgarians" to whom Romanus refers might not really be Serbs unhappy at being incorporated into the Bulgarian state.) As for emperor of the Romans: What Romans? Those who are captives in Bulgaria or does he have in mind those of Constantinople? Finally Romanus demanded the restoration of the fortresses in Thrace conquered by Symeon.

Symeon's Title

Emperor Romanus's letter states that Symeon was using the title "emperor of the Bulgarians and Romans." However, there is reason to raise the question: did Symeon really call himself by this title? After all it is preserved in a hostile Byzantine source. Furthermore, another source exists which gives Symeon another title. A seal used by Symeon renders his title simply "Emperor of the Romans"; Bulgaria is not mentioned on it. This title is certainly more reasonable for a man—like Symeon—acquainted with imperial theory, according to which there could only be one emperor on earth, the emperor of the Romans. The seal seems to indicate that at some time he simply took that title. And if his title included Romans, there would be no reason to add anything else (i.e., Bulgarians) for Romans was a universal title that encompassed the world.

When Symeon took the Roman imperial title is unknown, though many scholars give one of two dates—918/19 or 925—as a fact. Symeon had been crowned emperor of the Bulgarians by Patriarch Nicholas Mysticus in 913. Unless this coronation was in fact a sham which Symeon had come to realize, he would not have needed a second coronation for that title, despite Zoe's repudiation of it. To have had a second ceremony for it would have recognized that repudiation. By 925, when he wrote Romanus, Symeon had either added "and Romans" to "of the Bulgarians" or what is more likely replaced the phrase "of the Bulgarians" by the phrase "of the Romans." Since Symeon, as much if not more than most other medieval rulers, had a strong sense of theatre, we can assume this titular change emerged from a ceremony, one held in his Bulgaria. Many scholars have given 925 as its date. However, this date is based simply on Romanus's 925 letter objecting to his use of the title and shows only that the ceremony had occurred *by* 925.

The other date given is 918/19. It was advanced so positively by Zlatarski that many subsequent scholars have taken it as fact. Zlatarski, it should be noted, however, believed that Nicholas had crowned

Symeon caesar. Thus he argued for two Bulgarian coronations: 918 as emperor of the Bulgarians and 925 as emperor of the Bulgarians and Romans. Zlatarski states:

> A convocation of all the Bulgarian bishops first proclaimed the Bulgarian Church autocephalous and consecrated from its midst a patriarch, or at least the Bulgarian archbishop, who according to a Bulgarian Synodik [1211] was Leontius, was raised to the rank of patriarch. This event occurred in 918. That same year Symeon was triumphantly crowned by the hands of the new patriarch and in this way was fully legitimized his new title: Tsar (Emperor) and Autocrat of all the Bulgarians.[13]

Despite being given with no qualifications, this statement is entirely hypothetical. Though having a synod of the Bulgarian church raise the Bulgarian archbishop to patriarch and then having him crown Symeon is a likely scenario, no source mentions either event. "Patriarch Leontius" is mentioned only in a fifteenth-century copy of the decisions of a thirteenth-century Bulgarian church council, and that document simply has him listed as the first in a series of four Preslav patriarchs, none of whom is provided with dates at all. That this series, if the later church council was accurate about its existence, began under Symeon is a reasonable theory. After all Symeon almost certainly would have seen a patriarch as a necessary accompaniment to his being emperor; and if he dared call himself "emperor of the Romans," which his seal shows he did, he probably would not have hesitated to create his own patriarch. However, it must be emphasized, no source from the period mentions a Bulgarian patriarch existing before 927. Thus we can take Zlatarski's scenario only as a likely theory about the process of coronation. Moreover, it should be modified in two ways. First, since Symeon almost certainly from 913 was recognized at home as tsar of all the Bulgarians, the Bulgarian ceremony would have given him not that title but crowned him emperor of the Romans. Second, 918 as its date is only a guess; the ceremony could have occurred at any time between 914 and 925.

Finally it should be noted that regardless of what Symeon called himself and his chief prelate, the Byzantines—as is seen in Nicholas's and Romanus's letters—never recognized them with any higher titles. Symeon was always addressed as "prince" (archon) and the prelate continued to be referred to as an archbishop.

Symeon's Invasion of Croatia, 926

After Symeon's annexation of Serbia, the Bulgarian state bordered on the powerful Croatian kingdom, under its greatest medieval ruler, Tomislav (ca. 910–28), who was a Byzantine ally. Clearly Symeon saw Croatia, harboring his enemies and allied to the empire, as a threat. What was there to prevent Croatia, on Byzantine orders, from striking his rear, as Zaharije had done, when Symeon was directing his armies to the east against Byzantium? Therefore in 926 he sent a large army to invade Croatia. These forces met a disastrous defeat. Peace was then made between Tomislav and Symeon, with papal legates as mediators. Symeon then began planning a new campaign against Byzantium. He seems to have felt secure that Tomislav would honor the peace and not attack his rear. Since he was planning a new attack on Byzantium for 927 it is evident that he did not lose the bulk of his forces in Croatia as most scholars have claimed. He had probably sent only part of his army on that campaign and those forces had suffered heavy losses; but his overall army (having lost only a portion) was still a strong enough force to carry out a major invasion of Byzantium.

Death of Symeon, 927

In the spring of 927 Symeon once again led his armies on the route toward Constantinople, but this time, like his great predecessor Krum, he died en route. Symeon was about sixty-three. The cause of his death is given in a wide assortment of Byzantine sources.

In May 927 an astrologer named John discovered in the forum of Constantinople the double of the tsar Symeon. It was a statue which looked toward the west. The astrologer hastened to reveal his discovery to the emperor Romanus. "Your majesty," he said, "if you but strike that statue on the head, Symeon that instant will cease to live." The emperor ordered the destruction of the marble statue in which the shades of the Bulgarian sovereign resided. At the same hour that the statue was smashed, the heart of the old tsar weakened and he died.

NOTES

1. *The Letters of Nicholas I, Patriarch of Constantinople*, ed. and trans. R. Jenkins and L. G. Westerink, Corpus Fontium Historiae Byzantinae 6, Dumbarton Oaks Texts, Vol. 2 (Washington, D.C., 1973), p. 95.

2. Translation taken from M. Pundeff, "National Consciousness in Medieval Bulgaria," *Südost-Forschungen* 27 (1968):19–20.

3. G. Kolias, *Leon Choerosphactes* (Athens, 1939), pp. 76–77.

4. P. Karlin-Hayter, "The Emperor Alexander's Bad Name," *Speculum* 44, no. 4 (1969):585–96.

5. R. Jenkins, *Byzantium: The Imperial Centuries* A.D. *610–1071* (New York, 1966), pp. 229–30. Jenkins bases his account on the exaggerated and hostile life of Euthymius.

6. The war between Symeon and Byzantium continued from 913 to 927. Nicholas Mysticus lived through most of it, as patriarch, dying in 925. His letters to Symeon are preserved and are a major source for these events. See *The Letters of Nicholas I.*

7. Ibid., p. 187.

8. G. Ostrogorski, "Avtokrator i samodržac," in the volume of his collected works entitled, *Vizantija i Sloveni* (Beograd, 1970), pp. 303–17.

9. R. Jenkins, "The Peace with Bulgaria (927) Celebrated by Theodore Daphnopates," *Polychronion*, Winter, 1966, pp. 291, 295.

10. *The Letters of Nicholas I*, pp. 58–63.

11. Jenkins, *Byzantium: The Imperial Centuries*, p. 239.

12. *The Letters of Nicholas I*, p. 209.

13. V. Zlatarski, "Političeskijat život na B"lgarite pri car Simeona 893–927," in *B"lgarija 1000 godini 927–1927* (Sofija, 1930), p. 21. See also his general *Istorija na b"lgarskata d"ržava prez srednite vekove* (Sofija, 1938), vol. 1, pt. 2, pp. 389–91.

CHAPTER 6

Bulgaria after Symeon, 927–1018

Bulgaria and the Serb Lands, 927–65

Serbia Regains Independence under Časlav

Serbia almost at once after Symeon's death asserted its independence from Bulgaria. Bulgarian rule had not been popular and many Serbs had fled to Croatia (including the previous ruler Zaharije who soon died there) or to Byzantium. After Symeon's death Časlav escaped to Serbia. Ostrogorsky dates his escape reasonably to 927 or 928, though Constantine Porphyrogenitus states that it occurred seven years after his capture, which would place this event in 931. Časlav found popular support and restored a Serbian state. Many exiles quickly returned.

He submitted at once to Byzantine overlordship and gained Byzantine financial and diplomatic support for his efforts. Throughout his long reign, which lasted until about 960, Časlav maintained close ties with Byzantium.

Most scholars feel that during Časlav's reign Byzantine influence (including in particular that of the Byzantine church) greatly increased in Serbia. Orthodox influences in Slavonic were surely penetrating Serbia from Bulgaria during this period as well. This was a critical period in both the Christianization of Serbia and also in its becoming part of the Orthodox, rather than the Latin, church. Of course, as of yet the two branches of the one church had not split, but the ties formed in this period were to have great impact on how the different Slavic churches were to line up later when they did split. Many scholars have felt that, since the Serbs lived more or less in the middle between the regions under Roman jurisdiction and those under Byzantine jurisdiction, they could have gone either way. Speculations are, of course, interesting but it is unfortunate that so little is known about Serbia and the history of Christianity there in this key period.

The borders of Časlav's state are unknown, though eventually he extended them well into Bosnia. Časlav was killed in about 960, fighting the Hungarians in that region.

Michael of Zahumlje's Position in Balkan Politics

The other Serbian state of this period was that of Michael of Zahumlje, Symeon's loyal ally. It is generally believed that he remained loyal to Symeon until Symeon's death in 927, after which, lacking the Bulgarian prop, he made peace with the empire and accepted the court ranks of proconsul and patrician. Some scholars have argued that since he participated in a church council in Split in 925 along with a Byzantine client, Tomislav, whom Symeon was to attack the following year, he must have broken off with Symeon. However, this is poor reasoning; this church council decided on matters that affected churches all along Dalmatia, both in Croatia and Zahumlje. Both rulers, regardless of other alliances, were under papal jurisdiction. It was both their duty and in their interests to participate in this council. Thus there is no reason to see Michael's participation in the 925 council as evidence that he had abandoned his alliance with Symeon for one with Byzantium. Nor does his presence at the council with Tomislav show that he was allied with him. Furthermore Michael could have maintained good relations simultaneously with both Balkan rulers—despite the hostilities between them—and as far as we know Michael was neutral and did not participate in the 926 Bulgar-Croatian war. In any case, after Symeon's death, Michael patched up his relations with the empire, while maintaining good relations with the papacy. He remained as ruler of Zahumlje into the 940s.

Peter of Bulgaria's Reign to 965

Symeon had had two marriages; by the first he had a son, Michael (who became a monk), and by the second three sons (Peter, John, and Benjamin [Bajan]). His second wife was the sister of a prominent boyar, George Sursuvul. On Symeon's death Peter, the eldest son of the second marriage, succeeded. Why Michael had been ousted from succession is not known; possibly he lacked ability, possibly it was the result of the influence of the second wife and her family. Supporting the second possibility is the fact that on Symeon's death George Sursuvul was at first more or less a regent for Peter, illustrating his great influence at court.

Immediately after Symeon's death Peter and his uncle George Sursuvul renewed the war with Byzantium and raided Thrace to show that Bulgaria was still militarily strong. Then from a position of strength—as a result of this attack—they sent envoys with conditions for a peace to Byzantium. Since these conditions were brought by a secret mission, many scholars have felt that a segment of the Bulgar aristocracy was opposed to peace, wanting to pursue the war presumably for the booty it brought. By the early fall—late September, early October—of 927 Peter concluded peace with Byzantium. The Byzantine sources say the cause for his wanting peace was his fear that all his neighbors—the Hungarians, Byzantines, and Croatians—would take advantage of Symeon's death to attack Bulgaria. In addition Bulgaria had a major domestic problem, a severe famine resulting from an attack by locusts.

The peace was confirmed by Peter's marrying Maria Lecapena (the daughter of Christopher Lecapenus and the granddaughter of the emperor Romanus). The treaty restored the borders to those established by the 897 and 904 treaties (thus recognizing Bulgaria's possession of Macedonia). Thereafter the imperial frontier remained peaceful until war broke out in 965. Peter's title of tsar (emperor) of the Bulgarians was recognized, as was his autocephalous church under its own patriarch. A prisoner exchange was agreed upon. In addition the Byzantines were to pay the Bulgarians annual tribute. (Later, when objecting to its payment after Maria's death, the emperor Nicephorus Phocas was to claim that this was not tribute but money for the Byzantine princess's upkeep. This interpretation, however, may have been Nicephorus's and not that of the original treaty.)

Thus Peter succeeded in obtaining immediately all of Symeon's goals except for the Byzantine Empire itself. With Symeon dead the Byzantines could feel safer in making concessions. At the same time the empire may well have feared that if it did not make these concessions the pope would recognize the titles of tsar and patriarch, which would increase papal influence in Bulgaria. Considering Bulgaria's proximity, this would have been a distinct danger to the empire. The Bulgarians had been in communication with the papacy from late in 926 when the pope had mediated a conclusion to the Bulgarian-Croatian war. It seems that Symeon had also been seeking papal recognition for his titles, and Rome would have had little to lose by being generous. However, it should be noted that, though the empire recognized Peter's title of emperor, in its letters it called him "son" and not "brother." Thus he was recognized as an emperor, but one with a definitely inferior status. Symeon would surely have protested this slight, but there is no evidence that Peter did.

Along with Peter's wife a large Byzantine entourage came to

Preslav; most scholars speak about great Byzantine influence ensuing in Bulgaria. This is probably exaggerated and grounds exist to speak about Byzantine influence only at court, which presumably was considerable; now Bulgarian court officials began bearing Byzantine titles like logothete and protovestijar. Whether the Bulgarian bearers of these titles performed the same duties as their Byzantine namesakes is not known; in many cases they probably did not, for Bulgaria lacked the highly developed court and bureaucracy found in Constantinople. Since no evidence exists that this Byzantine influence—other than cultural influences in church art, architecture, music, and literature—associated with Maria's arrival extended into the society itself, scepticism should be shown to the claims, frequently seen in the historical literature, that such influence caused Bulgarian peasants to join heretical movements or drove Bulgarians into opposition to their tsar.

In 928 a revolt on behalf of Peter's brother, John, and supported by "Symeon's nobles" broke out in Preslav. It was easily suppressed. John underwent corporal punishment and a brief imprisonment before he was tonsured as a monk. His cohorts were tortured. Then John was sent off to Constantinople, probably to remove him as a potential focus for future plots. In Constantinople John shed his monkish garb, married an Armenian girl, and received lands, gifts, and high rank from the emperor Romanus. After this, John disappears from history. This exile shows the close ties between Peter and Byzantium at the time. The Byzantines were also presumably happy to have him, if needed, as a threat to hold over Peter's head. Zlatarski thinks John's revolt had been supported by the war party of old boyars opposed to peace and that is the reason the source spoke of "Symeon's nobles." This is a plausible suggestion, but, of course, further evidence is needed to prove it.

A more dangerous revolt followed. In 930 Symeon's eldest son (by wife number one), Michael, left his monastery and seized a fortress in the Struma region; here the population ceased to recognize Peter and accepted Michael. Operating from outside of Preslav, the capital, Michael was able to organize better and to build up a greater following than John had, making this revolt which led to the loss of some territory far more serious than John's. But when Michael died suddenly, his leading followers fled to Byzantium for asylum and the revolt fizzled out.

Zlatarski suggests their flight shows the Byzantines supported Michael's revolt; they wanted to cause chaos and weaken Bulgaria. Since the Byzantines regularly gave asylum to all sorts of rebels—pro-Byzantine or otherwise—the defeated rebels' flight thither can prove nothing. Since Peter was married to a Byzantine princess and was enjoying good relations with the empire, I doubt the Byzantines had any part in this particular uprising. Others have used the revolt to show Peter's unpopularity or boyar opposition to him. However, we know nothing about the motivations behind the revolt, about the ideology (if any) of the revolt or about why Michael obtained the support he did. Both of these revolts could well have been chiefly prompted by the two brothers' desires for the throne, supported by others counting on various rewards in wealth or position if the rebellions succeeded. But with sources so meager it is pointless to speculate on the aims, ideology, or composition of these rebellions.

The fourth son, Benjamin (or Bajan) had his own private form of revolt. According to Liutprand (a western imperial envoy to Constantinople in the second half of the tenth century), Bajan studied magic and possessed the power to transform himself suddenly into a wolf or other strange animal. Unfortunately nothing further is known about this talented young man; the reference just noted contains all the information about him preserved in our sources. Lycanthropy seems to have been a not uncommon form of mental illness in the Middle Ages—described as such by both Arab and Italian doctors who could not agree whether it was a form of mania or melancholy. Whether Bajan was struck with this form of insanity or achieved his transformations, as our source states, through magic practices, possibly through hallucinogens (a means which can be documented for seventeenth-century European werewolves), is unknown.

Other than four Magyar raids that passed through Bulgaria to hit Byzantine territory and the rise of the Bogomil heresy—to be discussed later—nothing else is known about Peter's reign until war broke out with Byzantium in 965. This is important to point out because normally Peter's reign has been depicted as one of decline and misery for Bulgaria. However, it should be emphasized that no sources show this and elsewhere I have presented an alternative hypothesis of peace and relative prosperity for Bulgaria for the bulk of Peter's reign until the warfare at the very end.[1]

Though the sources are lacking to prove either view, it should be stressed that evidence does not exist to support the bleak view universally presented in scholarship about Peter. There is no evidence that Bulgaria made peace with Byzantium because it was too weak to fight; a close look at the gains of the peace treaty show that Bulgaria came out very well by that treaty and there was no reason to fight further. There is no evidence that Bulgaria's manpower had been wiped out in Symeon's wars or that he had exhausted the state's economic resources. And, if he did not exhaust them, then there is no reason to postulate an economic decline as is usually done. In fact, peace with Byzantium meant increased trade, and a passage to be cited later shows the importance and wealth of Bulgaria as a trade center (particularly the city of Perejaslavec on the Danube) in the 960s. There is no evidence that the nobility opposed Peter, or that they asserted greater independence from the center than they had had previously, or that Byzantine influences, unpopular with this or that group, depending on which scholar is writing, spread throughout the society.

From the end of Michael's revolt in 930 Bulgaria under Peter enjoyed peace—excluding the four known Magyar raids that passed through Bulgaria and which may well have caused destruction along their route—until 965. Peter has also regularly been called weak, lacking in ability, and under his wife's thumb. Once again no sources show any of this. Peter has been one of the most maligned figures in Bulgarian history. But unlike some other historical figures depicted as incompetent, behind whose condemnation lie various sources, Peter has been unanimously denigrated without a single source speaking out against him.

Bulgarian Society and Administration

Before continuing the discussion of Bulgaria's political history and foreign affairs from the 960s and before examining the Bogomil heresy which arose under Peter, let us pause and examine to the very limited extent possible what Bulgarian society and administration were like.

We have discussed the gradual slavicization of the ruling group—both the increased number of Slavs rising to the top and the slavicization of the Bulgars themselves. By Peter's time the Bulgars retained few, if any, privileges. They seem to have merged into the mass of Slavs and become slavicized in language and Christianized. Other than Bulgar last names, no signs of Bulgar identity are found in tenth-century sources. Presumably many of the most important people, men like George Sursuvul, still were descendants of the old Bulgar aristocracy. But Sursuvul was a Christian—as his first name of George indicates—and loyally supported the crown (held by his nephew Peter) against the rebellious activities of Peter's brothers.

After Boris eliminated Vladimir in 893, Bulgaria experienced no more boyar revolts. There were none under Symeon and except for the possibility of some boyar support for one of Peter's brothers in 928, there were none under Peter either. Furthermore, that some of Symeon's nobles plotted with John against Peter need not reflect any ideological opposition to Peter by the boyars as a group. Their motives for joining John could simply have been that John promised these particular nobles great rewards.

Thus by Peter's reign the Bulgar and Slavic elements had merged to form a Slavic-speaking society of Bulgarians with a common national identity. The society was also Christian; the fact that the peasants in many cases were only nominally so, preserving many old pagan rites, need not militate against this. For there were no longer revolts or movements to restore paganism.

At the top of the society stood the boyars who by now were mostly—or entirely—Slavic-speaking Christians. Boris in a letter to Pope Nicholas I in the 860s spoke of two types of boyars—major and minor. This presumably just differentiated between those of greater and lesser wealth, with the wealthier ones holding greater estates, power, and influence. Later Constantine Porphyrogenitus refers to inner and outer boyars. There have been arguments as to what these two terms meant. Dujčev has argued convincingly that Constantine's terminology is not a translation of any Bulgarian titles but simply the Byzantine emperor using Byzantine terms to make Bulgarian reality intelligible to Greek readers. In this case inner boyars were those based at court; outer boyars were the provincial landlords, based on their own lands in the provinces.

Some scholars familiar with Byzantium have assumed Bulgaria duplicated the Byzantine situation, where there were two groups of nobles, the urban nobility of Constantinople closely tied to the court and the provincial landlords generally tied to the military. Because these two groups were great rivals in Byzantium, scholars have suggested that a similar rivalry existed in Bulgaria. However, we must pause at once. Surely Constantine was being loose in applying Byzantine terminology to Bulgaria. His terms were approximations to make it clear that there were some nobles based at court and others in the provinces. Neither group need be identical with its Byzantine parallel—and in fact, considering the different levels of development between the two societies, it would be strange if they were identical. Obviously the inner boyars at Preslav bore little resemblance to the educated urban nobles of Constantinople. Thus it cannot be assumed that rivalry existed between the inner and outer boyars or that the Bulgarian land owners were absorbing state lands and free villages in the same way that the Byzantine magnates were.

In the ninth century Bulgaria was divided into ten provinces, each under a Bulgarian noble. But, sadly, it is not known whether these ten provincial governors were appointees sent out from the capital to serve—and if so, for how long they served—or whether the ten were great local magnates holding lands in these provinces—having their own local power bases—who were recognized as rulers of their own counties by the ruler. To know which of these alternatives existed would tell us a great deal about the strength of the central government: whether it to some degree controlled the provinces with its administration or whether it relied on a loose federation of local autonomous counties which ran themselves, simply providing military service and taxes to the state on specified occasions.

The only two cases of provinces clearly being governed by outsiders appointed by the ruler were exceptional ones. Krum appointed three high Bulgars to govern the territory in Thrace which he had wrested from the Byzantines. And here, it may be noted, he had Greeks in the positions just beneath these Bulgars. Second, Omurtag sent Bulgar governors to rule over the Timok Slavs after he suppressed their rebellion. Since both these regions had just been conquered and considerable opposition to Bulgar rule might have been expected, it is impossible to draw conclusions from them about how the central Bulgarian lands were governed.

The prestige of the monarchy had increased through the success of various great war leaders and through the concept of the prince ruling by the grace of God. But poor communications and the lack of any sort of bureaucracy operating in the provinces indicate that central control of the provinces must have been weak. Either great power would have been left in the hands of local figures or a small number of men would have been sent out from the center who, lacking any sort of staff other than possibly a small garrison of troops, would have had to carry out their functions with local support. In these provinces presumably the nobles more or less ran their own lands, jointly took care of local problems and had little dealings with the state other than providing the military service required of them and paying whatever tribute or taxes were demanded. At times they surely tried to evade these two obligations. On such an occasion, if the ruler's representatives could not coax or threaten them to meet their obligation, the ruler would have had to bring them to obedience by a punitive action.

Thus one can assume that the state received loyalty and obedience through the carrot or the stick. That is, if a ruler—like Krum or Symeon—was a great warrior whose campaigns brought in great booty, then he would have obedience by the carrot of reward. If the carrot did not work, then he had to force obedience by a punitive raid, using sufficient loyal forces to bring the recalcitrant provincial to heel.

The great landlords were also probably the great military commanders. If the state had tried to thwart them, it risked turning them against itself. Other than particular state actions against disobedient individuals (executions and confiscations for particular crimes), the ruler probably left the land-owning aristocrats in possession of their privileges as a class. There was surely considerable brigandage and insecurity on the roads and this frequently may have been carried out by the nobles themselves (as well as by outlaw bands). In fact, it is often hard to distinguish between a noble warrior and a brigand chief.

Besides the normal administration whose authority presumably declined in direct proportion to the distance from the capital, extraordinary institutions could be convoked at critical moments to rally support for an important policy, such as councils which might be either secular or ecclesiastical. These had their roots in the earlier tribal councils where the clan or tribe was summoned to discuss important issues. Originally such a council would have been held in an open place, like a market; later it probably tended to be held at a church. In addition to small-scale (tribal or local) meetings which probably were held relatively often, though not on any kind of regularly scheduled basis, large national councils occurred (such as the Preslav council of 893). But though there were examples of national councils, there is no evidence that they were convened regularly. They seem to have been convoked for extraordinary situations like that in 893. Since they were not regular institutions, though some scholars have tried to make them so, it is meaningless to argue about whether they legislated policy or were only advisory. How decisive the vote of a council was would not have been based on any sort of constitution or defined set of rules, but rather, according to the balance of power between the different elements at a particular council. Since the ruler seems to have convoked them, presumably he would have done so only when he wanted to rally support for a particular policy and when he was sure his viewpoint would triumph.

In addition to council decisions and edicts by the ruler, which would be implemented throughout the country to the extent his representatives were able to enforce them, laws existed. Originally these probably consisted simply of charters and treaties. A subjected tribe accepted Bulgarian suzerainty which entailed a certain number of obligations. As long as these were met the tribe continued to administer itself by its own customs. From their early days in the Balkans the great boyars presumably also had agreements with the khan on mutual obligations. Eventually such obligations would have become recorded in individual charters of privilege. In addition to these charters, which were individual privileges or laws, the state, to maintain order, circulated specific commands to the general population. Presumably the khans from the start issued commands or edicts to raise troops or to meet crises.

The first coherent law code seems to have been issued by Krum. Unfortunately only a few excerpted articles of its text have survived. Thus we cannot speak of its tenor or determine the extent of control over the state by the central government. It also is not known whether Krum was able to enforce his code, or whether any of his sucessors even tried. When Boris turned to Christianity he requested and received Byzantine legal texts, some of which he seems to have tried to enforce, and whose contents seem to have troubled the old boyars— presumably overturning some of their established privileges; for the source on the 866 boyar revolt states that they revolted against the new laws. This suggests that more than paganism against Christianity had been at stake and that some of them were upset by new (and presumably secular rather than canon) laws coming in from Byzantium. That Boris continued his interest in acquiring secular law is seen in his correspondence with the pope. Thus Boris was clearly interested in revising Bulgaria's laws and was acquiring Byzantine laws to guide him.

Symeon had various Byzantine law codes translated into Slavic. He probably hoped that some of them might become standards for his state, particularly if he was to succeed in conquering the empire. He might well have hoped to have one code for the whole empire and may have planned to bring his people into line with imperial law. However, he may also have had the texts translated as handbooks for his officials. For it cannot be proven that these codes, though translated, had the power of law in Bulgaria. They may well have been given it; but even so their actual binding authority may have extended only to the capital and its environs and particular other places under tight control. In many regions of Bulgaria, local lords would have been ignorant of these codes and new laws and would simply have gone on living by and judging in the traditional manner.

After the conversion to Christianity various Christian institutions appeared, such as monasteries. Since it was traditional in the empire for them to be supported by large estates, this custom was carried over to Bulgaria and both the rulers and Christian nobles assigned large tracts of land to the monasteries. Thus the monasteries quickly became large landholders with large populations of peasants on their estates. The abbots judged the peasants on their estates—and also the monks under them—just as presumably the secular landlords judged peasants on theirs.

Under Peter, monasticism developed further accompanied by the increasing growth of monastery estates. At Rila, John of Rila estab-lished the greatest monastic center in medieval Bulgaria. Born in about 880 in a village near Sardika (Sofija), John, after a period as a monk in an established monastery, became a hermit in a forest cave. He gained a great reputation as a holy man. Disciples flocked to join him and a little community grew up at Rila. Eventually, feeling community re-sponsibilities detracted from his asceticism, in 941 John abandoned his growing monastery for a mountain retreat. He left behind a *Spiritual Testament* which contained a rigorous monastic rule, combining indi-vidual asceticism with community life. He stressed the value of manual labor and urged the monks to live in harmony, following the Christian faith taught by the church fathers, never aspiring to riches or power. The monks were urged to have nothing to do with the princes of this world, and the story has it that John refused to receive Tsar Peter when Peter came to his retreat.

The bulk of society was rural and peasant, whether free or bound to estates. Presumably land was held by a family and was inherited equally by all sons—though probably particular authority went to one son as elder. In general scholars believe that in the course of the ninth and tenth centuries more peasants were becoming bound to estates, landlords were increasing their holdings, and the number of free villages was declining. It should be stated that this is all hypothetical; such a trend was then occurring in Byzantium but no sources exist to prove a similar trend was occurring in Bulgaria. All that can reasona-bly be projected is the growth of monastic estates and an increased number of peasants under the control of monasteries. As far as secular landholding goes, nothing is known about the balance between estates and free villages, or whether this balance had changed from the eighth to the tenth century. I am not denying that Bulgaria was undergoing this process, I am simply saying no sources exist to demonstrate whether it was or not.

Bulgaria's small urban population included various foreign ele-ments, particularly Greeks and Armenians. Many of these foreigners, along with some Bulgarians, were involved in trade. Bulgaria was an important transit point, lying between the Byzantine Empire and either central Europe or Russia and the Steppes. Some towns, such as Perejaslavec on the Danube, were to acquire great prosperity from this trade. Svjatoslav of Kiev described Perejaslavec in the mid-960s as more prosperous than his own well-known trading center of Kiev.

The significance of commerce is also shown by the fact that the state concerned itself with it. Commercial clauses regularly played a part in Bulgarian-Byzantine treaties, and Symeon went to war with Byzantium in 894 over the commercial issue of the Bulgarian market being switched from Constantinople to Thessaloniki. Clearly then the state profited—through taxes and through goods acquired—from the prosperity of its merchants. Trade probably was a major source of cash in a state which lacked its own coinage, but which presumably needed coins to carry out foreign purchases or large-scale domestic ones.

Thus medieval Bulgaria enjoyed considerable commercial importance and its prosperity was likely to have increased during periods of peace with Byzantium, which is what existed between 927 and 965. Thus the frequently found depiction of Peter's reign (927–69) as a period of economic decline probably should be rejected.

Very little is known about taxes. Bulgaria had no coins yet, so whatever taxes the Bulgarian peasants paid were in kind. It is not known whether taxes were based on land, on hearth (or head), or on both units. In addition to paying taxes in kind, the common people surely had various service obligations—e.g., building or repairing roads, bridges, and fortifications. People probably also had obligations to billet and feed troops and to yield horses in requisitions.

Many scholars have assumed that foreign—particularly Byzantine—coins circulated in Bulgaria, that Byzantine gold coins were probably used for major purchases, and that the state may even have collected a portion of the taxes it received from the great magnates and from merchants in foreign currency. Cash could have been obtained by the state and by individual Bulgarians from booty taken in raids and from exports abroad. This assumption, though plausible, should not be accepted as fact. Very few Byzantine coins dating from the seventh through the mid-tenth centuries have been found in Bulgaria. They only become relatively common from the reign of John Tzimiskes (969–76); and he, as we shall see, was to annex part of Bulgaria.

Recent Bulgarian scholarship has emphasized social antagonisms between different classes in Bulgaria in the tenth century. No sources exist on this subject at all. Surely there were various tensions; throughout the history of mankind (the Balkans included) such conflicts have existed. However, in the absence of sources, specific statements cannot be made about the nature and importance of these conflicts in medieval Bulgaria. Moreover, even though most scholars have picked the mid-tenth century as a period of increased and bitter social antagonisms between classes and other groups, no sources exist to suggest that such conflicts were any more frequent or intense under Peter than under other rulers. Thus when we turn next to the heresy of the Bogomils, it cannot simply be assumed that the Bulgarian people were living in the midst of rampant social antagonisms at the moment the sect arose.

The Bogomil Heresy

The Bogomil heresy arose in Bulgaria during the reign of Peter. Presumably the Christianization of Bulgaria entailed the conversion of the elite, the formation of a priestly class, and subsequently the religion's gradual spread throughout society. By the time of Peter, some sixty years after the official conversion, most Bulgarians probably were at least nominally Christian; however, many of these nominal Christians must certainly have retained many pagan practices. But the established church—the Bulgarian Orthodox church—regardless of the beliefs of many of its uneducated members, was a duplicate of the Byzantine church, though with a Slavonic liturgy and with a leadership lacking the theological brilliance of its Byzantine counterparts.

The Bogomil heresy arose in Bulgaria, a state in which over ninety percent of the population was peasant and illiterate. Thus we should pause before we treat—as many scholars have—Bulgarian Bogomilism as an intellectual movement or stress its doctrinal aspects. Other scholars have treated the Bulgarian heresy as a popular movement; and though they may admit the leadership was primarily interested in theology, they argue that the heresy acquired its following for nondoctrinal reasons. In this way one can convert what may have originally been a more or less crudely expressed theological doctrine into an ideology for some sort of social protest. Recently a large proportion of writings on the heresy have been written by either theologians and church historians, who stress the doctrinal side, or by Marxists, who have stressed the social (and class struggle) side. But whether treated as a theological or a social movement, Bogomilism has always been considered by scholars as a large and significant movement, one of the major phenomena of medieval Bulgarian history.

Before turning to the heresy itself, it makes sense to stress the fact that an overwhelming majority of Bulgarians were peasants. As I have argued in detail elsewhere,[2] the religion of Balkan (and other) peasants is practice-oriented and deals primarily with this world. It has little or no doctrine and its emphasis is chiefly or even entirely upon practices that aim at worldly goals: at the health and welfare of family, crops, and animals. It clearly would be difficult to effectively propagate a new creed in such a society, indifferent to formal religion and already attached to old rituals which served these worldly needs. Moreover, furthering the difficulties of the new creed's dissemination would be the poor communications existing in Bulgaria. These difficulties are serious ones that require explanations; however, most scholars skim over them as if they were trivial matters and state or imply that heretical ideas simply swept across the land.

At the very beginning we must ask the vital question: how does a religious movement obtain a large number of adherents in a peasant society indifferent to formal religion? If the new religion is a state religion, where there is a policy of conversion implemented by state pressure, one can understand how members of that society can become nominally adherents of that religion (while, of course, in their homes many of them continue to adhere to and practice their old rites). This is what happened in Bulgaria at the time of the official conversion to Christianity. However, it is an entirely different matter when we try to explain the acceptance of a religion such as Bogomilism which was opposed by the state. Why would peasants be attracted to it? This is particularly important when the heresy in question, Bogomilism, is presented as a dualist, otherworldly, antimaterial religion, for such a world view is contrary to the materialistic peasant world view.

To resolve the question one can pose three alternatives: (a) Bogomilism was not really a dualist religion, (b) Bogomilism, though dualist, obtained its following for nontheological reasons (e.g., social protest, nativistic protest against Byzantium, or some such), which would make it a popular movement; thus it could—though not necessarily—have become a large movement, (c) Bogomilism, though dualist, was not widespread and had only a small semieducated following, but alarmist church sources exaggerated its danger and size.

Since the sources emphasize the religious side I shall treat the theological aspects of Bogomilism first and then later return to the questions which I have just raised.

Theological Aspects of Bogomilism

The three main sources about the Bogomils in Bulgaria—which all stress beliefs—are a letter from Theophylact, patriarch of Constantinople, to Tsar Peter written about 940; a tract written against the heretics by a Bulgarian priest named Cosmas (written probably about 970); and the edicts of a church synod held under Tsar Boril in 1211 which condemned the Bogomils.

Theophylact's letter is written in response to a nonextant letter from Tsar Peter which asked the patriarch for advice on how to deal with the heresy. Presumably the remarks about heretical beliefs given in Theophylact's letter were drawn from Peter's initial letter. The patriarch refers to a heresy newly appeared in Bulgaria which is given no name. He claims the heretics believed in two principles, the first of which created light and the invisible world and the second darkness, matter, and the human body. The heretics rejected the Old Testament, marriage, reproduction, and the reality of Christ's incarnation; these are said to be derived from the evil principle (the devil). The heresy is ancient but newly appeared, a mixture of Manichaeism and Paulicianism.

Paulicianism was an eastern heresy, generally depicted as dualist but recently shown by N. Garsoian to be an adoptionist movement. Adoptionists believe that Christ was simply a man until He was adopted by God and made divine by grace at the time of His baptism. The Paulicians lived in large concentrations in Armenia and eastern Anatolia. Over the years large numbers of them had been transferred by the emperors to the Balkans both to break up their concentrations in the east and also to defend the Thracian frontier because they were excellent warriors. Many had been settled in the region of Philippopolis (modern Plovdiv) near the Bulgarian border. The Paulicians have generally been credited with a major role in producing Bulgarian Bogomilism. If the Paulicians really were dualists, such a role is possible; however, if they were adoptionists, then an indigenous origin should be sought for Bogomilism.

The best and most detailed source about the heresy is a treatise by the Bulgarian priest Cosmas who had firsthand acquaintance with the heretics and who had the advantage of not being a sophisticated theologian, for most Byzantine antiheretical tracts tend to call heresies by classical names and then give the reader a mixture of new and relevant as well as classical and irrelevant beliefs when discussing their subjects.

Cosmas says that during the reign of Peter, a priest (pop) named Bogomil ("worthy of the pity of God" [a translation of his name] but, in truth, unworthy) preached heresy in the Bulgarian lands. Outwardly, the heretics seem like sheep; they are gentle, humble, and silent; they do not speak vain words or laugh or behave in such a way as to distinguish themselves from true Christians. But inside they are ravenous wolves. When they find the ignorant they sow the drunkenness of their teaching and blaspheme the doctrines transmitted by the Holy Church. They are worse than demons, for demons fear the cross of Christ and the images of the Lord. The heretics do not venerate icons but call them idols. The heretics mock the relics of the saints and mock us when we prostrate ourselves before them. They refuse to honor the saints and scorn the miracles of God as brought about by the relics of saints through the power of the Holy Spirit; they say that miracles have not occurred by the will of God but by the devil who makes them to seduce men.

They claim that not God but the devil was the creator of the visible world. They ask how can one adore the cross? It was on it that the Jews crucified the Son of God. The cross is therefore the enemy of God. They teach their adherents to detest it, saying that if someone killed the son of the king with a piece of wood, would that wood be dear to the king? Communion was not instituted by the command of God, and the Eucharist is not really the body of Christ but simple food like any other. They do not believe that the words of priests are sanctified by God. If priests are sanctified, then why do they not live as they should?

They are opposed to priests, churches, prayers (except for the Lord's Prayer), and reject the Law of Moses and the Books of the Prophets. They do not honor the Virgin Mary. They say a great deal of nonsense about her that Cosmas cannot even repeat. However, through fear of men they frequent churches and kiss the cross and icons as those who have been converted to Orthodoxy report to us. They say: all the honor we pay icons (and the like) is because of men and not because of the heart. In secret we keep hidden our beliefs. They do not accept the Old Testament, but only the Gospels. They live not according to the Law of Moses but according to that of the Apostles. They make the devil the creator of men and of all divine creation; some call him a fallen angel. (Cosmas then goes on to make it seem they worship the devil since they have made him the creator.)

The heretics spread their venom under the veil of humility and hypocritical abstinence; or, holding in their hands the Gospels, they give impious interpretations and try by these means to trap men. They say it is by will of the devil that all exists—the sky, sun, stars, air, earth, men, churches, the cross, and all that moves on earth. They make the Lord have two sons, Christ the elder and the devil the younger. It is the devil (Mammon) who commanded men to take wives, eat meat, and drink wine. They call themselves the inhabitants of heaven; they refuse all joys of life not by abstinence as we [Orthodox monks] do but because they claim these acts are impure. The Orthodox Christian, believing God made the world, sees nothing impure in these acts. Cosmas says that wine is fine in moderation whereas the heretics absolutely forbid touching it and meat. They reject baptism and hold in horror a baptized child. They call themselves Christians but do not have priests to baptize them. They do not make the sign of the cross or accept the chanting of priests and do not hold priests in honor. They do not believe in the miracles of Jesus Christ but claim that the devil was the author of them.

They pray, closing themselves up in their own houses, four times a day and four times a night. For prayers they say only "Our Father." They believe that men, not God, instituted the rites and practices of the Church and of Christians; these are not in the Gospels. The heretics do not celebrate church holidays. They do not commemorate the martyrs and saints. When faced with questions from the Orthodox they deny their heresy and affirm the Orthodox faith, and will do so under oath. They will deny their own practices; this they do as a ruse, saying if our works and practices become known to men, then all our labors will be lost. They confess their sins to one another and practice confession among themselves.

They also win converts by saying, do not fatigue yourself with work on the land for the Lord said "Take no thought about what we shall eat, drink, or be clothed in." This is why some of them become beggars and do not want to occupy their hands with any task. They go from house to house and devour the goods of others. They teach their adherents not to submit to authority; they slander the rich; they hate the emperors; they mock their superiors and insult their lords. They claim that God has horror of those who work for the emperor and recommend that all servants not work for their masters.

The third main source, written over two hundred years later (1211), is the edicts of a synod convened by a Bulgarian ruler named Boril (1207–18) against the Bogomils. It states that the devil has sown all the Bulgarian land with the heresy of the Manichaens and mixed it with that of the Massalians (an enthusiastic sect which flourished in some Byzantine and Syrian monasteries in the fourth and fifth centuries about which very little is known). Pop (priest) Bogomil in the time of the emperor Peter received this Manichee heresy and spread it in the Bulgarian lands. The heretics believe that it was only in appearance (not in reality) that Christ was born of Mary, crucified, and risen in the flesh. Satan was the author of all visible creation and the creator of Adam and Eve. The heretics reject Moses, the prophets, and the patriarchs and claim that these Old Testament writings contain the sayings of Satan. They reject the Old Testament. Woman conceives in the womb through the aid of Satan, and he remains there throughout and is not chased out by baptism but by prayer and fasts. They reject John the Baptist and his baptism with water; they oppose the mass and churches; their only prayer is "Our Father" and it matters not where it is said. They oppose the priesthood, communion, the Christian mysteries, the cross, and icons.

The three sources discussed above clearly demonstrate that the Bogomil heresy was a dualist one. This heresy spread from Bulgaria to Byzantium where it attracted many intellectuals and developed into a much subtler theological movement. From Constantinople it spread both east into Asia Minor and west along the Mediterranean to Dalmatia, Italy, and southern France. In these western European lands this same heresy—under different names (e.g., Cathars, Albigensians, Patarins)—flourished from the second half of the twelfth century. It was wiped out in France in the early thirteenth century but survived in Italy through the fourteenth.

Many sources exist which describe the beliefs and organization of these western heretics. These documents show that the western dualists shared many beliefs with the Bogomils. Since Inquisition sources state that the western heresy originated in Bulgaria, these similarities in views are hardly surprising. As a result, scholars have combined the information contained in eastern and western sources to produce a composite picture of medieval dualism. Then this picture is used to fill in the gaps in our knowledge about Bulgarian Bogomilism.

However, since new doctrinal ideas can be documented developing in the West, it cannot be inferred that every belief found in southern France, for example, was necessarily also held in Bulgaria. Thus most probably such composite pictures are not totally accurate for Bulgaria. Keeping this drawback in mind, a summary of the composite picture can still give the reader at least a rough outline of how the Bogomils viewed man's life on earth and how they sought salvation.

These heretics held a dualist world view: i.e., one which believes in two principles, one good (identified with the spirit world, who created that world and our souls) and the other evil (connected with matter, who created the visible world and human bodies). They had various cosmological myths but their basic idea was as follows: God had two sons, Satan and Christ. Both were entirely spiritual beings. Satan rebelled and created matter, made the world and everything on it including men. However, he could not create life by himself so he had to receive help from the spiritual father to put life in his creation.

There are different stories as to how this was done; the two commonest have God either breathing on the clay man or Satan imprisoning an angel in the clay. In the former God's breath and in the latter the angel becomes our souls, which are imprisoned in matter. Thus creation is identified with Satan who becomes the God of the Old Testament; for this reason the dualists rejected the Old Testament. Meanwhile the good principle and the good son (Christ) remained in the spiritual kingdom, while human souls, imprisoned in earthly bodies, desired to escape from matter and return to it. Since they did not know how, God sent Christ to earth with a message to explain the way. Christ, however, was entirely spirit. He only appeared to be a man but did not really undergo any of the earthly experiences attributed to Him. Thus He was not really born and did not really die, for He could not take on the evil of matter. His message of how to escape from matter is contained in the Gospels.

In simplified form He taught the following: souls through reproduction and sin on earth have become perpetually bound to this world; as a result when a man dies his soul is reborn in another earthly body. The only way to escape to heaven is to lead an ascetic life, praying so many times a day, and practicing only spiritual sacraments (avoiding in worship all material objects, baptism with water, crosses, icons, churches, etc.); one must avoid sex (and marriage) and anything born of sexual acts (e.g., meat).

Of course such an ascetic life is impossible for most people; thus western society was divided into two orders: the perfecti (priesthood) who have undergone a spiritual initiation and become possessed of the Holy Spirit, and the believers. The believers led normal lives and then late in life (when widowed or on their death beds) received the spiritual initiation and became perfecti. If one failed to receive this initiation, after his death he would be reborn as a man again. The perfecti led a wandering ascetic life, doing no manual labor, and being fed by the believers. If they sinned, they had to be initiated all over again. The western dualists were divided into many "churches," each under a bishop.

Some aspects of the composite picture outlined above cannot be corroborated in the Bulgarian sources and thus may not be accurate in respect to Bulgaria. For as noted this composite picture is drawn from many different places (Bulgaria, Anatolia, southern France, northern Italy) over a long period, from the tenth to the fourteenth centuries. It cannot be assumed that a foreign belief—even though ties between Bulgaria and the western heretics can be shown—was also held in Bulgaria if it is not documented there.

Though one can dispute whether the Bogomils held certain specific beliefs found in this composite picture, still a considerable amount is known from Bulgarian sources about Bogomilism's theology and general spirit. However, very little is known about other aspects of the heresy, even though some scholars present detailed accounts. The organization of the leadership given in the composite picture is drawn chiefly from foreign sources; it may well also be accurate for Bulgaria, but in the absence of evidence it must remain speculative. However, since the movement arose in Bulgaria, it does seem likely that many organizational aspects found in the West would have had the same or similar manifestations in Bulgaria. In fact, it is likely that much of the institutional structure found in the West even originated in Bulgaria. It can be proposed with some confidence that the Bulgarian Bogomils practiced spiritual initiation with a ceremony similar to that found in the west. This is suggested by the fact that an Italian dualist bishop named Nazarius is known to have gone to Bulgaria around 1190 to receive his initiation. Moreover, an Italian inquisitor, Rayner Sacconi, writing in about 1250, states that in the East there were six dualist churches (including Bulgaria and Dragovica in Thrace) which together had a total of five hundred perfecti. Thus it is evident that by the late twelfth and thirteenth centuries the Bulgarians, like the western dualists, had perfecti. There is no reason to believe this was a late innovation. And it seems likely that Cosmas is referring to perfecti when he states that certain Bulgarian Bogomils led wandering lives, doing no manual labor and being fed by others. But whether the Bogomils, like their western counterparts in the twelfth, thirteenth, and fourteenth centuries, had an organized hierarchy under the direction of one or more major bishops is unknown. All that can be said is that Boril's synod in 1211 condemned, among others, a ded'ec of Sardika (modern Sofija), who many scholars have plausibly suggested was some sort of bishop. (*Ded* is a Slavic word for grandfather which on occasion was used for an important elder.)

Social Aspects and Significance of Bogomilism

Now let us return to the questions raised at the start of this section. It is evident that very little information exists to settle the question of what appeal a dualist movement would have had in Bulgaria's peasant society. Was it a social movement (which for nonreligious reasons may have attracted a large following) or was it only a small sect?

To support the idea that Bogomilism was a social movement, there exists only the one brief paragraph in Cosmas about not obeying your superiors, etc. These adages were evidently preached but that is all that can be said. It is not known that they were effective in drawing converts. Since Bogomils are not found either leading or participating as a following in the various known social protests in medieval Bulgaria, it is hard to make a case for Bogomilism as a social movement. Since sources do not mention Bogomils active in any war against Byzantium or revolt against the empire—when Bulgaria was under Byzantine rule—it is even harder to make a case for Bogomilism as a national (nativistic) movement.

If it was not a practical movement for some worldly goal, be it national or social, it is hard to see why peasants would join it. And no source shows that they did. Thus, we probably should conclude that though Bogomilism had social aspects to its teachings, it did not become a peasant or social movement. When these facts are combined with the fact that there are only a handful of scattered sources about Bogomils in Bulgaria—sometimes with over a century between one reference and the next—and with the fact that none of these sources states it had a large following—though some state Bogomilism was scattered over a large area (e.g., throughout Bulgaria)—it seems that there are strong grounds to consider Bogomilism a small movement. Elsewhere I have argued this point at considerable length.[3]

Since the Bogomils cannot be found playing a role in any political or social event in Bulgarian history, Bogomilism probably had little impact on Bulgarian history. Thus I think it should be regarded as an interesting but small sect whose membership was attracted, on the whole, to a religious doctrine. These Bulgarian dualists had a major role in sowing the seeds of the dualist movement throughout the Mediterranean area (with a strong assist from Byzantine Bogomils who seem to have been the chief middlemen). Thus they acquired great prestige among foreign dualists.

However, if we are analyzing Bulgarian history as a whole and significant movements and causes of historical developments in Bulgaria, Bogomilism's importance has been tremendously exaggerated in all historical works. In fact—other than nuisance value to alarmist Orthodox churchmen and the curiosity value of its interesting world view—one would be justified in writing a history of medieval Bulgaria without mentioning the Bogomils at all, just as one could write a history of the United States without mentioning the Mennonites or the Shakers. The overwhelming majority of Bulgarians from their conversion to Christianity throughout their history have been members of the Orthodox church. In any case, the Bogomil sect which rose in the time of Peter lasted throughout the history of medieval Bulgaria, to be last heard of in Trnovo—the capital of the second Bulgarian Empire—in the middle of the fourteenth century.

Nicephorus Phocas, 963–69

In the empire, Romanus Lecapenus was overthrown in 944 and the legitimate monarch of the Macedonian house, Constantine VII Porphyrogenitus, who had been coemperor but had always taken a back seat, succeeded. He ruled until 959 when his son Romanus II succeeded him. Romanus II died early after only a four-year rule, in 963, leaving a widow and two small sons; the eldest, Basil II, was to become the greatest of Byzantium's military emperors. To preserve her position and that of her sons, Romanus's widow, Theophano, married Nicephorus, a military aristocrat from the important Anatolian landowning family of Phocas. He became coemperor in 963. These events occurred in the midst of a period of great Byzantine military successes. Crete had been recovered from the Arabs in 961 and Nicephorus led successful crusades to recover much eastern territory from the Arabs. Nicephorus was a great general, who loved nothing better than life on campaign. Sharing all the hardships with his men, he was extremely popular with them. When he was not on campaign he enjoyed the company of ascetics, and was one himself, sleeping on an animal skin on the floor and always wearing a hair shirt.

Development of Mt. Athos

During Nicephorus's reign Mt. Athos began to develop as a major religious center. He gave enormous gifts to it. Up until Nicephorus's reign Athos had been populated by hermits living in their own caves. Nicephorus supported and financed a monk named Athanasius, whom he greatly admired, to build a great *lavra*—monastery—there. The emperor put Athanasius, abbot of the lavra, over the prota of the mountain. The prota was a hermit, who until then had been a loose head over the whole mountain, standing over the hermits who all favored individual rather than community asceticism. The hermits and prota complained to Nicephorus about the change and the great authority given to the abbot of the new community monastery. By the time the complaint arrived, Nicephorus had been murdered (969) and the case was turned over to his successor, another general who also was regent coemperor for the two young boys, John Tzimiskes. He turned the case over to a Studite monk, a member of an enormous monastic community in Constantinople. Not surprisingly the Studite decided in favor of the abbot of the lavra.

In the centuries that followed, Mt. Athos—the Holy Mountain—became the greatest monastic, if not religious, center in the empire. Eventually the different Slavic nations (Bulgarians, Serbs, and Russians) also established their own monastic communities there. The monasteries are still active today, though now the number of monks is small. These monasteries have preserved great libraries with a vast number of manuscripts, valuable not only for religious history but also for the social and economic history of the empire, because the libraries contain a large number of charters which give a picture of the monasteries' landholding, of the status of people on their lands, and so on. From these documents a great deal can be learned about the legal and social position of peasants on monastic land and also about the immunities—tax and other legal exemptions—granted to the monasteries by the mountain's secular suzerains over the centuries. Mt. Athos has also been a center of male chauvinism. Even today no women are allowed on the mountain; in fact, even female animals (including until 1863 even hens) are banned from it.

The Russian and Byzantine War over Bulgaria, 965–71

In 965 Bulgarian envoys appeared at the court of Nicephorus Phocas to collect the annual tribute—prescribed by the peace treaty with Peter in 927—owed by the Byzantines. This was a period of extraordinary Byzantine military success against the Arabs in the east. Nicephorus was enraged that after all of his triumphs the "lowly" Bulgars would dare ask for tribute. Furthermore Maria Lecapena, Peter's wife, had by then died, and Nicephorus claimed that the annual financial gifts had not been tribute but money for her upkeep. As she was dead there was no further reason to send money. Whether this was an accurate interpretation of the 927 treaty or a way to escape payment is not known.

Deciding that the empire would pay tribute no longer, Nicephorus had the Bulgarian envoys whipped and sent home with stinging insults and the warning that he would come and personally deliver the tribute they deserved. He then attacked some Bulgarian border fortresses. Most scholars feel this was more than sufficient to quell the Bulgarians. Yet next the emperor summoned the Russians from Kiev, under their prince Svjatoslav, to attack the Bulgarians. Why would Nicephorus have called in a powerful state (which was to become a dangerous enemy when its troops overran Bulgaria) against a relatively weak enemy? And, if the emperor wanted to punish the Bulgarians, why did he not call in the Pechenegs as usual?

Stokes, a British scholar, argues convincingly that the Russian prince Svjatoslav, who had just destroyed the Khazars, opening his way into the Crimea, was threatening the town of Cherson, an important Byzantine commercial and intelligence center. Thus, Nicephorus's intention, when he invited Svjatoslav to plunder Bulgaria, was to draw him away from Cherson. Various sources support this theory; Yahyā of Antioch, a Christian Arab chronicler, speaks of Nicephorus making peace with the Russians before obtaining the agreement that they would attack Bulgaria. Furthermore a subsequent Byzantine-Russian treaty of 971—concluded after Tzimiskes had defeated Svjatoslav in Bulgaria and was forcing the Russians to withdraw—makes Svjatoslav promise to henceforth leave Bulgaria *and Cherson* alone. Thus the emperor seems to have hoped that the Russians and Bulgarians, as two troublesome enemies, would exhaust one another, and did not visualize other consequences.

Instead Svjatoslav arrived and in a matter of months crushed the Bulgarian armies and took over part of Bulgaria (presumably some of the territory along both banks of the Danube). There is no evidence that the Russians ever reached Macedonia at all. With Svjatoslav was Kalokyris, the Byzantine governor of Cherson, who had negotiated the initial treaty with Svjatoslav, and who, ambitious for the throne (to replace Nicephorus as regent coemperor), had accompanied Svjatoslav, encouraging him to attack the Byzantine empire, and offering Svjatoslav permanent possession of Bulgaria if he would help Kalokyris obtain the throne. Nicephorus, of course, had never agreed to Svjatoslav's conquering Bulgaria; all he had offered the prince was a chance for booty. Byzantine sources clearly show that the Russians were not expected to remain in Bulgaria and that Svjatoslav had, in fact, agreed to leave.

The chronology of the warfare in Bulgaria is complicated and the sources are at variance with one another; thus scholars disagree and one finds different dates in different studies. The most reasonable chronology is one worked out by Stokes, which places the initial Bulgar tribute demand in 965, Nicephorus's attack on the border fortresses and the invitation to the Russians in 966 and the Russian invasion and successes in 967.

After the Russian victory in 967 Peter, according to the Byzantine chronicler Leo the Deacon, suffered an epileptic fit and became incapacitated. Presumably the author meant an apoplectic fit or stroke. Peter then abdicated, entered a monastery, and died in 969. His son Boris had long been resident in Constantinople, possibly kept there partially as a hostage. Upon Peter's abdication Boris appeared in Bulgaria. Probably after the abdication of the father, the Byzantines had allowed the son to return to Bulgaria to try to regain his lost lands, hoping he would rule over them as a Byzantine vassal. To try to assure his loyalty, Boris's two daughters were engaged to the two young Byzantine emperors Basil II and his younger brother Constantine (VIII).

On his arrival in Preslav, he was immediately proclaimed as Tsar Boris II. Thus Svjatoslav clearly had not conquered all the Bulgarian state. Svjatoslav, however, held much of the territory of northeastern Bulgaria on both sides of the Danube including the important commercial town of Perejaslavec which he made his center of operations. The core of the original Bulgarian territory was thus divided, but it is impossible to say in general who held what and to determine how extensive Svjatoslav's conquests yet were. Bulgarian independence, however, was threatened by Svjatoslav's presence. Boris was too weak to oppose him and it is evident that if Boris was to have any hope of remaining the ruler of Bulgaria he needed Byzantine aid to oust Svjatoslav.

The Byzantine sources state that in 968 he sent an embassy to Constantinople for help against the Russians. The Byzantines, being occupied in the east, were unable to help. Instead they sent envoys to summon the Pechenegs to aid Boris by attacking Kiev. However, the Russian Primary Chronicle states that the Bulgarians summoned the Pechenegs themselves, without the Byzantines as middlemen. The Byzantine story seems more probable for it is known that in 968 an embassy sent by the Bulgarians arrived in Constantinople. Liutprand of Cremona, an emissary of Otto I, the German emperor, who was also there at the time, notes its arrival and complains that the Bulgarian envoys were seated higher than all other foreigners. This is often taken by scholars to be a sign of the general position of the Bulgarians in imperial eyes. However, considering the timing of this particular embassy (968), this precedence may have been special for that occasion rather than a general rule; for Nicephorus by then, realizing that the Kievans were far more dangerous than the Bulgarians, was actively trying to convert the Bulgarians into allies. He had allowed Boris to go to Bulgaria and had engaged the two Byzantine child-emperors to Bulgarian princesses; this situation may explain the seating of the Bulgarians. Furthermore, they may have been seated prominently to insult Liutprand since at the time the Byzantine emperor was angry at him because of his master Otto's imperial pretensions.

In any case in 968 the Pechenegs attacked Kiev. Svjatoslav left some of his troops in northeastern Bulgaria and returned to Russia, planning to return later to Bulgaria. He defeated the Pechenegs and drove them out into the Steppe; then he set up viceroys to rule his Russian territory. After this success and reorganization of his Russian realm, Svjatoslav, according to the Russian Primary Chronicle, announced to his mother (Saint Olga) and the Russian boyars,

> I do not care to remain in Kiev but should prefer to live in Perejaslavets on the Danube since that is the center of my realm, where all the riches are concentrated, gold, silks, wine and various

fruits from Greece, silver and horses from Hungary and Bohemia and from Rus furs, honey, wax and slaves.[4]

From this it is evident that Svjatoslav, having come to know Bulgaria, saw great possibilities for wealth there and decided not only to retain part of it but to make one of its cities his capital. This indicates the importance of trade to the Rus and the importance of Perejaslavec as a commercial center; presumably it was more important than the today better-known Kiev. Thus Bulgaria was a richer trade center than we have suspected till now. The chronicle also notes the countries with which Bulgaria had commercial contact and what the chief imports were.

Olga complained that she was old; why did her son want to leave her? She begged him to wait until she died and to bury her first and then he might go wherever he wished. She died three days later. Svjatoslav mourned her with many tears, buried her, and returned to Bulgaria in the middle of 969. It seems that in Svjatoslav's absence, Boris had driven the Russian troops which Svjatoslav had left behind back across the Danube and had retaken Perejaslavec. Svjatoslav quickly defeated the Bulgarians in a major battle and regained the city. He impaled three hundred Bulgarian boyars for disloyalty. This defeat seems to have ended Bulgarian resistance to the Russians. There would be no further Russian-Bulgarian battles.

Meanwhile in 969, in Constantinople a second general, John Tzimiskes, murdered Nicephorus Phocas and became regent for and coemperor with the two young emperors. He wrote Svjatoslav telling him to keep to the original agreement and return to Russia, which indicates that the original agreement of 965 or 966 had specified a Russian withdrawal. Svjatoslav replied that if the empire wanted peace, the Byzantines would have to withdraw to Asia Minor leaving Constantinople to him. Tzimiskes sent a second imperial embassy of warning. Disregarding it, Svjatoslav now took Preslav. There is no evidence that much fighting was necessary to take the city, and it seems it was surrendered immediately or after a very short time.

Since in 971, when Byzantium conquered Preslav, Boris was found freely wandering around the city (while Svjatoslav then was at Silistria) dressed in imperial robes, it seems probable that the city was surrendered promptly to Svjatoslav by agreement. After the Bulgarian defeat at or near Perejaslavec it must have been apparent to Boris that he was unable to resist Svjatoslav. Thus when the Russian prince appeared with troops, Boris probably surrendered on condition that he be allowed to retain his freedom and possibly even to continue to govern the city as Svjatoslav's vassal. This would have been a good opportunity for Svjatoslav; it would have given him the chance to obtain further Bulgarian support. The Bulgarians probably would have preferred being ruled by a Bulgarian than by a Russian and it would mean Svjatoslav would not have to spread his own commanders and troops too thinly. If Boris should turn out to be disloyal or fail to remit tribute or meet other obligations, then Svjatoslav could easily depose him and Boris knew it. Thus Boris seems to have been made not a prisoner but an ally, granted an ally in a very dependent position, retaining a title (though more or less a figurehead) and allowed to administer his capital for Svjatoslav as long as he behaved well.

That there was an agreement between Boris and Svjatoslav is confirmed by the subsequent actions of Bulgarian troops. In the warfare that followed against the empire, including a large battle at Arcadiopolis, the Byzantine sources report that Bulgarians were fighting on the Russian side. They remained with Svjatoslav until the end of the war; at that juncture some of them deserted him but that was after the Byzantine victory was assured. One Byzantine source mentions a specific Bulgarian-Russian alliance at this time. This is quite possible and could well have been part of the agreement which allowed Boris to retain his position in Preslav as a Russian ally and vassal. There is even mention of one skirmish between Bulgarians and Greeks with no reference to Russians at all.

This Bulgarian support of Svjatoslav is not surprising, considering the long history of anti-Byzantine feeling in Bulgaria. Svjatoslav gave them not only a chance to attack the Greeks but also to obtain great booty in his successful campaigns. In addition, despite a strong Scandinavian element in the Kievan ruling class, the Russians were fellow Slavs, which possibly created a bond against the alien Greeks. The fact that Svjatoslav decided to make a Bulgarian town his capital also reflects relative acceptance of him by the Bulgarians; if they had strongly opposed him he probably would not have chosen to live there but would have garrisoned it, collected income from it, and gone back to Kiev to reside. In addition the Bulgarians and Russians had also had earlier ties through trade and connections existed between Bulgarian clerics and the small Christian beginnings in Russia. However, Bulgarian support for the Russians was probably not a mass movement; surely the majority of Bulgarians were nonpartisan, trying to eke out some sort of existence and survive in a war-torn land.

The sources suggest that Svjatoslav, who now continued to move south, tried—usually with success—to restrain his troops and prevent them from looting thereby preventing them from antagonizing the Bulgarians. When cities surrendered immediately, which most of them seem to have done, he permitted no plundering; churches and their treasures were left intact. The only place where Svjatoslav met resistance was at Philippopolis, a Byzantine city south of the Balkan mountains in Thrace and a center of the Paulicians. When it fell Leo the Deacon, probably with exaggeration, states that Svjatoslav impaled twenty thousand people.

The first major Russian encounter with the imperial army was at Arcadiopolis (probably early in 970). Since this battle followed the fall of Philippopolis, it is probable that by then all of Bulgaria down to the Balkan mountains (though not including Macedonia which is mentioned in no sources at this time) had fallen to Svjatoslav. Some of this territory, however, seems not to have been occupied directly, but ruled indirectly through Boris.

The battle of Arcadiopolis—in Thrace not far west of Constantinople—was considered a Byzantine victory in Byzantine sources and a Russian victory in the Russian Primary Chronicle. Most scholars have accepted the Byzantine claim, but since Svjatoslav continued on south into Thrace after the battle, it is probable that either he won or else suffered only a minor defeat at Arcadiopolis. In fact, one Byzantine writer who says the Byzantines defeated one Russian division may be correct; if this had occurred, then Svjatoslav with the rest of his army would still have been in a position to push on south.

An important question at this juncture is whether or not a treaty was signed in 970 between the Russians and Byzantines. The Byzantines probably would have liked a treaty; in 970 they had been able to put only limited forces in the field against Svjatoslav since most of their forces were needed to oppose the revolt of Bardas Phocas—avenging the slain Nicephorus. Furthermore the existence of such a treaty would explain the puzzling fact that in 971, when Tzimiskes attacked Bulgaria (i.e., the Russians in Bulgaria), the mountain passes, ideal for ambushes, were unguarded. Svjatoslav at the time was back in Perejaslavec. Stokes speculates that a treaty had been signed which Svjatoslav trusted and thus, lulled into a false sense of security, he did not bother about border garrisons. Then Tzimiskes, seeing the open passes, decided to strike fast. In four months John Tzimiskes, leading the attack in person, had gained all of eastern Bulgaria. The Russians and their Bulgarian allies put up a heroic resistance first at Preslav (it is here at its fall that Byzantine sources note the capture of Boris) and then at the final fortress of Silistria on the Danube, which underwent a three-month siege.

At Silistria, short of supplies, the Russians charged out at the besiegers, were defeated in a wild battle, and agreed to a truce. A treaty was then signed; Svjatoslav was to be allowed to depart in peace up the Danube as a friend of the empire. Trade between the two states was to be restored; the Russian prince promised he would not return to Bulgaria again and would leave Cherson in peace. The emperor then promised food supplies to Svjatoslav's men.

After emissaries agreed to these terms, Svjatoslav expressed the desire to meet the emperor in person and the request was granted. The emperor appeared in all his pomp and splendor; Svjatoslav with a handful of other blond men naked to the waist arrived in canoes. Svjatoslav was distinguished from the others by a large gold earring. After the meeting, he left for home, wintering en route. In the spring of 972 he continued on his way, but was ambushed by the Pechenegs— possibly in the service of the Byzantines—and killed. His skull was made into a drinking cup.

During the period that Svjatoslav was active in Bulgaria (between 966 and 971), many Bulgarians went to Russia, some as prisoners, others as merchants, artisans, and craftsmen. After the 971 defeat still other Bulgarians emigrated to Kiev. Archaeologists have found "Preslav-style" tiles on Kievan floors from this period, showing Bulgarian influences in Russia. Bulgaria had long been an important center from which the small number of Russian Christians had obtained Slavonic clergy and texts. During the five years spent among Christians in Bulgaria, Svjatoslav's soldiers surely found themselves subject to many Christian influences. Some of them may well have maintained an interest in that religion on their return to Russia. Thus connections between Bulgarians and Russians, resulting from Svjatoslav's activities in Bulgaria, must be considered as an important part of the background to the official conversion of the Russians which occurred in 988 under Svjatoslav's son Vladimir.

Tzimiskes's Policy toward Bulgaria

Tzimiskes took Boris captive in Preslav. At first, however, to gain Bulgarian support he hailed him as ruler of the Bulgarians. During Tzimiskes's successful campaign in 971—through part of which he had the captured Boris at his side—various Bulgarians deserted Svjatoslav to join the Byzantines. A particularly large number of these desertions occurred in the final month of that campaign.

After the defeat of Svjatoslav, Tzimiskes annexed Bulgaria, and converted it into a theme; this annexation included only the northeastern part of the former state. Macedonia was not affected. Tzimiskes took Boris back to Constantinople and kept him there with his brother Romanus. This left no members of the royal family in Bulgaria. He also abolished the Bulgarian patriarchate. This victory restored the Byzantine border to the Danube for the first time since the arrival of Isperikh in the late seventh century. Of course, this annexed territory, despite becoming part of the empire, still remained settled overwhelmingly with people considering themselves Bulgarians.

Tzimiskes then turned to campaigns in the east, which included further warfare against the Armenians and Paulicians. This led to the transfer of more of these fine warriors to the region of Philippopolis, both to break up their concentrations in the east and to dilute the Slavs in Thrace. At the same time Tzimiskes removed various Bulgarian boyars from their homes and settled them in Constantinople and Anatolia, where they were given high titles and lands. Many came to serve the empire in high positions. Thus the Bulgarians were deprived of many of their natural leaders.

Samuel's Revived Bulgaria and Its Wars with Byzantium

Except for possibly a raid here or there, all the major Russian and Byzantine battles (e.g., Silistria, Perejaslavec, Preslav, Arcadiopolis, Philippopolis) took place in eastern Bulgaria. This was the region where both Svjatoslav and Tzimiskes were active. The western part of the state—Macedonia—which had belonged to Peter was untouched by the war. Boris II, though he presumably had title to this land, had had no opportunity to establish his authority there and there is no evidence that western Bulgarians sent him aid. Thus probably he had no control of this area. After defeating Svjatoslav, Tzimiskes returned to his eastern frontier to battle the Arabs. There is no evidence that he, during or after his victory over Svjatoslav, ever campaigned in Macedonia. There is also no indication that the western part voluntarily surrendered to him nor is there reason why it should have. Even though this territory may have been surrendered to Byzantium on paper (by Boris II) and have become officially part of the empire, in fact it probably remained on its own, under its own nobility, one family of which, that of Count Nicholas and his four sons, rose to dominance. Thus as Tzimiskes turned east and the rulers of eastern Bulgaria were eliminated and replaced by imperial officials, western Bulgaria (Macedonia) remained independent. Perhaps Tzimiskes had intended to direct a second campaign to annex this Macedonian territory. Such a plan might explain why easterners were subsequently settled in Thrace. But regardless of plans he never had the opportunity before his own death.

The Revolt of the Cometopuli

Soon after Tzimiskes's death in 976 there broke out in Macedonia the "revolt" of the four Cometopuli, sons of the Count Nicholas. Presumably this region had been independent all along but its inhabitants had not dared to do anything provocative in the lifetime of the able military emperor. The count's family had probably controlled only a county in the period 969–76, possibly gradually adding other counties to theirs. Presumably in 976 they pressed on to unite under their own rule all of Macedonia, and this constituted their revolt.

The four sons all had Old Testament names (Samuel, Aaron, Moses, and David), which is strong reason to assume that their parents had not been Bogomils, though it does not prove that some of them could not have been attracted to the heresy later in life. Some scholars suggest the family was of Armenian origin, and there has been considerable dispute among scholars on this; if so, it is not clear whether the Armenian ancestors came to Bulgaria in the ninth or tenth century. In addition the Middle Ages in Bulgaria was a period when nationality was not important; thus there is no reason why an Armenian in a position of power could not have united behind him a large number of Slavs against Byzantium. In any case, the family's nationality is not known.

The Roles of Romanus and Samuel in the New State

With the appearance of this new Bulgarian state in Macedonia, the ex-ruler of Bulgaria, Boris, and his brother Romanus set out for the Bulgarian border. It is not known whether they simply escaped or whether the Byzantines released them hoping that their attempt to regain the throne would set off a civil war, destroying whatever strength and unity the new Bulgarian state in the west might have. In any case, the two reached the Bulgarian border. There Boris was killed by a Bulgarian sentry (supposedly in error) but Romanus succeeded in arriving in Bulgaria. The sources do not agree on the role Romanus was to play or on the title he took.

According to the Byzantine chronicler Skylitzes, writing at the end of the eleventh century, Romanus, because he had been castrated by the Byzantines, was not eligible for the Bulgarian throne. (In Byzantium at least such a castration would have eliminated him as a candidate for the throne.) Thus, according to this source, leadership remained in the hands of the family of Count Nicholas. Nicholas by then had died, and power was divided among his sons, in particular the son named Samuel.

A second source is Yahyā ibn Saīd, an Arab Christian author who was writing ca. 1020 at Antioch. He states that Romanus was accepted as king of the Bulgarians, even by the family of Nicholas. That family served Romanus until his death as a prisoner in 997 after which—and not before—Samuel took the title of tsar. Yahyā's dating of Romanus's death is at variance with Skylitzes's and is not generally accepted. Samuel did take the tsarist title in 997, but Romanus probably did not die then. He was to be captured by the Byzantines—if we can believe Skylitzes, not the most reliable author—in 1004, when he surrendered the town of Skopje to them. Skylitzes, who states Romanus was never tsar of Bulgaria, refers to him here as the town commander.

However, it is possible that Samuel and his family did recognize Romanus for a while but in 997 some event other than his capture led the family to cease their recognition of Romanus and to crown Samuel tsar. Possibly Romanus, though at first accepted as tsar, abdicated in or before 997. Such an abdication would have allowed Romanus to remain alive and active in Bulgaria after Samuel's coronation.

It is also possible that the dates are wrong. Perhaps, as Zlatarski suggests, Romanus's capture described in the Byzantine source did not happen in 1004 but at an earlier date. No source confirms this; but since Yahyā has Romanus dying as a prisoner in 997 (thereby leaving the throne vacant for Samuel's coronation), we must either reject Yahyā's story entirely or redate Romanus's 1004 capture. Zlatarski chose this second alternative; and since the only known Byzantine pre-997 campaign—other than the disastrous one in 986—was 991, he chose that date for Romanus's capture. Thus Zlatarski, rejecting Skylitzes's dating of Romanus's capture to 1004, followed Yahyā and concluded that Romanus was captured prior to 997 (choosing 991 as the most likely time) and believed that Samuel then waited six years after this until Romanus died in 997 before he allowed himself to be crowned.

In any case, after Romanus's arrival in Bulgaria there seems to have been no friction between the four brothers and him (regardless of what title he did or did not get). The four brothers seem to have ruled jointly, each holding a portion of the territory. (Such a division of lands among sons was common among the Slavs in place of the primogeniture found in Western Europe.) On the basis of insufficient sources, some Bulgarian scholars have tried to work out who held what. Their conclusions can be ignored for the matter is impossible to prove and, more important, this arrangement was short-lasting.

Within about ten years all the brothers except Samuel were dead. One brother was killed by a Vlach, a second fighting against Byzantium, and a third, Aaron, was killed by Samuel. As a result, all the territory devolved upon Samuel, who was the most active and important individual in Bulgaria regardless of whether Romanus was tsar or not. The sources speak little of Romanus and emphasize Samuel. Thus it is clear that even though Samuel may not have been the titular ruler between 976 and his coronation in 997, he actually wielded power.

The Character of Samuel's State

Thus a new state appeared in Macedonia, with centers in Ohrid and Prespa. Scholars at times (particularly Macedonian scholars who want to depict this as a distinctly Macedonian state) have tried to stress the differences between Samuel's state and the earlier Bulgarian state. The main difference seems to lie in the geographical locations of their centers; the earlier state had been centered near the Danube while Samuel's state was centered to the west in Macedonia. However, this geographical difference is quite irrelevant. *Macedonia* was simply a geographical term; there was then no Macedonian ethnic awareness. And though some historians may stress the Slavic character of Macedonia and claim there had never been Bulgars here, this too has little meaning. By Samuel's time whatever Bulgars there had been anywhere in Bulgaria or Macedonia were slavicized; moreover, Kuver's activities in Macedonia would have given this area some earlier Bulgar background as well.

What is important is that Samuel called his state Bulgarian, a fact which shows that he considered it Bulgarian; furthermore, Byzantine sources called it Bulgarian also and treat Samuel simply as a ruler, continuing the former Bulgarian state. The fact that Samuel remained based in the west is also no evidence that he did not see himself as continuing the earlier state. In the west lay the center of his own support; furthermore, in Macedonia he was more distant from Byzantine attack, which enabled him to build up his state and army more easily. Thus he had no reason to move to Preslav and operate from the old capital.

Whether any of the leading figures of the previous Bulgarian state, centered in the northeast, came west to serve Samuel is not known. They would have supplied continuity between the two states, and one suspects some easterners must have fled west. But even if some had so fled, presumably Samuel still would have chiefly relied on his own servitors from the west whose loyalty he was assured of. The only émigré from the east whom the sources mention is the patriarch Damian who fled from Preslav when Tzimiskes conquered that city and abolished his office. Samuel shortly thereafter made Damian patriarch of a new patriarchate which Samuel established in Ohrid. This appointment at least provided continuity for the Bulgarian church between Preslav and Ohrid. With changes in title, up and down, between patriarch and archbishop, this see was to continue until the Ottomans abolished it in 1767.

Samuel was to expand his state from Macedonia in all directions. He seems to have launched his first attack right after the death of Tzimiskes in 976 (which would explain the reference to the revolt of the sons of the count in that year). Moses was killed in an unsuccessful attack against Serres. Samuel then raided Thessaly (at first he failed in a siege of Larissa; but he was to gain Larissa in 986 when he conquered all of Thessaly).

Samuel's Early Relations with Byzantium

It is apparent that if Byzantium had had a role in the escape of Boris and Romanus and had hoped thereby to cause a weakening of the Bulgarian state through civil war, the ploy had not worked. Romanus's presence had not diminished Samuel's actual power at all. Therefore, according to Yahyā, the Byzantines next tried to stir up rivalry between the two surviving brothers—Samuel and Aaron. Basil sent an envoy to Aaron who offered him aid against Samuel and Basil's own sister for a wife. Aaron, according to the story, was receptive and the metropolitan of Sebastea (modern Sivas in central Anatolia) arrived with a girl who in fact was a fake and not a princess at all. Furthermore, the metropolitan brought with him a document for Aaron to sign concluding peace and recognizing Byzantine suzerainty. Aaron, however, discovered the fraud about the girl, rejected the agreement, and killed the metropolitan of Sebastea.

After this failure, the young emperor, Basil II, decided to lead an expedition against the Bulgarians in 986. He attacked Sardika (modern Sofija); according to Zlatarski, this town was Aaron's, and Basil was angry at Aaron's rejection of the proposed agreement. He besieged the town for twenty days without success, and then ordered his troops to withdraw. Meanwhile Samuel had hurried thither to aid Aaron, and the combined armies of Samuel and Aaron pursued the withdrawing imperial troops. They succeeded in ambushing Basil's army, which they handily defeated though Basil himself managed to escape.

Samuel seems to have known of Aaron's treacherous dealings with the Byzantines. Thus his coming west to Sardika was probably designed both to thwart any further treachery as well as to prevent Basil from achieving his aims. Not trusting Aaron, Samuel then murdered him, probably still in 986. The Chronicle of the Priest of Dioclea—a twelfth-century source based on considerable oral tradition—says Samuel killed Aaron and a son. Skylitzes says he murdered all Aaron's family except for one son, John Vladislav, who was saved by the intervention of Samuel's son Gabriel Radomir.

After the elimination of Aaron and the defeat of Basil, Samuel was able to consolidate his hold over all the Bulgarian territory, and he now stepped up his raids against Byzantium, first attacking and annexing the territory of the original Bulgarian state and then the region of Thessaloniki (not including the city itself), acquiring several lesser forts. He then, probably still in 986, dispatched his army into Thessaly. Larissa fell. According to Skylitzes, Samuel then transferred many people from around Larissa to Bulgaria. Some of them were drafted into his armies. Next his troops pressed south and plundered parts of the Peloponnesus. Subsequently he attacked Epirus and the region of Durazzo between 986 and 997, a period for which almost no sources survive. By the end of it, Samuel held all Macedonia, Bulgaria, Thessaly, Epirus, Durazzo, and most, if not all, of what is now Albania. Basil, during this period, had been in no position to oppose Samuel because he was involved in putting down major rebellions by the great magnates of Anatolia—relatives of the former regent coemperors Phocas and Tzimiskes.

Samuel and John Vladimir of Duklja

With his hands tied by the Anatolian civil wars, Basil entered into negotiations with various other Slavic rulers, including Stjepan Držislav of Croatia and John Vladimir of Duklja. The name *Duklja* was derived from *Dioclea*—the name of a city (whose ruins lie just outside of Titograd) and of a Roman province roughly corresponding to modern Montenegro. The name *Dioclea*, in Slavic form, was retained as the name of the first Slavic state located there. Later this whole region came to be called Zeta, after one of the župas (or counties) within Duklja.

Duklja had greatly increased its strength and size after the death of the Serbian prince Časlav in ca. 960. Serbia had then disintegrated and Duklja had absorbed most of it along with Zahumlje and Trebinje. Duklja's ruler was John Vladimir, with whom Basil in the 990s entered into relations. These negotiations seem to have taken place in 992 after a campaign by Basil into Macedonia in 991 which seems to have achieved nothing (unless it succeeded in capturing Romanus as

Zlatarski speculates). This alliance, whenever concluded, was a cause of worry for Samuel; and in about 997, after he captured Durazzo, Samuel turned against Duklja and defeated John Vladimir. He thereby gained control over both Raška (Serbia) and Duklja. John Vladimir was imprisoned.

A romantic story is given in the Chronicle of the Priest of Dioclea. Since clearly the story is based on oral legends and written almost two centuries later, in the middle of the twelfth century, it is often felt to be unreliable. Sadly, there are no other sources about the event with which to compare the chronicle's information. In any case, the chronicle story reports that Samuel's daughter Kosara saw John Vladimir in jail, fell in love with him, and asked for his hand. Samuel allowed the marriage and the two were sent back to Duklja. John Vladimir received back his old principality and part of the duchy of Durazzo to rule as Samuel's vassal. An uncle of John Vladimir, named Dragimir, was given Trebinje and Zahumlje to rule also as Samuel's vassal.

There is much to wonder about in this story. John Vladimir clearly returned to rule in Duklja during Samuel's lifetime and one must therefore assume that he did so with Samuel's permission, presumably even as his vassal. Whether there is truth in the Kosara story is not known, but it is conceivable that, in restoring him to Duklja, Samuel did bind John Vladimir to him by making him a son-in-law. However, it is worth noting that after his restoration—and possibly his marriage—John Vladimir does not seem to have played any role in the warfare that followed between Byzantium and Bulgaria. Since Basil II never seems to have considered attacking Duklja it is likely that John Vladimir remained more or less neutral in the warfare.

Samuel and Ashot in Durazzo

Also to make us wonder about the romantic story is the fact that an almost identical story about two different figures is given by Skylitzes—a Byzantine source whose reliability may not be too much better than the Chronicle of the Priest of Dioclea. Skylitzes tells how a daughter of Samuel—this time called Miroslava—fell in love with a second captive of Samuel. This captive was Ashot, the son of Gregory Taronites, the Byzantine governor of Thessaloniki. Ashot married the girl, was released, and appointed governor of Durazzo (which Samuel captured in 997). He was not the only Byzantine in Samuel's service.[5]

It is hard to believe that two such romances happened. Possibly one of them occurred but one of the sources took the event and attributed it to the wrong pair. It is quite possible, however, that Samuel really did utilize these two men—possibly in both cases after capturing them—and bound them to him by marrying them to his daughters, thinking marriage would make them more loyal vassals. If so, Samuel's reasoning and hopes did not pay off. It seems John Vladimir contributed nothing to his cause, though, at least as one who seems to have remained neutral, he did not actually betray Samuel.

In Durazzo Samuel was less lucky. There he not only had his new son-in-law installed as governor, but Samuel himself was married to Agatha, the daughter of John Hruselios, a leading citizen of Durazzo. Once in power Ashot, until recently a Byzantine, entered into close relations with the leading citizens of the town (which up to 997 had been a Byzantine city and whose citizens had many economic reasons to prefer being under Byzantium) including John Hruselios. Together a plan to turn the city over to the Byzantines was hatched, which was eventually carried out in 1005 when, after Ashot and Miroslava (Samuel's daughter) were safely carried off to Constantinople on a Byzantine ship, the leading citizens opened the gates to the Byzantines. Thus in this case Samuel was directly betrayed.

Expansion of Samuel's State and His 997 Coronation

However, this betrayal was several years in the future when in 997 Samuel had subdued Duklja, conquered Durazzo, and installed Ashot. At that time he was moving from triumph to triumph. His state had expanded in all directions to incorporate Bulgaria, western Thrace and Macedonia (excluding Thessaloniki), Thessaly, Epirus, Albania, and Durazzo. In addition, the rulers of the states of Duklja, Raška (Serbia), Trebinje, Zahumlje, and some or all of Bosnia were his vassals. Thus he had an enormous kingdom stretching from the Black Sea to the Adriatic and from the Danube to the Aegean. Following these successes, Samuel had himself crowned tsar in 997. As noted above, it is not known why he waited this long before taking this step.

After describing the marriage between Kosara and John Vladimir, which settled Duklja's relations to Samuel for the moment, the Priest of Dioclea's chronicle states that Samuel marched up the Dalmatian coast as far north as Zadar and then returned via Bosnia (where he presumably asserted his suzerainty) and Serbia. In Dalmatia his activities were limited to raiding rather than conquest.

In the course of this campaign he also carried out negotiations with the king of Hungary, Stephen I. As a result Samuel's son and heir Gabriel Radomir married that king's daughter and briefly an alliance was established between the two states. But no permanent ties developed and a divorce soon followed which ended Samuel's alliance with the Hungarians. The Hungarians soon returned to the Byzantine camp and in 1004 participated along with Byzantine forces against Samuel. The Hungarian princess, however, who Skylitzes claims was driven out of Bulgaria, does seem to have left a son, the one child of the marriage, Peter Deljan, behind. Deljan was to lead a mid-eleventh-century revolt against Byzantium. His activities then and the different accounts of his ancestry (causing certain scholars to be sceptical that he really was Gabriel Radomir's son) will be discussed in the next chapter. After the Hungarian girl's departure Gabriel Radomir married a girl from Larissa by whom he had a large family.

Samuel and the Bogomils

Various scholars have tried to show—or have even stated as a fact with no discussion—that Samuel was a Bogomil or else that he supported that heresy or was supported by it. There is no evidence to support any such claim. His name shows he was not of Bogomil origin since Bogomils rejected the Old Testament. Of course, he could have converted later. But other facts do not support this. He restored the Bulgarian Orthodox patriarchate by establishing Damian in Ohrid. He transferred relics from a conquered Greek church in Thessaly to his town of Prespa on one occasion. He also built a church with carved crosses on it in 993 (which violated two Bogomil precepts). And when these facts are combined with the lack of any evidence about him in connection with Bogomils, it must be concluded that he was Orthodox. But it is worth noting that the building of at least one church does not prove outright he could not have been a Bogomil. He could have been a fairly indifferent one who built the church to please a wife or a local population. In Bosnia and Hercegovina, for example, in the fifteenth century rulers erected churches for wives of other faiths and later Turkish pashas on occasions built churches for Christian wives or concubines.

It is clear that Samuel was trying to unite considerable territory under his rule, and then rally it behind him for his Byzantine wars. If the Bogomils had a following of significant size—which is not known—he presumably would have tolerated them. And there is no evidence of any persecution under him. This tolerance could be expected in any case; for in the medieval Balkans—excluding occasional Byzantine actions in areas under imperial rule—very few acts of religious intolerance or fanaticism were carried out by Slavic rulers. But as noted, there is no reference in any reliable source about Samuel's relations with the heretics, and no source mentions them during Samuel's long wars with Byzantium, which suggests theirs was a small movement. Had they been a major force, the Byzantine sources, hostile to Samuel, would presumably have tried to link him or his cause to the heresy to discredit his movement. If Samuel himself had been a Bogomil, these sources surely would have damned him with that fact.

Basil II's Counteroffensive, 1001–18

In 1000 or 1001 the great counteroffensive of Basil II began, led by the emperor in person. It was a slow methodical reconquest with campaigns sometimes carried out through all twelve months of a year, instead of the usual briefer campaigning season with troops returning home to winter. He first recovered Sardika (Sofija) and then sent an army northward to cut Samuel off from the territory of the original Bulgarian state (Preslav, etc.) in the northeast. Next, after occupying this region, troops were sent south from Sardika into Macedonia where they took Berrhoia and opened the way to Greece. Shortly thereafter Byzantine rule was restored in Thessaly and in more of eastern Macedonia (including Voden). Then a major offensive was directed north again toward the Danube, and Vidin was taken after an eight-month siege—the emperor not letting himself be distracted from this venture when Samuel in person led a daring attack through the newly recovered territory against Adrianople. Samuel managed to capture that city, which he sacked, but could not hold.

Having captured Vidin, Basil moved south again, this time along the Vardar River, and in 1004 attacked Skopje. There an engagement was fought between Basil's and Samuel's armies, ending in a victory for Basil, but Samuel managed to escape. The city of Skopje then fell. It is here—if Skylitzes is to be believed—that the Byzantines captured Peter's son Romanus, who had commanded the city's Bulgarian garrison. After Romanus surrendered the city, he was received well by Basil and made strategos of the militarily unimportant theme of Abydos which, however, had an important customs station and was a lucrative post. By the end of 1004 Basil had conquered about half of Samuel's state. As a result of his gains to the north along the Danube and to the south in Thessaly, he had Macedonia in pincers. Next, in 1005, Durazzo was betrayed back to Byzantium by Ashot. (Parenthetically, it is worth noting here that in the course of this long war fortresses were betrayed by commanders to opponents in both directions and there were cases of Greeks deserting and seeking service with Samuel.)

After the surrender of Durazzo in 1005 the campaign continued for another decade but no sources survive about it. It seems to have consisted of a slow but steady Byzantine push to the west, presumably against stubborn resistance. Then in 1014 Basil surrounded the main Bulgarian army in the mountains near the River Struma; Samuel managed to escape to Prilep. But fourteen thousand men, we are told, were captured and Basil had them all blinded, sparing only one eye of every hundredth man, so that the one-eyes could lead the rest back to Samuel. When they arrived at Prilep, Samuel, at this grisly sight, fell unconscious to the ground and died two days later, on 6 October 1014.

Rule over what was left of Samuel's state went to his son Gabriel Radomir. From this point progress for the Byzantines was rapid and various Bulgarian commanders surrendered fortresses to Basil. In 1015 Gabriel Radomir was killed by his cousin John Vladislav (the son of Samuel's brother Aaron, whom Samuel had murdered). The Chronicle of the Priest of Dioclea says that he was pushed into this murder by Basil II and that he also killed Gabriel Radomir's wife and his eldest son by that marriage. Whether Basil was behind the murder is not known. Possibly it was simply a case of a blood feud. The Priest of Dioclea further claims that John Vladislav at first made peace with Basil and received a charter granting him lands in exchange for submitting to the empire; but subsequently, when he found the empire intriguing in his internal affairs, he became alarmed and renewed the war. Other sources do not describe this brief interlude of peace in the midst of the war.

Meanwhile John Vladislav murdered John Vladimir of Duklja. According to the not unbiased saint's life of John Vladimir, the murder could not have been done in more dastardly fashion. After sending John Vladimir a cross as a safe conduct, John Vladislav had him murdered in a church. Not surprisingly after his being struck down in such circumstances, John Vladimir's grave was to become a site of miracles. The motivation behind the murder is not clear: was it John Vladislav's ambition to annex Duklja? Was John Vladimir, as Samuel's son-in-law, another victim in the feud between the two branches of Count Nicholas's family? Or if John Vladimir had been neutral throughout the war and had not supported the Bulgarians against the Byzantines, was he possibly being punished for failing to help? Possibly John Vladislav felt that such an unreliable (at least nonsupportive) figure could be counted on to assist the Byzantines now that their victory seemed assured. Thus to prevent a second front against himself, he murdered him. The saint's life does not suggest any such intent by the murdered prince and makes him a man of peace who did not like war. But, of course, reality could have been considerably different.

In any case the Byzantine war continued. In 1018 John Vladislav led an attack against Durazzo but was killed fighting outside it in an unsuccessful effort to take the city. In that same year Basil reached the Macedonian capital of Ohrid where he received homage from Samuel's widow and other members of the family. All the Bulgarian state lay at his feet and he annexed it.

Basil's Administration of Bulgaria after the Conquest

After his victory Basil II was as moderate and sensible as he had been ruthless during the campaign. Though he annexed Bulgaria and Macedonia, he granted these regions special privileges. The rest of the empire paid taxes in gold, but Basil, having noted the absence of coinage in Bulgaria, allowed the Bulgarians to retain their existing tax system and pay taxes in kind. He also left the bishop's seat in Ohrid and even permitted the Slav, a man named John, who was bishop there under Samuel, to remain in office. He only reduced the prelate's title from patriarch to archbishop. However, he gave this archbishopric a special position. The see was not placed under the patriarch of Constantinople but directly under the emperor. The emperor, rather than the patriarch, was to appoint subsequent archbishops. In its ranking it was to stand higher than any archbishopric under the patriarch. In addition, he allowed the archbishop of Ohrid to retain all his suffragan bishops in Bulgaria and Macedonia. Not only did these sees remain under Ohrid but the Bulgarians who held office in them were permitted to remain in their positions. Basil thereafter tried as much as possible to utilize the church (rather than the military occupation) to administer these lands.

Basil transferred a considerable number of the leading Bulgarian boyars to Anatolia where they were given land grants. With the acquisition of lands, honors, positions, and often Byzantine wives, many of these transplanted Bulgarian aristocrats soon became Romans. Thus the Bulgarians were deprived of their natural leaders. But at the same time he left many of the middle-level nobles on their estates in Bulgaria, giving them privileges and a role in the local administration. Thus it seems he tried to gain the loyalty of the local populace by leaving them under their traditional leaders (after he had eliminated the major figures). Furthermore, Basil may have felt that the conquered area was too large to administer directly. Keeping these Bulgarian nobles in their customary positions spared utilizing for administration an extremely large number of Byzantines, possibly more than he had available. Finally, by giving the former nobility a stake in the new system revolts might be avoided.

At the top of the three themes into which Bulgaria was divided stood Byzantine generals appointed by the emperor. Therefore the highest and most responsible positions were in Byzantine hands. The Bulgarians were allowed a role only in local affairs and in these they were subordinated to and responsible to Byzantines. In addition to placing Byzantine officers at the top, Basil also established Byzantine garrisons in key towns to maintain order and razed the walls of the fortresses he lacked manpower to permanently garrison, thereby preventing them from becoming possible bases of resistance.

Byzantium's Position in the Balkans after 1018

All the Balkan area was now more or less Byzantine again. Basil divided what he directly governed into themes. The core of Samuel's state was divided into three themes: Bulgaria (with its capital in Skopje), Sirmium (with its capital in that city), and Paristrion (with its capital in Silistria). The former themes, which had lost some or all of their territory to Samuel, upon recovery were reconstituted: these were the themes of Macedonia, Strymon, Nikopolis, the Helladikoi, Dalmatia (with its capital in Zadar from which Dubrovnik was soon to break away as a separate theme), and the special duchies of Thessaloniki and Durazzo.

Durazzo was particularly important. It was the chief Byzantine port on the Adriatic, where a fleet was maintained and utilized to defend Byzantine interests along that coast. Furthermore it was both the center from which intelligence was kept on the local Slavs of the hinterland (Duklja and western Macedonia) and the base from which land attacks were generally directed at the Slavs located in those regions.

While the strategos in Durazzo directed military affairs in the Adriatic, in purely municipal affairs the local aristocracy played a major role. The activities of Hruselios were discussed above. The sources also mention a local archon in Durazzo who aided the strategos on occasion. When more troops were needed, the local archon levied Durazzans to supplement the troops permanently based there under the command of the strategos. In certain conflicts in the course of the eleventh century against Duklja the sources mention both thematic troops under the strategos and local militia troops under local Durazzan leaders.

Thus, in addition to the Balkan territories (chiefly in Greece and Thrace) long held by the empire, Bulgaria and Macedonia had now been directly annexed and made into themes. Despite various revolts—which were to be put down—these newly acquired regions remained part of the empire until 1186. Serbia (Raška), Bosnia, Zahumlje, Croatia, and possibly Duklja continued to be ruled by native princes who were vassals of Basil. During the rest of Basil's lifetime (until his death in 1025) Duklja, Raška, and Zahumlje stayed safely cowed. Croatia, more distant and stronger, was able to retain more independence, though it also did pay homage to Basil. After Basil's death, the empire began to show signs of weakening at the center, following a series of palace coups and weak emperors. The military declined as the civil bureaucracy asserted itself. As a result of these developments, the different Slavic peoples began to gradually reassert themselves. It became apparent that the enormous empire left by Basil on his death in 1025, which extended from the Adriatic to the Caucasus, was far too large for his less able successors to hold.

NOTES

1. J. Fine, "A Fresh Look at Bulgaria under Tsar Peter (927–969)," *Byzantine Studies* 5, pts. 1–2 (1978):88–95.

2. J. Fine, *The Bosnian Church: A New Interpretation*, East European Monographs, vol. 10, East European Quarterly, distributed by Columbia University Press (Boulder and New York, 1975), pp. 9–39.

3. J. Fine, "The Size and Significance of the Bulgarian Bogomil Movement," *East European Quarterly* 11, no. 4 (Winter 1977):385–412.

4. *The Russian Primary Chronicle*, ed. S. H. Cross, (Cambridge, Mass., 1953), p. 86.

5. For other examples, see V. Zlatarski, *Istorija na b"lgarskata d"ržava*, vol. 1, pt. 2, p. 677.

CHAPTER 7

Duklja and the Central and Eastern Balkans from the Death of Basil II, 1025, to the 1180s

Duklja after John Vladimir

The last chapter introduced Duklja—a region inhabited by Serbs whose territory coincided with what is now Montenegro—under John Vladimir. After he was murdered by John Vladislav of Macedonia in about 1016, the history of Duklja becomes obscure for a while. In view of the fact that John Vladislav was fighting for survival against Basil II, it is unlikely that he was able to annex Duklja.

The last prominent member of John Vladimir's family was his uncle Dragimir—ruler of Trebinje and Zahumlje—who was murdered in Kotor by some local citizens in 1018, the same year in which Basil destroyed the last remnants of Samuel's former state. Many scholars believe that at this point—if not a year or so earlier—Duklja was placed under direct Byzantine rule, under the authority of the strategos in Durazzo. There is no proof for this supposition but certain sources suggest it might have been the case. The Chronicle of the Priest of Dioclea (not an ideal source, and written in the mid-twelfth century) speaks of the dreadful situation in Duklja under Greek rule as the background to the revolt—to be discussed shortly—of Stefan Vojislav. Skylitzes says that in 1034 the Serbs renounced Byzantine rule. Since the sources do not mention any Serb rising other than Vojislav's and since there were anti-Byzantine military activities in Duklja in the middle of the 1030s, the Serbs to which Skylitzes refers were probably from Duklja. Thus these two sources do suggest that Duklja had been directly under Byzantine rule.

Some scholars, however, pointing to the fact that John Vladimir did not ever seem anti-Byzantine and had not aided Samuel in the war, believe it quite possible that Duklja was left under a member of his family—whose name has not survived—as a Byzantine vassal state. This flies in the face of the Priest of Dioclea's statement about *Greek* rule being dreadful. However, his chronicle, as has been mentioned, was partly based on oral traditions which may not always have been accurate. Thus possibly the reference to Greek rule is an error. If so, then this second interpretation that has Duklja remaining under its own princes as a Byzantine vassal state could be correct. In that case, one could interpret Vojislav's rising as being one to shed vassalage and its obligations for full independence.

In any case, when the sources again mention Duklja in the 1030s a certain Vojislav (or Stefan Vojislav) was ruling there. The most de-tailed of our poor sources, the Chronicle of the Priest of Dioclea, calls him Dobroslav and makes him the son of Dragimir, thus a first cousin of John Vladimir. This relationship is perfectly plausible but it is also possible that the chronicle was inventing a relationship to provide con-tinuity between Vojislav and the dynasty of Saint John Vladimir. It is not certain when after 1018 he took power.

At some time between 1034 and 1036 Vojislav refused homage to Byzantium. Byzantine troops were sent in from Durazzo; Vojislav was captured and taken off to Constantinople, and Duklja was put under the strategos of Durazzo. Not long thereafter (possibly in 1038 or 1039) Vojislav escaped from Byzantium and returned to Duklja where he took to the mountains with an ever-growing following; soon he had liberated most of Duklja again. Subsequent Byzantine expeditions against Duklja failed; in one of them the Byzantine commander was killed. This warfare followed a general pattern. When the Byzantine troops arrived in Duklja from Durazzo, the Dukljans retreated into the mountains from where they carried on a guerrilla war, marked by quick raids and ambushes, against the larger, better-equipped Byzan-tines. They defeated several Byzantine armies and the Byzantines were unable to subdue the Dukljans.

Peter Deljan's Rebellion

Though Duklja was able to assert its independence, Bulgaria and Macedonia remained under Byzantine administration. The late 1030s was a period of droughts and bad harvests for these regions. At the same time Basil II's successors—less sensitive than he to Bulgarian conditions—reversed Basil's tax policy which allowed the Bulgarians to pay taxes in kind and demanded payment in cash, while at the same time increasing the tax rate. To further exacerbate the situation, in 1037 Bishop John, the Slav whom Samuel had appointed as patriarch in Ohrid (and who had been left in office as archbishop by Basil II), died. The emperor, Michael IV, did not replace him with another Slav but with a Greek cleric named Leo who had served on the staff at Hagia Sofia. In addition the emperor seems to have made the appointment without consulting the Bulgarian bishops.

Rebellion swiftly broke out among the Bulgarians and very soon in 1040 it was joined and taken over by Peter Deljan (possibly more properly Odeljan) who claimed to be the son of Samuel's son Gabriel Radomir. The Byzantine sources give different versions as to who he really was: Gabriel Radomir's son, the son of Samuel's brother Aaron, or a man of low birth. (To be Aaron's son, Deljan would have had to be a fairly elderly man.) Most scholars have accepted his claim of descent from Gabriel Radomir, though others, led by the Soviet Litavrin, have been sceptical. Because of the disparity among the accounts in our sources, there is no way to be certain, and one could argue that the Byzantine authors who state Deljan's claims were false were trying to denigrate him and his whole rebellion. Indeed, subsequent developments connected with the appearance of Alusianus—to be discussed later—and his relations with Deljan suggest that Zlatarski may be right in opting for Skylitzes's version which makes Deljan the son of Gabriel Radomir and the Hungarian princess to whom he was briefly married.

In any case, the first stirrings of revolt occurred in the north further away from Byzantine control, and Peter Deljan was crowned in 1040 in Beograd (which seems to have been taken over by the rebels). After his coronation, Peter Deljan pushed south and, supported by large numbers from the local population, captured Niš and Skopje. The emperor called on the dux of Durazzo to send troops to put down the rebellion, but dissension in Durazzo prevented any effective action. First, the Byzantine second-in-command accused his superior, the strategos, of plotting against the emperor Michael. As a result of this charge and the confusion that followed— which eventually led to the removal of the strategos, who was replaced by his accuser—the rebels were given further time. Second, in the vicinity of Durazzo itself a second Slavic rebellion broke out under a certain Tihomir.

Deljan thought it would make sense to coordinate the activities of the two rebellions; possibly he aimed to take over the leadership of Tihomir's rebellion as well. In any case, there were differences between the two rebel commanders, and it was decided to hold an assembly in Skopje to settle the questions of leadership and the strategy to follow. Tihomir arrived and in the course of the meeting he was stoned to death. One source claims that this murder was the result of Deljan's deliberate planning. As a result Peter Deljan assumed control over the whole movement. Deljan then took Durazzo—it is not known whether he took it from the Byzantines or whether it had already been taken by Tihomir. One can assume that after Tihomir's murder his followers would have been disgruntled, to say the least, over Deljan's leadership.

Deljan meanwhile pressed further south with successes, capturing Prespa and occupying some of northern Greece (where were found not only Greeks, but also Slavs [labeled Bulgarians] and Vlachs). In the theme of Nikopolis in Epirus a revolt was already in progress over fiscal corruption in local imperial tax collection. These rebels joined Deljan, but they did so, according to Skylitzes, not for his sake but out of their hatred for excessive imperial taxes. Deljan's troops were active in Epirus and Thessaly. Possibly they briefly acquired control over parts of these regions.

Meanwhile a man called in the Byzantine sources by the hellenized name of Alusianus appeared on the scene. He was the grandson of Aaron and the son of John Vladislav of Macedonia, who had briefly ruled in western Macedonia from 1015 to 1018 after he had killed Gabriel Radomir. Thus, assuming Deljan was Gabriel Radomir's son, there would have been bad blood between Alusianus and Deljan. Up until this time Alusianus had been in Byzantine military service in Anatolia and had held fairly high commands. Presumably the Byzantines, knowing of the relations between the two branches of the Bulgaro-Macedonian royal family, unleashed him in the hope of causing a split in the rebellion.

Alusianus was ambitious and quickly advanced his own claims to lead the rebellion and began building up support. One may assume that many of Tihomir's former supporters would have gladly joined him. Although Alusianus and Deljan reached some agreement, the latter was highly suspicious of this newcomer who had arrived to challenge his leadership. After the agreement Alusianus was given troops and departed to attack Thessaloniki; this attack was a fiasco and Alusianus's army suffered great losses, which weakened Deljan's overall forces. As a result, Deljan, already hostile toward Alusianus, began to suspect treachery. Possibly Alusianus was a Byzantine agent who lost the battle intentionally to weaken the rebellion's strength. Next Alusianus's men captured Deljan when he was completely drunk and blinded him. As a result of this Alusianus was able to take over the whole movement. He seems to have attempted to keep the rebellion going, but he lost a second major battle to the Byzantines and the movement began to fall apart.

With the revolt fizzling, Alusianus's family contacted Michael IV and negotiated an amnesty for him. After the emperor agreed to this, Alusianus deserted to Byzantium where he was received with all honors. After this, the revolt died out completely; it was all over in 1041.

The evidence given here strongly suggests that Alusianus was a Byzantine agent throughout, whose only aim was to destroy the rebellion. After he had achieved this goal his family went through the motions of seeking amnesty which allowed him to return and reap the rewards of his great service to the empire. This is borne out by Kekaumenos's account of his activities; for his actions, as depicted, reflect such incompetence that one can only conclude they were deliberate. Soon thereafter his daughter married the prominent Byzantine aristocrat Romanus Diogenes who later took the throne as Romanus IV. None of the revolt's causes was to be alleviated. None of the privileges enjoyed under Basil II, which had been suspended, was restored and the Byzantines simply tightened their grip over these provinces.

Stefan Vojislav and Duklja in the Early 1040s

Though some scholars have suggested cooperation between Vojislav of Duklja and Deljan, no sources suggest that Duklja played any role whatsoever in these Bulgaro-Macedonian events. However, the Dukljans were able to take advantage of Byzantium's other worry to assert their own full independence. Vojislav established his capital at Skadar (Scutari, Skhoder) and maintained other courts in Trebinje and the coastal cities of Kotor and Bar. His territory stretched along the coast as far north as Ston, and included a portion of Zahumlje as well as Trebinje and Duklja. In about 1040 a Byzantine cargo ship was wrecked off Duklja's coast and Vojislav confiscated the rich cargo (including gold and other goods). He then refused Byzantium's request to return the cargo. The Byzantines, having regained Durazzo from the rebels, now sent another army against Duklja. Vojislav retreated into the mountains where he was able to ambush the Byzantines and gain a major victory.

The Byzantines did not accept matters but dispatched a couple of further expeditions, both of which were equally unsuccessful. In one of them, in 1042, the Byzantines built up against Vojislav a coalition including the ruler of Bosnia, the župan of Raška (Serbia), which had reemerged as a state (though one still under Byzantine dominance), and Ljutovid the knez (prince) of Zahumlje. Ljutovid led the allied troops (supposedly the largest force yet sent against Duklja). The Dukljans won a huge victory and the Byzantines temporarily gave up the fight, but Vojislav pursued the war against Zahumlje, defeating

Ljutovid. According to the Chronicle of the Priest of Dioclea, Ljutovid fled after he and a few of his retainers were defeated in a duel by Vojislav's son Gojislav and several of his followers. This victory resulted in significant territorial gains in Zahumlje for Vojislav. In fact, it seems he annexed most if not all of it. According to the Chronicle of the Priest of Dioclea he also was able to annex much of the hinterland territory of the Duchy of Durazzo. At this point then Duklja had become the leading Serbian state. It held this position until Raška rose to supplant it in the next century.

The lack of Byzantine success in the Balkans (namely against Duklja) seems to have been an excuse for an able Byzantine general named George Maniakes to raise a rebellion in 1043. He picked up support in Durazzo and then slowly began to move east across the Balkans. A scholar named Milobar has suggested he formed an alliance with Vojislav, and Milobar tries to connect Duklja's attack on the territory of Durazzo, leading to the Dukljan gains there, with such an alliance. Moreover Milobar sees confirmation for this theory in the fact that Maniakes in his march east kept well south of Dukljan territory. However, no source mentions such a specific alliance; and Maniakes would naturally have avoided the state of Duklja since, aiming for Constantinople, he would have had no reason to weaken his army by attacking Duklja. The Dukljan attack on Durazzo's hinterland can be seen simply as Vojislav taking advantage of Byzantine weakness at a moment of internal difficulties.

As Maniakes went east he promised to reduce taxes and quickly picked up considerable support from the inhabitants of Macedonia and Bulgaria. There is no evidence, as Milobar claims, that part of this increase was from troops given him by Duklja. The tax relief he promised affected only imperial territory and not Duklja; he seems to have built up his support in the dissatisfied Slavic provinces of the empire through which he was marching. However, in a skirmish near Thessaloniki which his side was winning, Maniakes was killed by an arrow and his rebellion ended. All the regions which had supported his rebellion were quickly restored to imperial control. Nevertheless, owing to the decline of the Byzantine army, actual Byzantine control over its Slavic provinces was less than had existed during the rule of Basil.

Vojislav died, probably in 1043, having greatly expanded his state and having achieved its independence from the empire. Many of the older works (such as Milobar's) go into great detail about Vojislav's aims and his conception of his state. It makes sense to think that he had some aims; however, since no sources survive about them there is no justification in speculating about them.

Raiders from the North, 1046 to the 1070s

The Pechenegs in the Balkans

Meanwhile the Turkic tribesmen called Pechenegs became a major problem for the empire during the period after Basil II's death. Prior to his annexation of Bulgaria, that state had been a buffer between the Pechenegs and the empire. In fact the Pechenegs had been useful to the Byzantines, for frequently when the Bulgarians had proved troublesome to the empire, the empire had been able to call upon them to raid Bulgaria. But now, with the annexation of Bulgaria, the Byzantines found themselves with a border along the Danube beyond which lived the Pechenegs. Now Pecheneg raids came to be directed against imperial territory, and the empire had the responsibility to defend these lands against their ravages, which became particularly troublesome in the 1030s. Eventually some of the Pechenegs sought and received permission in 1046 or 1047 to cross the Danube in large numbers to settle.

These Pechenegs, allowed to settle in the empire, were under a chief named Kegenis, an opponent of the great chief Tyrach. He and his following had split away from the main horde. Pursued and weaker than his rival, Kegenis had asked for and received permission to settle inside of imperial territory along the Danube with the responsibility of defending the river border. A condition of this arrangement was that Kegenis had to agree to be baptized. This is an excellent illustration of the Byzantine technique of settling foreigners on dangerous frontiers—like the former federates—to do the brunt of the fighting. It was a sensible policy if the foreigners were reliable, and since Kegenis's people were already enemies of Tyrach's Pechenegs across the border, one might expect that if they were well treated they would serve loyally.

Kegenis seems to have accepted his new role while retaining his hatred for Tyrach. Kegenis, therefore, sent frequent raiding parties across the Danube to plunder the lands and camps of Tyrach's Pechenegs. Tyrach, becoming exasperated and knowing that Kegenis was now an imperial subject, held the emperor responsible. In 1047 he sent an embassy to Constantinople to complain. The emperor, Constantine IX Monomachus, stupidly insulted the envoys; so, that winter, when the Danube was frozen, Tyrach led his hordes into the Balkans. Thousands poured in, plundering as they went. The raiders, however, were quickly struck with dysentery and thereby weakened. This enabled Kegenis's men and the Byzantine thematic troops from Macedonia and

Thrace to finally defeat them. Many prisoners were taken, including Tyrach, and the practical Kegenis suggested that they should be massacred; but the Byzantines did not follow this advice. Instead they settled them in various underpopulated parts of Bulgaria. It seems many were settled near Kegenis's Pechenegs, which created a great concentration of Pechenegs in the same general area.

In the following spring, 1048, the Byzantine emperor decided to send a large number of these newly captured Pechenegs to the east to strengthen the border defenses there against the Seljuks. The Byzantines took their leaders—including Tyrach—hostage and sent the rest across to Anatolia where they began their march east. The Pechenegs were not happy with this turn of events and began to wonder why they were obeying a silly order like this; and seeing no reason, they simply turned around and returned on their own to Europe. Byzantine troops were unsuccessful in preventing their return to Thrace.

Back in the Balkans, these captured Pechenegs were reunited with their compatriots who had not been sent east. After a meeting at Nikopolis on the Danube they organized a large army to conquer the fertile region of Bulgaria (the region between the Danube and the Balkan mountains). Kegenis and his men had not been involved in any of these events, and throughout them they had remained loyal to the empire. Now Kegenis was summoned to Constantinople to discuss matters with Constantine IX. He arrived with his full army, and camped outside the walls of the capital.

While Kegenis was camped there, three Pechenegs attacked and seriously wounded him. The three were arrested and for some reason taken to the emperor. They told him the fantastic story that they had committed their deed for the empire since Kegenis planned to seize Constantinople. The emperor foolishly believed this, and taking Kegenis into the city for medical treatment, locked him up. He also locked up Kegenis's two sons who had come into the city with their father, and then released the three would-be assassins. Then to try to win over Kegenis's armies to prevent a revolt Constantine sent out wine and meat to them. Kegenis's armies, though, were not so easily mollified. Angry at the loss of their leaders, they departed on the same night to join the rebels.

Thus Constantine succeeded in alienating all the loyal Pechenegs at this critical moment. After they had joined with the rebel Pechenegs, the whole throng marched south to avenge Kegenis and his two sons. The imperial army (the themes of Thrace and Macedonia) was sent out to meet them; but these troops, led by an incompetent court favorite, were defeated. Constantine IX, alarmed, now released the

Pecheneg leaders who had been taken hostage at the beginning of the year when the Pechenegs were being sent east. These leaders, including Tyrach himself, were sent to Bulgaria to pacify the rebels. At the same time the emperor summoned to the Balkans troops from the east. These troops were needed for defense there, and to allow for their departure the emperor had to conclude a humiliating treaty with the Seljuk leader Torghrul bey.

Tyrach and the other hostages, not surprisingly, upon rejoining the rebels, did not even attempt to pacify them; in fact they were restored to their old positions and took over the leadership of the rebellion. An imperial army sent out against them was defeated and the Pechenegs found themselves free to plunder not only Bulgaria but also Thrace. In May 1049, after the Pechenegs had freely plundered for almost a year, a third Byzantine army was dispatched against them. Once again its commander was chosen as a result of court intrigue rather than for talent and once again, this time near Adrianople, the Pechenegs won a major victory. This allowed their pillaging to continue unabated.

Finally in 1050, Constantine made peace with Kegenis and he was sent off to win his former tribesmen away from Tyrach. In the course of this attempt Tyrach had him murdered, so things remained the same until a Byzantine mercenary force of Varangians and Taurus mountaineers surprised a large Pecheneg force and defeated it. This led to peace between the two sides. Skirmishes occurred again in 1052, but then a thirty-year peace was agreed to by Tyrach.

In this way, and at the expense of imperial interests in the east, peace was briefly restored to the Balkans. However, Pecheneg raids did not cease; and the empire was to be faced with further brigandage and banditry from Pechenegs inside the empire and from others settled beyond its borders. They not only damaged the economy by plundering, but the state was also forced to buy protection or peace from them by further gifts, land grants, privileges, and titles.

Pecheneg raids continued throughout the 1060s, both by those from beyond the Danube and at times by those settled within imperial territory. Furthermore these Pechenegs, including some of the imperial colonists, carried out raids against the Hungarians (Magyars). The Hungarians, angry at this, complained to the emperor about these Pecheneg activities. When the emperor did nothing to stop them, probably because he could not, the Hungarians had an excuse to invade imperial territory. They launched an attack in 1059; but when the emperor Isaac Comnenus mobilized his forces, the Hungarians quickly made peace.

However, the problem of the Pechenegs remained, and in the late 1060s (possibly 1068) the Hungarians came to the conclusion that some Pechenegs, who were raiding Hungarian Srem, were working for the imperial governor in Beograd. In retaliation, the Hungarians attacked and took several towns on the Danube. The sources do not say which towns were taken, whether the Hungarians retained any of them, or whether they just looted and withdrew. The Pechenegs also continued their raids into the empire; in 1071 some from beyond the Danube penetrated as far as Thrace and Macedonia.

In 1071 or 1072 the Hungarians attacked the empire again and took Beograd; it seems they only plundered it and did not try to hold it. In any case, Beograd was clearly imperial when the First Crusade passed through it in 1096. Presumably, if it had been briefly retained it reverted to the empire in a 1074 treaty between the empire and the Hungarians, a treaty whose clauses have not survived. But though Beograd remained imperial, Sirmium was lost to the Hungarians who were in possession of it in 1071.

Ghuzz Turk Raids

The Pechenegs were not the only Turkic raiders who plagued the empire. A new Turkish people appeared in 1064 called the Ghuzz or Uze Turks. They had been pushed west by pressure from a third Turkish Steppe tribe to their east, the Cumans (Polovtsy). In 1064 the Ghuzz poured into the Balkans ravaging Bulgaria, Thrace, Macedonia, and northern Greece. Then they were struck by the plague, as a result of which many were wiped out. Others fled while still others entered imperial service. The Ghuzz did not disturb the empire again, but the Pechenegs still did and, later on, so did the Cumans.

The Balkans, 1043–1100

Michael Obtains Power in Duklja

Let us now return to Duklja after Vojislav's death which probably occurred in 1043. Our main source, the Chronicle of the Priest of Dioclea, gives a detailed story but there is serious doubt as to how much of its narrative can be believed. The chronicle was written more than a century after 1043. Much, if not most, of its eleventh-century material is from oral sources, whose accuracy cannot generally be confirmed by other sources. When it treats the twelfth century, the chronicle becomes partisan on behalf of one faction struggling for power and its bias may well influence its interpretation of events. But with this word of warning, alerting the reader that some items which follow may not be accurate, let us turn to the narrative.

According to the Chronicle of the Priest of Dioclea, when Stefan Vojislav died, his lands were divided between his widow and five sons (Gojislav, Predimir, Michael, Saganek, and Radoslav). Gojislav received the Trebinje region and shortly thereafter the local nobles rose up and killed him. They then installed one of their number, named Domanek, as prince. Michael attacked and defeated Domanek, who fled; Michael then put his own brother Saganek in. After Michael's departure Domanek returned and drove out Saganek who then decided not to return. Michael offered the territory to his brother Radoslav, who was afraid to go lest he lose Zeta (Luška župa).

Zeta at this time was one župa within Duklja. From the end of the eleventh century the name Zeta was also at times used to refer to all of Duklja. Zeta received this broad meaning for the first time in Kekaumenos's military manual written in the 1080s. The term *Zeta* gradually replaced *Duklja* over the succeeding decades and eventually became the standard term for this whole region until it was gradually replaced by the term *Montenegro* which was first to be used in the fifteenth century.

It seems that Radoslav was afraid that Michael or his other brothers would try to seize Zeta if he departed for Trebinje; it is also possible that Michael was trying to offer him a deal to take Trebinje in place of Zeta. Meanwhile Byzantium, wanting to take advantage of the death of the able Vojislav and the consequent instability in Duklja, was preparing for an offensive against Duklja. Faced with this threat, the four remaining brothers made peace and an alliance. A text of the agreement is given by the Priest of Dioclea; and though it should not be treated as a verbatim text, it probably conveys more or less the contents of that agreement. This is the oldest known treaty in Serbian history. After this agreement was made Radoslav felt safe to attack Trebinje, which he did successfully, and Domanek was killed. After this event their mother, who seems to have been a figure for stability—keeping any one brother from trying to oust the others—died.

Next Michael acquired the title king. It is not known whether his brothers agreed to this or whether Michael forced it upon them. It also is not known whether the remaining brothers retained local rights within their shares, or whether they were forced to surrender their appanages. But from here on it is clear that Michael was the ruler of all Duklja. At most his brothers were rulers only of appanages, with no independent foreign policy, owing tribute or taxes and service to the king. Trebinje seems to have maintained considerable autonomy in local affairs, and possibly certain other areas under other brothers did as well. However, Trebinje, as a region with its own special history and traditions, could well have been a special case.

If the Priest of Dioclea is correct in stating that Michael ruled for thirty-five years, then, since Michael died in 1081, he must have taken power in 1046. This would mean that the period of joint rule by the brothers lasted from 1043 to 1046. However, since on other occasions the chronicle gives inaccurate lengths of reigns, it is not certain that Michael actually did reign for thirty-five years.

The greatest threat to Duklja was from Byzantium. To reduce this danger and also to avoid giving his brothers the opportunity to utilize a Byzantine war to assert themselves against him, Michael made peace with the empire. He was a widower with, according to the Priest of Dioclea, seven sons; he now married a Greek, a relative of the emperor. The emperor at the time was Constantine IX Monomachus. The Byzantine sources do not mention this wedding but they do mention Michael obtaining the Byzantine court title of protostrator, which was presumably the result of a treaty. Treaties on occasion were sealed with marriages, and that such a marriage may well have occurred in this case is seen by the fact that two of his sons (the third and fourth) by his second wife had Greek names (Nicephorus and Theodore).

The treaty did not cause Michael to suffer any loss of independence nor to become a vassal of the empire, but it did allow the Byzantines to regain the part of the hinterland of Durazzo which Vojislav had taken in 1042 or 1043. After this agreement Michael began asserting himself against at least one of his brothers. He seized Radoslav's part of Zeta and assigned it to one of his own sons. Subsequently he regularly awarded territory which he conquered to his own sons. For example, between 1060 and 1074 he conquered Raška and assigned it to another son, Petrislav.

Vojteh's Rebellion in Macedonia

Despite the Byzantine alliance, Michael supported a rebellion against the Byzantines which broke out in Macedonia in 1072. Though there is no evidence that he had a planning role, the speed with which the rebels sought his aid suggests he may have been in communication with them earlier. In any case in 1072 an important Slavic landholder in Skopje named George Vojteh revolted against Byzantium. It was beautifully timed, for the Byzantines were at a military nadir. In the previous year they had suffered two major defeats—in the east at

Manzikert to the Seljuks, which opened up Asia Minor to the ravages of Turkomen tribesmen, and in the west at Bari in Italy, where the last Byzantine port there fell to the Normans. Michael of Duklja received a delegation from the rebels (showing the prestige and strength of Duklja) and immediately sent them an army under his son Constantine Bodin and a second army under a general named Petrilo.

On the way to join the rebels in the early fall of 1072, Bodin stopped at Prizren where he was crowned tsar of the Bulgarians. This coronation seems to have had the support of the rebel leader Vojteh; thus it did not cause a division in the ranks. Petrilo led his army south into Macedonia, where he took Ohrid, but then he was stopped at Kastoria. Kastoria was defended by both Byzantine troops and local aristocrats commanded by a Byzantine general who was a Bulgarian by birth, showing that other ties were at times stronger than ethnic ones. In fact, this general soundly defeated Petrilo's army and Petrilo returned to Duklja. Bodin meanwhile marched east by a more northerly route and took Niš. A Byzantine army was sent out against Skopje, the headquarters of Vojteh. Skopje was captured and Vojteh was taken prisoner. Hearing of this disaster, Bodin turned south to help, but near Skopje he was met by the Byzantine army which defeated his army and took him off to Constantinople as a prisoner. He remained a prisoner for several years until he was ransomed by his father or by his uncle or escaped (stories vary) around 1078. Bodin's capture occurred late in 1072 or early in 1073.

When Bodin's father, Michael, heard of his son's difficulties he at once dispatched new troops under a Byzantine general whom he had captured and subsequently married to one of his daughters. This general, however, did not feel particularly loyal to his new father-in-law and deserted to the Byzantines. After this final debacle, the rebellion quickly fizzled out and the region around Prespa suffered terrible devastation from the victorious Byzantine troops.

The Yugoslav scholar Ferluga[1] has concluded that the Vojteh-Bodin rebellion was a less substantial affair than Deljan's. It had a smaller following and involved a smaller region. This he attributes to less support from the Balkan nobles. By the 1070s many of them were established on successful estates. Having every reason to enjoy the status quo, they remained faithful to the empire. Ferluga argues that by the 1070s the interests of the Balkan landlords had come to resemble those of the aristocrats elsewhere in the empire. Furthermore, the peasants were more and more becoming enserfed on estates, leaving fewer free peasants to provide manpower for rebel armies, and the many landlords who did not join certainly were not encouraging their peasants to do so. The sources do not provide any numerical data or any solid evidence on how members of different social classes stood. All any scholar can do is come up with an impression, which he can support with a small number of illustrations, but which he cannot prove. Ferluga's impressions are reasonable and plausible but they still could easily miss the mark.

Position of the Church in Duklja

Michael, by sending Bodin to aid the rebels, was moving further away from Byzantium. He was soon in communication with the pope from whom he received a crown in 1077. He may have had several reasons for turning to Rome. Having earned the Byzantines' enmity by his Balkan policy, he needed a powerful ally. Furthermore, the Normans were also papal vassals; thus becoming a papal vassal could help Michael in his relations with them and facilitate cooperation with them against the Byzantines. In addition, Michael's being a papal vassal made it more likely that the pope would act to prevent the Normans from attacking Duklja. Moreover, Michael wanted an independent church for his state. Presumably he saw this as the prerogative of an independent ruler. At that moment the churches of Duklja were subjected to one of two if not three superior metropolitans: Ohrid, Durazzo, and possibly Split. Not one of these suzerain metropolitans lived within Michael's state. Since his relations were not particularly friendly with Constantinople, it made sense for Michael to seek his own archbishop from the pope, who might be expected to approve it since Rome could thereby add to its jurisdiction further territory, for both Durazzo and Ohrid were subject to Constantinople.

The only part of Duklja that might then have been under Rome—through Split—was coastal territory. Duklja's future archbishopric, the port of Bar, was said to have been under Split in the middle of the eleventh century. However, the one source which states this is the very partisan supporter of Split, Thomas the Archdeacon's chronicle. This is clearly not an ideal source to settle the question and his statements are not supported by traditions preserved in the later records of Dubrovnik and Bar. If, as was probably the case, Bar was not a suffragan bishop of Split, then probably it was under Durazzo, an important nearby coastal see under Constantinople. It is also possible that some churches in Bar recognized one suzerain while other Bar churches recognized the other. Michael, it seems, had been pressing the pope to raise the bishop in Bar to the rank of archbishop and place him directly under the pope. Some studies have stated that Michael's request was

granted and a bull of Pope Alexander II of 1067 to this effect is frequently cited. However, it seems that this bull is not authentic and
most scholars now believe that Bar had to wait until 1089 to receive
this elevation. In confirmation of this later date is a letter of 1078 to
Michael from Pope Gregory VII which refers to a certain Peter, *bishop*
of Bar. Had he possessed a higher title the pope clearly would have
used it.

1066 Revolt in Thessaly

In 1066 a serious revolt had broken out against the empire, this time in
Thessaly. The rebels were Bulgarians and Vlachs; this shows that both
of these peoples existed in significant numbers this far south. In fact so
many Vlachs lived in Thessaly that part of it was then called Valachia
in the sources. The rebels were chiefly free men, not living on estates,
but paying their taxes directly to the state. The revolt began in the
region of Larissa, where in 1065 there was a great deal of dissatisfac-
tion among the local populace over increases in taxation and corruption in its collection. The Bulgarians and Vlachs began to speak of
revolt, and came together, deciding to revolt jointly.

Word of their plans reached a powerful magnate of Larissa named
Nikulica Delfin, who had his own fortress, garrisoned with his own
men and supplied with his own weapons. He was one of the most
powerful men in Thessaly and the population looked to him as their
lord. He, disgruntled with Constantinopolitan politics, rarely went to
court, and stayed at home as a provincial strong man. But he was not
happy about the brewing rebellion, so he went to Constantinople to
warn the emperor of the situation that was developing in Larissa and
to call on him to reduce taxes to appease the potential rebels. The
emperor brushed him off and took neither reform nor defensive mea-
sures, so Nikulica returned to Larissa.

The Vlach and Bulgar allies, meanwhile, had increased their
propaganda and had drawn into the movement many people from the
town of Trikkala. Nikulica, seeing the movement growing, tried to talk
them out of a revolt. Unimpressed by his arguments, the rebels called
on him to lead them. After all, he had a fortress and a well-equipped
private army. He tried to avoid involvement by pointing out to them
that his two sons were then in Constantinople and would be sure to
suffer if he joined the revolt. The rebels, however, forced him to take
a leadership position.

The revolt was soon in full swing. Supported by both townsmen and
countrymen, it spread north toward the Bulgarian border. But though

he was now one of its supposed leaders, Nikulica was not pleased with the situation and managed to write secretly to the emperor trying to mediate a peace. At first the Byzantine governor in Bulgaria did not take his letters seriously, finding it inconceivable that one leading a successful rebellion could actually be seeking peace; but eventually Nikulica did succeed in mediating a peace between the two sides and it seems that he did win a relaxation in taxes (surely one that would be short-lasting). This revolt was ended easily, in spite of its strength and success, because it lacked a serious leader. The man chosen was not interested in rebelling and succeeded in alleviating some of the grievances, which presumably defused much of its following.

Even though it was a minor event, its narration is valuable for us because of the light it sheds on the population and local history of Thessaly at the time. It shows that there were abuses in the tax system. These abuses are confirmed by other sources, in particular the letters of Theophylact, the Greek who was archbishop of Ohrid from about 1090 to 1109. Theophylact complained greatly about the amount collected in taxes as well as the behavior of the tax collectors; even the privileges held by church properties in the Ohrid archdiocese were ignored by the imperial tax officials.

Rise of Great Magnates in the Byzantine Balkans

The Nikulica Delfin story also sheds light on an important stage in the evolution of the great magnates who, in their own localities, possessing their own private armies and fortresses, were becoming more or less a law unto themselves. In the century that follows more and more such figures appeared and their rise is a sign and further cause of the decline of the central government of the empire. Before Constantinople's fall to the Crusaders in 1204, whole areas of Greece and Macedonia had become more or less autonomous under local strong men, each of whom had his own private military force. Nikulica was in a position to become such a warlord in the 1060s; however, he did not have such ambitions and remained loyal to the government in Constantinople throughout.

This all reflects a major change which had been occurring gradually in the empire. At the time of *The Farmer's Law,* many free villages had existed in the Byzantine Balkans. Such villages probably outnumbered villages on estates. However, a process was also underway by which estates absorbed free villages. This process was stepped up through the eighth, ninth, and tenth centuries until these great estates created a state problem—in the same way as they had under

Justinian. The wealthy magnates were acquiring vast tracts of populated land and the number of free villages was declining. The magnates acquired these lands through purchase, through foreclosure (after lending money to villagers who had put up lands as security), and even through gift.

In the case of a gift from a peasant (as in some cases of foreclosure and purchase) the peasant remained on his lands with a right not to be removed from them. This was in the landlord's interest, for at a time of manpower shortage lands were of limited value if they lacked peasants to farm them. The peasant, though retaining his hereditary right to his plot and his livelihood, had exchanged his free status (by which he paid taxes directly to the state) for the status of a serf, whose obligations were to a landlord. If, on occasion, magnates acquired peasant lands through gifts, clearly then there were advantages in being a serf rather than a free peasant. What were these advantages? First, the great magnates, through services to the state and through pull, had acquired a variety of fiscal immunities; thus peasants on their lands paid lower taxes. Moreover, the magnate, who clearly would be interested in the prosperity of his estates for years to come, himself collected these taxes. Furthermore, in bad years the magnates, as a result of their influence, could wangle waivers of taxes through the courts which free villagers could not. The free villager faced an imperial tax collector who was obliged to collect for the state the whole sum that was owed and who usually hoped to line his own pockets as well. If this meant taking all the peasant's seed for the next year's planting, the tax collector would not have cared; as an outsider assigned to a particular province for a short term, he had no interest in what happened to a village the following year. Bad weather conditions or raids could also ruin small freeholders, whereas peasants under the protection of a magnate were better protected; since the magnate was interested in the prosperity of his villages, peasants could count on him to supply seed and other necessities in critical moments when they had none. Finally, his armed retainers could also provide defense against raiders. Thus peasants sometimes voluntarily gave up legal freedom to become bound to estates. The magnates also seem to have absorbed thematic villages—weakening the military defenses of the state—and some of the great magnates in the tenth and eleventh centuries created large private armies.

The state started issuing edicts against the absorption of land in the 920s under Romanus I and such edicts continued through the reign of Basil II. The frequency with which these edicts were issued shows it was a losing battle, and by the eleventh century the state had lost.

Though free villages were to remain—such as those supporting the 1066 rebellion—a great portion of the empire was in the hands of these great magnates.

Because this change had a detrimental effect on military service, a new military system, known as the pronoia system, was worked out late in the eleventh century, becoming common under the Comneni. By this system a source of income (usually a manned estate belonging to the state) was assigned to a powerful magnate; this was called a pronoia. In exchange for the income from this grant, the magnate was obliged to serve on call leading a contingent of armed retainers. The size of his contingent depended on the size of his pronoia. Since these lands were not to be alienable, and since title to them remained with the state, the state could reclaim them if a magnate failed to provide the expected service. On a magnate's death, his pronoia reverted to the state to be reassigned. A holder could not leave, sell, or even donate it to a church.

The pronoia system shows that by the late eleventh century the state had given up trying to oppose the magnates. Furthermore, since the thematic units were on the decline it was apparent the state could not depend for its defense on the theme system. Thus the state recognized the existing situation and turned to the triumphant magnates, and by increasing their privileges and powers, placed a large proportion of the empire's defenses in their hands. As the central bureaucracy declined, these magnates acquired greater and greater control of their own areas. At times they were able to ignore orders from the center and even, by the end of the twelfth century, carve out their own private petty principalities. It should also be mentioned here that, with the decline of the thematic armies, the Byzantine state came also to use more and more mercenary troops.

Byzantium's Religious and Cultural Policy in Occupied Bulgaria

In addition to the fiscal and social grievances which caused the revolts of the various Balkan peoples against Byzantium, there must also have been dissent at Byzantium's culturo-religious policy. To what extent this dissent played a part in causing these revolts is unknown. However, it is worth noting that Deljan's revolt followed shortly after Michael IV reversed Basil's Bulgarian church policy and, without consulting the Bulgarian bishops, appointed a Constantinopolitan Greek (Leo) as archbishop of Ohrid. From then on Basil's conciliatory church policy was forgotten and Michael's successors continued to appoint Greeks as bishops throughout Bulgaria and Macedonia.

By the end of the century, the language of the Bulgarian church became an issue. Byzantium's tolerance of Slavonic was a feature of its foreign policy; the annexation of Bulgaria and Macedonia made the liturgical-literary language a domestic matter. Efforts toward the hellenization of the Bulgarian church may well have been the cause for the murder of the Greek bishop of Sardika by a mob in 1082. This policy of hellenization became particularly intense under Archbishop Theophylact of Ohrid (ca. 1090–1109), whose surviving letters are a major source for this period. Theophylact closed Slavic schools, introduced Greek-language services in many places, and encouraged the translation from Slavonic into Greek of many local texts. Theophylact himself translated into Greek the life of Saint Clement.

There also seems to have been a systematic destruction of Slavic manuscripts. Not one Slavic manuscript written prior to the establishment of the Second Bulgarian Empire in the 1180s has survived within Bulgaria. Scholars have long blamed the Ottoman Turks for the destruction of Bulgarian texts. But though it is certain that many Bulgarian manuscripts were destroyed during and after the Ottoman conquest, still this, as the Yugoslav scholar Vladimir Mošin has shown, is not sufficient explanation. If the Ottomans had been responsible, one would not expect any medieval Bulgarian texts to have survived. However, several hundred manuscripts from the Second Bulgarian Empire have been preserved in Bulgaria. Furthermore, many Greek manuscripts from as far back as the ninth and tenth centuries have been preserved in Ohrid. Thus, Mošin reasonably concludes, a systematic destruction of Slavic manuscripts evidently occurred prior to the thirteenth century, namely during the period when the Byzantines ruled Bulgaria.[2] (Those writings from the First Bulgarian Empire which have been discussed in this work were all preserved abroad, chiefly in Russia.)

Not surprisingly, in this atmosphere Bulgarian culture seriously declined. No major Bulgarian writers were active during the Byzantine period.

Constantine Bodin Obtains Rule over Duklja

Meanwhile in 1081 or 1082 Michael of Duklja (or Zeta as that state was by then often coming to be called) died. The last reference to him alive is in 1081. No source gives a date for his death. According to most sources, Bodin succeeded him immediately; one source even suggests that Bodin had been coruler with Michael since his return from

Byzantine captivity in about 1078. According to the Priest of Dioclea, Michael's immediate successor was Michael's brother Radoslav. This version has many odd features; it claims that Radoslav, Bodin's uncle (rather than Michael, Bodin's father and the king), purchased Bodin's freedom from the Byzantines; next it states Radoslav succeeded Michael and ruled for sixteen years, which is a clear impossibility. Thus one can have little confidence in the chronicle here. It then states that Radoslav, on obtaining the throne, gave appanages to a large number of people; but after a time a revolt broke out on behalf of Bodin, led by his four half-brothers, the four sons of Michael's Greek second wife. (Bodin was a son of Michael's first marriage.) This revolt supposedly drove Radoslav out of the kingdom to Trebinje where he remained until his death as an old man.

In any case, in the very early 1080s when Bodin was already king the župa of Zeta was held by Radoslav's sons. Bodin saw them as a threat and tried to expel them; however, the bishop of Bar intervened and made peace, as a result of which the brothers submitted to Bodin, presumably still holding some of their Zetan appanages. This story of Radoslav's sons suggests a way to reconcile the two accounts: Bodin immediately on his father's death succeeded to the throne, but his succession was greeted by a rebellion led by Radoslav (or his sons—of whom there were supposedly eight, the eldest being Branislav—using Radoslav as a figurehead) in his lands in the župa of Zeta. The inhabitants of the župa of Zeta in supporting Radoslav recognized him as king of Duklja. Thus, the Priest of Dioclea simply followed an oral tradition from the župa of Zeta when he stated Radoslav became king. Bodin then suppressed this revolt, forcing Radoslav to flee to Trebinje; but he was stopped from destroying his cousins by the intervention of the bishop of Bar.

In any case Bodin—if not from the death of Michael—was clearly ruler of all Duklja by 1085.

Bodin's Relations with Byzantium

Also in 1081 the Normans launched an attack against the Byzantine city of Durazzo; the Byzantine emperor Alexius Comnenus went out to meet the attack. The actual fighting around Durazzo will be discussed later, but what is relevant here is that Bodin appeared as an imperial ally to aid in the defense of Durazzo. Whether he was already the Dukljan ruler or whether he had simply been sent by his father King Michael to lead the Dukljan troops is not known. However, at the key battle in October 1081 the Dukljans sat on the sidelines, and their neutrality contributed to the Norman conquest of Durazzo.

Milobar believes that Bodin was already a secret Norman ally because that same year (in April 1081) he had married an Italian girl from Bari, whose father was head of the Norman party in Bari—a city which had been conquered from the Byzantines by the Normans in 1071. That there may have been an agreement, Milobar feels, is seen by the fact that when, after their victory, the Normans marched east, on their way toward Thessaloniki, they bypassed Duklja, marching well to the south of its borders. This last argument is unwarranted because the best route to Thessaloniki in any case lay south of Duklja and the Normans presumably would have taken it with or without an agreement. Furthermore, the imperial cities along that route were more important for both the strategic and plundering interests of the Normans.

However, whether or not there was an alliance, it would have made sense for Michael to keep his army out of the fray and intact to defend his country from the victor should it choose to attack him. For had the Byzantines repulsed the Normans, they would have been free to turn against Duklja; and one might not have foreseen that victorious Normans would not have decided to seize further ports in southern Dalmatia (including those belonging to Duklja). In fact, shortly thereafter the Byzantines were to turn against Duklja. Milobar sees this attack as further evidence that Bodin was allied to the Normans; however, Bodin's neutrality alone, since the Byzantines had counted on his participation on their side, would have been sufficient reason for the empire to have seen him as unreliable and deserving of punishment if not removal.

Bodin and Raška

In the midst of the domestic and Norman-Byzantine confusion, it seems that Raška broke away from Duklja and asserted its own independence. Though no source mentions a revolt there, Bodin—once his hands were freed from these issues—marched against Bosnia and Raška and in both cases was successful. Since Raška had already been annexed by Michael, a conquest by Bodin would only have been necessary if it had broken away. The period right after Michael's death when Bodin was faced with these other problems would have been a natural time for this breakaway to have occurred.

Bodin put two župans—Marko and Vukan—over Raška. These two men were from his court, and recent scholarship[3] considers them two sons of Petrislav (a son of Michael and his Greek second wife); Petrislav had been placed by Michael over Raška between 1060 and 1074. In any case, these two men swore an oath of loyalty to Bodin and took power as his vassals in Raška. Most scholars date this action in Raška to 1083 or 1084. Marko immediately disappears from the sources but Vukan remained in power in Raška for many years and became a very prominent figure in subsequent Balkan history. Byzantium, still concerned with the Norman threat, was not able to intervene in these events involving Raška.

Neither Bosnia, Zahumlje, nor Raška was ever incorporated into an integrated state with Duklja. Each retained its own nobility and institutions and simply acquired a member of the Dukljan royal family to head the local structure as prince or župan.

In 1085 the Norman leader Robert Guiscard died, and the Byzantines were quickly able to regain Durazzo. According to Anna Comnena, the Byzantines simply recovered it, which is probably correct; according to the Priest of Dioclea, Bodin captured it but, afraid to provoke the Byzantines further, and wanting to conclude peace with them, restored the town to the emperor. In any case, the Byzantines, because of Bodin's behavior when he, though an imperial vassal, sat on the sidelines in 1081 when the Normans took Durazzo, did not trust Bodin. When the Norman threat was over and Durazzo, the leading center for mobilizing forces to go against Duklja, was recovered, the Byzantines began preparing for a new offensive against Bodin.

Bar Raised to an Archbishopric

In the meantime, and probably just on the eve of the Byzantine attack against Duklja, Bodin succeeded in achieving one thing that Michael had tried but failed to do. By supporting the pope against an antipope in 1089, he got the bishop of Bar raised to the rank of archbishop. The historical basis for this promotion was that in the early church an archbishop had existed in the nearby Dukljan city of Dioclea. Under Bar as suffragan bishops would be: Kotor, Ulcinj, Svač, Skadar, Drivast, Pula (Polati), Serbia, Bosnia, and Trebinje. It is noteworthy that Zahumlje was not included under Bar. Possibly Zahumlje had already broken away from Duklja. Thus in obtaining its promotion to an archbishopric Bar acquired a much larger diocese, and it obtained much territory that earlier had not been under the pope but had been included in the dioceses of the metropolitan of Durazzo and the archbishop of Ohrid, two sees which recognized the jurisdiction of Constantinople.

However, much of Bar's new territory was certainly only theoretical, for in fact the pope's edict could only have affected those churches which recognized Rome or were willing to do so. Thus making Serbia a suffragan bishop had little meaning because most of the churches in Serbia were under Constantinople. There is no evidence that Bodin's governor there, Vukan, tried to swing the churches in his territory over to the pope, and besides, Vukan was to become an independent actor two or three years from then. Thus probably Durazzo and Ohrid suffered only slight territorial losses, presumably chiefly along the coast. But briefly the Dukljan church would be subject to Rome, and Bar itself was to remain a Roman Catholic bishopric throughout the Middle Ages. However, most of inland Duklja was not much affected and subsequently, along with much of the Dukljan coastal population (like most of the population of Kotor), was to retain its loyalty to Orthodoxy. Possibly Bodin's turning to the pope at this time was motivated by a search for allies on the eve of the Byzantine attack.

Duklja Loses Peripheral Territories

It seems the Byzantine campaign did not actually take place until some time between 1089 and 1091. Then the Byzantines directed a major attack against Duklja which was successful not only in defeating Bodin's army, but also in taking him prisoner again. Some scholars think it a bit too much to believe that he could have been captured twice and doubt that this second capture took place. They argue that sources making this claim have mixed in an account of his initial capture.

In any case a civil war soon broke out in Duklja among Bodin's many relatives which greatly weakened Duklja and gave the Serbs of Raška a chance to assert themselves and break away from Duklja's control. Bosnia and Zahumlje also seceded from Dukljan control. The leader of Raška in this venture was Vukan, who, as noted, was a Dukljan—possibly a nephew of Bodin—placed over Raška by Bodin.

Up to this point—through the eleventh century—the leading Serbian center (and also Balkan center of resistance to Byzantium) had been Duklja. But now because of Duklja's defeat by the Byzantines and the civil war that followed—which we shall shortly turn to—this role passed to the Serbs of Raška whose prestige rose. In the twelfth century Serbs based in Raška (rather than Duklja) became the leading opponents of Byzantium. Because of the loss of Bosnia, Zahumlje, and Raška, Duklja became much weaker and was left with little territory other than Duklja itself and Trebinje. Not surprisingly, Bodin's heirs were forced to recognize the overlordship of Byzantium.

Vukan of Raška and Byzantium

In the course of our study, we have found Serbs living in many regions of what is now Yugoslavia: Raška, Duklja, Zahumlje, Trebinje, and parts of Bosnia. By the end of the eleventh century Raška had come to be the most powerful Serbian state, and it was to remain so throughout the Middle Ages. Henceforth in this work the terms *Raška* and *Serbia* will be used as synonyms. Furthermore, the term *Serb*, unless otherwise modified, will refer to a person from Raška.

In the early 1090s Vukan of Raška took the title of grand (veliki) župan. His state was centered in the vicinity of modern Novi Pazar. Under him were a series of local župans (each over a župa or county) who seem to have been more or less autonomous as far as the internal affairs of their župans were concerned, but who were obliged to be loyal to the grand župan and to support him in battle. It seems the župans were hereditary rulers of their counties—local Raškans with their own local support who had had authority in that land before the Dukljans annexed Raška. In about 1090 Vukan began raiding into imperial territory, first in the vicinity of Kosovo.

Initially the Byzantines were unable to take serious steps against Raška for once again they were faced with a serious threat from the Pechenegs. In 1090 a horde of these Turkish tribesmen reached the walls of Constantinople, plundering along their route to the city. They then formed an alliance with the emir of Smyrna (modern Izmir on the west coast of Asia Minor) who provided ships. The emperor in this desperate situation called upon a second Turkic people living beyond the Danube, the Cumans (or Polovtsy). They responded to the call and, joining the imperial troops, battled the Pechenegs in a wild battle on 29 April 1091 which lasted the whole day. It resulted in a massive victory for the Byzantines and the whole Pecheneg force was destroyed. Anna Comnena writes, "An entire people numbering myriads was exterminated in a single day." Most scholars believe she was a bit too optimistic and feel this victory only destroyed a particular group of Pechenegs, leaving others still beyond the Danube, who were to be a problem again in the 1120s. However the Rumanian scholar Diaconu persuasively argues that Anna was, in fact, accurate. The nomadic barbarians who were to attack the empire in the 1120s were Cumans, not Pechenegs.

With the Pecheneg problem solved, Alexius Comnenus was able to turn to the Serbs of Raška. Owing to the vagueness of sources, the dates of some of the events that follow are not certain; thus the reader may find that some of the dates given here are different by a year or so from those in some other studies. There really is no way to be certain of the dating; all that seems secure is the sequence of events. In any case, Alexius first sent out an army led by the governor of Durazzo. The Serbs defeated this army in 1092, so in 1093 Alexius mobilized a larger army under his own leadership and marched on Raška. Vukan immediately sent envoys to the emperor seeking peace and offering homage which Alexius quickly accepted because a new problem had arisen at home. The Cumans from beyond the Danube had broken their alliance with the empire and had begun to plunder imperial territory, penetrating as far as Adrianople. The emperor accepted Vukan's homage and returned east to meet and drive out the Cumans.

As soon as the emperor departed, Vukan broke his treaty and began to expand along the Vardar obtaining much booty and taking the cities of Vranje, Skopje, and Tetovo. Once again in 1094 or 1095 the emperor marched out to meet the Serbs. Vukan with his župans arrived at the emperor's tent to make peace and to give the emperor hostages, including his own son Uroš. Throughout the twelfth century it was usual to find a son or other close relative of the Serbian grand župan in Constantinople as a hostage; these hostages were one factor keeping the Serbs in semiorder vis-à-vis the empire. Vukan seems to have carried out these actions entirely on his own. He was no longer a Dukljan vassal but an independent actor; and Duklja, because it was so involved in its own civil strife, did not involve itself in these Raškan-Byzantine wars.

Byzantium and the First Crusade

Byzantium had long been hard pressed by the Moslems from the east—particularly by the Seljuks and Turkomen—and by Alexius's reign much of the east had been lost, not only the Holy Land (of interest to all Christians) but much of Anatolia as well. In 1090, threatened by the alliance between the emir of Smyrna and the Pechenegs, Alexius had sought help, hoping for mercenaries, from the West. The West was slow to respond, and by 1095, when Pope Urban went into action, the crisis had passed. Furthermore the pope did not do what Alexius had wanted. The emperor had thought that the pope, a figure in contact with all the western rulers, was an ideal person to widely disseminate word of Byzantium's need for mercenaries who could come east and fight under imperial command. However, instead of asking the secular rulers to recruit such mercenaries for the hard-pressed Byzantines, the pope in 1095 called for a crusade to march under its own leaders and recover the Holy Land.

This massive venture was not at all to the emperor's liking. Large armies loyal to their own leaders and hostile to the Greeks had to pass through imperial territory. They included Normans, one of the major enemies of the empire, who had ambitions toward imperial territory; the Crusaders had to be fed somehow and kept in order; their obedience to imperial wishes was doubtful; furthermore mercenaries would have fought where needed, particularly in nearby Anatolia, whereas the Crusaders' ambitions lay toward the Holy Land, and once there they became more interested in hacking out independent kingdoms than in restoring the former imperial lands to the Byzantines.

To make matters worse, news of their arrival came late and the empire expected them to land at Durazzo and come via the Via Egnatia through Ohrid and Thessaloniki. Instead the largest groups appeared via Hungary at Beograd, planning to take the Orient Express route (Niš, Sardika), where they were not expected. The Byzantines, on short notice, were not able to have sufficient supplies for them, so the Crusaders began looting. This led to skirmishes with the local population and also with Byzantine units sent out to guard the roads and to try to keep order.

None of these occurrences increased the good will between Crusaders and Byzantines, and the issues noted earlier divided them as well. Thus the Crusades can be seen as a major factor in causing hatreds on a popular level between easterners and westerners, and in making the people themselves opposed to any compromise to heal the rift that had developed between the two churches. The split had officially occurred in 1054. However, at that time all that had taken place were mutual excommunications between a papal legate, representing a deceased pope, and a Byzantine patriarch. Neither had excommunicated the other church as a whole. Though communion had not been restored after that, relations had been continued between the two sides, as is seen in Alexius's request to the pope for mercenaries.[4] But now as a result of the Crusades more and more bad feelings developed and each society came to look upon its own practices (leavened or unleavened bread in the communion wafer, shaven or bearded priests, *Filioque* or not,) as superior and would brook no change.

As time went on the Crusades became more and more directed at schismatic and, possibly more important, wealthy Constantinople. Finally in 1204 Crusaders were to take Constantinople itself and for fifty-seven years occupy the capital from which they directed an inefficient Latin Empire. We shall be devoting considerable attention to the Crusaders off and on in this history. But what is relevant here is that Vukan took advantage of Alexius's difficulties with the Crusaders to

assert himself once again. He pressed south into Macedonia, and Alexius was able to do nothing about him until 1106, when the dust settled
from the Crusaders. Then once again Vukan submitted.

This Serb drive to the south was to be a constant one over the
next two and a half centuries. At this time Raška was still too weak to
successfully expand against the Byzantines and establish any sort of
permanent hold over this territory. To do so it needed a strong ally
and in the twelfth century it was to find this ally in the Hungarians.
This Hungarian-Raškan alliance was to exist throughout most of the
twelfth century, a period during which the Hungarians greatly increased their activities and influence in many regions of the Balkans,
particularly after 1102, when they incorporated Croatia and Dalmatia
into their kingdom. Thus from the early twelfth century the Hungarians became a major factor in Balkan politics.

Civil War in Duklja

Controversy over Bodin's Position in the Civil War

It is not known what happened to Bodin of Duklja after the Byzantine
war. Milobar, following the Chronicle of the Priest of Dioclea, which
does not refer to Bodin being captured by the Byzantines, believes he
was not captured; Milobar suggests that the Greek source, Anna Comnena, which notes this capture has taken the story of his first capture in
1072 and mistakenly placed it later. Milobar thus believes that Bodin
ruled without a break straight through until 1108. Milobar, following
the Priest of Dioclea's account, believes that the civil war which occurred in Duklja was against a present Bodin.

The other extreme view is that of Zlatarski who has so low an
opinion of the Priest of Dioclea that he ignores his information entirely. Zlatarski—doubting that the Byzantines, once freed of the Normans, would have waited five or six years to attack Zeta—dates the
Byzantine invasion right after 1085. He thus believes Bodin's defeat
took place in 1085; he also believes Bodin was captured, as Anna
Comnena states; and since he discounts the Priest of Dioclea's chronicle, Zlatarski claims that from this point onward Bodin disappeared
from history.

A modified view, frequently found, argues that Bodin was captured; during his absence civil war broke out as rivals tried to oust his
wife from power; then Bodin returned to Duklja to find a weakened
state with Raška and possibly Bosnia gone. Bodin was able to regain
his throne but could not reassert his authority over the neighboring

regions; thus he ruled over a weaker state until his death which occurred after 1101. It is impossible to choose among these various views because sources are lacking with which to compare the Priest of Dioclea's data. In any case, all views allow for some sort of civil strife leading to the loss of some territory and the weakening of the Dukljan state.

First Phase of the Dukljan Civil War

Let us now summarize the account of the civil war given by the Priest of Dioclea. As noted, the chronicle does not have Bodin captured. Presumably, however, Bodin could have been captured and then have returned to face the situation described in the chronicle's account.

Bodin's wife is depicted as the moving force behind the throne. She was of Italian origin and was named Jakvinta. She was worried that Michael's brother Radoslav's son Branislav (who was the eldest of the eight sons of Radoslav) would threaten the future of Bodin and her children; her sons were younger and thus weaker, and should Bodin die before they reached their majority Branislav could well have ousted them from succession. Her children's ages are not known; but since Bodin and Jakvinta were married in 1081, the children could not have been much older than ten or fifteen, depending on when in the 1090s the action taken against Branislav and his family, described by the Priest of Dioclea, occurred. Milobar believes it took place around 1093–95, which would explain Bodin's noninvolvement in the war between Vukan and Byzantium.

Branislav, Branislav's brother, and a son, unattended and expecting no trouble, arrived at some time in Skadar. They were quickly seized and jailed on Bodin's orders at Jakvinta's urging. Branislav very soon thereafter died in jail; at liberty were six more brothers and six other sons of Branislav who were furious and also afraid for their own lives. They temporarily found asylum in Dubrovnik. Bodin then demanded that Dubrovnik expel them, but the town, faithful to a tradition it upheld—often at great risk—throughout the Middle Ages of granting asylum to all who sought it, refused. So Bodin besieged the city. In the course of the siege a favorite of Jakvinta was killed. In fury she convinced Bodin to take the two remaining prisoners (Branislav's brother and son) before the walls of Dubrovnik to be beheaded.

After these events the church succeeded in mediating a peace, but the desire for revenge remained strong in Branislav's family, several of whose members departed for Constantinople as émigrés, and were to contribute to further weakening Duklja after Bodin's death. Not surprisingly Bodin, occupied with these matters, was in no position to restore Duklja to its former state.

The Situation at Bodin's Death

After the death of Bodin in the first decade of the twelfth century (the actual date is unknown; scholars accept different dates between 1101 and 1108) chaos broke out in Duklja. Originally it seems Duklja, like Raška, had been divided up into župas each under a hereditary local nobleman (župan); however, Stefan Vojislav had started placing members of his enormous family over the local leadership as governors of the župas. Thus the old system, working from the bottom up, continued to exist but a royal relative was now sent out from the center to stand at the top of this provincial structure (e.g., Gojislav who was sent off to rule Trebinje).

Michael on occasions and Bodin even more frequently began trying to deprive many members of their own broad family from a ruling role over provinces; in their place they tried to establish rule by their own descendants alone. Thus Bodin tried to break the starešina (elder) principle which would have given rights to all descendants of Vojislav or of Michael, and to limit the rights to his own descendants; he also tried to establish for his succession a principle of primogeniture (with his own eldest son succeeding) rather than the senior member of the broad family. This conclusion is Milobar's; however, by thinking in terms of systems and rights, he may have been too systematic. Possibly Bodin simply aimed to install his own children in de facto authority and never concerned himself with the theory behind matters.

In any case at Bodin's death chaos was created by the ambitions of others to succeed, by the hatreds produced during his rule (which were particularly directed at his widow who was supporting her own sons), and by the return of many exiles. The two major groups of contenders for power seem to have been (1) the four sons of King Michael by his second, the Greek, wife, the eldest of whom was Dobroslav who then was about twenty-five, and (2) Bodin's widow working on behalf of her four sons, the eldest of whom, Michael, was a teenager.

Dukljan Civil War: Second Phase

When upon Bodin's death, his eldest son Michael tried to establish himself, Bodin's half-brother Dobroslav was also declared king. At the same time word of Bodin's death reached the emperor Alexius in Constantinople and he decided to meddle in Dukljan affairs by utilizing one of several Dukljan exiles then in his capital. He ordered the brothers and sons of Branislav sent to Durazzo from where one brother, named Kočapar (with Byzantine support), went to Raška to seek from Vukan aid against Dobroslav. At this moment Vukan was at peace with the empire, recognizing Byzantine overlordship. Seeing an untenable situation developing, Dobroslav, to save his throne, sought Byzantine suzerainty and Alexius accepted his request.

Vukan and Kočapar, however, then attacked Duklja and won a battle on the Morača River in which they captured Dobroslav, who was taken off to Raška as a prisoner. Vukan and Kočapar occupied Duklja and even pillaged part of Dalmatia. Then Vukan returned to Raška, leaving Kočapar as his man on the throne of Duklja. (This reverses the eleventh-century situation when the Dukljans were putting their men on the Raškan throne.) But very quickly, for some unknown reason, a break occurred between Vukan and Kočapar; possibly Kočapar was not satisfied to remain in this subordinate position. In any case Vukan sent troops to Duklja, forcing Kočapar to flee first to Bosnia and, later, to Zahumlje where he died. Next "the people" (presumably nobles) of Duklja held an assembly and ignoring the outside powers, elected as their ruler one Vladimir, the son of a Vladimir who was a son of King Michael. Milobar tentatively dates his reign 1103–14; these dates are by no means secure.

Meanwhile the Byzantines, to face a Norman attack, had assembled a large army which was gathered on the borders of Vukan's Raška. Vukan was worried that this army might attack him for eliminating the Byzantine vassal Dobroslav. Vukan's fears were quickly realized; the Norman Bohemund delayed his campaign, freeing Alexius to turn against Raška. Vukan immediately sent an embassy for peace and, though he had not kept promises before, Alexius accepted, for the emperor, worried about Bohemund, wanted in an emergency to be able to count on neutrality if not help from the Balkan Slavs. According to the Priest of Dioclea, twelve years of peace followed in Duklja, which suggests that to pacify the Byzantines, Vladimir must have accepted Byzantine suzerainty. Moreover, Vladimir married Vukan's daughter; thus good relations were reestablished between the two Serb states.

But all was not well, for Jakvinta, still ambitious for her sons, continued to intrigue. Now she was working on behalf of her (and Bodin's) son Juraj. She succeeded in giving Vladimir in Kotor a dose of a slow-working poison. He was carried ill to Skadar. Jakvinta arrived there right after him to try to secure the succession for Juraj. She tried to put the blame for the murder on Dobroslav (who had been transferred from a Raškan jail to one in Duklja where he had languished for about a decade). Vladimir did not listen to her but had her driven from Skadar; but Jakvinta continued to plot against Dobroslav whom she expected to be released from jail and restored to the throne on Vladimir's death. Therefore at Vladimir's death, Jakvinta's henchmen attacked the jail and captured Dobroslav whom they castrated and blinded. He was tonsured as a monk and then placed in a monastery in Skadar.

Jakvinta's son Juraj then ascended the throne. Milobar dates his reign 1114–18. However, more recent scholarship places all these events later and sets his accession at about 1118. Juraj seems to have had support from a local party opposed to the empire; after his succession, members of the family who had had close ties with the Byzantines fled to Durazzo. These included the surviving sons of Branislav who all escaped except for a certain Grubeša who was captured and jailed. Not surprisingly, the refugees sought and obtained Byzantine support. Soon a Byzantine army, accompanied by various members of the Dukljan royal family, was dispatched into Duklja from Durazzo. Juraj was driven out and Jakvinta was arrested and sent to Constantinople where she died.

Grubeša, released from jail, was then declared king. Since the invasion had been carried out in his name, perhaps he had been plotting prior to his arrest. Thus possibly Juraj, rather than being an initiator (who groundlessly tried to arrest the sons of Branislav), had been reacting to their plots against him, and thus had arrested Grubeša in self-defense.

In its discussion of these events the Chronicle of the Priest of Dioclea strongly favors the descendants of Branislav and thus depicts them as heroes while Bodin's heirs (particularly Jakvinta and Juraj) are cast as villains. Bias, therefore, should be added to the other difficulties presented by this source. As a result, this chronicle in supporting its favored family ends up also favoring the pro-Byzantine party, whose policy brought Duklja into a dependent position under Byzantine overlordship, and opposing Bodin's son who aimed for fuller independence.

After Grubeša gained the throne, word reached the Byzantine troops, stationed in Duklja in support of Grubeša, that Alexius was seriously ill in Constantinople. Thus finally a definite date exists—1118. The Byzantine commander, John Comnenus, was heir to the throne. Since he was faced with a possible challenge to his succession, the Byzantine forces withdrew to Durazzo, leaving only a few troops behind to support Grubeša. Juraj meanwhile fled to Raška to seek asylum from Vukan. Grubeša ruled until 1125 and during his reign Duklja enjoyed a period of peace.

However, in 1125, in the midst of a Hungarian-Byzantine war, Uroš I of Raška and Juraj, who lived at his court, attacked Duklja, ruled by the Byzantine ally Grubeša. Grubeša was killed and Juraj again became ruler of Duklja; but it seems that he did not hold it all. By then various cousins held territories and soon quarrels broke out between them and Juraj. The most prominent dissidents were Grubeša's three brothers, who had fled when Grubeša was killed. To prevent further intrigues which might have brought the Byzantines in to depose Juraj again, Juraj had invited the three back under oath and had given each an appanage. This peace did not last and two of the brothers fled to Durazzo. The Priest of Dioclea (who is biased in favor of the brothers and against Juraj) blames Juraj for this and claims he intended to jail them.

Once again a large Byzantine army entered Duklja and occupied much of the coast and the inland territory as far as Podgorica (modern Titograd). Juraj fled after blinding two prisoners—the third brother of Grubeša whom he had jailed and also ex-King Vladimir's son Michael. Michael had been plotting against Juraj (whose mother had murdered his father) and it seems he was also intriguing with the Byzantines. According to the biased Priest of Dioclea, the people hated Juraj and did not support him. The Byzantine commander next declared Gradinja, one of the brothers of Grubeša who had fled to Durazzo, king. He was to be the last ruler of Duklja to bear the title king. Juraj remained in the woods, carrying on a guerrilla war while Gradinja strengthened his ties with both Serbia and Byzantium. This phase of the struggle lasted for some time and was probably the most destructive part of this long civil war. Eventually another Byzantine expedition from Durazzo succeeded in capturing Juraj, and he was carried off to Constantinople where he died.

Gradinja ruled into the 1140s as a Byzantine vassal. As was usually the case, when a ruler of Duklja accepted Byzantine suzerainty (and when the leading fighters for independence were in exile) peace followed. Various people who had fled during the last civil war returned; however, intrigues and arrests continued. Gradinja eventually died a natural death in about 1146 and his eldest son, Radoslav, succeeded. He was personally installed, during a visit to Constantinople to pay homage, by the emperor Manuel Comnenus. He bore the title prince (knez) rather than king. Radoslav was hard pressed to maintain his state against pressure from the Serbs of Raška, who, by this time, had developed ambitions toward Duklja.

Hungary, Byzantium, and Serbia (Raška), 1100–1180

The Hungarians had gradually become a more active factor in the Balkans. They had occupied considerable territory nominally Byzantine, conquering Sirmium and the surrounding region of Srem. In addition they annexed Croatia in 1102 and took over, as well, various cities in Dalmatia which belonged to the empire. The Byzantines naturally felt concerned about this expansion and about the danger of further Hungarian actions against imperial territory.

King Koloman of Hungary, meanwhile, trying to guarantee succession for his own son Stephen, had blinded his own brother, Almos, and Almos's son, Bela. These two had then fled to Constantinople which was becoming a center for Hungarian dissidents. Constantinople may well have been chosen as a refuge partially because John Comnenus, heir to the throne, had married a Hungarian princess. When in 1116 Koloman died, his son Stephen succeeded as Stephen II.

A few years later a huge horde of "Scythians" crossed the Danube and plundered Thrace and Macedonia. Scholars have usually concluded these were Pechenegs but recent scholarship has shown them to be Cumans. John Comnenus marched out against them and won a terrific victory over them in 1122 or 1123. Many were captured; some of those taken as prisoners seem to have been settled in the empire and drafted into the imperial army. This event is relevant to our discussion of the Hungarians and Serbs because it is dated and chroniclers have placed other Balkan events in sequence with it.

According to one Byzantine source, Niketas Choniates, John, after his victory over the "Scythians," immediately turned against the Serbs and defeated them. However, a second Byzantine historian, Kinnamos, makes the war against the Serbs follow the Hungarian wars (to be discussed shortly), and since there is no sign of any Serb provocation this early, probably Choniates's story about the Serb war should be placed a little later. Kinnamos states that after his victory over the Scythians, the emperor was involved in affairs in Asia Minor.

Next, the Hungarians protested to the emperor about his harboring the blinded Almos and other Hungarian dissidents, but the Byzantines refused to give Almos up. Choniates adds that the Hungarians were also objecting to the treatment of Hungarian merchants by the local inhabitants of the important Byzantine border town of Braničevo (at the junction of the Morava and Danube rivers).

Since they received no satisfaction from the empire, the Hungarians attacked Byzantine territory. Choniates depicts it as an attack upon the relevant city of Braničevo. He states that the town was destroyed and the stones were taken from it to build the Hungarian city of Zemun (just across the river from Beograd). He claims they deeply penetrated imperial territory, reaching Sardika (Sofija) which they plundered. The emperor then sent out troops, defeated the Hungarians, and reestablished peace.

Kinnamos describes two Hungarian attacks. The first was directed against Beograd, from which Kinnamos says stones were taken to build Zemun. (Since Beograd is just across the river from Zemun, it is a more likely source for the stones than Braničevo.) The emperor responded by driving the Hungarians back and obtaining a peace which Kinnamos claims was immediately broken, for the next year the Hungarians launched a second attack, this time against Braničevo. Then the Serbs rose up and destroyed the fortress of Ras (then Byzantine but soon to be Serbian).

Unfortunately, neither author gives a date for any of these events. B. Radojčić believes that two Hungarian attacks occurred, and dates the attack on Beograd to 1125, the imperial campaign the same year, followed by a peace over the winter 1125–26, followed by the Hungarian attack on Braničevo in 1126 at roughly the same time as the Serb rising.[5]

The emperor immediately went into action; he attacked the Serbs first (and now we can utilize the data from Choniates's story which that author implies occurred three or so years earlier). The emperor won a decisive victory over the grand župan of Raška and seized much booty and took many prisoners. Some of the latter were settled as tax-paying farmers and as soldiers in Asia Minor, in particular in the region of Nicomedia. As a result the Serbs were forced again to acknowledge Byzantine suzerainty.

Having settled the Serbian question, the emperor moved on and defeated the Hungarians again, still in 1126, and forced peace upon them. The Hungarians were driven out of whatever eastern Balkan territory they had held and the empire recovered Braničevo, Beograd, Zemun, and the region of Sirmium (which had been Hungarian since the 1060s). Soon a major cause for the differences between the two states was removed when in 1129 Almos, the exiled claimant to the Hungarian throne protected by the Byzantines, died.

Radojčić's chronology makes sense, and I think it superior to other versions which assign different dates to these events; most frequently scholars have dated the Hungarian-Byzantine war to the period 1127–29 and some scholars have even placed the Serbian revolt as early as 1123 or 1124.

One addition should probably be made to Radojčić's version. If Yugoslav scholars have correctly dated events in the Dukljan civil war, then Raška's active opposition to Byzantine interests preceded the 1126 attack on Ras and went back at least to 1125—a year when the empire was also concerned with the Hungarians—for in 1125 Uroš aided Juraj to oust the pro-Byzantine ruler, Grubeša, and to recover the throne of Duklja.

The Hungarian king Stephen died in 1131. Having no son, shortly before his death he recognized as his heir Bela "the Blind," the son of Almos, also blinded by Koloman. Bela by then was back in Hungary and had married in about 1130 Jelena, daughter of Uroš I, grand župan of Raška. When he came to power Bela II (1131–41), presumably because of his blindness, relied a great deal on others and had particular confidence in his wife Jelena and her brother Beloš who also came to the Hungarian court. Thus with these two Serbs in such prominent positions it is not at all surprising that extremely close ties were established between Hungary and Raška in the years that followed. As Jelena's dowry the Hungarians received part of northern Serbia (probably northeastern Bosnia and Mačva, lying along the lower Drina) and the Serbs in exchange received further support in their struggle against Byzantium. Secondly both the Serbs and Hungarians negotiated with the Normans and marriage ties were established between the Hungarian and Norman royal houses.

In 1141 Bela II died and was succeeded by his son Geza II, who was still a child. Thus the Serbs at court—the boy's mother and uncle—not only retained power under the new ruler but increased it. Beloš became the official regent; in 1142 he took the title of ban of Croatia and Dalmatia (a position later often given to a younger son of the Hungarian king who was not heir to the throne) and in 1145 he became *comes palatinus* (count palatine), the highest Hungarian court title, the holder of which was a substitute for the king when necessary. Beloš was able and retained close ties with Serbia where by now his brother Uroš II had become grand župan. In times of trouble each was able to count on the other.

By this time the emperor in Byzantium was Manuel Comnenus (1143–80). He was attracted to the west and had visions of recovering Italy, but he also had serious reasons to worry about the west because of the Normans. In 1147 the Normans under Roger II seized Corfu, Corinth, and Thebes (the center of the Byzantine silk industry, whose weavers were captured and taken off to Palermo in Sicily to establish a weaving industry there). Manuel, having defeated a Cuman attack in 1148, made an alliance with the Germans to support his war against the Normans. In 1149 he began his offensive against them. In that year with Venetian aid he recovered Corfu.

Meanwhile the Serbs, Hungarians, and Normans were exchanging envoys; it is not clear who initiated these discussions but it certainly was in the Normans' interests to stop Manuel's plans. In any case, Manuel was at Avlona preparing to launch an offensive across the Adriatic when he learned that the Serbs had revolted. This uprising entailed more than just throwing off allegiance to Byzantium. First there was danger that the Serbs might strike at the Byzantine Adriatic bases while the Byzantines were attacking Italy. Secondly, the Serbs had taken the offensive against a loyal Byzantine vassal; they had attacked Radoslav of Duklja and had forced him to take refuge in Kotor. The Serbs (Uroš II and his brother Desa) occupied much of inland Duklja and Trebinje, leaving Radoslav only the coastal territory. Thus with Radoslav driven into the very southwest corner of his realm, about two thirds of Duklja was in Serbian hands. Radoslav turned for help to his Byzantine overlord, and aid was sent from Durazzo. Just at this moment the Chronicle of the Priest of Dioclea ends; presumably its author died.

A major Balkan war was on the verge of breaking out; for after their attack on Duklja, making probable a major Byzantine response, the two Raškan brothers, Uroš and Desa, had sought aid from their third brother Beloš in Hungary. It is not clear whether any aid was sent at once but Hungarian troops were to play an active role in Serbia by 1150.

Manuel, seeing this situation developing in his rear, decided to delay his attack on the Normans. He sent troops from Avlona into Raška where they quickly captured the Serbs' major fortresses including Ras (by now Serbian). Uroš fled to the mountains, carrying on a guerrilla war marked by hit-and-run attacks and ambushes and the avoidance of any major encounters. Thus the Byzantines achieved no major success against his armies, despite their capture of various forts. In 1150 more Byzantine troops arrived, and in that year for the first time sources mention the presence of Hungarian troops who had responded to the Serbian call. After several minor skirmishes the Byzantine army met the Serbs and Hungarians on the River Tara in 1150 and the Byzantines gained a major victory. A great deal of devastation of Serbia followed. After this victory, Manuel, following the policy of his father, resettled many captured Serbs elsewhere in the empire; some were settled in the region around Sardika.

After the Byzantine victory, the defeated Uroš was briefly deprived of his rule; the Byzantines replaced him with his brother Desa. However, Uroš asked for mercy from the emperor and was allowed to regain his position as grand župan of Serbia. Thus the old ties of vassalage were restored between Raška and the empire. By the treaty Serbia promised military aid for Byzantine wars and recognized the obligation to provide two thousand men for western campaigns and five hundred men for eastern campaigns. This turns out not to be a new obligation, for the agreement states that previously the Serbs had owed three hundred men for Asia and implies that the obligation to send two thousand men for western campaigns had applied earlier. A final result of this warfare was the restoration of Radoslav as the ruler of all of Duklja. He remained a Byzantine vassal. If previous Byzantine action in 1149 had not succeeded in driving the Raškans from Duklja, them presumably the treaty in 1150 brought about their withdrawal.

The Hungarian assistance to the Raškans must have wakened Manuel to the Hungarian danger, for in 1151 he declared war against Hungary and sent troops through the Balkans into the region of Sirmium and then across the Danube. Zemun was besieged. These armies caused a great deal of destruction, and took many captives, who were subsequently settled in underpopulated regions of the empire. There was no occupation of Hungarian territory, however, for this was purely a punitive campaign; after its completion the Byzantine armies withdrew. Geza soon negotiated a treaty with Byzantium. Over the next twenty years, however, there were to be ten Byzantine campaigns against Hungary. As a result of them Manuel was able to keep the Hungarian advance into the Balkans under control but this was at the expense of his goals against the Normans in Italy. Manuel did not consciously give up his Italian goals, but they were nevertheless abandoned because of his Balkan activities.

In 1150 the defeated Uroš had been forced to accept Byzantine overlordship. This pro-Byzantine result seems to have been upsetting to the pro-Hungarian faction at the Raškan court and in 1155, these people ousted Uroš and replaced him with his brother Desa. The Byzantines sent troops in, deposed Desa, and restored Uroš. Uroš on the occasion reaffirmed his Byzantine alliance and renounced any alliance with Hungary. Desa was granted the region of Dendra (near Niš) and a definite border was established between his appanage and the lands of Uroš. The Byzantine armies then withdrew taking Serbian hostages back to Constantinople.

In 1162 Geza died, leaving two sons. The elder was his successor Stephen III and the younger son was named Bela (later to become Bela III). However, in Constantinople resided two younger sons of Bela II "The Blind" (grandsons of Almos, younger brothers of Geza, and uncles of Stephen III), and unfortunately the one who concerns us was also named Stephen; since he briefly was to hold the Hungarian throne he was to become known as Stephen IV. The Byzantines supported Stephen IV and succeeded in placing him on the Hungarian throne for a short time. But then Beloš, the regent and brother of the Raškan ruler, ousted him from power and took him prisoner. However, through an agreement he released Stephen IV and allowed him to return to Byzantium. Once there in ca. 1163, Stephen IV and the Byzantines immediately began planning a new campaign to recover the Hungarian throne.

Meanwhile in Serbia, Desa had once again replaced Uroš as grand župan. What had happened there is not at all clear. According to Kinnamos, who gives no dates, at some time before 1163 the Byzantines removed a Serbian grand župan named Primislav; they briefly replaced him with his brother Beloš; but then Beloš went off to Hungary and the emperor replaced him with his younger brother Desa. This account provides one more example of successful imperial interference inside Serbia and shows the balance of power between the two states. But beyond these obvious conclusions, scholars have argued heatedly about this story.

Until now Kinnamos has not referred to Primislav, nor is this name mentioned in any other source. Since he is clearly a brother of Desa, either Primislav was another name for Uroš II (as probably the majority of scholars have concluded) or else Primislav was a fourth brother who had somehow replaced Uroš and had a brief fling at ruling before he was overthrown.

Next comes the question, did Beloš leave Hungary briefly to take the Raškan throne? If Kinnamos is accurate here, that must be what happened, for the Hungarian official Beloš was Desa's brother, and the Hungarian connection of Kinnamos's Beloš is clearly stated; for after a very brief rule Kinnamos states Beloš left for Hungary. Thus, if his account is correct, Beloš had left Hungary for a short time; perhaps he had been forced to flee by events following the death of Geza II in 1162. He may have had to flee when Stephen IV took over in Hungary.

However, as noted above, Stephen IV had held power only briefly and then Beloš had quickly overthrown him. Quite possibly Beloš had gone to Serbia, raised an army, and then launched his successful campaign against Stephen from Serbia. The victory over Stephen IV would then have made it possible for Beloš to return to Hungary. Quite possibly Kinnamos had such an event in mind when he said Beloš went off to Hungary. Beloš, by departing, evidently preferred Hungary to Serbia; quite possibly he voluntarily gave up his rule there. It is also possible that he had tried to hold both states but Manuel objected to seeing so much power in the hands of one Serb, particularly an unreliable one who had fought Byzantium before. In any case, Desa was the Raškan ruler by 1163. Presumably the initial Byzantine interference came about because the Serbian grand župan Primislav (or Uroš if the two are the same) had shown too much independence. These events occurred at some time between 1155 and 1162. Most scholars place them 1161–62.

The Byzantines meanwhile were bent on restoring Stephen IV to the throne of Hungary. They aimed thereby to obtain a loyal vassal and to regain the Sirmium region and Hungarian Dalmatia. The emperor with his army marched northward and called on Desa as his vassal to mobilize his army and meet the emperor and imperial army at Niš, after which the two armies together would march on Hungary. Desa, as the brother of Beloš who was supporting the legitimate King Stephen III, was not enthusiastic about this plan and only the threat of a Byzantine attack against Serbia (or possibly a real attack because one source has Desa taken prisoner) forced Desa to appear at Niš with his army. Since the sources tell different and not particularly precise stories it is not certain exactly what happened. In any case in one way or another Desa was forced to comply with Manuel's wishes.

The Byzantine army then proceeded to march toward Hungary. Most scholars date this march to 1163 though Browning suggests it occurred in 1164.[6] En route Manuel came to realize how unpopular Stephen IV was in Hungary. Presumably Desa, if he was present on this march, played a role in causing the emperor to change his mind. When the emperor reached the border he sent an envoy to the Hungarian court to treat with Stephen III.

The treaty recognized Stephen III as ruler of Hungary. His younger brother Bela was to come to Byzantium and be betrothed to Manuel's daughter. If Manuel did not have a son, Bela would become heir to the Byzantine throne, and if Stephen III had no children, Bela would also become king of Hungary. Thus on paper, if neither ruler had a male heir, Bela would become emperor of Byzantium and king of Hungary and thereby unite the two states and form a vast empire.

If realized, such a union would have doomed the independence of the Slavs—the Serbs and Bulgarians—living between Byzantium and Hungary for however long such a union lasted. Whether such a thing was feasible in reality in the context of actual Byzantine politics is a matter for dispute, but Manuel, as we shall see, was serious about the idea.

Moreover, it had already become customary for the Hungarian king to make a younger son who was not heir to the throne ban of an independent banovina or appanage as compensation. The ban was able to rule this territory and collect income from it, but was not allowed independence in foreign affairs. He remained subject to the Hungarian king and was obliged to provide military service to the king. In the course of the twelfth century it had become customary to make Croatia that appanage, and Geza II had therefore made his younger son Bela ban of Croatia and Dalmatia. Croatia in this context included the territory south of the Krka River. Furthermore this banovina included part of the region of Srem (Sirmium). According to the treaty between Manuel and Stephen III, Bela should be allowed to retain this appanage even after he came to Constantinople. In this way Byzantium would regain this long-disputed territory.

What immediately followed this treaty is not clear. But it seems that the Hungarians did not consider Srem as part of the territory to be included in Bela's appanage, and thus they continued to occupy it. Angry, Manuel in 1165—claiming Srem was Bela's—sent troops against Hungary to occupy Zemun. The Hungarians then besieged the city and retook it. As a result Manuel himself led a second Byzantine army and retook the city for the Byzantines. A new treaty followed in which the Hungarians again recognized Bela's possession of his appanage and now admitted that the appanage included Srem—meaning Byzantine occupation of Srem—while the Byzantines once again recognized Stephen III as king of Hungary.

Bela meanwhile was living in Constantinople; there he took the name Alexius, accepted the Orthodox faith and received the title of despot (an honorary court title which by then was the second title in the empire after emperor). Two years later he was officially engaged to Manuel's daughter Maria and the two were declared heirs to the throne; Byzantine generals and court officials were made to take oaths to them. Protocol lists placed Bela's name right after Manuel's. Thus it is evident that Manuel was serious about this plan and really intended Bela to be his heir.

Meanwhile almost immediately after the second treaty between Byzantium and Stephen III, the dropped candidate Stephen IV made a new attempt for the Hungarian throne (presumably on his own initiative). The Hungarians had, according to the second treaty, evacuated Srem; but now Stephen IV appeared in Srem, trying to contact supporters in Hungary and planning an attack on Hungary. He then invaded Hungarian territory in 1165 or 1166, but picking up little support, he quickly retreated to Srem. The Hungarian troops of Stephen III, not surprisingly, pursued him into Srem; as a result of this pursuit the Hungarians found themselves in Byzantine territory, though of course attacking Stephen IV and not Byzantium. It is also evident that the Byzantines by not stopping Stephen IV's activities had failed to live up to the treaty. In any case in the course of this attack the Hungarians overran the Byzantine garrison and occupied the fortress of Sirmium.

Manuel once again accused Stephen III of violating their treaty, and the emperor began negotiating with Venice for joint action against the Hungarians in Dalmatia. A major Byzantine invasion of Dalmatia followed which took Trogir, Šibenik, Split, Skradin, Ostrovica, Salona, and a town whose name varies in different manuscripts but probably is Klis (one later manuscript, often cited, says Dioclea; but its conquest would be highly unlikely in this context). The Kačići (the ruling family of the Neretljani on the lower Neretva) were also subdued. Altogether, Kinnamos tells us, fifty-seven towns were taken. Next the Byzantines sent troops to aid Stephen IV. But he was poisoned and the Byzantines ascribed this act to the machinations of Stephen III. The Byzantine armies then regained Sirmium and also Zemun and a new peace was concluded between the Byzantines and Hungarians.

Matters were not yet quiet for later in 1166 warfare again broke out, though it is not known what provoked it. At that time a Hungarian army defeated a Byzantine army in Srem while a second Hungarian army attacked Dalmatia. Finally in July 1167 a massive Byzantine victory took place at Zemun which smashed the Hungarian armies and peace followed. The Hungarians now accepted the loss of Srem, Dalmatia, and part of Croatia (i.e., that part included in the banovina under Bela). Inland Croatia south of the Krka River, including Bosnia, went to Byzantium while the rest of Pannonian Croatia north of that river remained Hungarian. It is not clear whether in 1167 Byzantium had recovered all the relevant Dalmatian cities or whether some were surrendered by treaty. But in any case after 1167 Byzantium held Dalmatia, part of Croatia, Bosnia, and Srem. It retained this territory for the rest of Manuel's reign. He was to die in 1180.

Byzantium and Venice

Venice was most unhappy with the renewed Byzantine presence in Dalmatia. Tensions soon developed between the two states, leading to a sudden overnight arrest of all Venetians in the Byzantine empire on 12 March 1171. At the same time the Venetians' property was confiscated from their warehouses. This set off a Byzantine-Venetian war which seems to have continued for a decade during which the Venetians sacked various Greek islands. This war was a factor in turning Venice even more strongly against Byzantium; relations went from bad to worse until the Venetians turned the Fourth Crusade against Constantinople itself in 1204 and conquered it, establishing the Latin Empire.

Byzantium and Hungary, 1169–80

Meanwhile in 1169 Manuel finally had a son (Alexius) and made him his heir. Bela lost the title of despot for the lesser title of caesar. His engagement to Maria was also broken off. Thus the plans to unite Byzantium and Hungary were now scrapped. However, Manuel still hoped to make Hungary a closer vassal of Byzantium through Bela who remained the heir to the Hungarian throne since Stephen III was still childless. Bela, though demoted, was not disgraced; he remained a member of the imperial family and soon married the stepsister of Manuel's wife.

In 1172 Stephen III died childless at the age of twenty-four, and Bela, according to the agreement, was escorted by the Byzantine army to the Hungarian border. There he was met by a Hungarian escort. Most of the country was ready to accept him and the little opposition to him that existed dissolved when Bela returned to Roman Catholicism. Before his departure Bela took an oath of allegiance to Byzantium and Manuel. He strictly observed this oath for the duration of Manuel's life, eight more years. During this period Bela never tried to regain Srem, Croatia, or Dalmatia and he even sent troops to aid the Byzantines against the Seljuks of Iconium (Konya) in Anatolia in 1176.

Stefan Nemanja Establishes a New Dynasty in the Serbian Lands

Up to this point a variety of Serbian revolts (often aided by Hungary) had occurred. The Byzantines each time were able to put down the uprising but Serbia never remained pacified. Even when the Byzantines changed rulers in Serbia—as they did upon occasion—they could not prevent new revolts from breaking out. Between 1166 and 1168 a major change occurred in Raška. The old dynasty was replaced by a new one, headed at first by a certain Tihomir who was quickly replaced by his brother Stefan Nemanja. This dynasty was to reign in Serbia until 1371.

Where the founders of this new dynasty came from and what—if any—connection they had to the preceding dynasty is a matter of great controversy and unfortunately is really unknown. It is possible that this family was installed by Manuel. A Byzantine oration, published by Browning, referring to events of about 1166 states that Manuel easily reduced the Serbs to submission; they repented and accepted the ruler you [Manuel] appointed over them.[7] This suggests a change of ruler occurred there in about 1166—roughly the date Tihomir came to power. Thus quite possibly Desa did something to displease Manuel leading once again to Byzantine intervention and a change on the Serbian throne. Since the time is right perhaps Tihomir was the ruler appointed over the Serbs by Manuel.

In any case by 1168 Serbian territory was divided among four brothers (or cousins as one scholar has suggested since the term *brother* on occasion can mean a cousin): Tihomir, Stefan Nemanja, Miroslav, and Stracimir. The eldest, Tihomir, bore the title of grand župan. Nemanja quickly drove him out of Serbia and assumed that title. Tihomir fled to Byzantium where he sought aid. He returned with Byzantine troops but in the ensuing battle he was killed. The Byzantine army was also defeated. This occurred in about 1171.

Since the Byzantines were becoming involved in a war with Venice they could not immediately become engaged in Serbian affairs, but in 1172 the emperor Manuel led an army into Serbia. Like Vukan before him, Nemanja saw it was pointless to resist; so he went forth to surrender and submit to the emperor. The emperor made him go through a humiliating ceremony at the imperial camp and then took him back to Constantinople for another humiliating ceremony there, featuring long orations celebrating his submission. (Some wall paintings depicting this ceremony survive to the present day.) Then, as a sworn loyal vassal, Nemanja was allowed to return to Serbia as its grand župan. Nemanja, too, remained loyal to this oath for the duration of Manuel's life.

While Nemanja held Raška, his brother Miroslav became ensconced in Hum (formerly called Zahumlje). Duklja, which by this time was coming to be called Zeta, was soon conquered by Nemanja and became a possession of his family. The conquest of Zeta may well have occurred in the 1180s. When Nemanja abdicated in 1196 Zeta was assigned to his eldest son, Vukan, as an appanage.

Byzantium's Position in the Balkans in the 1170s

Thus, by 1172, Manuel had recovered all of the Balkans except for what is now Slovenia and the Croatian territory north of the Krka River which was retained by Hungary. But the Hungarian presence was not a major danger because the Hungarian throne was then occupied by a king (Bela III) who had sworn allegiance to the empire. Dalmatia, part of inland Croatia, Bosnia, and Srem had been recovered from Hungary. One suspects that in part of this recovered territory—Croatia and

Bosnia—there was little or no direct imperial rule and these lands remained in the hands of local nobles who only nominally accepted Byzantine suzerainty.

Byzantine control of Dalmatia suffered one brief setback. In the course of the Venetian-Byzantine war in ca. 1172, Venice was to attack and capture certain Dalmatian cities—including Trogir and Dubrovnik—but an epidemic and Byzantine military action soon forced them out. The Serbian lands—Raška, Zeta, and Hum—were under vassal princes who at the time were loyal to the empire; and Bulgaria and Macedonia were of course still annexed and under the regular Byzantine theme administration.

Postscript to This Section

It is here that this volume's coverage of the central and eastern Balkans ends. Their subsequent history will be traced in the second volume. This postscript will present just a brief look ahead at the immediate aftermath which will be treated in detail in the second volume.

Manuel died in 1180 and a brief and unsuccessful regency for his minor son Alexius followed. What had held Bela III of Hungary and Nemanja of Serbia loyal had been personal ties to Manuel. Now those ties were broken, and in 1181 Bela recovered Srem, Dalmatia, and most probably Croatia as well. It seems this was a bloodless recovery, and perhaps the Byzantines even acquiesced in it. It was a time of anarchy and intrigue at home and Byzantium was in no position to send troops to Dalmatia. Presumably it seemed better to have friendly Hungary obtain Dalmatia than Venice with whom Byzantium was at war. Venice in fact had already recovered Zadar and the Hungarians had to take it by force in February 1181. Venice, after an unsuccessful attempt to regain Zadar in 1193, was to obtain it in 1203 when it turned the Fourth Crusade against the city. Immediately after Manuel's death Nemanja declared his independence.

Meanwhile the regency for young Alexius was unpopular, and an elderly cousin named Andronicus Comnenus, who had long been a dissident against Manuel and had been exiled all over the map, appeared with an army in Asia Minor. At first he seemed appealing to the population of Constantinople. He was willing to pose as being anti-western (and the westerners under Manuel's widow held great influence) and antirich; and he was to ride to power on the coattails of a revolt in which hundreds of westerners in the city of Constantinople were massacred. He awaited the end of the bloodbath, and then entered the city, whose gates were opened to him. He became regent for the little boy in 1183. He quickly had Alexius's mother murdered, then made himself coemperor, and finally had Alexius strangled. As a result he became the sole emperor. These murders gave Bela the opportunity to step forward to avenge the victims. Bela's wife was the stepsister of Manuel's murdered widow. Bela moved at once and occupied Beograd and Braničevo, and then picking up the Serbs as allies, he headed down the main invasion route (the Orient Express route), driving out imperial garrisons from Niš and Sardika and sacking both towns. Six years later passing Crusaders spoke of both towns being deserted and partly in ruins. The allies then moved through the Balkans toward the capital. The Hungarians were to keep control of this route and the towns along it for the next three years.

Stefan Nemanja, meanwhile, if he had not earlier, began expanding both to the south and west to annex all of Zeta which was now incorporated into his state of Raška. Thus Raška and Zeta became a single principality under him and no territory remained in the hands of the old Dukljan-Zetan dynasty.

At home Andronicus was fighting corruption, but he also seems to have been intent on eliminating the powerful and avenging himself on those who had opposed him before. Falling victim to a persecution mania, he unleashed a reign of terror in the city, leading to various plots against him. The Hungarians, in occupation of much of the central and eastern Balkans, were approaching the capital, and then in 1185 the Normans launched an attack on Durazzo. The commander immediately surrendered the city to them, for he was opposed to Andronicus. The Norman army then moved across the Balkans toward Thessaloniki while the Norman fleet occupied Corfu, and then sailed around into the Aegean, occupying various other islands. In August 1185, this fleet finally reached Thessaloniki. The army arrived there at about the same time and after a brief siege the Normans took Thessaloniki and sacked it. Part of the Norman army then moved on toward Serres while the rest headed for Constantinople. This set off a revolt in the city against Andronicus, who was overthrown and tortured to death.

The revolt placed Isaac Angelus (1185–95), a cousin of the Comneni, on the throne. He soon succeeded in chasing the Normans out of the Balkans. Bela then withdrew his troops as well, and recognized Isaac as emperor. Shortly thereafter Isaac married Bela's daughter Margaret. In the marriage agreement Bela consented to withdraw all his troops beyond the Danube in exchange for Byzantine recognition of Hungarian possession of the Dalmatian cities. In 1195, Bela was prepared to aid Isaac against a rebellion in Bulgaria; but then, later in

1195, Isaac was deposed by his brother and the campaign never took place.

Bela's death in the following year ended the period of cooperation between Byzantium and Hungary. In the next decade this alliance was totally disrupted, and communications were cut off by the emergence of independent Slavic states in the territory between them—in Raška (under Nemanja), in Bulgaria (which revolted successfully against the Byzantines in 1185 and established once again an independent state north of the Balkan mountains known as the Second Bulgarian Empire), and in Bosnia (which though under theoretical Hungarian suzerainty was able to establish an independent state in the 1180s under Ban Kulin). These three states, all emerging at roughly the same time (accompanied by the successful attempts of great magnates in Greece and Thrace to secede from the empire and hack out independent petty principalities) mark the beginning of a new period for the Balkans. That period will be treated in the second volume.

NOTES

1. J. Ferluga, "Les insurrections des Slaves de la Macédoine au XIe siècle," in J. Ferluga, *Byzantium on the Balkans* (Amsterdam, 1976), pp. 379–97.

2. V. Mošin, "O periodizacii russko-južnoslavjanskih literaturnyh svjazej X–XV vv," *Trudy otdela drevnerusskoj literatury* 19 (1963):54–69.

3. *Istorija Crne Gore*, vol. I, od najstarijih vremena do kraja XII vieka [a collective work] (Titograd, 1967), p. 396.

4. Little attention is paid to the split between Rome and Constantinople in this volume since in this early period it had little effect on the South Slav states. The different states remained under the jurisdiction of their previous church suzerain; their rulers on occasions carried on relations with both Rome and Constantinople and showed no particular hostility toward either side on this issue. Probably the majority of the population was unaware that the break had even occurred. Readers interested in learning more about the background and immediate causes of the schism which was to have such tremendous consequences for Christians of both the East and the West are referred to S. Runciman, *The Eastern Schism* (Oxford, 1955).

5. B. Radojčić, "O hronologiji ugarsko-vizantijskih borbi i ustanku Srba za vreme Jovana II Komnina," *ZRVI* 7 (1961):177–86.

6. R. Browning, "A New Source on Byzantine-Hungarian Relations in the Twelfth Century," *Balkan Studies* 2, no. 2 (1961):173–214.

7. Ibid.

CHAPTER 8

Croatia and Dalmatia

Sources on Medieval Croatia

Early medieval Croatian history fits the concluding line to the old jingle: the more you study the less you know. When I was an undergraduate studying Balkan history I thought I knew quite a bit about Croatia; but as I study more about Croatia, one by one the "facts" that I knew before turn out to be dubious, based on questionable sources or no sources at all. Most of the existing literature in western languages on medieval Croatia is extremely poor; and frequently it is marred by nationalistic bias.

A basic problem making early Croatian history difficult for everyone—including the most serious scholars—is the scarcity of sources and the question of the authenticity of some of the few that do exist. Furthermore, the authors of most of the sources for early medieval Croatia were distant from the events they described. Either they lived in places distant from Croatia (e.g., Byzantium, Italy) or they lived several centuries later. Byzantine writers knew little about Croatia. Examples of the difficulties they had in understanding Croatia were seen in chapter 2 when we discussed Constantine Porphyrogenitus's treatment of the early history of the Croatians. Most Byzantine historians did not mention Croatia at all.

Much of the information about medieval Croatian history comes from later (seventeenth- and eighteenth-century) narrative histories. These were written by enthusiastic people but contain a mixture of fact and legend; and since many of the documents they based their works on are now lost, it is extremely difficult to judge whether their information came from reliable sources or not.

Typical is a massive history of the South Slavic bishoprics, carried out by three Jesuits (over three generations), which was published between 1751 and 1819. The work is attributed to Farlati—the Jesuit of the second generation—who brought out the first and next several volumes. This project was far too ambitious, and though the attempt was highly admirable, many of their results must be treated with scepticism. Their method was to rapidly visit all the archives and monasteries they knew of and to hire in them monks or scribes to copy documents for them while they rushed off to the next archive. Eventually their volumes were compiled chiefly from these copies.

By now many of the original documents from which their copies came are lost, so modern scholars cannot properly evaluate much of their information. Some of their documents can now be shown to have been forgeries. Farlati and his associates were not experts in the study of documents and in addition when they were compiling their work they were not working with the original documents but with copies, which not only could contain copying errors but also lacked the external features (handwriting, paper, watermarks, seals, etc.) that might show that certain documents were not what they purported to be. Thus, like most of the early historians of the seventeenth and eighteenth centuries they were uncritical of their texts. They seem to have concluded that each document was of equal value and as a result they have presented a mixture of authentic sources and forgeries; in the absence of the originals in many cases no way is provided for us to judge which is which.

In fact, when we discover in secondary works very strange myths and often impossibilities for which no medieval documentation exists, the best place to seek their source is in Farlati and in some of the other early narrative historians of the South Slavs. Thus these early historical works are the basis for a vast number of errors, stories, and legends passed off as history in subsequent works on Croatia and Bosnia and the basis for much of the poor historiography of these regions.

One must treat these regions on the basis of existing documents whose authenticity can be verified and not accept as certain anything in these earlier historians that is not confirmed by other sources. Thus one must rely on Byzantine contemporary writing (keeping in mind Byzantium's distance from Croatian events), papal letters, Hungarian letters, conciliar records and diplomatic reports from Dubrovnik, and the existing charters. However, one must also beware of charters for many of them are later fabrications; some are clearly so (though even these are still used from time to time by various historians) while the authenticity of others is in dispute among scholars.

Many Croatian documents, including the texts of certain charters and church council acts, have not survived in the original but exist only as they have been copied in later historical accounts. In some cases these documents appear in Latin translations instead of Slavic originals. In others, documents appear in histories aimed at building up the prestige of a family, city, or bishopric, e.g., Thomas the Archdeacon of Split's *History of Split*. This history presents a vast number of problems. Its author died in 1268; his work survives in a short version and a long version. The long version—known as *Historia Salonitana maior* (HSM)—is a sixteenth-century expansion of Thomas by an unknown author. Whether any of these additions go back to Thomas's time (or close to it) or whether some or all were added in the sixteenth century is not known. We also do not know what the documentary base for the additions was and whether reliable sources about some or many of these earlier events still existed in Split in the sixteenth century. Various documents which these works—particularly HSM—provide are given nowhere else; for example, HSM is the only source to describe the important church councils in Split in 925 and 928.

Thomas's *History* and HSM were both written to glorify the city of Split and its church. Both claimed that Split was a successor to the ancient metropolitanate of Salona (which fell in 614). According to HSM, the two church councils of 925 and 928 gave Split jurisdiction over all the Adriatic cities from Kotor to Istria on the basis of this historical succession. Thomas's work (the earlier source) ignores both councils. Did they really take place? Most scholars conclude that they did. If so, Thomas probably omitted them because their decisions gave to Split what he claimed Split had possessed ever since the seventh century (i.e., suzerainty over the Byzantine Dalmatian churches). But if this conclusion is a correct one, can HSM's account of the councils be trusted? Did the sixteenth-century author of HSM have accurate sources to work with some six hundred years after the councils had taken place? And, if he did have good sources, can the author of HSM be trusted not to have altered certain canons to serve the interests of his see?

Both authors—in particular Thomas—had contempt for the Slavonic liturgy. Thomas gives an account of the 1060 Council of Split which condemned this liturgy. No other text of this council's deliberations has survived, though in this case a papal letter from 1063 confirms in general terms what Thomas says in more detail; both Thomas and the pope claim that the 1060 council passed articles against Slavonic. But Thomas reports that this council condemned Methodius as a heretic, stating,

> The council condemned the Service of God in Slavic and only allowed it in Latin or Greek and stated that Gothic [*sic*] letters were created by a certain heretic Methodius who wrote in the

same Slavic language many lies against the doctrines of the Roman Catholic Church.

Could the council really have stated this? Methodius (in the mid-ninth century) had had papal support at first and had even been appointed bishop of Sirmium by the pope. Had the Roman Catholic view—or at least the view of certain Catholic circles—of Methodius changed that much by the 1060s? Or was Thomas inserting his own views and claiming they were the views of the council?

The question of sources is basic for other major issues too; for example, the so-called pact between the Hungarian king and the Croatian nobility of 1102 which set up a dual monarchy under the king of Hungary survives only in a fourteenth-century manuscript. Many scholars feel this text reflects the fourteenth-century situation and not the twelfth. Was there really any such agreement in 1102? If so, does the fourteenth-century manuscript render its terms accurately or were these terms altered in the fourteenth century to serve the purposes of fourteenth-century figures?

These problems shall be discussed in the narrative that follows, but it seems important to preface this discussion of Croatian history with a word of warning about the nature of the sources and the problems connected with them.

Croatia from the Seventh Century to 969

Although some of the Croatians who lived in central Croatia and what is now Bosnia threw off the Avars in the seventh century and lived in independent groups under their župans (Constantine Porphyrogenitus listed eleven župas), the Croatians to the north in Pannonian Croatia, though under their own prince, seem to have remained in a position of some dependence on the Avars. By the late eighth century the original Iranian Croatians had become assimilated by the Slavs, and became for all practical purposes Slavs speaking a Slavic language.

Franks Establish Overlordship over Pannonian and
Dalmatian Croatia

In 788 Charlemagne (Charles the Great, king of the Franks), having conquered Lombardy, turned further east and subjugated Istria. This brought him into contact with the declining but still existing Avar khaganate in Pannonia with its center on the Tisza River. Charles launched his first campaign against the Avars in 791, and after gaining various successes returned for a second campaign in 795–96, which more or less destroyed Avar power. At least, it seems to have eliminated an independent Avar state. A small khaganate, vassal to the Franks, under Christian khagans, existed until at least 822. Bands of Avar nomads are mentioned off and on in the ninth century. Krum had dealings with them in the first decade of the ninth century and Frankish troops defeated some Avars as late as 863. After that they disappear from history. Charlemagne took possession of the incredible booty amassed by the Avars over the centuries and needed fifteen large wagons each with four oxen to cart the gold, silver, and gems back to Aachen.

Refugees from the Avar khaganate—both Avars and Bulgars—fled east, many settling in Bulgaria or in the regions near its western borders, and it seems likely that the great Bulgar khan Krum had his origin among these Bulgars from Pannonia. In any case when the dust settled at the beginning of the ninth century the Franks were overlords over the territory as far east as the Tisza River.

The Croatians of Pannonia and Slavonia were under a prince named Vojnomir who had supported the soldiers of Charlemagne in the Frankish campaigns against the Avars. After the defeat of the Avars, in the 790s, he accepted Frankish overlordship. The Franks placed these Croatians under the margrave of Friuli, who tried to extend his rule over the Croatians of Dalmatia. Soon, with Frankish blessing, missionaries began entering the territory of the Pannonian Croatians from Aquileia. The Franks assigned this region to the bishop of Aquileia, a city in the March north of Slovenia and on the northern coast of the Adriatic in the border region between modern Italy and Yugoslavia. Possibly some missionaries from Dalmatia had entered Pannonian Croatia earlier; but probably most of their efforts had been among the Slavs along the Dalmatian coast.

On Christmas Day 800, the pope crowned Charlemagne emperor. According to the belief at the time, there was one God, one world, one church, and one empire; hence there could be but one emperor. Thus this coronation was a direct challenge to Byzantium's claim to be the one—the Roman—empire. Charles's justification was that the Byzantine Empire was at the time being ruled by a woman (Irene) and a woman could not be emperor. Thus he was the one emperor. At first Byzantium simply ignored his pretensions but then in 802 Nicephorus became emperor in the east; once again there was a man bearing the title emperor on the Byzantine throne. At the same time Charles's subordinates were pressing into Dalmatia which was theoretically Byzantine territory.

Dalmatia was chiefly in the hands of Slavic tribes. North of Dubrovnik these came to be under Croatian župans and eventually came to consider themselves Croatians, while many of those to the south of Dubrovnik were coming to consider themselves Serbs. Many of these Slavs were active and successful pirates against the settled Roman society which still existed in their midst. We have noted that most of the islands and a small number of walled cities held out (e.g., Budva, Kotor, Dubrovnik, Split, Trogir, Zadar). They were Roman or Italian in character and language and still nominally under Byzantine suzerainty, but administering themselves under their own town councils and law. They maintained contact with the Italian towns by sea and very rarely communicated with Constantinople. After the fall of Salona, Zadar became the most important city in Dalmatia from an administrative standpoint whereas Split became the cultural center.

The more southerly coastal regions (Ionian) were being reclaimed by the empire in the early ninth century and the Byzantines established a theme in Durazzo. This was a small theme which included only the city and its hinterland. It was established, probably in the first decade of the ninth century, and was the only place on the Adriatic directly under Byzantine rule. A fleet was based there and Durazzo was the center for Byzantine activity for the whole Adriatic. From here expeditions were sent out to patrol the coast, suppress piracy, and defend the coast from the Arabs.

Meanwhile the Franks were pressing into Dalmatia. From 803, Frankish overlordship was recognized in most of northern Dalmatia. As a result of this expansion, Frankish missionaries under the jurisdiction of the metropolitan of Aquileia appeared in Dalmatia as well. Nin, a port near Zadar, became the residence of a Croatian prince named Višeslav (ca. 800–ca. 810). He is spoken of as a Christian, which reflects at least some success by the missionaries. Most of Croatian Dalmatia (i.e., the towns and countryside settled by Slavs along Dalmatia, but not including the Byzantine cities) was under Višeslav. It seems his territory stretched from the Adriatic inland to the Vrbas River and extended roughly from modern Rijeka down the coast as far south as the Cetina River. Possibly he was pro-Frank and had obtained their aid in extending his control over Dalmatia. In any case it makes sense to conclude that the campaigns of the Franks, followed by their recognition of a single Croatian prince (or duke) in Dalmatia, had done much to unite under one Croatian leader the many Croatian counties or tribes in Dalmatia, which previously had been separate and under their own leadership. It is often said that the Franks established a bishopric at Nin in about 803. However, there is little evidence for this and probably the Nin see dates from the middle of the ninth century.

The Roman Dalmatian cities, meanwhile, each had a bishop, who presided over a tiny diocese including little more territory than the city itself. They were, it seems, under the archbishop of Split, who, though his city was politically under the Byzantines, was under papal jurisdiction. (The act of Emperor Leo III which transferred the sees of Calabria and Illyricum from Rome to Constantinople had not affected Dalmatia which remained under the pope.) Thus Split and its suffragans administered the churches in a limited number of coastal cities, but prior to 925 did not control the Slavic hinterland in between. But presumably missionaries from Split and the other old Dalmatian cities were active in the Slavic interior along with the Frankish missionaries, and surely there was no clear-cut border between those accepting Christianity from one mission or the other.

Thus in the first decade of the ninth century the two Croatian states of the future (Dalmatian Croatia and Pannonian Croatia) existed each under Frankish suzerainty and each under its own native prince. The Franks meanwhile gained possession of Venice in 810. The loss of Venice plus the accession to the Byzantine throne in 811 of the incompetent Michael I resulted in a Byzantine-Frankish treaty in 812 (the Peace of Aachen). By it the Byzantines recognized Charles's title as emperor (though as emperor of the Franks and not as emperor of the Romans) in exchange for the return of imperial territory: Venice and the Roman cities of Dalmatia (i.e., whichever of the Roman, non-Slavic, walled cities the Franks had been able to subdue). The Franks were allowed to retain Istria and suzerainty over some (I suspect all) of the Slavic towns in Dalmatia (i.e., suzerainty over Croatian Dalmatia). Thus the checkered map of Dalmatia with no single clear-cut border continued. Almost all its territory, including some towns (e.g., Nin, Šibenik, Omiš, and Biograd [n.b., not Beograd]), was in the hands of Croatians who recognized Frankish overlordship. Then within this territory were a few walled coastal cities (named above) which remained Roman-Italian in character. They and most of the islands off the coast continued to recognize Byzantine suzerainty and in theory paid tribute to the empire.

In both original sources and modern works the term *Dalmatia* can refer to the whole coast or to just the Byzantine towns. Thus the reader, coming across this term, should always be alert to the fact that it can have either of these two meanings. By the ninth century *Dalmatia* was also coming to refer to a fairly narrow strip of territory along the coast, whereas earlier it referred to the old Roman province which included a wide inland hinterland, including much of Bosnia, as well as the coastal territory. In Constantine Porphyrogenitus's account, Dalmatia was still given the older and broader significance. Readers must be alert to this distinction as well.

In 814 Charlemagne died. Some of the Croatians seem to have considerably resented the behavior of Frankish officials and desired to be independent from these overlords. At that time in lower Pannonia (with his chief residence at Sisak) lived the Croatian prince Ljudevit (ca. 810–23) who was a Frankish vassal. Concurrently Višeslav's successor Borna (ca. 810–21), who resided at Nin and seems to have been the ruler of most of the Croatians in northern Dalmatia, was also a Frankish Vassal. Rivalry seems to have existed between the two Croatian princes (who between them seem to have ruled over most all the Pannonian and Dalmatian Croatians).

In 819, Ljudevit revolted against the Franks. He began his uprising in Kranj, supported by the Slavic tribes in the vicinity. He was also joined by some Slovenes and the Timok Slavs. This last group lived between Vidin and Braničevo and in theory was under the Bulgarian state of Omurtag. Initially the Timok Slavs had sought an alliance with Ljudevit and the Franks against the Bulgarians, but then when Ljudevit broke with the Franks they decided to stay with him. The Franks took no action at first, so Ljudevit pressed on in his aim to unite to his Pannonian state the Slavs of Istria and Dalmatia. This, of course, led to an open conflict with Borna whom he defeated. Many scholars assume that he gained control over Croatian Dalmatia after he defeated Borna. This assumption may be unwarranted. He next defeated a couple of small Frankish armies sent out against him in 820 and 821. Eventually in 822 a large Frankish army appeared and forced Ljudevit to flee to a Serbian tribe and the Dalmatian and Pannonian Croatians found themselves under the Franks again. Borna's nephew and successor in Nin, presumably in power as a result of the Frankish 822 campaign and thus their vassal—the source states he was chosen by the people and confirmed by the Franks—promised asylum to Ljudevit who came to him only to be murdered in 823.

The Timok Slavs then found themselves under the Franks much to the displeasure of the Bulgar khan Omurtag; having these tribesmen on the Timok River loyal to the Franks meant that the Frankish border (i.e., the borders encompassing the lands of people subject to the Franks) was now extended much further east, beyond the Timok River. Omurtag sent embassies to the Franks to settle the border problem in 824 and in 826. They achieved nothing, so in 827 Omurtag launched an attack to the west, penetrated this disputed territory and pressed well into Pannonia. He expelled the local Slavic chiefs and installed Bulgarian governors over these unreliable tribesmen. Furthermore, it seems that south of the Sava River, Bulgarian overlordship was extended over territory which had until then been under Frankish suzerainty. It is not clear where the actual borders ran after this campaign, but Sirmium, Beograd, and Braničevo were now Bulgarian. Some of these Bulgarian gains into Pannonian Croatia were to be restored to Frankish overlordship by a treaty in 845, but the Bulgars retained what is now northern Serbia and Srem (the region between the Danube and Sava, including Sirmium from which the place-name *Srem* is derived).

In 843 the Frankish empire was divided. Frankish Italy became suzerain of Istria and Dalmatian Croatia while Frankish Germany directed Pannonian Croatia and what is now called Slavonia. The Bulgars seem to have had a border not only with the Pannonian Croatians but also one with the Dalmatian Croatians, since in 855 Khan Boris attacked the Dalmatian Croatians. The attack presumably occurred at a common border, and it has been proposed that it was somewhere along the Bosna River. Presumably the Bulgarians had occupied all the territory of northern Serbia and northern Bosnia as far west as the Bosna (or wherever) bringing their western borders up to the two Croatian states; the Pannonian state lay to their northwest and included part of Slavonia, while the Dalmatian state lay to the south of the Sava and stretched as far east as the Bosna (or wherever) where it had a border with the expanding Bulgarian state. The Serbs lay to the south of this western Bulgarian wedge. N. Klaić believes the Bulgar borders extended even further west at the expense of the Pannonian Croatians; she feels the Bulgars held Slavonia.

Meanwhile in the second quarter of the ninth century the Dalmatian Croatians, under Frankish suzerainty, began developing a navy. The most active Slavic fleet in the Adriatic was that of the Neretljani, who occupied the territory between the Cetina and Neretva rivers and took to piracy, striking across the Adriatic at Italy, and especially Venice. They, along with the Arab corsairs present in the Adriatic, made shipping in that sea hazardous. The Neretljani were still pagan and occupied a variety of villages in the marshes of the wide, multichanneled Neretva mouth. They had become so troublesome that finally in 839 the Venetians (their major victims) launched a major campaign against them; in it the Neretljani were supported by the Roman city of Dubrovnik (a commercial rival of Venice). The Venetians succeeded in forcing a treaty upon the Neretljani, but it was to be short-lasting and again in the 840s they are mentioned as dangerous pirates irritating the Italian coast.

The Dalmatian Slavs' Relations with the Byzantines

These Slavs along the coast, though still remaining under Frankish suzerainty, began developing friendly relations with the Byzantines in the 830s. This was to pave the way for some of them to seek Byzantine suzerainty later. One gets the impression that despite Frankish overlordship, the Franks had almost no role in Dalmatia in the period from the 820s through the 840s; the Dalmatian towns and sailors seem to have acted pretty much according to their own wishes. Relations with the Byzantines greatly improved under the Dalmatian Croatian prince Trpimir I (845–64) who moved the prince's main residence from Nin to Klis. On his death in 864 he was succeeded by his son Zdeslav—one of three sons. In the very year of his succession Zdeslav was overthrown by a Knin nobleman, Domagoj (864–76), and had to flee to Constantinople.

This was a period of intense Arab marauding along Dalmatia. By then the Byzantines had restored their fleet. In 866, a major Arab raid along Dalmatia struck Budva and Kotor and then in 867 laid siege to Dubrovnik. That city appealed to Basil I, who responded by sending over one hundred ships which rescued Dubrovnik after a fifteen-month siege. After this success the Byzantine fleet sailed along the coast collecting promises of loyalty to the empire from the (Byzantine) Dalmatian cities. At this moment of increased Byzantine prestige various of the local Slavic tribes of the southern Adriatic also accepted Byzantine suzerainty—the Slavs of Trebinje, Duklja, and Zahumlje. Only the Neretljani refused until finally in 871 the Byzantine fleet forced them to end their resistance.

At this time Slavs from Dalmatia and Zahumlje are mentioned participating in Byzantine military ventures against the Arabs in the Adriatic and against the Arab-held ports in Italy (e.g., against Arab-held Bari in 870–71). They seem to have served both on their own ships and on regular imperial ships.

The Roman cities in Dalmatia had long been pillaged by the Slavic tribes in the mountains around them. Basil, between 882 and 886, allowed the towns to pay the tribute formerly owed to Byzantium (and still owed at that moment) to the Slavic tribes; thus the raiding was reduced by buying the Slavs off with protection money. Presumably a large portion of this tribute went to the prince of Dalmatian Croatia.

The Byzantine Theme of Dalmatia

To the 870s must be dated the establishment of the theme of Dalmatia. This included the Byzantine towns on the coast and most of the islands off it. Though much is still unknown about this theme, Ferluga has succeeded in demonstrating that it was different from all other themes. In fact when the Byzantine fleet was not present in Dalmatia, even in the late 860s (when the fleet was most active) and the 870s, there is no sign of any real Byzantine authority there. The Byzantine towns and islands continued to administer themselves as had been their custom. In this period—and subsequently as well—Byzantine authority in the general area was chiefly exercised from Durazzo, where the main Byzantine Adriatic fleet was based and where a strategos stood over not only a fleet but thematic troops (which at least later could be supplemented with local levies). From Durazzo troops were sent inland to deal with the neighboring Slavic states while its ships handled problems of Adriatic security.

In the late 860s and 870s Byzantium was particularly active in the Adriatic, preparing campaigns against the Arabs in Italy. But from the late 870s this activity decreased and presumably Byzantine influence in Dalmatia declined, leaving the Byzantine cities there to administer themselves as they had previously. When war with Symeon of Bulgaria broke out in the beginning of the tenth century, surely distant Dalmatia had to be left mainly to its own devices.

How was Byzantine Dalmatia organized? After the fall of Salona in 614, Zadar had become the first Roman city in Dalmatia and capital of the archonate of Dalmatia (under a leader called an archon). Zadar is referred to as the capital of this Dalmatian archonate in the second half of the eighth century. In the 820s the archon was a local figure and the town of Zadar enjoyed autonomy under him. The other Roman cities in Dalmatia were independent too, each responsible for its own administration (with its own laws and town council) and for its own defense. Despite the existence of the title archonate of Dalmatia, there is no sign of any intercity organization.

From about 870 sources begin mentioning a theme of Dalmatia with Zadar as its capital. A strategos is also mentioned there. Scholars usually assumed that a Byzantine general had been sent there from the capital to head a military-civil administration as strategoi did in the other themes. And the sources show that for the rest of the ninth century a Byzantine commander was in fact sent thither from the capital (since this was a period of intense naval activity there). It is not certain, however, that this situation continued in the tenth century, for between 900 and 950 no details about the strategos are given in any source; no names are mentioned and nothing is known of his subordinate officials.

During the period following 870 the Dalmatian theme seems to have been very different from the other themes. There is no evidence that the Dalmatian strategos ever had a civil role. The traditional local institutions continued to exist and the strategos is found only with a military role in the Byzantine naval campaigns along the coast against the Arabs. Furthermore, though at first the strategos was sent from Constantinople and at times commanded a Byzantine fleet also sent from there, and did levy certain locals for campaigns, there is no evidence that at any time there were regular thematic troops based in Dalmatia. The sources also do not mention the territorial divisions (tourma) seen in other themes or the subordinate commanders who stood over these districts (the tourmarchs). Therefore it seems no thematic structure was established under the strategos.

The individual character of the Dalmatian theme increased between the late ninth century and the 950s when sources appear again. The head of the town government of Zadar, who stood over the locally elected town council, was a local citizen entitled the prior. From the 950s the prior was also recognized as the head of the Byzantine administration in Dalmatia. Soon thereafter the prior acquired also the title of Dalmatian strategos. Thus the institution of strategos had changed in Dalmatia in the tenth century. Faced with other priorities and problems, the empire had been forced to give up its naval presence in the Adriatic, and in time, it ceased sending commanders (strategoi) thither and came to recognize the headman of its main town there as that strategos.

When this recognition came is unknown, but it had happened by the 950s; whether this had occurred shortly before that date or back toward the beginning of the tenth century is not known. From here on (except for roughly twenty years of Venetian rule later) the prior of Zadar, also called strategos, was the imperial representative in Dalmatia. This continued until 1067, when the prior came to bear the title of katepan (a change, however, of little significance because *katepan* is a term equivalent to *strategos* and used often in Byzantine Italy). From at least 950 when the Byzantines came to utilize this local figure as strategos, there is no further direct Byzantine administration in Dalmatia.

The prior was more or less only an honorary head of the theme. He had no role in any other Byzantine city in Dalmatia. Each city continued to operate under its own councils and headmen; there was no intercity administration. Each city had its own militia and ships; there was no intercity military organization. The prior functioned only in Zadar, and what role he had there seems to have been simply that which he would have had anyway as prior or headman. Thus he was responsible only for the defense and administration of Zadar. In terms of the theme the prior's position as strategos was nominal and seems to have simply symbolized Byzantium's theoretical overlordship over these Dalmatian cities without entailing any actual duties or functions.

This situation (with the prior as strategos) is documented for the period after 950. Some scholars have felt—with no evidence to prove it—that from 870 until some point just before 950 the Dalmatian theme had been like other themes. But because of the distance and the decline of Byzantine interest and possibilities in Dalmatia, the Byzantines had finally turned responsibilities over to the Dalmatians themselves. Yet Ferluga argues that under different names the situation in the 950s and after was the same as it had been in the 820s. In both periods each city was responsible for itself, there was nominal Byzantine suzerainty, there was no intercity military or administrative organization, and Zadar was considered the capital of Dalmatia. Pre-theme Dalmatia was headed by a locally elected man of Zadar called an archon who was recognized as the head of Dalmatia and upon whom was bestowed the honorary Byzantine court title of proconsul. Thus the only difference in administration between 820 and the period after 950 seems to be one of titles; the archon became a strategos and the archonate a theme.

Ferluga stresses with very strong arguments that from the start the Byzantine theme of Dalmatia was different from other themes, lacking the normal theme organization, the civil role of the strategos, locally based thematic units, tourmarchs, and the like. Thus, what existed in the 950s was the old system under new nomenclature. Though briefly after 870 a man who was called strategos had been sent out from the capital to head the fleet, his presence had not affected the local administration of any of the Dalmatian towns, and though he had commanded military operations briefly, he had not established any of the other features of a theme in Dalmatia. When Byzantine activities in Dalmatia ceased, no more commanders were sent from the capital. The towns continued to function as they had previously under their own administrations, but the Byzantines, to maintain a symbol of their suzerainty, simply gave the title strategos to the prior of Zadar. Since the pre-theme structure had not been altered by the establishment of the theme, the earlier system still remained in its entirety in 950; nothing was really new except for a couple of titular changes. What is not known is when the prior acquired the strategos's title which he is found holding in the 950s.[1]

End of Frankish Suzerainty over Dalmatia

Since 843, as a result of the division of the Frankish empire, Dalmatian Croatia had been under Italy. However, in 875 it found itself under the suzerainty of Carloman (son of Louis the German), holder of the German half. And like other states under Carloman (Bavaria, Bohemia, Pannonian Croatia, Italy, etc.), the Dalmatian Croatians continued to have their own local ruler. In 875, the Franks, who had had little role in Dalmatia for years, tried to reassert their authority and regain a role there. Perhaps they were worried about the increased Byzantine influence in Dalmatia. These Frankish actions led to a revolt by Prince Domagoj and the Dalmatian Croatians in 876. The revolt succeeded and the Dalmatians won their independence from the Franks, whose overlordship in Dalmatia was now ended. Frankish suzerainty was to continue for a little longer over Pannonian Croatia. Domagoj tried to liberate Istria too, but this attempt failed as the Venetians drove his troops out.

Afterward the same general situation continued in Dalmatia, except for the removal of Frankish suzerainty. The Dalmatian Croatians (now independent), under their own prince, continued to rule over most of the coast, while in their midst were scattered a few walled cities, not part of their state, populated chiefly by Italian-speakers who governed themselves but recognized Byzantine suzerainty and were theoretically included in a Dalmatian theme.

Soon after eliminating Frankish suzerainty, probably still in 876, Domagoj died and his son succeeded, only to be overthrown by Zdeslav of the legitimate dynasty, who had close ties with Byzantium and who had been living in exile in Constantinople. He may even have briefly recognized Byzantine suzerainty. He was eventually replaced by a nobleman named Branimir, who secured the throne in about 879 by means of a revolt. In 879, under him, Dalmatian Croatia, now free of Frankish suzerainty, received papal recognition as a state. In about 892, a representative of the legitimate dynasty, named Mutimir, succeeded in gaining the throne. Mutimir, who was the son of the earlier ruler Trpimir (d. 864), ruled until about 910, when he was apparently succeeded by Tomislav, probably his son. I shall avoid the controversy as to whether Tomislav succeeded Mutimir directly in about 910 (which is the most widely accepted view) or whether Mutimir died in about 900, to be succeeded by four different figures before Tomislav came to the throne between 910 and 914. Scholars have written a great deal about all sorts of political, diplomatic, and social motivations behind alleged factions in regard to the various changes on the throne.

However, the sources are so meager that none of it is more than speculation. In any case, after various rulers and enormous gaps in our knowledge, Tomislav, the greatest of medieval Croatian rulers, gained the throne of Croatian Dalmatia at some time between 910 and 914.

Tomislav

Tomislav set to work increasing the strength of both his army and navy. Constantine Porphyrogenitus states, probably with considerable exaggeration, that before the civil wars in the late 940s Croatia's army included sixty thousand horsemen and one hundred thousand foot soldiers while its navy included up to eighty galleys and one hundred cutters. The Hungarians, who had moved into present-day Hungary in the 890s, had immediately begun raiding far and wide as well as expanding their territory. They had become the greatest threat to the independence of the other states in the area. They particularly threatened the Pannonian Croatians, still nominally under Frankish suzerainty. The chiefs of Pannonian Croatia sought aid against the Hungarians from Tomislav, who marched against them, defeated them in several battles, and established a lasting border between the Hungarians and Croatians along the Drava River. In so doing he took over all of Pannonian Croatia and added it to his own state, thereby eliminating all Frankish overlordship over Pannonian Croatia. Some credit for ending Frankish suzerainty should also go to the Hungarians, for in a sense their presence and activities had actually ended the Frankish suzerainty.

Tomislav now found himself master of both Croatian states, which were united for the first time. Other than the Drava border, it is not known exactly where his state borders lay. To the south of the Drava he held what we think of as modern Croatia, Slavonia, northern and western Bosnia, and the territory along the Dalmatian coast from what is now Rijeka to at least the mouth of the Cetina River (excluding the scattered Byzantine towns). His state was divided into three main regions: (1) Slavonia, the most northern territory from the Drava extending beyond the Sava and Kupa rivers, seems to have retained considerable autonomy, only rendering tribute to the Croatian ruler. Constantine Porphyrogenitus calls it an archonate. It was to keep this autonomous, but subordinate, position until the early eleventh century; (2) the banovina of Lika, Krbava, and Gacka seems to have maintained considerable autonomy—the ban of this region held a high position at court and probably after Tomislav's death became a more or less independent figure; (3) Tomislav's original Dalmatian lands, including the northwestern Bosnian territory, which contained the eleven županijas (župas) which Constantine Porphyrogenitus mentions. Under their own local nobles, who presumably had less autonomy than those of the other two regions, the eleven župas were: Livno, Cetina, Imotsko, Pliva, Pset, Primorje (the coast), Bribir, Nona, Knin, Sidraga, and Nin. (Since Nona refers to Nin, controversy exists over what the Nin he lists refers to.) Presumably within his state there were actually more than eleven župas. Of the Pannonian Slav territory only Srem (with Sirmium), still held by the Bulgars, remained outside of his state. In the middle of the tenth century the Hungarians drove the Bulgars out of Sirmium and annexed it to their state.

Tomislav had no permanent capital (like many other early rulers; e.g., the Roman emperors of the late third and part of the fourth century and the later medieval Serbian rulers) but traveled from one royal residence to another (his chief residences being Biograd and Klis), collecting taxes, assuring himself that things were in order, and judging legal disputes. His household and retinue traveled with him. This movement meant that no single locality would be responsible for maintaining this expensive contingent, but, rather, that the burden would be divided. Up to this time there had been no distinction between personal (or palace) finances and state treasury or between palace servants and state officials. In fact most tasks which one associates with state offices were charges assigned on specific occasions to anyone in his retinue—soldier or servant—whom he appointed. Thus servants were assigned to look after taxes, diplomacy, and the like. Under Tomislav some specific offices and some sort of state administration began to develop. He had a chancellery with permanent scribes to draw up charters and issue decrees. He carried on diplomatic relations with his neighbors as well as with the pope.

In the course of the war between Byzantium and Symeon, in about 923, the Byzantines sent an embassy to Tomislav and the two concluded an alliance. It seems it was concluded at the moment the Byzantines had Zaharije in their fold as ruler of Serbia and had hopes of building a large coalition against Symeon. But then, as we saw, in 924 Symeon invaded Serbia and Zaharije fled to Croatia. It is frequently stated that at this time, hard-pressed by the Bulgarian threat and with no manpower to intervene in Dalmatia, the Byzantines surrendered the administration of the Dalmatian theme to Tomislav. However, there is no evidence for this view.

Tomislav was clearly a power in Dalmatia and surely was influential even in the Byzantine cities; but if the argument is correct that the Byzantine Dalmatian theme was different from other themes, and that by this time no strategos was sent thither from Constantinople, but instead the locals ran their own cities with the prior of Zadar holding the strategos's title, then there was no reason for the Byzantines to call in Tomislav. Most likely the Byzantines simply allowed the prior to continue through this period to be strategos as well. Even if the prior did not yet hold that title but acquired it nearer 950, as some think, still there would have been little reason to invite Tomislav in. Why assign a powerful figure, even if presently an ally, a role in one's possessions? Maybe he could not be removed later. The only apparent reason to have brought Tomislav in at this time would have been to defend Dalmatia from a direct attack by Symeon; but there is no reason to suspect Symeon had such an attack in mind or that the Byzantines believed he was planning one. And presumably if he had attacked, as an ally whose territory lay all around the Byzantine cities, Tomislav would have opposed Symeon with or without a position in Byzantine Dalmatia. Finally, and most importantly, no source states that Tomislav was given this role.

However, as we have noted, relations were cordial between Byzantium and Tomislav and they formed an alliance against Symeon, who was a threat to both states. In concluding the alliance the Byzantines granted Tomislav the court title of proconsul. However, this was an honorary title which in itself had no functions. It also was not an uncommon title, so no particular significance should be drawn from the fact that the earlier archon of Dalmatia (the leader of Zadar who stood over the archonate of Dalmatia) also held it. Thus there is no evidence that the Byzantines ever recognized the loss of their rights in the theme to Tomislav.

As a result of the alliance, which led to Symeon becoming alarmed about being caught between Croatia and Byzantium, plus Tomislav's asylum to Zaharije, Symeon attacked Tomislav. Symeon's invasion of Croatia was an utter disaster for him and Tomislav soundly defeated the invading Bulgarian troops. This success demonstrates Tomislav's ability as a military leader and also shows that he had created in Croatia a truly powerful military force.

It is generally said that Tomislav was crowned king in 924 or 925; like most other things about medieval Croatia this is not certain. It is not known when or by whom he was crowned. The only piece of evidence about this is a letter—whose authenticity has been questioned—from Pope John X allegedly written in 925 calling him king.

It seems that Tomislav died in 928, though Farlati, whose information is frequently questionable, on the basis of an unknown source has him live on to 940. Farlati and Constantine Porphyrogenitus each gives a totally different list of rulers after Tomislav, just as each gives a different list of his predecessors and different dates for Tomislav's accession. This issue is debated at great length among scholars but we need not concern ourselves with it since there is no way to resolve it. Moreover (except for Tomislav between 915 and 928) nothing is known about any of these rulers or their policies; so even if the lists could be straightened out, there would be only an accurate list of names and dates which would have no real significance. After all, it is only important that a Mutimir rather than a Trpimir was king if something is known about the two men and what they represented.

Constantine Porphyrogenitus says a civil war broke out in 949 in which an important nobleman, Pribina (the ban of Lika, Krbava, and Gacka), overthrew and killed a ruler named Miroslav and put Miroslav's brother Kresimir II (949–69) on the throne. Thus in the period after Tomislav, this ban had great influence in the state, perhaps the strongest Croatian military force, and had risen to become a kingmaker. However, since he was the most powerful nobleman, the ruler of three districts, he may have been a special case. Thus one probably should not infer from this, as some scholars have, that the nobles in general had increased their power. However, the civil wars after Tomislav's death most probably did hasten the decline of central authority. Various peripheral territories took advantage of unsettled conditions to secede. The Neretljani broke away and returned to their old piratical ways (if they ever had stopped and ever were really subdued); they were joined in this activity by sailors from the islands of Hvar, Brač, and Vis.

Furthermore much of Bosnia was lost to Časlav's revived Serbia. However, Časlav was to die in ca. 960. This led to unsettled conditions among the Serbs which allowed Kresimir of Croatia to regain western (if not all) Bosnia in the 960s. Through all these events the Pannonian Croatian lands between the Drava and Sava seem to have remained unaffected and under the Croatian state.

Those who argue that Tomislav had taken actual control of the Byzantine theme in Dalmatia now argue that as a result of the chaos of the 949 civil war, Croatia lost control there and direct Byzantine suzerainty was restored. However, the Byzantines were in no position to take a direct role, so now—according to this view—in ca. 950 the Byzantines recognized the prior of Zadar as strategos of Dalmatia. Thus these scholars believe it is only from ca. 950—when sources for the first time mention him in this role—that the Zadar prior became the strategos also. However, though documents referring to the prior as strategos are found only from the 950s, I still find Ferluga's theory that the prior actually had this double position and title throughout the tenth century more convincing.

The loss of part of Croatia's territory in the period after Tomislav's death, like the breaking away of Serbia after Symeon's death or of parts of Duklja after the death of its stronger rulers, all illustrate the weakness of these early Slav states. The core areas might be retained but the outlying regions, annexed by the strongmen, did not become integrated into the states owing to the absence of any serious administrative structure. The retention of outlying territories by these states was dependent on the local nobles in these lands rendering obligations. It seems that only rarely did rulers send more than a governor (often a royal cousin or brother)—presumably accompanied by some retainers—into these areas to keep order. This was obviously insufficient to create lasting large territorial units, loyal to a given dynasty.

The Church in Dalmatia in the Tenth Century

Now let us turn to the controversial church affairs. The most discussed and supposedly best-known events of this period are the church councils held in Split in 925 and 928. The first, in particular, was a major affair attended by clerics and laity including Tomislav of Croatia and Michael of Zahumlje. It was under the chairmanship of a papal legate and attended by clerics from both Croatian and Byzantine Dalmatia. Yet, despite the importance of these councils, almost everything about them turns out to be uncertain.

Ecclesiastical Jurisdictions in Dalmatia

Before Tomislav, politically there were two Dalmatias (Byzantine and Croatian). Yet despite Byzantine political suzerainty over its cities and islands it seems that the churches in Byzantine Dalmatia remained under the jurisdiction of the pope throughout. Dvornik convincingly argues that though Sicily, Calabria, and Illyricum were transferred to the patriarch of Constantinople in 732, Dalmatia was not. The chief ecclesiastic in Dalmatia was the bishop (probably archbishop) of Split. Despite Zadar's political and administrative importance, Split was the cultural center of Dalmatia and Dvornik believes its bishop had authority as suzerain archbishop over the other Byzantine Dalmatian towns. However, he did not have authority over the Croatian Dalmatian towns. But though Split had no jurisdiction over the Croatian territory, Dvornik believes—and produces evidence to support his contention—that some of the missionary activity into the Slavic hinterland originated from Split (or churches under Split) and therefore some of the early Christian communities in the Slavic hinterland were under Split's jurisdiction.

The original Dalmatian cities, the old Roman-Italian towns whose populations had long been Christian, had Italian-speaking majorities and maintained ties with Italy. Not surprisingly as part of the Italian world the language of their church services was Latin.

In the Croatian regions of Dalmatia, despite some proselytism from Byzantine Dalmatia, the chief missionary activity had been from the Franks, under the direction of the metropolitan of Aquileia; these efforts dated from the beginning of the ninth century. The Frankish mission seems to have been centered in the princely residence of Nin where in roughly 850–60 a bishopric was established by the pope for Frankish Dalmatian Croatia. Dvornik believes Nin was directly under the pope; other scholars have considered Nin a suffragan of Aquileia.

The Pope Summons a Council

In 924 or early 925—if the texts of two letters given in HSM are authentic—Pope John X sent a legate with a letter to call a church council. In the letter he referred to Tomislav as a king and attacked the Slavonic liturgy. Thus, though the Franks clearly had not spread it, the Slavonic liturgy had entered Dalmatia; presumably it had entered from Pannonian Croatia (which had been under the bishopric of Sirmium, a post held previously by Methodius until his deposition and during whose episcopate that liturgy had been favored) or from the Byzantine theme (which though ecclesiastically under Rome still could have had in it Slavs loyal to the Slavonic liturgy which the Byzantine government supported). Since actual Frankish influence on the Croatians was slight, one might expect that by 925 Slavonic letters would have been quite widespread in both Dalmatia and Pannonian Croatia. Various early Slavonic texts have survived from these regions.

The contents of Pope John X's letters are given in the long version of Thomas (HSM) from the sixteenth century. Various other later manuscripts giving their text exist as well. But in no case is it known where the copiers of these manuscripts or the author of HSM found the texts. Various views as to the letters' authenticity exist. Some scholars believe they are forgeries, others believe they are totally genuine while still others consider them later reworkings of genuine letters. But since the original texts have not survived and since the letters' authenticity is questioned in varying degrees, the letters cannot be used as proof to confirm the existence of the 925 council; this is especially true since the only sources about the council—the two letters of Pope John about it and the council's edicts—are contained only in the same sixteenth-century history. However, if authentic and rendered accurately, the papal letters would be confirmation for the existence of the 925 council and would show that Tomislav was already a king, Split was already an archbishopric, and that the pope wanted action against Slavonic in Dalmatia. But though the pope may have wanted such action, it does not mean that the council necessarily took this action.

The Need to Establish a Rational Hierarchy

Meanwhile another problem existed in Dalmatia which was probably far more important than that of the language of the liturgy. The patchwork political geography of Dalmatia has been discussed; this pattern carried over to the church. The bishop of Nin headed a new see responsible for a large territory, including the Croatian Dalmatian cities and the hinterland of Croatian Dalmatia (i.e., of Tomislav's Dalmatian lands). At the same time in each of the old Roman towns, which had been Christian for centuries, there was a bishop. Each of these urban bishops stood over little more than his town itself, plus whatever missionary communities the town may have established among the Slavs in its hinterland. Dvornik shows evidence of such missionary communities being loyal to mother churches in the old Roman cities; thus some of the Slavic communities might have looked to a Roman town bishop or to Split rather than to Nin. This resulted in there being overlapping jurisdictions between Nin and Split, assuming, as most scholars do, that Split was an archbishopric already and stood over the dioceses of the old Roman towns.

Now if we can believe HSM, the pope, following canon law, did not favor major bishoprics in new and minor places (like Nin). Therefore it made sense to establish a rational hierarchy for all Dalmatia where two separate churches then existed—Nin (for Croatian Dalmatia) and Split (for Byzantine Dalmatia)—whose jurisdictions probably overlapped in places. To do this it was necessary to create a metropolitan see for all Dalmatia. Clearly it was impossible to have subordinated the old Latin sees (with their ancient traditions) to the new Slavic see in Nin; the older churches would never have accepted that and, moreover, since each of the older cities had a bishop they could have outvoted Nin at any council.

Decisions of the Council of Split, 925

When the council met, Tomislav supported the archbishop of Split against Nin, and the council therefore made the archbishop of Split metropolitan for all Dalmatia (both Byzantine and Croatian). Nin and the other sees were subjected to Split. According to HSM, historical justification for this decision was presented: Salona had been the metropolitan for all Dalmatia. When Salona fell in 614, its population fled to Diocletian's palace at Split, creating a definite continuity between Salona and Split. Hence the bishop of Split was the bishop of Salona. (Throughout the Middle Ages the archbishop of Split called his seat "Salonitana" [Salona].)

Split thus at the council received jurisdiction over Croatian Dalmatia; and assuming Split already was suzerain archbishop of the Byzantine cities and islands, it was confirmed in its jurisdiction over them. The council recognized Split's possession of the hereditary rights of the Salona church, which the council stated had been founded in apostolic times by Saint Dujam (a disciple of Saint Peter). Split was thus given jurisdiction over the territory from the Raša River in Istria to Kotor. Šišić points out that the Saint Dujam story was entirely legendary; however, it was at the time accepted by the pope, Split, and, it seems, all of Dalmatia.

Thomas's *History of Split* does not mention the council at all. According to Thomas, Split's succession to Salona went back to the seventh century and from that time Split had had hereditary rights over all Dalmatia though it had exercised them only over Byzantine Dalmatia. The council appeared to give these rights to Split, thereby contradicting Thomas's claim that they had been acquired in the seventh century. Presumably Thomas ignored the council so as not to undermine this claim.

Why did Tomislav support the Split bishop living in Byzantine territory against the Croatian bishop residing in his own town of Nin? We do not know. Possibly Tomislav had received his crown shortly before the council from the pope, who had demanded support of Split as a condition for the crown. Perhaps he wanted the support of the older bishoprics to further his own coastal ambitions; this was a time of Byzantine weakness, and if Tomislav, as is likely, wanted to acquire the older Roman towns, possibly he felt it sensible to woo the churches in these towns. And, of course, if Byzantium had in fact given Tomislav the position of head of the Dalmatian theme—which I doubt but Dvornik believes—then all the Dalmatian towns were already under Tomislav and it made sense to unite all his cities under one bishop to rationalize the hierarchy; and since the older towns, newly under him, would not have accepted Nin, he might have hoped to gain their acceptance of his political leadership by supporting Split against the pretensions of his bishop in Nin.

Grgur of Nin's Reaction and the Split Council of 928

Nin under Bishop Grgur protested vehemently against the council's decision, and as a result a second council was held in 928 which abolished the see of Nin. Grgur was then given a new appointment as bishop of Skradin. According to HSM, the archbishop of Split was now placed over the whole Croatian state and the bishop of Sisak, the leading bishop in Pannonian Croatia, was subjected to Split. This would mean that in 925 Dalmatia, with two political loyalties, Byzantine and Croatian, but one religious loyalty (the pope) was all put under the metropolitan of Split under the pope and then in 928 all Croatia (Dalmatian and now Pannonian) was subjected to Split. N. Klaić, however, believes that the subjection of Sisak and Pannonian Croatia to Split was an invention by the author of HSM.

Was the Slavonic Liturgy an Issue at the Councils?

The discussion of the Split councils, which stresses the jurisdictional issue, has followed the emphasis of recent scholarship. However, until the middle of the twentieth century most scholars had depicted these councils primarily as the scenes of a language battle where Grgur of Nin, the great defender of Slavonic, was crushed by the establishment. This older view claimed that as a result of his struggle for Slavonic, Grgur's see of Nin was placed under Split and then, when he continued the fight, the second Council of Split, in 928, abolished his see and condemned Slavonic as a religious language. The older view thus made the language question the major issue of the councils and saw the jurisdictional change as a result of the language fight: i.e., to effectively crush the Slavonic language championed by Nin, it was necessary to subordinate and eventually abolish the see of Nin.

This view of Grgur became popular in the nineteenth century when the Croatians had to fight for their own language and culture against the threat of magyarization. Not surprisingly Grgur then became a great national symbol for the Croatians. His struggle was depicted not only in historical writing but also in literature and art. This image of Grgur has remained popular in this century; it is reflected by Meštrović's magnificent statue of Grgur which stands in Split.

Over the last thirty years or so this romantic story of an early fight for nationality and language has been replaced by a less dramatic but more realistic one which describes a jurisdictional fight between the ancient see of Split and the ambitious Croatian bishop in Nin. According to this recent view, language, if it was an issue at all at the councils, was a very minor one.

If HSM accurately gives the contents of the pope's letter, it is evident that the pope sought to condemn Slavonic (something the author of HSM believed in condemning). But this is not necessarily something that the local bishops were interested in doing. In fact, Article Ten of the 925 council (by N. Klaić's corrected version) specifically allows Slavonic for secular priests and monks, though it bars the advancement of Slavonic-liturgy priests to better positions. This shows that the members of the council did not share the pope's wish to ban Slavonic entirely. At this council, the language issue, though meriting discussion, was clearly less important than the jursidictional one. The material given by HSM on the council of 928 never touches on the issue of Slavonic, which suggests that the 928 council made no significant pronouncement on the language question. Thus the recent view, emphasizing a jursidictional quarrel rather than a language one, should be accepted.

Scholarly Debate on the Councils and Their Cause

Even though most of the leading contemporary scholars of Croatian history share the view that emphasizes the jurisdictional fight, they still disagree among themselves on all sorts of particular issues. These disputes all arise from the unsatisfactory sources; for, as noted, there are no contemporary sources on the 925 and 928 councils. The only information existing about them is that given by the author of the long version of Thomas (HSM) who compiled his work in the sixteenth century. It must be asked in what documents did this author, writing six hundred years after the councils, find his material? No satisfactory answer to this question has been found. But those scholars who believe that reliable sources on the tenth-century councils still existed in Split in the sixteenth century must still ask whether this author's biases caused him to alter the information given by his documents. There is a wide range of opinion on this question, from those saying that Thomas and HSM are not to be trusted at all, to those saying that despite their passions and editorial comments they faithfully recorded their sources. Let us examine two examples of scholarly opinion.

Dvornik's Interpretation

Dvornik (with whom I more or less agree and have basically followed) believes that Thomas is accurate when he claims that in the seventh century (ca. 640) Split was raised to an archbishopric and succeeded to the position of Salona. Dvornik notes a recently discovered inscription referring to an Archbishop John—the name given by Thomas for the first Split archbishop in the mid-seventh century. Dvornik notes the archaic style of its writing and declares the inscription is certainly pre-tenth-century and could well be seventh-century. Thus here and elsewhere he finds evidence to support Thomas's account of the early history of Split, an account which many scholars have rejected as fiction. Dvornik thus believes that from the mid-seventh century Split was an archbishopric over the Byzantine Dalmatian cities and under the pope. Then, in the middle of the ninth century a bishopric at Nin was established for Croatia by the pope and also placed under the pope. Rivalry, owing to overlapping jurisdictions over various Croatian communities, followed, so the council of 925 met to solve this issue. The council put Nin and all Croatian Dalmatia under Split and of course left Byzantine Dalmatia under Split.[2]

Klaić's Interpretation

Nada Klaić takes a totally different view; and though I do not share various of her conclusions, I applaud her work. She is one of the most critical historians of medieval Croatian history and has done a marvelous job in showing how weak many of our sources are.

Klaić rejects all the information about Split in the seventh century given by Thomas. She believes Split was just a bishopric, one among many in Byzantine Dalmatia. The bishop of Zadar (in the administrative center) was probably more important. But no city stood over the others. Thus there existed a collection of more or less equal and separate bishoprics without a suzerain archbishop. She believes they were subject to the patriarch of Constantinople, not to Rome. She believes an 879 letter of Pope John VIII to the Dalmatian bishops under him is not to be taken literally. Though most scholars have seen this letter as proof that the Byzantine cities were under the pope, Klaić sees it as advancing a claim rather than expressing reality. She feels that until 879 or so Split was just a bishopric and that it probably received the higher rank of an archbishopric about then, though this is not entirely certain. But despite the higher title, Split received no authority over the other cities.

In the early 920s, according to Klaić, during their negotiations with Tomislav, the Byzantines transferred the churches of Byzantine Dalmatia from the patriarch of Constantinople to the pope. Now having obtained superior jurisdiction over all Dalmatia, the pope wanted to set up a sensible hierarchy there. There were three contenders for the metropolitan position: Split, Zadar (which Klaić feels was a serious rival), and the Croatian see of Nin, which from its creation in about 860 to 925 Klaić believes was not directly under the pope but under the Frankish metropolitan of Aquileia. Only after the 925 council did Split obtain authority over any other Dalmatian city. This is a fact that Thomas the Archdeacon intentionally hid; for this reason he did not mention the two tenth-century councils, instead implying that the decisions the councils reached had been in effect over the previous three hundred years. To mention the councils would have refuted what he had already written about the earlier history of Split. And since he had misrepresented that to so great an extent, Klaić believes his general account of the earlier history of the Split church is most unreliable. Thus she concludes that Split's suzerainty over the Dalmatian churches—both Byzantine and Croatian—was established in 925 and was based on historical succession to Salona; however, this succession was created by the council and, despite Thomas's claims to the contrary, had not previously been recognized or been in effect. She also believes that HSM is not to be trusted when it states that the 928 council placed Sisak (a bishop for much of Pannonian Croatia) under Split.[3]

Position of Split's Archbishop after 928

In any case, most scholars agree that if Split had not had some bishoprics as suffragan sees before 925, at least after 928 Split had all Dalmatia (and maybe Pannonian Croatia) under it. The following bishoprics were under Split: Osor, Krk, Rab, Zadar, Skradin (to which Grgur formerly of Nin had been sent), Ston (bishop of Zahumlje), Dubrovnik, Kotor, Duvno, and Sisak. The list of suffragan bishoprics has generally been accepted (except for Klaić's doubts about Sisak). In time new bishoprics were to be created within this broad territory (Trogir before 1000, Knin after 1042, Biograd replaced Skradin in about 1058, and Nin was restored in 1074). Furthermore certain bishoprics were to be raised to archbishoprics and gain their independence (e.g., Dubrovnik).

Croatia, 969–1075

Croatia and Byzantium in the Late Tenth Century

In the second half of the tenth century Byzantium was involved in a series of major campaigns which utilized the state's military energies to their capacity; these campaigns were all basically land wars, comprising expansion to the east, suppression of the rebellious magnates in Anatolia, and the Bulgarian wars. As a result, the navy and Adriatic affairs took a low priority and the empire soon found itself in no position to participate in defending the Adriatic towns against the Saracens or pirates. When Byzantium withdrew its forces from that area, it left responsibility for the Dalmatian theme to the individual cities and appointed the prior of Zadar as the imperial representative there.

Very little is known about either part of Croatia in the late tenth century. Stjepan Držislav ruled Croatia from 969 to 997, and was crowned king in about 988. Some scholars, including Šišić, have claimed that the Byzantines recognized Držislav as the head of their Dalmatian cities. The mid-to-late 990s, of course, was the time of Samuel's westward expansion when he reached Dalmatia, after making client states out of Duklja and Zahumlje. Byzantium needed allies against him; and since his activities threatened Croatia, Croatia was a natural ally. However, this does not mean that Držislav was made head of the Byzantine theme. This theory is based on the fact that in addition to the patrician rank awarded him, the Byzantines granted him the title of eparch of Dalmatia. However, the title of eparch was not one ever given by Byzantium to one holding authority in its Dalmatian towns and the title is not attested in any Byzantine theme. More likely it was an honorary title or, less likely, one connected with Držislav's rule over his own Croatian Dalmatian towns.

Držislav died in 997 and left his lands to be divided among his three sons (another case of the Slavic division of lands among heirs rather than primogeniture); the sons were ordered to cooperate with each other and the eldest, Svetoslav, was to have primacy over the younger two (Kresimir and Gojislav). This situation did not last long and troubles broke out from several directions. First Svetoslav, it seems, tried to oust his brothers and assert his sole authority, causing his brothers to rise up in revolt. At the same time marauding by the Neretljani against the Latin towns and Venetian ships increased; these pirates had close ties with Svetoslav. These relations turned the Latin Dalmatian towns and Venice against Svetoslav. Moreover, to support the Slavic Dalmatian sailors and merchants (his allies and vassals),

Svetoslav tried to limit the privileges of the Venetian merchants in his towns. Byzantium, occupied with Samuel, needing allies and seeing Croatia becoming weaker as a result of these troubles, allowed the angry Venetians to intervene themselves.

Period of Venetian Overlordship in Dalmatia, 998–1024

Since the beginning of the ninth century, the Venetian merchant and fighting fleet had grown in size and become increasingly powerful. By the second half of the tenth century it had become a major force in the Adriatic. Its active opposition to piracy was appreciated by the Byzantines. In 997 Samuel conquered Durazzo. He then raided up the coast as far as Zadar; but though his troops did a great deal of damage they did not occupy any Dalmatian territory. However, the Byzantines, already at war with Samuel, saw these western activities as a threat to the empire while it found itself helpless to oppose him there. Its troops were fighting him in the eastern Balkans. Because its fleet was weak and its Croatian ally was in the midst of a civil war, not surprisingly, the empire turned to Venice for aid in defending Dalmatia.

In 998 Basil II recognized the doge of Venice as his official representative in Dalmatia, giving him the title of dux of Dalmatia and the court rank of proconsul; Byzantine suzerainty remained but it was now to be exercised through Venice. No Venetian representatives entered any of the Dalmatian cities yet; the cities continued to administer themselves but now they took oaths of loyalty to Venice. The doge added "et Dalmatiae" to his title. Thus the de facto situation remained unchanged. It is worth stressing here that changing overlords had little effect on these towns; they continued to administer themselves as before, simply taking an oath to the new power and at times supplying sailors to whichever power it was.

However, many of the Dalmatian towns were suspicious of Venice; for unlike Byzantium, Croatia, or the early Franks, Venice was a sea and trading state like the Dalmatian towns. Thus Venice was a rival, and increased Venetian authority in the area could threaten Dalmatian interests and give Venetians commercial advantages over the Dalmatians. This was not a serious danger yet; but Venice was to realize their fears in the fourteenth and fifteenth centuries. As a result of these worries some Dalmatian towns became more assertive of their independence and some even refused to submit to Venice. Dubrovnik, for example, continued to remain directly under Byzantine suzerainty. At this time Dubrovnik was developing as a commercial power with a growing fleet. To avoid falling prey to Venetian influence, Dubrovnik strengthened its ties with the empire and in so doing increasingly separated itself from the rest of Byzantine Dalmatia. In a few decades it was to be officially separated from the Byzantine Dalmatian theme and made into a small theme in its own right.

In 998, then, Venice was exercising suzerainty over the Byzantine Dalmatian towns in the name of the emperor while the Croatians of Dalmatia were in the throes of a civil war and the semi-independent Neretljani pirates were marauding along the Adriatic (particularly against Venice). Because the Venetians had gained increased authority in Dalmatia, some of the Dalmatian towns, feeling threatened, allied themselves with the Neretljani against Venice. Venice then intervened and won a decisive naval battle over the Neretljani and their Croatian allies. In consequence the Neretljani entered a period of decline.

Whether Venice had had any role in supporting either side in the Croatian dynastic war to this point is not clear—though many scholars have suggested that they supported Kresimir; this would have made sense considering Svetoslav's policy and the allies he had. In any case in 1000, Svetoslav was ousted, and, needing support, he turned to his ex-enemy Venice. He recognized Venetian overlordship over Dalmatia (which of course was just a nominal act since his brothers by then actually held Dalmatia) and as an ally of Venice obtained a promise from the doge to support him in regaining his lost throne. His son Stjepan went off to Venice, more or less as a hostage. Svetoslav then disappears from the sources; possibly he died. But his son Stjepan remained in Venice and soon married the doge's daughter. Thus the doge seems to have been building up a potential ally who could be useful if Stjepan could be restored to the Croatian throne. This meant that Kresimir III (1000–1030) and Gojislav (1000 to ca. 1020) had to worry about Venice and oppose all Venetian activity in Dalmatia.

The Venetians meanwhile were increasing their involvement in the area and were trying to convert the titles given them by Basil II into something of substance. The doge, though verbally retaining his loyalty to the empire, sent envoys into various Byzantine Dalmatian towns to extract oaths of loyalty to himself. Zadar, Trogir, Split, and the isles of Krk and Rab submitted in this way. As far as we can tell, this brought about no changes in the internal affairs of these towns, and presumably the prior continued to administer Zadar. Most probably, however, during this period of Venetian overlordship he lost the title of strategos.

As tensions increased between Kresimir and the Venetians, Venice directed its attention to some of the Croatian ports. Soon Venice became overlord over Biograd, the important Slavic port which had been the favorite coastal residence of Tomislav. Very likely various other Slavic ports came under Venice as well. However, even in the Slavic towns it seems no direct Venetian rule followed. No Venetian representatives entered them; these towns too just swore allegiance to Venice and went on administering themselves. But the towns were unhappy with the Venetian presence and, in the years that followed, various Dalmatian towns, when the opportunity presented itself, rejected Venetian suzerainty. The Croatian rulers then asserted their suzerainty over them. Who was overlord over a given town and for how long is usually not clear and we need not trouble ourselves with the details.

In 1018, the Venetians returned to Dalmatia for a major offensive and drove the Croatian leaders from various towns; but then, in 1019, Basil II, having triumphed over Samuel, asserted his own authority in Dalmatia. He now claimed and took direct suzerainty (minus the doge as middleman) over the *central* Dalmatian Byzantine towns.

At the same time Kresimir, the Croatian ruler, fearing the Hungarians who were becoming more active to his north and also fearing Basil who was now interesting himself in Dalmatia, sent his submission to Basil. Basil accepted it and gave Kresimir the patrician title and left him as ruler of Croatia, which meant that he was now a vassal prince of Byzantium. Kresimir was to rule until 1029 or 1030. The Venetian role in Dalmatia was thus reduced, though it seems that Byzantine authority over some of the *northern* Dalmatian towns was still exercised through Venice. Moreover the quarrels between Venice and Kresimir over the Slavic towns in northern Dalmatia continued.

Byzantine Dalmatia after 1024

In 1024 a civil war erupted in Venice which encouraged Kresimir to take advantage of Venice's problems to reassert himself. But Byzantium intervened immediately and succeeded, by the end of 1024, in regaining all of Byzantine Dalmatia. Venice had lost its role as Byzantine representative. Very likely the prior of Zadar regained his former position immediately in 1024. However, documentation of this comes a bit later. In 1029 the prior is again mentioned as the Byzantine representative in Dalmatia and in 1036 he is referred to as strategos. He continued to be called strategos until 1067 when he came to be called katepan (a title with the same meaning, then regularly used in Byzantine Italy). So the prior regained his old role which, as before, seems to have been entirely symbolic; he exercised no actual functions in any of the other towns.

Meanwhile Dubrovnik increasingly separated itself from the rest of Dalmatia. It had never accepted any Venetian overlordship, and throughout the preceding period had recognized Byzantium directly. It increased its ties with Basil between 1016 and 1018. By 1030 (and possibly as far back as 1018) it is found as a separate theme under its own strategos. Thus two so-called themes had come into existence in Dalmatia; that of Dalmatia, including all the Roman towns and islands under their own leaders with nominal authority belonging to the prior of Zadar as strategos of the theme, and that of Dubrovnik, including Dubrovnik and environs. Dubrovnik, though tiny, was more like a typical theme for it received its strategos from Constantinople and he most frequently was a Greek. Dubrovnik retained close ties with the empire. It sent sailors regularly to serve on imperial campaigns and its strategos had a role in coastal patrols.

Croatia, 1025–75

Kresimir, still a Byzantine vassal, also took advantage of the Venetian civil war of 1024 to restore his rule over the Croatian Dalmatian towns. After 1025, when Basil II died, the Byzantines became less concerned with military projects. The civil bureaucracy acquired a greater role in setting policy and took little interest in distant Dalmatia. Kresimir now ceased to pay homage to Byzantium and became an independent ruler again in theory. He suffered some loss of territory to his nephew Stjepan (the son of Svetoslav). After the overthrow of the doge, his father-in-law, in ca. 1024 Stjepan had fled to Hungary. The Hungarian king had then seized part or all of Slavonia, which he gave to Stjepan to rule as an appanage.

Under Kresimir's son and successor Stjepan I (1030–58) (not to be confused with Svetoslav's just-mentioned son Stjepan), the Croatians increased the size of their navy. They had successes against both the Venetians and Byzantines, and maintained control over the Dalmatian Croatian towns. Stjepan I also expanded his authority to the northwest, annexing Carinthia; the jurisdiction of his bishop of Knin was extended up to the Drava.

But though tensions existed between Stjepan I and Byzantium, Byzantium was to reestablish and maintain cordial relations with his son Peter Kresimir (known as Kresimir IV) who succeeded to the throne in Croatia in 1058 and ruled until 1074 or 1075. The Byzantine empire was declining militarily, while the Croatians were coming to be the major power in their area. By the 1060s the Byzantines were tied down by two major enemies, the Seljuks in the east and the Normans in Italy. They were in no position to act in Dalmatia, which was now threatened by the Normans. The Croatians were in a position to threaten the Byzantine cities there as well. Thus it made sense to cultivate good relations with Kresimir.

Finally in 1069 the empire made him imperial representative in Dalmatia (i.e., over the Dalmatian theme; not including the theme of Dubrovnik and the duchy of Durazzo). The katepan Leo (presumably the prior of Zadar who had been the Byzantine representative in 1069) was allowed to remain in his post and retain his title, but now he was to serve Kresimir. Thus it seems that no changes occurred in Zadar; the prior continued 'his administrative role there and possibly even retained some sort of titular role for the rest of Byzantine Dalmatia. Kresimir respected the autonomy of the towns. Thus Byzantine suzerainty was not renounced but was just wielded for the empire by Kresimir.

In the 1060s Croatia included three banovinas: (1) Bosnia, (2) a coastal banovina mentioned between 1060 and 1069 under Ban Gojčo, (3) Slavonia, between the Sava and the Drava under Zvonimir. Very little is known about them. How independent were the first two? Were the bans local figures or were they appointed by the Croatian ruler? Since the coastal banovina is mentioned for only that one decade, possibly it was a very temporary affair. The third, Slavonia, between the Sava and the Drava, was administered by the autonomous ban Zvonimir, son-in-law of the Hungarian king Bela I. Zvonimir was found as an autonomous ruler in Slavonia by 1065. In the course of the next four years he came to accept Croatian suzerainty. It seems he accepted this in an agreement by which his region (Slavonia) was restored to the Croatian state but in such a way as to retain its autonomy, leaving him as its ruler. It also seems that the region which the Croatian king confirmed as Zvonimir's banovina was more extensive than his initial territory, which suggests he was given further lands by the Croatian king.

Zvonimir joined his territory to Croatia in exchange for continued local independence, an important role in general Croatian state affairs, and for his own succession to the Croatian throne should Kresimir be childless. (Kresimir had had a son named Stjepan who predeceased him.) Croatian charters were issued in the names of King Peter Kresimir and Ban Zvonimir. After late 1074, Kresimir disappears from the sources. A year later, in the fall of 1075, his junior coruler Zvonimir was crowned king of Croatia.

Some studies state that a nobleman named Slavac succeeded, but the only source for this is Lucius—a late Renaissance historian. Slavac, it seems, was in reality an early-twelfth-century figure from the Neretva who had no connection with the Croatian throne.

The Slavonic Liturgy Becomes an Issue in the 1060s

In the mid-eleventh century the Slavonic liturgy became an issue in Croatian Dalmatia. Written in Glagolitic, it was widely used particularly in northern Dalmatia, where its chief centers were on the islands lying in the Gulf of Kvarner, formed by the Istrian peninsula. In this regard the island of Krk was the most important. In the 1060s, when the pope was demanding general church reform, many high clerics in the old Roman towns of Dalmatia, which had always used the Latin liturgy, wanted to prohibit Slavonic and standardize church practices. Kresimir IV, a religious man who had founded a Benedictine monastery at Biograd, his favorite residence, sympathized with the latinizers. One wonders why: perhaps he wanted papal support; perhaps he sought support from the Latin Dalmatian cities, toward which he may already have had ambitions; perhaps it was a result of his Venetian upbringing. (His mother was a Venetian and he had been educated in Venice.)

In any case the reformers or latinizers were upset by the situation in the Croatian church; many priests (like the Greeks) married and wore beards. Many of them did not know Latin. A synod was held in Split in 1060 which declared that priests must know Latin and declared it the language of the church. The council condemned Slavonic. It also banned priestly beards and marriages. Some churches were closed as a result and there seems to have been a degree of unrest. Parties developed for and against Latin, with the high clergy and nobles tending to support Latin. In 1063 the pope demanded application of these decisions and he too called Slavonic heretical.

In 1064 a rebellion for the Slavic church broke out on the isle of Krk under a man named Vuk. He set up an autonomous church under its own bishop and wrote the pope. Various misunderstandings followed and envoys from each side were rebuffed by the other. Kresimir then sent a naval expedition against Krk (whose church was branded heretical by the pope). By the end of 1064 Vuk's rebellion was crushed and Latin clerics were in control of the church of Krk. Thus the national church organization suffered a further blow and its organization rapidly died out. Surely, however, in inland villages Slavonic priests continued to function over the next several centuries, owing to the lack of an educated clerical class there. In addition, though the established church opposed it, Slavonic seems to have survived in places along the coast presumably because the local population tolerated it. Glagolitic manuscripts from Croatia survive from each subsequent century throughout the Middle Ages. But as an established accepted movement the Slavonic church collapsed and the main reason for its collapse was that the leading Croatian political and religious figures opposed it. In 1074 a second council was held in Split which reissued the edicts of 1060 against Slavonic. This second council also reestablished the bishopric of Nin.

Norman Balkan Activities in the Late Eleventh Century

Meanwhile in the 1060s the Normans were completing their conquest of Byzantine Italy and Sicily. In 1071 Bari, an important port in Apulia and the last Byzantine possession in Italy, fell to them. They next began looking toward the Byzantine Empire, and the first step in that direction was clearly the Balkans.

During this period, Duklja was the leading Balkan power opposed to Byzantium. Its ruler, Michael, eventually concluded an alliance with Rome, bringing him a crown from the pope in 1077. He also exchanged embassies with the Normans in Apulia and in 1081 a marriage took place between Michael's son Constantine Bodin and an Italian princess of Bari. The girl's father was a leader of the pro-Norman party in Bari. Thus the possibility of the Normans acquiring allies inside the Balkans increased Byzantium's dangers.

The Normans struck first against northern Dalmatia in 1074; they briefly made themselves overlords over Split, Trogir, Biograd, Zadar, and Nin. But within the next three years the Venetians sent a fleet to Dalmatia and drove them out. The doge of Venice again took the title of dux of Dalmatia (the title given an earlier doge in 998 by Basil II which had expired in the 1020s when Venice ceased to be the imperial representative in Dalmatia). Venice was now using Basil's 998 grant as a basis for its Dalmatian claims. Venice was growing ever stronger. Despite its close ties with Byzantium and its supposed vassal status, Venice was truly an independent force in the Adriatic.

The focus of the next Norman attack was directed further south, where Byzantium was still active, against Durazzo. Here a Byzantine dux was present. Durazzo was the city from which Byzantine reinforcements had been sent to relieve the siege of Bari in 1071 and from which any Byzantine attempt to recover parts of Italy would be most probably launched. In 1081 a Norman joint land-sea attack was sent against Durazzo. When the new emperor, Alexius I Comnenus, marched out to meet the invaders his armies included Serbs from

Duklja under Bodin. Bodin, though allied to the emperor, had just married the daughter of the leader of the pro-Norman faction in Bari. Bodin also had had hostile relations with the Byzantines before. He had actively supported the Bulgarian rebellion in the 1070s and had then been carted off to Constantinople as a captive after the Byzantines had defeated him in battle. The Byzantines, however, had serious support from Venice. Since the Byzantine navy had so greatly declined, Venice's strong fleet was vital to oppose the Norman sea attack. In fact, the Venetians defeated the Norman fleet and broke the naval part of the Norman siege.

For its services Venice in 1081 or 1082 gained a large number of privileges; duty-free trade throughout the empire; the right to establish colonies and warehouses in any port it wanted, the right to have its own administration for its colonies; the right to use its own laws and judges for its people; and various gifts and titles for the doge. The Venetian merchants, enjoying these privileges, came to acquire great advantages over the Byzantine merchants who had to pay duties. Soon the Venetians acquired an economic stranglehold over Byzantium and came to dominate the carrying trade of the empire. In addition, as the Byzantine fleet was allowed to deteriorate, the Venetian fleet came more and more to replace it. This process continued until it was too late. Then the Venetians were able to demand further privileges; if rebuffed, they could and did raid the poorly defended Greek islands and ports to force the Byzantines to capitulate. Thus the long-run effect of these 1081 capitulations was the ruin of Byzantine commerce and the further decline of its already poor navy.

Despite their naval defeat, the Norman land attack continued and in a critical battle in October 1081, the Normans defeated the Byzantines and took Durazzo. In this battle Bodin and his Dukljans sat on the sidelines and watched. According to the Byzantine sources, their nonparticipation was an important factor in the Norman victory. The Normans then, from their base in Durazzo, pushed on into imperial territory. They marched through Epirus and Macedonia into Thessaly, where they laid siege to Larissa. At this moment an uprising broke out in Italy and the Norman leader, Robert Guiscard, had to return to quell it. In his absence the emperor Alexius was able to clear Thessaly of the Normans. By 1085 things were settled in Italy and Guiscard was ready to return to recover his recently lost conquests; but the plague carried him off first and confusion followed in Italy. As a result, the Byzantines were to be spared the Normans for a while, and in 1085 the empire regained Durazzo.

Croatia, 1075–1102

Zvonimir of Croatia

Meanwhile Zvonimir (1075–90), upon succeeding Kresimir IV as ruler of Croatia, turned to the pope and received papal blessing to be crowned king of Croatia. He was crowned in late 1075 or early 1076 by a papal legate at Split. He then accepted the status of papal vassal and thereafter maintained close ties with Gregory VII—the reform pope. Since the old Dalmatian city bishops regularly supported the reform papacy, and since a Croatian ruler, who wanted to hold power over these cities, needed the bishops' support, it made sense for Zvonimir to support a reform line and agree with the papal policy against the Slavonic language in church. In addition it made sense to have good relations with the pope since the Normans, who were now threatening Dalmatia, were papal vassals. The pope might be able to hold them back. Zvonimir found himself opposed by Byzantium and Venice. The Venetians, allied to Byzantium, had all sorts of ambitions in Dalmatia which Zvonimir stood in the way of.

Zvonimir aimed to subdue the nobility—the independent hereditary provincial nobles, the old župans, who for generations had been governing the provinces (županijas, župas). They had their own local power bases and great internal independence; according to some later sources, the king had even been forced to recognize a diet of the nobles. This diet, however, may not have existed that early. It may have been a fourteenth-century institution projected back on this earlier time by fourteenth-century authors. In any case, it seems that Zvonimir sought to gain firmer control of his state by ousting various local nobles from local administration and replacing them with his own supporters—court nobles and high clerics. His use of clerics in administrative positions was a natural outgrowth of his close ties with the papacy; he could count on the church to support his centralizing activities. Needless to say, his policy was opposed by the local nobles.

In 1089 or 1090 Zvonimir died. Legend has him killed in a brawl during a council. He had been married to the sister of the king of Hungary; they had had one young son—his heir—but that boy died almost immediately afterward in 1090. The deceased son was the last of the Trpimirović dynasty, and with its end, a "Time of Troubles" began. The widow took over, but she was unpopular with the nobles who had hated her husband. This was a moment of weakness for the forces of centralization, and a perfect chance for the nobles to reassert their traditional rights in their own counties. In addition, as some scholars point out, the queen was a foreigner, a Hungarian. However, it is not certain that her nationality really mattered to anyone then.

Hungarian Intervention in Croatia in the 1090s

The Hungarian king quickly intervened to protect his sister's interests (a fine excuse for what were probably his own ambitions) and occupied much of Croatia, including part of Dalmatia. However, some "wild people" (Pechenegs, according to Šišić, but more probably Cumans as argued by N. Klaić) then attacked Hungary, causing a partial withdrawal of the Hungarians. They pulled out of Dalmatia, but kept inland (Pannonian) Croatia. Between the Drava River and the Gvozd mountain they created a special Croatian banovina ruled by Almos, the nephew of the king. Almos was to hold this territory from 1091 to 1095. The Hungarians also established a bishopric in Zagreb in 1094 whose borders coincided with Almos's banovina. To separate the church in Pannonian Croatia from Split, the Zagreb bishopric was placed under a Hungarian archbishop in Ostrogon. Later Zagreb was to be subjected to another Hungarian archbishopric, Kalocsa.

What was left of Croatia (primarily Dalmatia and any part of the interior not included in the Hungarian-occupied banovina of Almos) was then taken over by a certain Peter (1093–97), whose main residence was in Knin. He soon recovered Croatia, expelling Almos in 1095. Then, late in 1095, Koloman (1095–1116) succeeded to the Hungarian throne. Immediately in 1096 his armies retook Pannonian Croatia and pushed into Dalmatia. Peter was killed in this warfare on the Gvozd mountain which was to be renamed Petrova gora after him. Peter was to be the last independent Croatian king. The Hungarians, who had long needed a port, occupied Biograd in 1097. The other Dalmatian cities, now alarmed, quickly turned to Venice. The Hungarians, having just won their first port, had no navy yet, and needed naval help against Venice. They turned to the Normans and made an alliance with them. But soon Koloman concluded it was a poor idea to press matters against the Venetians, and he signed a nonaggression treaty with them.

The Hungarian Annexation of Croatia, 1102, and Its Aftermath

Croatia

In 1102 Koloman moved against Croatia again but this time he stopped at the Drava and there, a late source reports, he met with twelve leading Croatian nobles. As a result of this meeting, he obtained Croatia by agreement (the so-called *Pacta Conventa*). He then proceeded to occupy the Dalmatian towns (Zadar, Trogir, Split) one by one; probably his conquest of them (or possibly more accurately his obtaining submission from them) was completed between 1105 and 1107. There seems to have been no attempt at common action by the Dalmatian cities. Koloman allowed them to keep their former autonomy and issued them charters guaranteeing this.

Thus by 1107, Koloman had annexed Croatia and secured his overlordship over Dalmatia. But, though it is certain that he acquired these territories, the circumstances surrounding his annexation of Croatia remain problematical. Therefore let us examine more closely Koloman's dealings with the Croatian nobles. Koloman is said to have met with the Croatian nobles and obtained their acquiescence in his taking the Croatian crown by promising to respect their ancestral privileges. Having received these promises, the nobles elected him king of Croatia and Dalmatia. The Croatian diet was retained, with representatives from each of the twelve Croatian tribes. It is implied that at some point this diet or assembly had become a regular Croatian institution.

However, before going into detail on this important agreement it is worth noting that our source for Koloman's relations with the Croatian nobles is no older than the fourteenth century. In addition, that document is probably not even a copy of a lost twelfth-century original. Evidence of these twelve families as class representatives exists only from the middle of the fourteenth century. The earliest reference to them as an "institution" is in 1350/51 and the earliest text of the 1102 pact (the Trogir manuscript) dates from 1387/88. N. Klaić thinks that probably some sort of surrender had occurred in 1102 by which the Croatians were given light terms. But what the Trogir manuscript contains is not the text of that surrender but a fourteenth-century legend, which described contemporary relations between king and nobility and then traced that current fourteenth-century reality back to an initial agreement. Some of the features mentioned in the document did go back to 1102, but other items (including the diet) could have been later developments which were then attributed to 1102 to give them an aura of tradition. To formalize a present-day reality which was satisfactory to the fourteenth-century Croatian nobles and base it on a binding treaty would have increased their security in dealing with the king. Thus, even if there had been an original agreement, as most scholars believe, this fourteenth-century text probably does not contain its original text.

Although the text probably includes some questionable historical events and various later features, much of its contents does depict the situation that actually was created in 1102. A summary of its germane points, therefore, is a fitting introduction to a discussion of Croatia under Hungarian rule.

The document stipulates that the two kingdoms were not to be merged; they were to remain separate kingdoms with a common king. Thus Croatia was still an independent state; however, the Hungarian dynasty had succeeded the Croatian kings. Each Hungarian king would have to come to Croatia for a separate coronation. The separate coronation in Croatia lasted until it was dispensed with in 1235. Latin was made the official language of state. This basic situation was to last from 1102 (with an interruption for much of Croatia by the Ottoman period) to 1918.

The Croatian nobles (i.e., the hereditary provincial leaders and landlords) were thus recognized in their positions by the Hungarian king and they in turn recognized him as king of Croatia (by a separate coronation). These nobles were probably relatively content since they had just escaped from an attack by the Croatian rulers (particularly Zvonimir) on their positions and privileges. Thus they were allowed to remain as basically independent lords on their lands and as local leaders. They were to continue in this position throughout the medieval period up to the Ottoman conquest of most of Croatia.

By owing loyalty to a Hungarian king who was also crowned king of Croatia they sacrificed little: (1) Foreign affairs were in the hands of the king of Hungary. (2) The king was the commander-in-chief of the army and the nobles owed him military service when summoned (but this had been owed earlier to the Croatian ruler); however, if they had to cross the Drava, the Hungarian king had to pay. And the king had the mutual obligation to defend Croatia from attack. (3) The Hungarian king appointed a ban of Croatia; but it seems that other than being a military leader for campaigns this ban interfered little in local affairs. Later, some of these local bans would be Croatian noblemen. General Croatian matters were to be discussed at the Croatian diet (whenever this section of the treaty appeared, be it originally or later). The king did have to confirm decisions of the diet before they became law. But if the diet did exist prior to 1102, the Croatian ruler presumably would have had to confirm its decisions too. And the Hungarian king confirmed these decisions as king of Croatia.

Other than these few items everything else was left in the hands of the nobles: internal administration, judicial matters, land policy, and the like. There was no integration of the Croatian state with the Hungarian. Except for the ban, no Hungarians were sent to administer in Croatia. In fact, there was very little integration in Croatia at all. Power remained basically on a county level under local nobles, which was how matters had been until then. Though the king seems to have received some taxes and customs duties in Croatia, it seems that the nobles owed no tax to the king. They rendered him only military service. The king, however, did receive for his personal use the estates of the extinct Croatian royal family.

Occasionally later, individual nobles were to try to break away from Hungary. For example, some of those near Bosnia later accepted the suzerainty of the king of Bosnia instead of the Hungarian king. Some succeeded for a while, and at times the Hungarian kings had to send troops thither to reassert their authority. At times there also were civil wars over the Hungarian throne. On these occasions the Croatian nobles often split, some for each rival, and civil wars were then fought throughout Croatia. There also were to be cases of civil wars within Croatian families or between different Croatian families for local power. Thus despite the long-lasting system established by the Hungarians, there often was anything but tranquility in Croatia. But despite these stormy events, Croatia remained a region in the hands of its nobles, not integrated into the Hungarian state.

Just as almost no Hungarians came to Croatia—excluding Slavonia—few Croatians went to Hungary. In the following centuries a few Croatians, along with members of other nationalities, could be found at the Hungarian court; but it is necessary to emphasize again that Hungary was constructed like other medieval empires (e.g., like Byzantium), having multinational populations united around a common religion (in this case Roman Catholicism). Though the largest element at the Hungarian court was Hungarian, all the nationalities of the kingdom could be found there; and little favoritism along national lines existed.

A second unifying factor was Latin, which was dominant in the whole kingdom as the official church and court language. Almost all documents (including nearly all the medieval royal letters) in Hungary until the middle of the nineteenth century were to be in Latin. (Clearly vernacular dominated among the people, and presumably even at court among Hungarians; but Latin did give members of the different nationalities at court a common language in which to communicate.) In addition almost all Croatian documents, charters, and land grants were in Latin. Whether the nobility all spoke Latin well may be doubted—though presumably those resident at the Hungarian court did—but there existed a large number of scribes (many of whom were priests) to draw up documents.

Thus was established a dual monarchy with the king of Hungary monarch for two states originally with two coronations. At home in Croatia the local nobles retained their local independence, caring more about their own privileges and local power than about maintaining an independent Croatian state. This "contract" of 1102—regardless of whether it actually took place as claimed—became the legal basis not only for the Hungarian king's rule in the Middle Ages, but also for the Hungarian claim—which was allowed—that Croatia be in the Hungarian part of the Habsburg Dual Monarchy in 1867.

The verdict given in the previous paragraph, which is seen in most Croatian works, is seriously criticized by N. Klaić. She believes that the events of 1102 did not consist of a loss of Croatian independence. Since the Croatian nobles kept their autonomy, Croatians continued to rule Croatians in the counties. The peasants remained under Croatian nobles. Feudalism was a tie to a dynasty and not to a nation. The change in 1102 was one of dynasties—accepting the Hungarian—and of capitals. But the nation remained. The aim of the nobility had been to keep the ruler weak, and it was unimportant what language he spoke. Why should a nobleman or any other Croatian have supported a dynasty just because it originated from his own region and its representative had a common language with him? The nobles after 1102 were able to keep their autonomy and life remained unchanged for their villagers, who knew neither dynasty. Thus, Klaić concludes, there was a change of dynasty but not the end of the Croatian nation. One should not, as many later historians have, see 1102 as a national collapse or the end of the state. The Croatian nation survived throughout the Hungarian period, as did the ethnic consciousness of its people.

Bosnia in the Twelfth Century

It was only Pannonian Croatia which remained permanently with Hungary. Two other regions also went to Hungary: Bosnia in 1102, and Dalmatia by 1107. Bosnia as a distant region was hard to control and soon is found under its own ban who in theory remained under Hungarian suzerainty. In the 1150s, its ban, Borić, was to lead Bosnian troops to Beograd to aid the Hungarians against the Byzantines. In the 1180s Bosnia for all practical purposes became an independent state, though through much of its independent period suzerainty was to be claimed by the Hungarians.

Dalmatia in the Twelfth Century

Dalmatia was too important for other powers to sit back and allow Hungary to keep. Right after the death of Koloman in 1116, Venice attacked Hungary's Dalmatian holdings. The Dalmatian cities seem to have been unhappy with Hungary for one after another they opened their gates to the Venetians (who were working with the Byzantines). Zadar, Split, Trogir, Biograd, and much of the rest of Dalmatia came over to Venice. In 1117 Hungary invaded Dalmatia to try to regain its lost cities, but the attack failed even though the doge of Venice was killed in the fighting. Again in 1124 the Hungarians attacked the Dalmatian cities, which were still held by Venice. But though the Hungarians found the Dalmatians more friendly to them now, they still could not regain Dalmatia.

By the 1150s Hungary had reestablished cordial relations with the German empire which freed it once again to give its attention to Dalmatia which was still under Venice. Geza led an attack which recovered Zadar in 1158. In the course of the wars between Manuel and Hungary, noted earlier, the Byzantines invaded Hungarian Dalmatia in the mid-1160s. In 1167 after the major Byzantine victory at Zemun, the Hungarians recognized Byzantine rule over the empire's former Dalmatian towns. After the mass arrest of the Venetians resident in the empire in 1171 set off a ten-year Venetian-Byzantine war, Venice in 1172 took certain of these Dalmatian towns, including Trogir and Dubrovnik; but Byzantine action and an epidemic led to a quick Byzantine recovery.

In 1180, while the Venetian war was still in progress, the emperor Manuel died, leaving a weak regency. It was apparent that Dalmatia would fall to either Venice or Hungary, and clearly, since the empire was at war with Venice and since the Hungarian ruler was Bela III, with whom the empire had close ties, Hungary was preferable. Thus seemingly without bloodshed and with imperial consent Bela recovered the Dalmatian cities in 1181. The Venetians had already occupied Zadar, however, and the Hungarians had to take that city by force in February 1181. Since Zadar was in danger from a Venetian counterattack, a Hungarian governor was established in Zadar. The Venetians made an unsuccessful attempt to recover Zadar in 1193. They gained it only in 1203 when they utilized the Fourth Crusade to take it from the Hungarians. The Venetians insisted that the Crusaders do this service for them to pay for their transport east. The fact that the Hungarian king was a Catholic who had already pledged himself to take the Cross for the crusade was immaterial. But by this time we are in the midst of the subject matter of the next volume. As the present volume draws to a close in the 1180s, the Hungarians were once again in possession of Dalmatia with the Venetians hovering in the wings, with their ships dominating the Adriatic, just waiting for a chance to regain the Dalmatian towns.

Summary

In this work we have traced the history of the Balkans from the sixth century to the 1180s. We have seen established the foundations of the contemporary Balkans. The Greeks and Albanians were already old-timers there in the sixth century—when this volume began. They were jolted by the arrival of the invaders who were to establish the Slavic states in the Balkans. We have traced the development of the Slavs into different ethnic groups and have seen how each (except the Macedonians) acquired an ethnic consciousness that has lasted to the present time. These developments, as well as the first state formations of all these Slavic peoples, occurred in this critical period. We have also seen the conversion of the new peoples to Christianity and have seen that whether a region was to be Catholic or Orthodox (after the church split) had been determined for everyone but the Albanians and Bosnians in the period we have covered.

We have examined the states which these different peoples established in the early medieval period. Except for the Bulgarians all produced relatively short-lasting and unstable states. The proximity to Bulgaria of Byzantium, both as a model and as an enemy to unite the Bulgarians to defend themselves against, was a major factor in the greater stability of the Bulgarian state. But now as we enter the end of the twelfth century, we see that the Byzantine Empire was declining in strength. We shall see in the next volume how separatism by powerful noblemen in various provinces of the imperial Balkans was increasing. And, as the empire succumbed to feudalism and as its central government became less and less able to control its provinces, the Bulgarians got a chance to liberate themselves from the empire and recreated an independent Bulgarian state. At the same time the Serbs were able to shed their vassalage to Byzantium and assert their full independence. These two developments—along with the establishment of an autonomous Bosnian state (in theory under Hungarian overlordship)—were features of the 1180s. With the establishment of these new states— each of which was to develop and increase in power—we enter a new period of medieval Balkan history. The history of these independent states will be dealt with in the second volume of this history.

NOTES

1. This section is heavily indebted to the conclusions of J. Ferluga, *Vizantiska uprava u Dalmaciji,* Serbian Academy of Sciences, posebna izdanja, 291, Vizantološki Institut, knj. 6 (Beograd, 1957).

2. For Dvornik's views see F. Dvornik, *Byzantine Missions among the Slavs* (New Brusnwick, N.J., 1970).

3. For Klaić's views see N. Klaić, *Povijest Hrvata u ranom srednjem vijeku* (Zagreb, 1971).

Medieval Rulers

Byzantine Emperors to 1204

324–37	Constantine I
337–61	Constantius
361–63	Julian
363–64	Jovian
364–78	Valens
379–95	Theodosius I
395–408	Arcadius
408–50	Theodosius II
450–57	Marcian
457–74	Leo I
474	Leo II
474–75	Zeno
475–76	Basiliscus
476–91	Zeno (again)
491–518	Anastasius I
518–27	Justin I
527–65	Justinian I
565–78	Justin II
578–82	Tiberius I Constantine
582–602	Maurice
602–10	Phocas
610–41	Heraclius
641	Constantine III and Heraclonas
641	Heraclonas
641–68	Constans II

668–85	Constantine IV
685–95	Justinian II
695–98	Leontius
698–705	Tiberius II
705–11	Justinian II (again)
711–13	Philippicus
713–15	Anastasius II
715–17	Theodosius III
717–41	Leo III
741–75	Constantine V
775–80	Leo IV
780–97	Constantine VI
797–802	Irene
802–11	Nicephorus I
811	Staurakios
811–13	Michael I Rangabe
813–20	Leo V
820–29	Michael II
829–42	Theophilus
842–67	Michael III
867–86	Basil I
886–912	Leo VI
912–13	Alexander
913–59	Constantine VII
920–44	Romanus I Lecapenus
959–63	Romanus II
963–69	Nicephorus II Phocas
969–76	John I Tzimiskes
976–1025	Basil II
1025–28	Constantine VIII
1028–34	Romanus III Argyrus
1034–41	Michael IV
1041–42	Michael V
1042	Zoe and Theodora
1042–55	Constantine IX Monomachus
1055–56	Theodora (again)

1056–57	Michael VI
1057–59	Isaac I Comnenus
1059–67	Constantine X Ducas
1068–71	Romanus IV Diogenes
1071–78	Michael VII Ducas
1078–81	Nicephorus III Botaneiates
1081–1118	Alexius I Comnenus
1118–43	John II Comnenus
1143–80	Manuel I Comnenus
1180–83	Alexius II Comnenus
1183–85	Andronicus I Comnenus
1185–95	Isaac II Angelus
1195–1203	Alexius III Angelus
1203–04	Isaac II (again) and Alexius IV Angeli
1204	Alexius V Murtzuphlus

Bulgarian Rulers
From the arrival of the Bulgars in the Balkans to the Byzantine conquest in 1018

House of Dulo

670s–701	Isperikh (Asparukh)
701–18	Tervel
718–25	(unknown)
725–39	Sevar

Rulers during "Time of Troubles"

739–56	Kormisoš
756–ca. 761	Vinekh
ca. 761–ca. 764	Telec
ca. 764–67	Sabin
767	Umar
767–ca. 769	Toktu
ca. 770	Pagan
ca. 770–77	Telerig
777–ca. 803	Kardam

House of Krum

ca. 803–14	Krum
814–31	Omurtag
831–36	Malamir
836–52	Persian (Presiam; possibly same as Malamir)
852–89	Boris I
889–93	Vladimir
893–927	Symeon
927–67	Peter
967–71	Boris II

Descendants of Count Nicholas (The Cometopuli)

from 976	Four brothers (Samuel, Aaron, Moses, David)
986–1014	Samuel (ruling alone)
1014–15	Gabriel Radomir
1015–18	John Vladislav

Rulers of Croatia

Dalmatian Croatia

ca. 800–ca. 810	Višeslav
ca. 810–21	Borna
821–?	Borna's nephew
	(gap)
845–64	Trpimir I
864	Zdeslav
864–76	Domagoj
876	Domagoj's son
876–79	Zdeslav (again)
879–92	Branimir
892–910	Mutimir (possibly Mutimir died ca. 900 and was succeeded by several rulers with brief reigns to 910)

Dalmatian Croatia United with Slavonia

ca. 910–28	Tomislav (king by 925)
ca. 928–49	(somewhat confused situation follows Tomislav, including rule by a Kresimir I)
949–69	Kresimir II
969–97	Stjepan Držislav (king from ca. 988)
997–1000	Svetoslav (with brothers Kresimir and Gojislav)
1000–30	Kresimir III (with Gojislav to 1020)
1030–58	Stjepan I
1058–74/5	Peter Kresimir IV
1075–89/90	Zvonimir
1090–93	"Troubles"
1093–97	Peter

After Stjepan Držislav's coronation in 988 all Croatian rulers had the title of king.

Serbian Rulers

mid-ninth century	Vlastimir
mid-ninth century	(succeeded by 3 sons: Mutimir, Strojimir, and Gojnik)
? –891	Mutimir (sole rule)
891–92	Prvoslav
892–917	Peter Gojniković
917–21	Pavel Branović
921–24	Zaharije Prvoslavljević
924–ca. 927/28	(Bulgaria annexes Serbia)
ca. 927/28–ca. 960	Časlav Klonimirović

Rulers of Duklja (Zeta)

late-tenth century–1016	John Vladimir
	(thereafter possibly annexed by Byzantium or possibly a vassal state under a local prince whose name has not survived)
ca. 1034–43	Vojislav (or Stefan Vojislav)
1043–ca. 1046	(joint rule by several family members)

ca. 1046–1081/82	Michael (king from ca. 1046)
1081/82–ca. 1101	Constantine Bodin (but see chapter 7 for other views on Bodin's reign-dates)
ca. 1101–02	Michael and Dobroslav
ca. 1102–03	Kočapar
ca. 1103–18	Vladimir
ca. 1118	Juraj
ca. 1118–25	Grubeša
ca. 1125–27	Juraj (again)
ca. 1127–46	Gradinja
1146–?	Radoslav (with title knez)

The dates for the successors of Bodin are all approximate and it is possible, since our source is based on oral tradition, that even the list of names might have inaccuracies. The rulers from Michael in ca. 1046 through Gradinja (dying in ca. 1146) all bore the title king.

Raška

1083/4–ca. 1122	Vukan (governor of Raška for Zeta, who became independent ruler of Raška with title grand župan in early 1090s)
by 1125–early 1140s	Uroš I
by 1145–early 1160s	Uroš II (Desa briefly replaced Uroš II, 1150, 1155)
ca. 1162	(possibly brief rule by a Primislav and/or Beloš)
ca. 1162–ca. 1166	Desa (again)
ca. 1166–67	Tihomir (brother of Stefan Nemanja)
ca. 1168–71	Joint rule (Tihomir, Stefan Nemanja, Stracimir, Miroslav)
ca. 1171–96	Stefan Nemanja

Hungarian Rulers Discussed in Text

1095–1116	Koloman
1116–31	Stephen II
1131–41	Bela II
1141–62	Geza II
1162–72	Stephen III (throne briefly lost twice to rival Stephen IV, 1163 and ca. 1165)
1172–96	Bela III

Glossaries

Terms

Adoptionists: People who believed that Jesus was a man adopted by God as the "Son of God." This current (associated with Paul of Samosata) was widespread in Syria, Armenia, and the Greek East in the third and fourth centuries and probably survived as the theological basis for the Paulicians (active in the empire from the eighth to the eleventh century). Adoptionism was considered a heresy by the Orthodox church.

"Adulterer": A term of abuse used by Extremist Byzantine clerics for their Moderate opponents in the eighth and ninth centuries. It goes back to the Moderates condoning a second marriage, while his first wife was still alive (hence adulterous), for the emperor Constantine VI in 793.

Albigensians: The dualist (or Cathar) heretics of southern France derived from the town of Albi, one of their main centers.

Appanage: A large land grant by a ruler to a member of his family. Usually not hereditary. Holder usually has rights of internal administration but owes military service to his superior, and is allowed no independence in foreign affairs.

Archon: A leader; used in a variety of ways by the Byzantines, e.g., the ruler of Bulgaria, the leader of their Dalmatian holdings in the eighth century, etc.

Archonate of Dalmatia: The cities held by the Byzantines along the Dalmatian coast from the late seventh century through the first half of the ninth century. The archonate had no overall intercity organization; Zadar was the capital of the archonate, the seat of the archon, who was a local Zadar leader.

Arians: Followers of Arius, an Alexandrian theologian, who taught that Jesus Christ was neither fully God (consubstantial with God) nor coeternal but a subordinate creature. This view was condemned at the Councils of Nicea (325) and Constantinople (381). However, the Germanic Goths were converted by an Arian missionary and Arianism survived as the dominant form of Christianity among them while they resided in the Balkans (fourth to late fifth century).

Ban: A ruler or governor of a large province, usually a subordinate of a king. The title was found used in the western Balkans, in Bosnia, Croatia, and Slavonia. On occasions the ban-ship became hereditary. Bans also sometimes were able to achieve considerable, if not complete, autonomy.

Banovina (sometimes banate): The territory ruled by a ban.

Basileus: A Greek term for king which under the Byzantines came to signify emperor, and was the term used in the title of the Byzantine emperor.

Basilica: A type of building used for Roman official buildings taken over by the church in the fourth century to become the major form of early Byzantine churches. A basilica was a rectangular-shaped church with a semicircular apse at the end and three aisles separated by two rows of columns. Basilicas were common in the Balkans prior to the Slavic invasions and this style was also used by the Slavs after their conversion.

Bogomilism: A heretical current arising in Bulgaria in the mid-tenth century, believing in two principles (i.e., dualistic) which spread beyond Bulgaria into the Byzantine Empire and from there along the Mediterranean to the south of western Europe.

Boyar (bojar): A member of the military aristocracy in Bulgaria. In the early period the boyars were drawn from leading Turkic Bulgar families. The term was also used in Russia.

Caesar: The second title (after emperor) in the Byzantine Empire until the late eleventh century, frequently given to the heir to the throne.

Cathars: Dualist heretics found in southern France.

Cometopuli: The four sons of Count Nicholas in Macedonia who rose in 976 to unite Macedonia. By 986 only one, Samuel, survived. He created a brief but powerful state centered in Macedonia, but called Bulgarian, which was eventually conquered by Basil II for Byzantium.

Count palatine: The highest figure below the king at the Hungarian court who governed in the absence of the king.

Cyrillic: The alphabet used for the Slavic languages of the Orthodox Slavs (e.g., Bulgarians, Serbs [including Montenegrins], Macedonians, and Russians). It was named for Saint Cyril (Constantine), one of the two apostles to the Slavs who worked out the first Slavic literary language (what we now call Old Church Slavonic).

Despot: An honorary court title of the Byzantine Empire, introduced in the twelfth century to be the second highest title (after that of basileus).

Doge: The title for the ruler of Venice.

Dragovica: (Church of) a dualist (Bogomil) church based in Thrace in the thirteenth century; (tribe of) a Slavic tribe found in Macedonia and Thrace in the seventh and eighth centuries.

Dualist: Religiously, one who believes in two opposing gods or principles: generally good vs. evil (or spirit vs. matter). Under this heading one finds the Manichees, Gnostics, the medieval Bogomils, and their western off-shoots (Patarins, Cathars, etc.).

Dulo, house of: The ruling house of the Onogur Bulgars, ruling north of the Sea of Azov early in the seventh century, one branch of which conquered the territory of modern Bulgaria in the 670s. The dynasty died out in 739.

Dux: A Roman military commander. In the Byzantine period the title was given to the military commander of a small theme (military province), such as Durazzo or a frontier duchy in the east, such as Antioch. The doge of Venice was also recognized as dux of Dalmatia in 998. This signified Venice was to represent Byzantium in Dalmatia.

Emir: A prince or governor of an Islamic territory.

Emirate: The territory ruled by an emir.

Emperor of the Romans: The Byzantine emperor's title, and believed to be the only true and rightful emperor on earth.

Eparch: A Greek title used for a governor (and in the church for a bishop). It was granted to Držislav of Croatia (eparch of Dalmatia) in the 990s. In his case it was probably an honorary title.

Exarch: A high military commander, generally standing over a large province, an exarchate; e.g., Ravenna (Byzantine Italy), Carthage (Byzantine North Africa). Also occasionally used in Byzantine sources for a tribal military leader.

Extremists: A group of Byzantine clerics in the late eighth and ninth centuries who believed in rigorously observing church laws and were frequently in opposition to Byzantine state policy.

Federates: Barbarians settled within the Roman Empire, under their own leaders, who were responsible for the defense of the region of their settlement.

Fibula: In archaeology, a buckle or clasp.

Filioque: "And the Son," an addition to the Nicene Creed, making the Holy Spirit descend from the Father *and the Son.* Arising in Spain in the sixth century, by the ninth it had become regular usage by the western (Catholic) church. After the 1054 break it became the major theological point of difference between the Orthodox and Catholic churches.

Glagolitic: The first alphabet worked out by Cyril and Methodius for Slavic. It was soon replaced in most places by the Cyrillic alphabet. However, it survived for many centuries in Croatia.

Hellene: A Greek; however, since the term connoted a pagan, the Greeks did not call themselves Hellenes in the Middle Ages, but Romans (since they considered themselves citizens of the Roman Empire).

Hippodrome: A stadium for horse races. In this book, it generally refers to the great stadium in Constantinople.

Icon: A religious picture.

Iconoclasm: The belief that there should not be religious pictures, generally seeing them as a form of idolatry. The term literally means icon-breaking. This view was state policy in the Byzantine Empire from 730 to 787 and from 815 to 843.

Iconoclast: One practicing Iconoclasm, an opponent of icons.

Iconodule: One supporting icons, literally a slave (servant) of icons.

Immunities: Exemptions, usually attached to an estate. They could be financial (from certain taxes) or judicial (allowing the landlord to judge his tenants for certain types of crimes or law suits).

Inner (or Interior) boyar: A term used for certain Bulgarian boyars in Byzantine sources. It most probably refers to the boyars based at court as opposed to those resident on estates in the provinces.

Katepan: A Byzantine title arising in Italy for the commander of a military province. The katepan was the equivalent of a strategos, and in addition to his military duties also had certain civil functions.

Kavkhan: Bulgarian title; second title in the state. Held by the leading military commander, excluding the ruler himself, and possibly also regent in the absence of the khan.

Khagan: Turkish title for a supreme chief used, e.g., by the Avars and Khazars.

Khan: The same word as *khagan;* however, scholars usually use the form *khan* when describing the pre-Christian rulers of the Bulgars.

Knez (in Serbian or Croatian; *knjaz* in Bulgarian): Prince.

Libellus: A written declaration; often the basis for a prosecution's case. The term is a Latin diminutive of *liber* (book).

Limitanei: Roman troops settled on a border and responsible for its defense.

Logothete: In the Middle Byzantine period, a high Byzantine court secretary standing at the head of a bureaucratic office.

Manichee: A member of a dualistic religion (opposing light against darkness) based on the teaching of a third-century Persian named Mani. Damned as a heresy by the Christian church.

Massalians (or Messalians): Members of an enthusiastic Christian sect. They believed salvation came from prayer and asceticism and not sacraments. Little is known about them since all that survive are highly slanderous attacks by their enemies (accusing them of licentiousness). They arose in the fourth century in Syria and seem to have died out in the seventh century. However, attacks upon the later Bogomils frequently use *Massalian* as a label of abuse for the Bogomils.

Metropolitan: A major bishop, standing over a major diocese, ranking below the patriarch and above the archbishops.

Moderates: In the eighth and ninth century, the Byzantine church party opposed to the Extremists. The Moderates were willing to interpret canons flexibly. They were willing to tolerate repentant ex-Iconoclasts in church positions and were willing to bend church canons for the needs of state.

Nicea, Council of: The first ecumenical (universal) church council held at Nicea in 325 to condemn Arius. It passed the Nicene Creed.

Nicene: One who accepts the creed of the Council of Nicea.

Obščina: The village commune in early modern Russia, a taxable unit.

Old Church Slavonic (OCS): The name recently given by scholars to the Slavic language devised by Constantine (Cyril) and Methodius in the middle of the ninth century. The first written Slavic language, they translated the Bible into it and it became the language of church services for the Orthodox Slavic churches. It was based upon a spoken Macedonian dialect to which various Greek features were added. The words *Old Church* distinguish it from the various literary languages that evolved from it on the basis of local spoken languages, e.g., Bulgarian Slavonic, Russian Slavonic, etc.

Orthodox: Correct belief. A term used for the mainstream church in East and West until the church split. Subsequently the term came to refer to the eastern churches in communion with Constantinople, while the term *Catholic,* also originally used to refer to the church both in the East and West, came to refer solely to the Roman Catholic church.

Outer boyar: A term used for certain Bulgarian boyars in the Byzantine sources. It most probably refers to the boyars resident on their estates in the provinces as opposed to those resident at court.

Pallium: A cloak worn by a bishop which was considered a major symbol of his office.

Patarin: A name used for the dualist heretics in Italy, who were part of the Cathar movement.

Patriarch: A major bishop who was the independent head of a major diocese. In the early church (from the mid-fifth century) there were five recognized patriarchates: Rome, Constantinople, Antioch, Alexandria, and Jerusalem. After their conversions the various Slavic churches sought (and at times unilaterally assumed) this title for the heads of their various churches, sometimes even achieving recognition of this title from the Constantinopolitan patriarch. The first Slavic patriarch was the Bulgarian, probably declared by Symeon, recognized by Byzantium in 927. When Byzantium conquered Bulgaria this patriarch's title was reduced to archbishop.

Patriarchal family: A family unit, often a large one including several generations, which is autocratically run by the family "patriarch" (usually the eldest male).

Patrician: Member of an order of high nobility in Byzantium appointed by the emperor; on occasions foreign princes were honored with this rank by the Byzantine emperor.

Paulicians: Members of a religious sect, seen as heretical by the Orthodox church, arising in Armenia and eastern Anatolia. Long considered to be dualist, but more recently shown to be adoptionist. Many Paulicians, after suffering military reversals at Byzantine hands, were then transferred to the Balkans to defend the border with Bulgaria where (centered in Philippopolis) they continued to retain their individuality.

Perfectus: A Cathar who had received spiritual baptism and thus was considered to possess the Holy Spirit. As such he could be considered clergy as opposed to the larger number of unbaptized (lay) followers.

Perun: The Slavic god of thunder.

Philhellenes: The Europeans and Americans who actively supported the Greeks in their war of independence against the Turks, 1821–33.

Prefectures: The late Roman–early Byzantine Empire was divided into huge administrative provinces called prefectures, each under a Praetorian prefect.

Prior of Zadar: The head man of the city of Zadar who, when the Byzantines in the tenth century were no longer able to take an active role in their Dalmatian theme, was given the entirely nominal title of strategos of Dalmatia.

Proconsul: Derived from the title of a Roman governor, this term in the Byzantine period became an honorary rank which was granted at times to important foreign leaders.

Pronoia: In the Byzantine empire (and later Bulgaria and Serbia), a grant of a source of income (usually land) given in exchange for service (usually military) to the state. The grant was temporary and reverted back to the state when the holder died or ceased to carry out the duties for which it was given.

Protostrator: A high Byzantine court title which occasionally was granted to foreign leaders.

Protovestijar: The title of a Byzantine palace official in charge of the imperial wardrobe which was taken over by the Slavs. Though it is not certain what the early Slavic protovestijar's functions were he seems to have been some sort of financial official.

Sbornik: A collection of texts.

Solidus: A Byzantine coin. Seventy-two of them equaled a Roman pound of gold. (A Roman pound equaled about twelve American ounces.)

Stefanos: The wreath-shaped crown worn by a Byzantine caesar.

Stemma: The crown worn by the Byzantine emperor.

Strategos (pl. strategoi): A Greek term for "general"; from the seventh century used, however, specifically for the military commander of a theme (military province). He not only commanded the local troops but was also more or less the governor of the province.

Studites: Monks of the great monastery of Studios in Constantinople. They were very influential in Byzantine church politics and usually a bastion of support for the Extremist faction.

Suffragan bishopric: A lesser bishopric subordinate to a greater one.

Synod: A Church council.

Synodik: A text presenting the decisions of a synod.

Theme: Originally a Greek term for an army corps, it came in the seventh century also to refer to a Byzantine military province defended by that corps. Soon thereafter the whole Byzantine Empire was divided into these themes (military provinces) each under the direction of a strategos.

Toponym: A place name.

Tourma: A military district within a theme. Each theme was divided into two to four such districts, each commanded by a tourmarch.

Tourmarch: The military governor of a tourma.

Tsar: The Slavic translation of the Greek *basileus,* emperor. The Slavs used the title when referring to the Byzantine emperor. In time when certain Slavic rulers (starting with Symeon in Bulgaria in the 910s) claimed for themselves the imperial title they called themselves tsars.

Zadruga: A scholarly term for the South Slavic extended family, i.e., a household where several generations of the same family lived together.

Župa: A territorial unit (roughly equivalent to a county) found in Croatia, Bosnia, and Serbia.

Župan: The lord of a county.

Peoples

When a people is referred to below as, e.g., Indo-European or Turkic, it refers to language spoken rather than to race or ethnicity.

Albanians: An Indo-European people, probably descended from the ancient Illyrians, living now in Albania as well as in Greece and Yugoslavia.

Antes: An ancient tribe. Though their name is of Iranian origin, by the time they came into contact with the Byzantine Empire, the Antes were Slavic-speaking. They appeared from the Steppes in the fifth century in what is now eastern Rumania and Bessarabia.

Armenians: An Indo-European people living in the Caucasus and in parts of eastern Anatolia. In the course of the Middle Ages many migrated or were transferred to other regions of Anatolia and the Balkans. They had their own church which, owing to an interpretation of how the human and divine were mixed in Christ which differed from that of the Orthodox church, was considered heretical by the Byzantines.

Arnauts: Another name for the Albanians.

Avars: A Turkic people who migrated into what is now Hungary in the late sixth century and established through their dominance of other peoples (including Bulgars and Slavs) a huge empire that included most of what is now the Ukraine, Rumania, Hungary, Yugoslavia, and Czechoslovakia. Their empire began declining after successful rebellions by various subject people in the second quarter of the seventh century. Their independent power was destroyed by Charlemagne in the 790s.

Belo Croats (White Croats): The Croatians of a Croatian state existing in the seventh century north of the Carpathians whence, according to Constantine Porphyrogenitus, the Croatians who migrated into the Balkans in the seventh century came.

Bulgars: A Turkic people, divided into various tribes, found north of the Black Sea and Sea of Azov. In the late seventh century some of them migrated across the Danube into what is now northern Bulgaria, where they conquered the Slavs already settled there. By the late ninth or early tenth century the Bulgars had become slavicized. However, their name was given to the Slavic people (and its language) that resulted. From the tenth century on the term refers to a Slavic people.

Byzantine: A term invented by scholars to distinguish the later Roman Empire beginning with Constantine in the 320s, after the empire became centered in the East and Christian, up to its fall in 1453. However, throughout this period those we now call Byzantines called, and considered, themselves Romans even though most of them were Greek-speakers.

Celts: An ancient people which included the Britons, Gauls, and modern Irish. On their migration west in the fourth century B.C. some settled for a time in the Balkans, leaving behind certain cultural influences.

Croats: A people, probably of Iranian origin, who migrated into the western Balkans in the seventh century and subjected the Slavs settled there. In time they became slavicized but gave their name to the Slavic people (and its language) of what is now Croatia, Dalmatia, and part of Bosnia. From the ninth century, if not earlier, they are clearly a Slavic people.

Cumans (Also called the Polovtsy): A Turkic people who appeared in the Steppes in the eleventh century after the decline of the Pechenegs. They were a problem for the eastern Balkans for the next two centuries owing to their raids. However, others settled in Bulgaria and provided a valuable portion of the armies of the Second Bulgarian Empire.

Dacians: An ancient Indo-European people settled in what is now Rumania, northern Bulgaria, and northeastern Yugoslavia. They were scattered by the Slavic invasions but survived to become the ancestors of the modern Rumanians and Vlachs.

Dragovica Slavs: A Slavic tribe settled in Thrace and parts of Macedonia noted in sources of the seventh and eighth century, who gave their name to a region of Thrace in the Middle Ages.

Ezeritae: A Slavic tribe in the mountains of the Peloponnesus which unlike most of the other Slavs of Greece did not become hellenized but retained its identity and remained Slavic-speaking throughout the Middle Ages into the Ottoman period.

Fātimids: A Muslim dynasty in North Africa founded early in the tenth century. In 969 they conquered Egypt and ruled their empire from Cairo.

Franks: A Germanic tribe which conquered most of Gaul and eventually established a powerful state centered in what is now France and Germany, but whose borders extended well beyond. Charlemagne, the greatest Frankish ruler, in 800 won recognition from the pope that his state was an empire. In this period the Franks were active in the northwestern Balkans, and for a while were overlords over most of the Croatians.

Gepids: A Germanic tribe found in the fifth and sixth centuries in the northwestern Balkans, and what is now Hungary.

Ghuzz Turks: A Turkish tribe that swept across the Steppes and raided the Balkans in 1064.

Goths: Germanic tribes, consisting chiefly of Ostrogoths and Visigoths, who raided and then settled in large numbers (causing considerable chaos) in the Balkans from the fourth century until the very end of the fifth.

Greeks: The ancient settlers of Greece who also lived along the Thracian coast and existed in large numbers in Anatolia. They became the dominant people of the Roman Empire in the period after Constantine moved its center to the east.

Huns: Asiatic nomads who dominated the Steppes and the Hungarian plains and raided central Europe and the Balkans during the fifth century. Their famed leader was Attila.

Hungarians (or Magyars): A Finno-Ugric nomadic people who moved into what is now Hungary at the end of the ninth century. They established a powerful state that has survived to the present.

Illyrians: An ancient Indo-European people dominating the western Balkans (what is now Dalmatia, Bosnia, Albania, Epirus), though conquered by Rome, until the Slavic invasions. They have survived in a much more restricted area as the Albanians.

Khazars: A Turkic tribe dominating the Steppes with centers on the lower Volga and Don. They were a major power in that area from the seventh century until their destruction by Svjatoslav of Kiev in 965. They were generally allies of the Byzantines.

Kutrigurs: A Bulgarian tribe noted in the late fifth and sixth centuries living north of the Black Sea and in what is now Bessarabia.

Lombards: A Germanic people living in the northern Balkans and Pannonia in the sixth century who migrated into Italy in the late sixth century when the Avars appeared on their borders.

Magyars: See Hungarians.

Melingi: A Slavic tribe in the mountains of the Peloponnesus which unlike most of the other Slavs of Greece did not become hellenized but retained its identity and remained Slavic-speaking throughout the Middle Ages into the Ottoman period.

Neretljani: A Slavic people, living between the Neretva and Cetina rivers, very active as sailors and pirates from the ninth through eleventh centuries.

Normans: By the time they hit the Balkans they were French-speaking, having come from Normandy. Most of those active in campaigns in the Balkans were based in southern Italy which they had conquered in the course of the eleventh century.

Onogur Bulgars: A Turkic Bulgar tribe first mentioned in the early seventh century living north of the Black Sea and Sea of Azov. From this group, led in the 630s by Kovrat, emerged various Bulgar groups including those led across the Danube by Isperikh in the 670s to found the Bulgarian state in the Balkans.

Ostrogoths (East Goths): One tribe of Goths which was active in the Balkans in the fourth and fifth centuries until, led by Theodoric, they conquered Italy in the 490s, which they ruled until conquered by Justinian in the 550s.

Ottomans (Osmanlis): A Turkish tribe ruled by the dynasty founded by Osman (1299–1326) which expanded from a small principality in northwest Anatolia to conquer the whole Byzantine Empire during the late fourteenth and fifteenth centuries.

Pechenegs (also Patzinaks): A Turkic tribe which dominated the Steppes from the end of the ninth to the end of the eleventh centuries. They were frequently raiders of the Balkans and also participated as mercenaries or allies in various wars in the Balkans.

Polovtsy: See Cumans.

Roman: A citizen of the Roman Empire. In the Byzantine period (324–1453) the citizens of that empire, though chiefly composed of Greek-speakers, continued to call themselves Romans.

Sarmatians: An Iranian tribe originating in the Steppes but settled in the territory north of the Danube in the third, fourth, and fifth centuries.

Saxons: Germans from Saxony; however, in time many migrated to Hungary where some became active as miners. Some came from Hungary into various Balkan regions between the thirteenth and fifteenth centuries, where they were known as Sasi.

Scythians: An Iranian people which dominated the Steppes during the first millennium B.C.

Seljuks: A Turkish dynasty establishing itself in Iraq (Baghdad) in the middle of the eleventh century as protectors of the caliph. Their tribesmen (with other loyal Turkish tribes) expanded to control almost all of Anatolia by the 1080s.

Serbs: A people, probably of Iranian origin, who migrated into what is now southeastern Yugoslavia in the first half of the seventh century and subjected the Slavs settled there. In time they became slavicized but gave their name to the Slavic people and its language of what is now Serbia, Montenegro, part of Bosnia, and most of Hercegovina. From the ninth century, if not earlier, they are clearly a Slavic people.

The Seven Tribes: A group of Slavic tribes (probably having formed some sort of confederation) existing in Bulgaria in the 670s who were conquered by the invading Bulgars.

The Severi: A Slavic tribe in Bulgaria which even after the arrival of the Bulgars still was found maintaining considerable independence during the eighth century.

Slaveni: A Slavic tribe mentioned living north of the Danube in the fifth and sixth centuries which provided much of the manpower which over-whelmed the Balkans in the sixth and early seventh centuries.

Slavs: A major Indo-European group of people speaking one of several Slavic languages. In this study we are concerned with South Slavs: the Bulgarians, Serbs, Croats, Macedonians, and Slovenes.

Slovenes: The South Slavic people found occupying what is now Slovenia and speaking Slovenian.

Smoljane: A Slavic tribe mentioned living in the vicinity of the Struma River in the ninth century.

Thracians: An Indo-European people living in Thrace and much of what is now Bulgaria prior to the Gothic and Slavic invasions. In the period after the Slavic invasions they disappeared completely.

Timok Slavs: Slavs settled on the Timok River who were active politically, trying to assert their independence from the Bulgarians, in the ninth century.

Turkomen (or Turcomen): Turkic nomadic tribesmen from Central Asia who began pouring into Anatolia in the eleventh century. Many were associated with the Seljuks.

Turks: A major linguistic group of people originating in Central Asia, many of whom swept across the Steppes, some migrating as far west as the Hungarian plain. They had impact on the Balkans as raiders or as overlords of people settled within the Balkans. The major Turkic people discussed in this study were the original Bulgars, Avars, Khazars, Pechenegs, Cumans, and Ghuzz. In Byzantine sources the term *Turk* was regularly used for the Hungarians (Magyars), though they are not really a Turkish people.

Utigurs: A Bulgarian tribe living north of the Black Sea in the late fifth and sixth centuries.

Uze: See Ghuzz.

Varangians: Originally a particular Scandinavian people who were active in Russia. The term soon came to mean a military servitor hired for service in Kievan Rus (and subsequently hired via Kiev for service in the Byzantine Empire). Varangians formed a famous bodyguard corps in Constantinople in the eleventh century.

Visigoths (West Goths): A Gothic tribe that carried out raids in the fourth century in the Balkans before moving further west.

Vlachs: A pastoral people, related to the Rumanians and presumably descended from the Dacians, found in large numbers in certain parts of the Balkans. In the Middle Ages so many were found in Thessaly that that region was known for a while as Valachia. Many others were found in Macedonia, Bulgaria (where they played an important role in forming the Second Bulgarian Empire), Hercegovina, and northeastern Serbia.

West Turks: A group of Turks based in western Central Asia who were overlords over the Utigur Bulgars in the second half of the sixth century.

White Croats: See Belo Croats.

Sources and Authors of Sources Referred to in the Text

Anna Comnena (1083–ca. 1148): Daughter of the Emperor Alexius I Comnenus (1081–1118) and author of a history of her father's reign, *The Alexiad;* the work was completed in 1148.

Arethas: Byzantine author and churchman active in the late ninth and early tenth centuries. Bishop of Caesarea, exiled to Greece, owing to his opposition to the fourth marriage of Leo VI in 906. His letters from exile are a valuable source on early-tenth-century Athens. He was also involved in copying classical manuscripts.

Boril's *Synodik:* The results of the synod held by Tsar Boril of Bulgaria against the Bogomils in 1211.

"On the Bulgarian Peace": An anonymous Byzantine court oration from ca. 927 which discusses Nicholas Mysticus's dealings with Symeon of Bulgaria.

Choniates, Niketas (died 1210): Byzantine historian whose history deals with the period from the death of Alexius Comnenus in 1118 to 1206.

Chronicle of the Priest of Dioclea: See *Dioclea, Chronicle of the Priest of.*

Constantine Porphyrogenitus: Byzantine emperor, born 905, died 959, who was a coemperor with his father, Leo VI, from 907, was titular emperor under various regencies 913–19, shared the throne with Romanus I Lecapenus (919–44), and then ruled alone from 944 to 959. Since Romanus I ran the state, Constantine was diverted into literary activities, which he continued even after 944. His three major works are *De administrando imperio* (an unfinished work from the 950s) dealing with the foreign policy of the empire, diplomatic techniques, and sketches of the neighbors with whom the Byzantines had to deal—the most important of his works for this study; the *Book of Ceremonies;* and the *Book of Themes* (describing the Byzantine military provinces, known as themes).

Cosmas the Priest: A Bulgarian priest and author of a tract against the Bogomils. Written in about 970, it is the most important source we have on the beliefs of the Bogomils in Bulgaria.

Court Law for the People [*Zakon sudnyi ljud'm*]: A legal text in Slavic, based upon the Byzantine law code known as *The Ecloga,* adapted to Bulgarian conditions, appearing during the reign of Boris I (852–89). Scholars are not agreed on whether it was compiled in Moravia and brought from there to Bulgaria or whether it was compiled in Bulgaria.

Demetrius, St., Miracles of: See *Miracles of Saint Demetrius.*

Dioclea (Duklja), *Chronicle of the Priest of:* A mid-twelfth-century chronicle, possibly originally written in Slavic, but surviving only in Latin translation. Much of it is based on oral tradition and thus there is considerable debate about the reliability of much of its contents. It is, however, the most detailed source we have for the early history of Duklja, what is now Montenegro, and Hum (Zahumlje—which roughly consists of modern Hercegovina). It also has information on the history of Bosnia, Croatia, and Macedonia.

Ecloga, The: Byzantine law code issued by Leo III (717–41).

Euthymius, Life of: Saint's life of Euthymius, an ascetic made patriarch by Leo VI when Nicholas Mysticus refused to accept the emperor's fourth marriage. It is an important, but biased, source for Byzantine events, particularly church-related ones, during the reigns of Leo VI and Alexander.

Evagrius: Byzantine church historian who died near the end of the sixth century. His history covers the period 431–593.

Farlati, D. (1690–1773): A Jesuit historian of the church in the western Balkans. His work (done in conjunction with two other Jesuits, but published under Farlati's name) *Illyricum Sacrum* was published in Venice in nine volumes between 1751 and 1819. Though basically a work of synthesis (thus a secondary work rather than a primary source), it does contain many no-longer-extant documents, some of which are of doubtful authenticity, about the history of the church in Bosnia, Croatia, and Dalmatia.

Farmer's Law, The: A Byzantine legal text (though probably only a guide for judges in a particular province of the Byzantine Balkans) issued in the late seventh or early eighth century. It almost entirely treats issues that might arise within a village and is a major source for village conditions at that time. A controversial document, it is discussed in detail in chapter 3.

Fredegar's *Chronicle:* A late-seventh-century Frankish chronicle.

Gregory the Decapolite, Life of: A ninth-century saint's life which has some information on conditions in and communications across the Balkans of that time.

Hambarli Inscription: An inscription in Greek found in a village of that name in Thrace put up by Krum's occupation authority describing how the territory he had taken from Byzantium in 812–13 was to be administered.

Hincmar (806–82): Frankish churchman and chronicler writing the period 861–82 of the *Annales Bertiniani.* Though primarily a source on western events, he does give information on the establishment of Christianity in Bulgaria.

Historia Salonitana maior (HSM): A sixteenth-century expansion of Thomas the Archdeacon of Split's *History of Split* (written in the middle of the thirteenth century). Since it is not clear when and under what circumstances these additions came to be added to Thomas's text the HSM is a controversial source. It is discussed in some detail in chapter 8.

Hrabr's *Defense of Slavic letters:* A defense of Slavic letters written by an anonymous Bulgarian monk (writing under the pseudonym of Hrabr [the Brave]) in the early tenth century. It is discussed in detail and quoted from at length in chapter 5.

HSM: See *Historia Salonitana maior.*

Isidore of Seville (ca. 560–636): Spanish churchman, encyclopedist, historian, and theologian. In one of his historical works he refers to the Slavic presence in Greece at the time of Heraclius.

John of Ephesus (ca. 505–ca. 585): Syrian church historian, writing in Syriac, whose *Ecclesiastical History* has a detailed description of the Slavic penetration of the Balkans after 578.

John the Exarch: Bulgarian churchman and author from the time of Symeon (893–927), whose major work, the *Šestodnev* (the Six Days) is an account of creation based heavily on Saint Basil's *Hexaemeron*. Its preface, however, is original; a panegyric addressed to Symeon, it also praises (and briefly describes) his capital of Preslav.

John of Rila: Born ca. 880, founder of the Rila monastery, medieval Bulgaria's greatest monastic center, and author in about 941 of a *Spiritual Testament* which established a rigorous monastic rule for his monastery.

Kekaumenos: An eleventh-century Byzantine general who in the 1070s wrote a military manual (*Strategikon*), which not only has descriptions of military tactics but also describes particular military events including eleventh-century uprisings in the Balkans.

Kinnamos: Byzantine historian, born after 1143, disappearing from the sources after 1185. Author of a history covering the period 1118–76.

Leo Choerosphaktes: Byzantine envoy to Symeon during the Bulgarian-Byzantine war (894–97) whose letters survive and are a major source on the war and on Symeon.

Leo the Deacon: Tenth-century Byzantine historian whose history covers the period 959–76 and is the major source for the war of Svjatoslav against Nicephorus Phocas and John Tzimiskes in Bulgaria.

Liutprand of Cremona: Western envoy who twice visited Constantinople, once during the reign of Constantine VII Porphyrogenitus and once during the reign of Nicephorus Phocas. He wrote up both these embassies.

Logothete, Chronicle of the: A chronicle written by a tenth-century high court official (bearing the title of logothete) covering the period 813 to 948. A large portion of the chronicle known as the *Continuator of Theophanes* consists of the Logothete's chronicle.

Lucius (1604–79): A historian from Dalmatia who wrote about Croatia and Dalmatia.

Al-Mas'ūdī: A tenth-century Arab geographer (died 956) whose wide travels included Russia. Among other things he confirms the existence of the White Croatians whom Constantine Porphyrogenitus discusses.

Menander: A sixth-century Byzantine historian whose history covers the period 559–82 and provides considerable information about the Antes, Slaveni, and Avars. His work only partially survives in extracts incorporated in the works of later authors.

Miracles of Saint Demetrius: A collection of tales concerning miracles performed by Saint Demetrius after his death for the benefit of Thessaloniki. The *Miracles* were compiled in that city in the seventh century and are a major source for the history of the Slavic settlement in that region and the relations Thessaloniki had with these Slavs and with the Bulgar Kuver.

Monemvasia, Chronicle of: A late-tenth- or early-eleventh-century anonymous chronicle from Monemvasia (on the southern tip of the Peloponnesus) which Charanis has shown to be based partially on earlier written sources. It provides considerable material on the Peloponnesus from the seventh to the ninth centuries.

Nicephorus (ca. 758–ca. 829): Byzantine churchman, patriarch of Constantinople (806–15), opponent of iconoclasm, wrote a history of the empire covering the years 602–769.

Nicholas III: Patriarch of Constantinople (1084–1111). Some letters of his survive including one to Alexius I referring to Slavic control of Greece during the late sixth to ninth centuries. His information was clearly derived from some other source.

Nicholas Mysticus: Patriarch of Constantinople (901–07, 913–25). Many of his letters survive, including his side of the correspondence with Symeon during the long Byzantine-Bulgarian war (913–27). His letters are a major source on Symeon and the war.

Philotheus's *Kletorologion* (899): A guide listing whom to invite to imperial ceremonies and the order of precedence of different positions. A major source for the administration and social hierarchies of the empire.

Procopius: Byzantine historian, contemporary of Justinian (527–65). His works are the major source on Justinian's reign: *History of the Wars, Secret History,* and *On Buildings.* A very opinionated writer whose views differed from work to work. He has considerable material on the Slavs of his time.

Pseudo-Maurice, *Strategikon:* A military manual attributed, perhaps correctly, to the emperor Maurice (582–602). If he was not the actual author he may well have ordered the work done. Among other things it discusses methods of warfare against the Slavs and contains information on their way of life.

Rayner Sacconi: An Italian inquisitor of the mid-thirteenth century who wrote a tract on the Cathars, which also presents information about the organization of the dualist churches of the east in his day. Having been a Cathar in his youth, Rayner is considered a more accurate authority about the heretics than many other Catholic inquisitorial sources.

Russian Primary Chronicle (Povest' vremennyh let): A chronicle compilation from the early twelfth century, containing both oral and earlier written material. I have used it chiefly for the information it contains on Svjatoslav's warfare in Bulgaria (965–71) and on the condition of Bulgaria at the time.

Skylitzes: A Byzantine official who at the end of the eleventh century wrote a chronicle covering the period 811 to 1057. The work is original only from 944; his coverage of the years prior to that date is chiefly from the *Continuator of Theophanes.* Recent scholarship is showing Skylitzes to contain many inaccuracies.

Strabo, Abbreviator of: A medieval (eighth- to tenth-century) editor of the classical geographer Strabo (ca. 63 B.C.–A.D. 21) whose comments note the presence of the Slavs in Greece.

Strategikon, attributed to Maurice: See Pseudo-Maurice, *Strategikon.*

Svjatoslav's *Sbornik:* Svjatoslav's collection. A collection of texts, probably a translation of a popular Byzantine encyclopedia. Usually named after

Prince Svjatoslav II of Kiev (1073–76) since the text survived in his copy, the work actually goes back to Symeon of Bulgaria.

Taktikon of Uspenskij: A military manual from the ninth century, compiled between 842 and 846. It contains considerable information about the themes (military provinces) that existed in the empire at the time it was composed. It is named for the Russian Byzantinist who edited its text.

Theophanes: Byzantine monk and chronicler who compiled his chronicle between 810 and 814. His chronicle covers the period from 284 to 813. His work is the major source for Byzantine events of the seventh and eighth centuries.

Theophanes Continuatus (or the *Continuator of Theophanes*): A compilation drawn up in the middle of the tenth century at the orders of Constantine VII Porphyrogenitus. It picks up where Theophanes ends (813) and continues the history to 961. It is not the work of a single author but a collection of different works stuck together: e.g. Constantine VII's *Life of Basil,* the *Chronicle of the Logothete.*

Theophylact, Patriarch of Constantinople (933–56): His letter to Peter of Bulgaria from ca. 940, and presumably based on a no-longer-extant letter from Peter, is the earliest source about the Bogomils in Bulgaria and sheds some light on the heresy itself.

Theophylact of Ohrid: A Greek who was bishop of Ohrid (ca. 1090–1109), many of whose letters from Ohrid survive and are a major source for conditions in Bulgaria at his time.

Thomas the Archdeacon of Split: Thomas died in 1268. He was the author of a *History of Split* which is a most important but biased source for the history of Split from the seventh to the thirteenth centuries. An expanded version of his work from the sixteenth century, known as *Historia Salonitana maior,* also exists.

Willibald: Bishop of Mainz and a pilgrim to Jerusalem in the 720s who refers to Monemvasia being a Slavic land.

Yahyā ibn Saīd of Antioch (ca. 980–1066): An Arab Christian living in Antioch who wrote in Arabic a chronicle covering the period 936–1034. In addition to eastern events, he has considerable material on Byzantine events including the warfare between Samuel of Bulgaria and Byzantium.

Zakon sudnyi ljud'm: See *Court Law for the People.*

Selected Bibliography

Ashburner, W. "The Farmer's Law." *Journal of Hellenic Studies* 30 (1910):85–108; 32 (1912): 68–83. Includes an English translation.

Balcanoslavica. Vol. 1. Beograd, 1972. Contains a variety of important papers on the results of archaeology.

Barišić, F. "Car Foka (602–610) i podunavski Avaro-Sloveni." *Zbornik radova Vizantološkog Instituta* (Serbian Academy of Sciences) 4 (1956):73–86.

———. *Čuda Dimitrija solunskog kao istoriski izvori.* Serbian Academy of Sciences, posebna izdanja, 219, Vizantološki Institut, knj. 2. Beograd, 1953.

———. "Proces slovenske kolonizacije istočnog Balkana." In *Simpozijum predslavenski etnički elementi na Balkanu u etnogenezi južnih Slovena,* edited by A. Benac. Sarajevo, 1969. Pp. 11–27. See also Barišić's remarks in the general discussion, ibid., pp. 122–23.

Barker, J. *Justinian and the Later Roman Empire.* Madison, Wis., 1966.

Benac, A., ed. *Simpozijum predslavenski etnički elementi na Balkanu u etnogenezi južnih Slovena.* Academy of Sciences and Arts of Bosnia and Hercegovina, posebna izdanja, knj. 12, Centar za Balkanološka ispitivanja, knj. 4. Sarajevo, 1969.

Birnbaum, H. "The Original Homeland of the Slavs and the Problem of Early Slavic Linguistic Contacts." *Indo-European Studies* 1, no. 4 (Winter 1973):407-21.

Bon, A. *Le Peloponnese byzantin jusqu'en 1204.* Paris, 1951. Especially pp. 1–76.

Brand, C. *Byzantium Confronts the West, 1180–1204.* Cambridge, Mass., 1968.

Browning, R. *Byzantium and Bulgaria.* Berkeley, Calif., 1975.

———. "A New Source on Byzantine-Hungarian Relations in the Twelfth Century." *Balkan Studies* 2, no. 2 (1961): 173–214.

Bury, J. *A History of the Later Roman Empire.* New edition covering the period 395–565. 2 vols. London, 1923.

Cankova-Petkova, G. "Bulgarians and Byzantium during the First Decades after the Foundation of the Bulgarian State." *Byzantinoslavica* 24, no. 1 (1963):41–53.

———. "Contribution au sujet de la conversion des Bulgares au Christianisme." *Byzantinobulgarica* 4 (1973):21–39.

———. "O territorii bolgarskogo gosudarstva v VII–IX vv." *Vizantijskij vremennik* 17 (1960):124–43.

Charanis, P. "The Chronicle of Monemvasia and the Question of the Slavonic Settlements in Greece." *Dumbarton Oaks Papers* 5 (1950):141–66.

————. "Kouver, the Chronology of His Activities and Their Ethnic Effect on the Regions around Thessalonica." *Balkan Studies* 11, no. 2 (1970):229–47.

————. "Nicephorus I, The Savior of Greece from the Slavs (810 A.D.)." *Byzantina-Metabyzantina* 1, no. 1 (1946):75–92.

————. "Observations on the History of Greece during the Early Middle Ages." *Balkan Studies* 11, no. 1 (1970):1–34.

————. "The Significance of Coins as Evidence for the History of Athens and Corinth in the Seventh and Eighth Centuries." *Historia* 4 (1955):163–72.

Čremošnik, I. "Die Chronologien der aeltesten slavischen Funde in Bosnien und der Herzegovina." *Archaeologia Iugoslavica* (Beograd) 11 (1970):99–103.

Constantine Porphyrogenitus. *De Administrando Imperio.* Vol. 1, Greek text and English translation, edited by Gy. Moravcsik and R. Jenkins. Dumbarton Oaks Texts, vol. 1. Washington, D.C., 1967. Vol. 2, Commentary, edited by R. Jenkins. London, 1962.

Cosmas, Presbyter. *Le Traité contre les Bogomiles de Cosmas le Prêtre.* Edited and Translated by H-C. Puech and A. Vaillant. Travaux publiés par l'Institut d'Études Slaves, no. 21. Paris, 1945.

Dewey, H. W., and Kleimola, A. M. *Zakon sudnyi ljudem (Court Law for the People).* Michigan Slavic Materials, no. 14. Ann Arbor, Mich., 1977.

Diaconu, P. *Les Coumans au Bas-Danube aux XIe et XIIe siècles.* Bucharest, 1978.

————. *Les Petchénègues au Bas-Danube.* Bucharest, 1970.

Dujčev, I. "La Chronique byzantine de l'an 811." *Travaux et memoires* 1 (1965):205–54.

————. *Medioevo Bizantino-slavo.* 3 vols. Rome, 1965–71.

————. "Protobulgares et Slaves." In I. Dujčev, *Medioevo Bizantino-slavo.* Vol. 1. Rome, 1965. Pp. 67–82.

Dvornik, F. *Byzantine Missions among the Slavs.* New Brunswick, N.J., 1970.

————. "Deux inscriptions Greco-Bulgares de Philippes." *Bulletin de Correspondance Hellenique* 52 (1928):140–43.

————. *The Making of Central and Eastern Europe.* London, 1949. Appendices, pp. 268–304, discuss the Serb and Croat states beyond the Carpathians.

————. *The Photian Schism in History and Legend.* Cambridge, 1948.

Farmer's Law, The. For this text see Ashburner, W. "The Farmer's Law." *Journal of Hellenic Studies* 30 (1910):85–108; 32 (1912):68–83.

Ferjančić, B. *Vizantija i južni Sloveni.* Beograd, 1966.

Ferluga, J. *Byzantium on the Balkans.* Amsterdam, 1976.

————. "Drač i Dračka oblast pred kraj X i početkom XI veka." *Zbornik radova Vizantološkog Instituta* (Serbian Academy of Sciences) 8, no. 2 (1964):117–30.

————. "Les insurrections des Slaves de la Macédoine au XIe siècle." In J. Ferluga, *Byzantium on the Balkans.* Amsterdam, 1976. Pp. 379–97.

————. "Sur la date de la création du Thème de Dyrrachium." In J. Ferluga, *Byzantium on the Balkans.* Amsterdam, 1976. Pp. 215–24.

————. *Vizantiska uprava u Dalmaciji.* Serbian Academy of Sciences, posebna izdanja, 291, Vizantološki Institut, knj. 6. Beograd, 1957.

Fine, J. *The Bosnian Church: A New Interpretation.* East European Monographs, vol. 10, East European Quarterly, distributed by Columbia University Press. Boulder and New York, 1975.

————. "A Fresh Look at Bulgaria under Tsar Peter (927–969)." *Byzantine Studies* 5, pts. 1–2 (1978):88–95.

————. "The Size and Significance of the Bulgarian Bogomil Movement." *East European Quarterly* 11, no. 4 (Winter 1977):385–412.

Garsoian, N. *The Paulician Heresy.* The Hague, 1967.

Georgiev, V. "The Genesis of the Balkan Peoples." *Slavonic and East European Review* 44, no. 103 (July 1966):285–97.

Gimbutas, M. *The Slavs.* New York, 1971.

Gjuzelev, V. *Knjaz Boris P"rvi.* Sofija, 1969.

Istorija Crne Gore. Vol. 1. Titograd, 1967. A collective work covering the period from prehistory to the end of the twelfth century.

Jenkins, R. *Byzantium: The Imperial Centuries* A.D. *610–1071.* New York, 1966.

————. "The Peace with Bulgaria (927) Celebrated by Theodore Daphnopates." *Polychronion,* Winter 1966, pp. 287–303.

Jireček, K. *Istorija Srba.* Translated into Serbo-Croatian and updated by J. Radonić. 2 vols. Beograd, 1952.

Jones, A. H. M. *The Later Roman Empire.* 2 vols. Norman, Okla., 1964.

Karlin-Hayter, P. "The Emperor Alexander's Bad Name." *Speculum* 44, no. 4 (1969):585–96.

Kinnamos, John. *Deeds of John and Manuel Comnenus.* Translated by C. Brand. New York, 1976.

Klaić, N. *Povijest Hrvata u ranom srednjem vijeku.* Zagreb, 1971.

Kolias, G. *Leon Choerosphactes.* Athens, 1939.

Kovačević, J. *Avarski Kaganat.* Beograd, 1977.

Lemerle, P. "Invasions et migrations dans les Balkans." *Revue historique* 211 (1954):265–308.

Liutprand of Cremona. *The Works of Liutprand of Cremona.* Translated by F. A. Wright. London, 1930. See in particular Liutprand's *Legatio.*

M., F. "Dukljanska kraljevina." *Glasnik Zemaljskog muzeja* (Sarajevo) 11 (1899):237–315, 611–97; 12 (1900):1–63. The initials by which the article is signed stand for F. Milobar.

Mošin, V. "O periodizacii russko-južnoslavjanskih literaturnyh svjazej X–XV vv." *Trudy otdela drevnerusskoj literatury* 19 (1963):28–106.

Nicholas I, Patriarch of Constantinople. *The Letters of Nicholas I, Patriarch of Constantinople.* Edited and translated by R. Jenkins and L. G. Westerink. Greek text with English translation. Corpus Fontium Historiae Byzantinae 6. Dumbarton Oaks Texts, vol. 2. Washington, D.C., 1973.

Obolensky, D. *The Bogomils.* Cambridge, 1948.

————. *The Byzantine Commonwealth.* New York, 1971.

Ostrogorsky, G. [Spelled Ostrogorski in Yugoslav publications]. "Avtokrator i samodržac." In G. Ostrogorski, *Vizantija i Sloveni.* Beograd, 1970. Pp. 281–364. Discussion on Bulgaria, pp. 303–21.

————. "The Byzantine Empire in the World of the Seventh Century." *Dumbarton Oaks Papers* 13 (1959):3–21.

————. *History of the Byzantine State.* 3d ed. New Brunswick, N.J., 1969.

————. "Postanak Tema Helada i Peloponez." *Zbornik radova Vizantološkog Instituta* (Serbian Academy of Sciences) 1 (1952):64–75.

————. *Vizantija i Sloveni.* Beograd, 1970.

Pundeff, M. "National Consciousness in Medieval Bulgaria." *Südost-Forschungen* 27 (1968):1–27.

Radojčić, B. "O hronologiji ugarsko-vizantijskih borbi i ustanku Srba za vreme Jovana II Komnina." *Zbornik radova Vizantološkog Instituta* (Serbian Academy of Sciences) 7 (1961):177–86.

Runciman, S. *The Eastern Schism.* Oxford, 1955.

————. *A History of the First Bulgarian Empire.* London, 1930.

Russian Primary Chronicle, The. Edited by S. H. Cross. Cambridge, Mass., 1953.

Šišić, F. *Pregled povijesti hrvatskoga naroda.* Zagreb, 1962.

Stokes, A. D. "The Background and Chronology of the Balkan Campaigns of Svjatoslav." *Slavonic and East European Review* 40 (1961):43–57.

————. "The Balkan Campaigns of Svjatoslav Igorevich." *Slavonic and East European Review* 40 (1962):466–96.

Sullivan, R. E. "Khan Boris and the Conversion of Bulgaria: A Case Study of the Impact of Christianity on a Barbarian Society." *Studies in Medieval and Renaissance History* (University of Nebraska) 3 (1966):51–139.

Swoboda, V. "L'origine de l'organisation de l'église en Bulgarie et ses rapports avec le patriarcat de Constantinople (870–919)." *Byzantinobulgarica* 2 (1966):67–81.

Vaklinov, S. *Formirane na starob"lgarskata kultura.* Sofija, 1977.

Vasiliev, A. A. *History of the Byzantine Empire.* 2 vols. Madison, Wis., 1958.

Venedikov, I. "La population byzantine en Bulgarie au début du IXe siècle." *Byzantinobulgarica* 1 (1962):261–77.

Zakon sudnyi ljudem. For this text see Dewey, H. W., and Kleimola, A. M. *Zakon sudnyi ljudem (Court Law for the People).* Michigan Slavic Materials, no. 14. Ann Arbor, Mich., 1977.

Zlatarski, V. *Istorija na b"lgarskata d"ržava prez srednite vekove.* Vol.1, pt. 1. Vol. 1, pt. 2. Vol. 2. Vol. 3. Sofija, 1938–40.

————. "Političeskijat život na B"lgarite pri car Simeona 893–927." *B"lgarija 1000 godini 927–1927.* Sofija, 1930. Pp. 3–49.

Index

For major events, see the Contents. Since Č, Š, and Ž are the equivalents of Ch, Sh, and Zh, words using these letters are alphabetized as if they were written Ch, Sh, and Zh. Italicized numbers in the index refer to items referred to, but not by name (e.g., Constantinople being referred to as "the capital," Jakvinta being referred to as "Bodin's wife"). The limited number of topical headings are not complete; they are intended to pick up more sustained discussions and do not attempt to include all passing references.

Map 6. The Modern Balkans